I0893074

Advanced praise for *Botha, Smuts and the Great War*

An important contribution to our knowledge of not just South Africa but of the British Empire in the Great War. Professor van der Waag is one of the leading scholars of the military history (broadly defined) of South Africa, and Dr Garcia is one of the best of the new generation of South African military historians. The authors, by placing the South African experience into the wider context of the war effort of the British Empire, have written a book that is relevant to global as well as national history. While much has been written about Smuts, and, to a lesser extent, on Botha, producing a joint military/political study of the two men during the First World War is largely innovative. So is placing the study of Smuts and Botha into the modern context of culture wars...the authors' moving beyond the White population to include Black, Indian and Coloured perspectives; the reassessment of Smuts' period of command in East Africa, and South African manpower problems, particularly the difficulty of keeping the Brigade in France up to strength; and the creation of the South African intelligence service.

Professor Gary Sheffield, University of Wolverhampton, Kings College London, University of Buckingham

The authors correctly point out that regarding the military and political, Botha and Smuts had not been covered in comprehenisve fashion, and that there is a significant gap in the historiography. The result is this outstanding academic biographical study with the thematic focus on the First World War. In the process, by drawing on extensive archival sources, especially the use of personal papers, the authors bring a fresh and new interpretation on Smuts and Botha. Apart from the new information on their military campaigns, I can especially refer to their analysis of the 1915 general election in South Africa. This is a significant contribution to South African historiography by reflecting what a challenging and bitter campaign it was for the two generals.

Professor Alex Mouton, University of South Africa

Original research that contributes to the national and international scenes ... provides a useful comparative on a long-standing political partnership which has until now been neglected. By exploring the unique friendship of two powerful and influential men like Botha and Smuts, a firmer understanding of the dynamics of these two men at work, their strengths, weaknesses, hopes and ambitions for their country at a pivotal time in their nation's history can be investigated. The book will serve a useful benchmark ... an archivally-driven book, they have argued, quite convincingly, that to examine this partnership between Louis Botha and Jan Smuts, an important gap in the literature and historiography of South Africa has been filled. In this they have succeeded very well ... and by comparing and contrasting the leadership styles and characteristics of both men over a fraught period of South Africa's history, the strengths and weaknesses of these men have been highlighted as never before.

Professor Kent Fedorowich, University of the West of England, Australian National University.

*I*t provides much needed insights into South African military politics during the Great War. It is certainly original and thought-provoking as it departs from the traditional narrative concerning race and also illuminates the networks that underpinned the higher direction of the war. It has been well-researched and makes good use of archival collections... Apart from its national significance, it also enhances our understanding of the British Empire during the Great War as well as the relations between the United Kingdom and South Africa. Overall, it brings together a number of key themes while also shedding much light on hitherto obscure personal relationships.

Dr Ross Anderson, independent scholar, Lieutenant Colonel (ret).

A very strong piece of scholarship based on some extensive archival research.

Professor Andrew Stewart, National Danish Defence College, Kings College London, Australian National University.

Botha, Smuts and the Great War

Antonio Garcia and Ian van der Waag

Wolverhampton Military Studies Series No. 40

Helion & Company

Helion & Company Limited
Unit 8 Amherst Business Centre
Budbrooke Road
Warwick
CV34 5WE
England
Tel. 01926 499 619
Email: info@helion.co.uk
Website: www.helion.co.uk
Twitter: @helionbooks
Visit our blog at blog.helion.co.uk

Published by Helion & Company 2023
Designed and typeset by Mach 3 Solutions (www.mach3solutions.co.uk)
Cover designed by Paul Hewitt, Battlefield Design (www.battlefield-design.co.uk)

ISBN 9-78-19151137-7-1

British Library Cataloguing-in-Publication Data.
A catalogue record for this book is available from the British Library.

To my dad Jose Manuel Barbon Garcia and my mum Magdalene Phelps Garcia

To my parents – J.C.J.M. van der Waag (1922-1993) and J.M. van der Waag-Ellis (1933-2023)

Contents

List of Illustrations

List of Maps

List of Figures

List of Tables

The Wolverhampton Military Studies Series
Series Editor's Preface

As series editor, it is my great pleasure to introduce the *Wolverhampton Military Studies Series* to you. Our intention is that in this series of books you will find military history that is new and innovative, and academically rigorous with a strong basis in fact and in analytical research, but also is the kind of military history that is for all readers, whatever their particular interests, or their level of interest in the subject. To paraphrase an old aphorism: a military history book is not less important just because it is popular, and it is not more scholarly just because it is dull. With every one of our publications we want to bring you the kind of military history that you will want to read simply because it is a good and well-written book, as well as bringing new light, new perspectives, and new factual evidence to its subject.

In devising the *Wolverhampton Military Studies Series*, we gave much thought to the series title: this is a *military* series. We take the view that history is everything except the things that have not happened yet, and even then a good book about the military aspects of the future would find its way into this series. We are not bound to any particular time period or cut-off date. Writing military history often divides quite sharply into eras, from the modern through the early modern to the mediaeval and ancient; and into regions or continents, with a division between western military history and the military history of other countries and cultures being particularly marked. Inevitably, we have had to start somewhere, and the first books of the series deal with British military topics and events of the twentieth century and later nineteenth century. But this series is open to any book that challenges received and accepted ideas about any aspect of military history, and does so in a way that encourages its readers to enjoy the discovery.

In the same way, this series is not limited to being about wars, or about grand strategy, or wider defence matters, or the sociology of armed forces as institutions, or civilian society and culture at war. None of these are specifically excluded, and in some cases they play an important part in the books that comprise our series. But there are already many books in existence, some of them of the highest scholarly standards, which cater to these particular approaches. The main theme of the *Wolverhampton Military Studies Series* is the military aspects of wars, the preparation for wars or their prevention, and their aftermath. This includes some books whose main theme is the technical details of how armed forces have worked, some books on wars and battles, and some books that re-examine the evidence about the existing stories, to show in a different light what everyone thought they already knew and understood.

As series editor, together with my fellow editorial board members, and our publisher Duncan Rogers of Helion, I have found that we have known immediately and almost by instinct the kind of books that fit within this series. They are very much the kind of well-written and challenging books that my students at the University of Wolverhampton would want to read. They are books which enhance knowledge and offer new perspectives. Also, they are books for anyone with an interest in military history and events, from expert scholars to occasional readers. One of the great benefits of the study of military history is that it includes a large and often committed section of the wider population, who want to read the best military history that they can find; our aim for this series is to provide it.

Stephen Badsey
University of Wolverhampton

Acknowledgements

This project is ultimately an output from my partnership and friendship with Ian van der Waag, my teacher, co-author and fellow historian. The concept for this book took shape over many years, over various coffees and other drinks, many conversations, and much research. Starting with my PhD thesis, Ian was my supervisor, and we spent much time evaluating biography as a discipline, and its importance in South African history. This volume was the result.

I need to say a word of thanks to the many who have assisted in different ways at different times in my professional and academic career: Kent Fedorowich, Albert Grundlingh, Fankie Monama, Evert Kleynhans, Nicholas Southey, Tilman Dedering, Abel Esterhuyse, Andrew Dinwoodie, Fransjohan Pretorius, Gary Sheffield, Sam Tshehla, Ross Anderson, Paul Rich, Manuel Trucco, Max Lauker, Eddie Watson, Jason McDonald, and Alex Mouton.

Mentioned in dispatches are also Hex Novoa, Cobus Buitendag, Dewald du Toit, Bonakele Msimango, Jacques de Vries, Johan Pieterse, Pierre Lombard, Theuns Barnard, Sifisu Masuku, Steve Maluleka, Derek Van Wyk, Derick Wells, Allan Bantom, Will Gordon, Clyde Koen, Maurice Snell, Jonathan Thompson, Anri Delport, P.C Manser, Gilmour Gordon, Nardus Haarsbroek, and my old unit 2 Field Engineer Regiment.

Duncan Rogers, Helion's managing director, has been patient and considerate, as well as Michael LoCicero our book editor – a word of thanks to you both as well as the staff at Helion & Company. My thanks to Stellenbosch University, Department of Military History and Open University. And finally to the most important person, I thank you Tara, my love, my friend and my wife. A word of appreciation to my kids, Rafa and Emilio who had to put up with me while working on this project – there will be even more play time now.

Antonio Garcia
Edinburgh

I am delighted to co-write this book with Antonio Garcia – a young colleague, serious scholar, and most of all a friend. We conducted the research on which this book is based over an extended period of many years, and it draws on our mutual endeavours to find a better understanding of two complex and persistently provocative South African figures. Our debts are many: to the staff and colleagues at the various libraries, archival repositories and records offices where we have trawled the material; and to colleagues and friends with whom we have sound-boarded ideas. For my part I need to mention first and foremost, Kent Fedorowich to whom my debt only grows – Kent introduced me inter alia to the Viscount Long of Wraxall Papers and the Wiltshire Research Centre at Chippenham; the late Jeff Grey (Canberra) who so generously introduced me to his circle and opened the wider, academic world to a young, novice colleague; Albert Grundlingh and Fransjohan Pretorius, who have equally given succour and support in South Africa; Brigadier General (Dr) Nuno Correia Barrento de Lemos Pires, for inviting me to a stimulating First World War conference at the Academia Militar in 2016, and Ambassador Keitumetse (Kitty) Matthews for hosting me at her residence in such grand fashion and sharing her Lisbon – interspersed with reminiscences of her grandfather, Z.K. Matthews – with me; Gary Sheffield and the colleagues at the Western Front Association; Sandra Swart, Andrew Stewart, Douglas Delaney and Ross Anderson for so many years of friendship and scholarly engagement; and Anne Samson, who in 2016 co-hosted the Great War in Africa conference in Stellenbosch with Ross and me.

My heartfelt thanks also go to my colleagues at Rabdan Academy and Zayed Military University, and to Duncan Rogers and the team at Helion & Company. But the greatest debt is owed to my family and particularly to Noëlle – partner, confidant, closest friend.

Ian van der Waag
Abu Dhabi

Introduction

Botha's memory is the shared heritage of all South Africans.
Smuts on Botha[1]

Botha is not our hero and cannot be a hero of a democratic South Africa.
Malema on Botha[2]

The biographies of Louis Botha and Jan Smuts are undeniably intertwined, and their histories are still emotive both in South Africa and abroad. Two historical figures, they survive in dusty books, hardcopy, and digital tomes, kept on the bookshelf, in libraries and the cloud; only to be pulled out when the old debate between the past and the present rears its head; summonsing them to answer new questions on historical matters – a Socratic dialogue on South Africa's contested history. The spate of statue vandalisms in South Africa, the United Kingdom, the United States, and various African countries, is testament to the reopening of the historical conversation and feelings of frustration.

The vandalism of Botha's and Smuts's statues was an outcry to their pride of place in central public spaces in South Africa – their prominence no longer chimes with majority South African public opinion, with contemporary politics and with modern heroes. Throughout the twentieth century powerful British and South African leaders erected statues to Botha and Smuts and mainly White South Africans and Britons paid homage to their former leaders, their likenesses trapped in their antiquated stone, bronze, and concrete structures.

1 Smuts quoted in Anon., *Louis Botha Album*, published by the Louis Botha Memorial Committee for the unveiling of the Botha equestrian statue in 1946 (Pretoria: Wallachs' & Co, 1946). EA: Box 1/13 Enkelargiefversameling.

2 T. Zwane, 'EFF and ANC at odds over "offensive" statues', *Mail and Guardian*, 8 April 2015 < http://mg.co.za/article/2015-04-08-eff-and-anc-at-odds-over-offensive-statues-1> accessed 01/02/2016.

Starting in the Present

Following Botha's death in 1919, Smuts ensured that Botha would not be forgotten – he advocated for the creation and display of Botha's statues across South Arica. Despite his busy schedule, Smuts kept the position of Chairman of the Louis Botha Memorial Committee. At the unveiling of Botha's statue at parliament, Smuts gave tribute to his friend stating that Botha was the chief architect of the Union of South Africa and claimed that his memory was the shared heritage of all South Africans.[3]

Smuts unveiled Botha's statues in Durban in 1923 and outside parliament in 1931, the latter one on horseback. Engelenburg quoted Botha who jokingly said that if a statue of him was ever to be erected he would want it on horseback.[4] The effigy of Botha at the Union Buildings in Pretoria, also equestrian, was erected 27 years after his death and Smuts gave a speech at its unveiling in 1946. Smuts commented that he had to wait a long time to commemorate his friend at the Union Buildings – the Nationalist Party had blocked previous requests.[5]

Smuts has several effigies, including but not limited to statues at Smuts House, the Union Buildings in Pretoria, and a few in Cape Town. An artistic interpretation of Smuts outside the National Art Gallery in Cape Town, unveiled in 1964, was met with considerable protest – the *Cape Times* referred to it as a monstrosity. This led to a more conventional representation of Smuts, a statue that can be found in Adderley Street in Cape Town.

Smuts was a powerful voice for Botha, but he had even more powerful advocates, in none other than Winston Churchill, who in his second stint as British prime minister requested a statue of Smuts be erected outside parliament. Smuts who claimed to 'belong to antiquity'[6] was immortalised in London, his hands behind his back looking ahead, appearing to be skating,[7] searching the horizon for answers to practical and theoretical questions.

John Buchan, who first met Botha and Smuts at Vereeniging and knew both men well, paid homage:

> Botha [was] built on lines of a primitive simplicity and wise with the elemental wisdom; Smuts, the acute legal intelligence and the philosophic mind who saw the problems of the day in the light of eternal principles – the two statesmen who between them made the early grant of responsible government to the new colonies a success, when otherwise it might have been a fiasco.[8]

3 Smuts quoted in Anon., *Louis Botha Album*. EA: Box 1/13 Enkelargiefversameling.
4 F.V. Engelenburg, *General Louis Botha* (Pretoria: J.L. Van Schaik BPK, 1928), p.9.
5 Anon., *Louis Botha Album*. EA: Box 1/13 Engelenburg argiefversameling.
6 See A. Lentin *Jan Smuts* (Johannesburg and Cape Town: Jonathan Ball, 2010), p. x
7 Thanks to Gary Sheffield for this description.
8 John Buchan, *Memory Hold-The-Door* (London: Hodder & Stoughton, 1954), pp.118–119.

Since their statues were first put up, much has changed, and democracy of thought and universal franchise in South Africa has started to re-balance the unequal landscape of Apartheid, and earlier forms of oppressive legislation. The result – we live in a time where the older heroes of some, are fading away, making space for new figures to emerge.

Several universities have statues of Smuts and halls named in his honour, including but not limited to the University of Cape Town, and his *alma mater*, Cambridge University. The University of Cape Town had the name of Smuts Hall changed due to protests, and the new campaign '#Smuts Has Fallen' demands the removal of his statue – this mirrors the '#Rhodes Must Fall' campaign which led to the removal of Cecil's bust in 2015. In 2018 Smuts's portrait and bust at Cambridge University was taken down, and in 2022, his statues at the University of Cape Town were defaced.

Botha's statues in Cape Town, Durban and Pretoria were defaced in a spate of vandalisms starting in 2015 and going on to 2022, at the time of completing this book. Julius Malema, the leader of the Economic Freedom Fighters (EFF), observed:

> Louis Botha is not our hero and cannot be a hero of a democratic South Africa … The statue of Botha outside this Parliament must go down, because it represents nothing of what a democratic South Africa stands for.[9]

Contemporary comments from EFF members, in 2022, reinforce the position, 'It's not a misnomer to call for any of these statues to be removed.'[10]

A number of scholars and politicians reflected on the statue debate. In October 2018, Pretoria Executive Mayor, Solly Msimanga, commented that the people of South Africa should remember its history both good and bad and that the youth should be encouraged to participate in such debates. He went on to say, 'If you go to the Union Buildings, you'll find the statue of Louis Botha and in front you'll find the statue of Nelson Mandela. You can actually have a perpetual discussion around them…'[11] In 2018, the South African Minister of Arts and Culture, Nathi Mthethwa, worked towards creating a national consciousness of shared symbols,[12] and in 2022 his attempts to push forward the so-called 'Flag Project' was met with public and political

9 Zwane, 'EFF and ANC at odds over "offensive" statues', *Mail and Guardian*, 8 April 2015.

10 J. Evans, 'Parliament's Louis Botha statue targeted with spray paint and an angle grinder', *News 24* < https://www.news24.com/news24/southafrica/news/parliaments-louis-botha-statue-targeted-with-spray-paint-and-an-angle-grinder-20220316> (accessed 25/09/2022).

11 J. Mahlokwane, 'Remember History, Good and Bad, Msimanga says as Church Square reopens', *IOL*, 27 October 2018 < https://www.iol.co.za/news/politics/remember-history-good-and-bad-msimanga-says-as-church-square-reopens-17666029> accessed 25/05/2019.

12 Editorial Leader, 'Transforming Pretoria's heritage landscape', *IOL*, 26 February 2018 < https://www.iol.co.za/pretoria-news/opinion/transforming-pretorias-heritage-landscape-13490847> accessed 25/05/2019.

disapproval. The 100-metre pole and South African flag, was apparently designed to promote social cohesion, but received significant backlash for wasteful spending of public funds.[13] The cost of new symbols is certainly a constraint and something that needs consideration during the cost of living crisis.

A key point in the debate are the values linked to the figures represented in statues. A report from the Department of Arts and Culture recommended that certain statues which did not represent constitutional values should be removed.[14] Values are subjective and need to be considered in their historical context, however there are situations where values are almost universally regarded as unethical, an example being Nazism. S. Marschall, professor of cultural and heritage tourism at the University of KwaZulu Natal, said, 'for the majority of South Africans, Botha remains first and foremost a white oppressor'.[15] She added that Botha had freed King Dinizulu – there is nuance in South African history, and the statues of Botha and Dinizulu in Durban, similar in style and size, represent contested histories and their positioning also cleverly shows their friendship.[16] S. Ngubane, professor of African languages at the University of KwaZulu Natal, commented that it was not about replacing one symbol with another but rather placing different statues together, adding 'that is what will make history come alive'.[17]

History has certainly come alive, and it remains an emotive topic. Who could blame South Africans who are offended by these statues – who could blame those who want to see a change in art and sculptures in public spaces. Equally we cannot fault many South Africans and the government who want a more balanced response to the statue debate. Answers are hard to come by, where norms, politicisation of grievances, historical links to the past, and law and order must be considered – in the age of social media, organising protests, mobilising political messages, and spreading information has become easier. For those suffering, learning about the link between older leaders, reflected in bronze busts, and the poverty caused by the Land Act, could only make matters worse.

13 Anon, 'Nathi Mthethwa's 100-metre R22m flag monument still on department's agenda', *IOL*, 28 September 2022 <https://www.iol.co.za/pretoria-news/news/nathi-mthethwas-100-metre-r22m-flag-monument-still-on-departments-agenda-1c869327-1c93-4a98-9d07-d5d6c144df2e> (accessed 28/09/2022).

14 S. Stuurman, 'Report Recommends that Colonial Statues must Fall', *SABC News* < http://www.sabcnews.com/sabcnews/report-recommends-colonial-statues-must-fall/> (accessed 25/05/2019).

15 S. Marschall, 'What South Africa's Monument Debate Taught Us About Our History, And Ourselves', *Huffington Post*, 25 August 2017 < https://www.huffpost.com/entry/south-africa-charlottesville-monument_b_599ef3c9e4b0821444c18516> (accessed 25/05/2019).

16 Marschall, 'What South Africa's Monument Debate Taught Us About Our History, And Ourselves', *Huffington Post*, 25 August 2017.

17 L. Rondganger, '#KnowYourLand: Dick King is here, but where is Ndongeni?', *IOL*, 1 September 2018 <https://www.iol.co.za/dailynews/knowyourland-dick-king-is-here-but-where-is-ndongeni-16822664> (accessed 25/05/2019).

Until perhaps the impact of older politicians, generals and leaders are no longer felt on contemporary society – when the historical record, within reason, no longer offends people in the present, when past decisions no longer directly touch the food, and purse of South Africans; and when our oppressive past is no longer in living memory – then maybe the heroes of old will have a rediscovered place in South African memory – perhaps like those from the classics, whose distance from the current moment is so detached, their main purpose is only ancient inquiry.

Like all leaders, Botha and Smuts have points on both sides of their narrative ledger, credit and debit. But when they made mistakes, they were massive – the Native Land Act of 1913, is a case in point. Their victories too were colossal – facilitating the formation of Union, contributing to the First World War and helping to form the League of Nations are examples of such immense achievement.

This book was conceived as a comparative study and an inquiry into the lives of the two main characters, Botha and Smuts. We placed the current debate upfront, and we call out the errors of our subjects. The manuscript finds its place in the historiography as a comparative biography focusing on the First World War, it is anything but a hagiography, it is also not a full life reflection of the two generals – what we offer is a fresh view of Botha and Smuts and their role in the First World War, through significant archival research. The primary material provided the bulk of the evidence, but our methodology was formed by asking ourselves a few key questions.

We Start With Three Questions

When we, the authors, decided to write this book, we discussed ideas for the project. Initially it was to be a biography on only one of the two generals. Then we considered how difficult it would be to understand the role of one without the other, especially in the First World War. We decided that we needed both Botha and Smuts. We zoomed in on their lives and considered why a historical subject should be studied. We asked three key questions: Firstly, did they play a significant role in the history of South Africa? Secondly, is there in fact a story to tell? Or rather do we have something new to add? And lastly, does the subject or subjects interest us or is there a fascination? The answers to all three questions needed evaluation.

The answer to the first question was critical– did Botha and Smuts play an important role in South Africa's history? It was Botha and Smuts's leadership during the First World War that put South Africa's footprints on the global stage. They in fact decided on much of the key domestic and international policy questions facing a young South Africa. The difference between the South Africa into which they were born, and the one they helped create was striking. They grew up in a mixture of British colonies and Boer republics, a mixed bag of competing interests, and contested spaces. The unlikely pair came from very different backgrounds and were not similar in appearance or personality – Botha a big built farmer, born in 1862 in the Natal Colony, and Smuts, a bookish boy, who joined the world in 1870, in the Cape Colony. The fact that they found each other and forged the relationship they did, was in part due to coincidence – both coming to serve in Paul Kruger's Transvaal government. They strengthened their bond during the Anglo-Boer War 1899–1902, which forever changed the South African political landscape. It was in war that their relationship was forged, and it was in politics that their partnership would find its ultimate expression.

Following the Anglo-Boer War, they played a critical role in the formation of the Union of South Africa in 1910. Botha had the vision – he gave the 'what' – a united British and Boer South Africa (no Black, Coloured or Indian franchise), and Smuts provided the 'how' – the constitutional democratic mechanism and the constructive ways of achieving change. By first securing the independence of the Transvaal and then the Free State, they attempted to bring together British and Boer interests, while Black, Coloured and Indian voices remained unheard. It was their revolutionary experiment – a united White South Africa, a change for republican Afrikaners, and Imperial Britons that showed Botha as a visionary for his time. His idealism was backed up by his credentials as the former commandant-general of the Transvaal, his disarming charm and the undisputable intellect of Smuts, the talented former Transvaal State Prosecutor-cum-general, whose genius underpinned the whole initiative.

The two generals were on a roll – they worked night and day to create the Union. It was an amalgamation of its component parts; historic Boer republics and British colonies, each with different cultures, demography, and distinct political and military establishments. Botha became prime minister in 1910, and Smuts, true to his ability, took on triple ministerial portfolios, defence, mines, and interior – a sure way to wrest control of the military, finance and home affairs, thereby controlling all bases of power. It would become a trend with the powerful pair directing key areas and only delegating to those in their inner circle. The newly formed Union, which had historic debts, and informal cultural, financial, and familial networks required an army – of course two Boer generals could not rule a dominion without an army, and in 1912 the Defence Act provided the legislative base to unite the various military organisations. Botha and Smuts were quick to commit the newly formed Union Defence Force to an active role in the First World War.

The war aims were without a doubt imperialist, something that is worth reflecting on – to Botha and Smuts it was clear – realpolitik – it was the world that they inherited and the world they helped create. South African expansionism was not a foreign idea to Boer republicans and the commandos of old. In that fashion but donning, new and khaki uniforms, Botha and Smuts led campaigns in German South West Africa, German East Africa, and supported fighting in the Sanusi campaign, and on the Western Front. Smuts uniquely went on to serve in the Imperial and British War Cabinets, holding the highest levels of office, influencing policy at the administrative heart of the Great War.

At the start of the First World War, in 1914, republican minded Afrikaners rebelled. Botha and Smuts used the Union forces to quell this uprising, but it indicated a deep dissatisfaction. Rebel grievances which combined, political, historic, and personal issues, found violent expression. Our book shows how Botha and Smuts created a system that would give Boer republicans the political means to express their choice, and after 1914, there was no need to take up arms again. This was one of the central reasons that a second rebellion did not take place. It was Botha and Smuts's Union of South Africa – a dominion, with political franchise, at least for White South Africans – a constitutional democracy, with a constituency system. It was in fact this system that allowed Botha and Smuts to decide to join the war in an active way, and facilitated increased participation in the campaigns in Africa, and on the Western Front. It was these decisions, that disadvantaged South Africans with a stronger pigment make up; these policy decisions also helped shape the modern world, resulting in South Africa finding a role on the international stage, colonising Namibia in all but name, influencing the Treaty of Versailles, and contributing in no small part to the formation of the League of Nations. This answers the first question as to whether Botha and Smuts played a key role in South Africa's history, and the First World War.

The above discussion, begs the question, 'so what?' – and we asked ourselves the second question – do we have something to add? At first, we thought 'maybe we do but we need more evidence', and we scanned the historiography. We started to consider the combined role of Botha and Smuts in the First World War. The various books, chapters, articles, and papers addressed a wide range of areas, but the political and military Botha and Smuts in the First World War was not covered in a comprehensive fashion. A gap in the historiography started to emerge. We did further research on each of the generals. In their individual capacities, they both have a considerable historiography. On Smuts in particular, biographies, studies, and histories abound.[18] On Botha there is a more select reading list, but only six

18 Although hardly an exhaustive list, see F.S. Crafford, *Jan Smuts: A Biography* (New York: Doubleday, Doran & Co., 1944); W.H. Hancock, *Smuts: Study for a Portrait* (Cambridge: Cambridge University Press, 1965); C. Danziger, *Jan Smuts* (Cape Town: MacDonald, 1978); J.C. Smuts, *Jan Christian Smuts* (London: Cassell, 1952); T. Cameron, *Jan Smuts: An Illustrated Biography* (Cape Town: Human and Rousseau, 1994); Z. Friedlander, *Jan Smuts Remembered: A Centennial Tribute* (London: Wingate, 1970); O. Geyser, *Jan Smuts and his International Contemporaries* (Johannesburg: Covos Day, 2001); H.C. Armstrong, *Grey Steel, J.C. Smuts: A Study in Arrogance* (London: Arthur Barker, 1937); A. Lentin *Jan Smuts* (Johannesburg and Cape Town: Jonathan Ball, 2010); N. Levi, *Jan Smuts: being a Character Sketch of Gen. the Hon. J.C. Smuts*, (London: Longmans, 1917); K. Ingham, *Jan Smuts: The Conscience of a South African* (New York: St Martin's Press, 1986); R.H. Kiernan, *General Smuts* (London: Harrap, 1943); R. Kraus, *Old Master: The, Life of Jan Christiaan Smuts* (New York: E.P. Dutton 1944); S.G. Millin *General Smuts* (Boston: Little, Brown & Co., 1936); J. Joseph, *South African Statesman: Jan Christiaan Smuts* (New York: J. Messner, 1969); F. van Damme, *Jan Smuts* (Antwerp: Standaard Boekhandel, 1956); B. Friedman, *Jan Smuts: A Reappraisal* (New York: St. Martin's Press, 1976); P. Meiring, *Smuts the Patriot* (Cape Town: Tafelberg, 1975); R. Steyn, *Jan Smuts: Unafraid of Greatness* (Johannesburg: Jonathan Ball, 2015); P. Beukes, *The Holistic Smuts: A Study in Personality* (Cape Town: Human and Rousseau, 1989); G. Natrass and S.B. Spies, *Jan Smuts: Memoirs of the Boer War* (Johannesburg: Jonathan Ball, 1994); T.J. Haarhoff, *Smuts the Humanist: A Personal*

biographies have emerged.[19] Of these the only study involving extensive primary research[20] was by one of the authors, Antonio Garcia, who wrote his PhD thesis on Louis Botha's life, supervised by Ian Van Der Waag.[21] Our personal biographies date back to the South African military, Stellenbosch University Faculty of Military Science, and a professional relationship and friendship that is founded on the deep reading of military history, and a never-ending dialogue, often over coffee, on South Africa's fascinating past.

Not only does the subject of military history fascinate us but also that of the discipline of biography. It was in this area that Ian cut his teeth, writing his PhD thesis, a biography on Hugh Wyndham. He was a contemporary of Botha and Smuts, but perhaps a secondary figure.[22] Ian's doctoral study made a greater body of historical knowledge available. The eminent historian and biographer John Cooper says that he learned the trade of life writing by studying 'lesser' luminaries, before moving on to the central figures in early twentieth century American history, Woodrow Wilson and Theodore Roosevelt. Taking a page out of Cooper's book, this work is built on our previous studies, and is an attempt to fill a gap in the historiography.[23]

The authors build on their previous works but also the broader historiography – Antonio, wrote a number of papers, later published as a book *The First Campaign Victory of the Great War*,[24] whereas Ian covered the First World War and South Africa in various publications including his book *A Military History of Modern South Africa*.[25] The broader historiography shows a rich variety of books, papers and articles

Reminiscence (Oxford: Blackwell, 1970); and W.F. Burbidge, *Smuts, Soldier and World Statesman* (London: W.S. Coswell, 1943).

19 E.H. Spender, *General Botha: The Career and the Man* (London: Constable & Co., 1916); S.C. Buxton, *General Botha* (London: Hazel, Watson & Viney, 1924); Engelenburg, *General Louis Botha* (an English version of the book was subsequently published in 1929); J. Meintjes, *General Louis Botha* (London: Cassell & Co., 1970); and R. Steyn, *Louis Botha: A Man Apart* (Johannesburg: Jonathan Ball, 2018).

20 F. Pretorius, 'General Louis Botha's Role in the South African War, 1899–1902', *War and Society*, 2022, no.2.

21 See A. Garcia, 'General Louis Botha: Farmer, Soldier, Statesman, 1862–1919', PhD thesis, Stellenbosch University, 2019.

22 See I. van der Waag, 'Hugh Archibald Wyndham: His Life and Times in South Africa,', 1901–1923, PhD thesis, University of Cape Town, 2005.

23 See J.M. Cooper Jnr, 'Conception, Conversation and Comparison' in L.E. Ambrosius (ed.), *Writing Biography: Historians and Their Craft*.

24 See A. Garcia, *First Campaign Victory of Great War: South Africa, Manoeuvre Warfare, the Afrikaner Rebellion and the German South West African Campaign* (Warwick: Helion, 2019), p.31; A. Garcia, 'Manoeuvre Warfare in the South African Campaign in German South West Africa during the First World War', MA thesis, University of South Africa, 2015.

25 See I. van der Waag, *A Military History of Modern South Africa* (Johannesburg: Jonathan Ball, 2015); I. van der Waag, 'The Battle of Sandfontein 26 September 1914: South African Military Reform and the German South West Africa Campaign, 1914–1915',

covering South Africa's First World War, including campaign, strategic, and military histories.[26]

First World War Studies, vol.4, no.2 (2013), I. Van der Waag, 'Smuts's Generals: Towards a First Portrait of the South African High Command', *War in History*, vol.18, no.1 (2011).

26 See for example, J.J. Collyer, *Campaign in German South West Africa, 1914–1915* (Pretoria: Government Printer, 1937); Anon., *Union of South Africa and the Great War, 1914–1918: Official History* (Pretoria: Government Printer, 1924); W.W. O'Shaughnessy and W.S. Rayner, *How Botha and Smuts Conquered German South West* (London: Simpkin 1916); G. L'ange, *Urgent Imperial Service* (Rivonia: Ashanti, 1991). Regimental histories which address tactical and lower-level aspects of SA's participation in the First World War include B.G. Simpkins, *Rand Light Infantry* (Cape Town: Timmins, 1965); N. Orpen, *The History of the Transvaal Horse Artillery, 1904–1974* (Johannesburg: Alex White, 1975); A.C. Martin *The Durban Light Infantry, Volume 1, 1854 to 1934* (Durban: Hayne & Gibson, 1969). Sources on the Union's First World War efforts which cover the Afrikaner Rebellion of 1914 include T.R.H. Davenport, 'The South African Rebellion of 1914', *English Historical* Review, vol.78 (1963); S. Swart, 'The "Five Shilling" Rebellion: Rural White Male Anxiety and the 1914 Boer Rebellion', *South African Historical Journal (SAHJ),* vol.56, no.1 (2006); Anon., *Judicial Commission of Inquiry into Causes and Circumstances on the recent Rebellion in South Africa* (Pretoria: Government Printer, 1916); K. Fedorowich, 'Sleeping with the Lion? The Loyal Afrikaner and South African Rebellion of 1914–1915', *SAHJ*, vol.49, no.1 (2009); Anon., *Report on the Outbreak of the Rebellion and the Policy of the Government with Regard to its Suppression* (Pretoria: Government Printer, 1915); P.J. Sampson, *The Capture of De Wet: The South African Rebellion 1914* (London: Arnold, 1915); S. Swart, "Desperate Men': The 1914 Rebellion and the Polities of Poverty', *SAHJ*, vol.42, no.1 (2000); and A. Grundlingh and S. Swart, *Radelose Rebellie: Dinamika van die 1914–1915 Afrikaner Rebellie* (Pretoria: Protea Bookhouse, 2009). Nasson, *Springboks on the Somme*; T. Couzens, *The Great Silence* (Johannesburg: Sunday Times, 2014); A.M. Grundlingh, *Fighting their Own War: South African Blacks and the First World War* (Johannesburg: Ravan Press, 1988); J. Stejskal, *The Horns of the Beast: The Swakop River Campaign and World War I in South West Africa, 1914–1915* (Solihull: Helion, 2014); I. Gleeson, *The Unknown Force: Black indian and Coloured Soldiers through Two World Wars* (Rivonia: Ashanti, 1994); D. Williams, *Springboks, Troepies and Cadres: Stories of the South African Army 1912–2012* (Cape Town: Tafelberg, 2012).

The East African campaign is covered by, R. Anderson, *The Forgotten Front: The East African Campaign* (Stroud: Tempus, 2004); Anon., *The Union of South Africa and the Great War* (Pretoria: Government Printer, 1924); J.J. Collyer, *The South Africans with General Smuts in East Africa* (Pretoria: Government Printer, 1939); A. Samson, *Britain South Africa and the East African Campaign* (London: Tauris, 2006); F.B. Young, *Marching on Tanga: With General Smuts in Africa* (London: W. Collins, 1917); P.E. von Lettow-Vorbeck, *My Reminisces of East Africa* (London: Hurst & Blackett, 1920); T.J. Stapleton, *No Insignificant Part: The Rhodesia Native Regiment and the East Africa Campaign of the First World War* (Ontario: Wilfred Laurier University, 2006); J.R. Sibley, *Tanganyikan Guerrilla: East African Campaign 1914–1918* (London: Pan, 1973); E. Paice, *World War 1: The African Front* (New York: Pegasus 2008). The Sanusi campaign and operations on the Western Front is covered in J. Buchan, *The History of the South African Forces in France* (London: Nelson, 1920); I. Uys, *Rollcall: Delville Wood Story* (Johannesburg: Uys, 1991); Anon., *Union of South Africa and the Great War*; P.K.A. Digby, *Pyramids and Poppies: The 1st SA Brigade in Libya, France and Flanders, 1915–1919* (Johannesburg: Ashanti, 1993); and G.W. Warwick, *We Band of Brothers: Reminiscences from the 1st S.A. Infantry*

This book is not a campaign or strategic history – these have a strong historical base. One of the areas that needed attention was that of Botha and Smuts. We could not find a book length comparative biography of Botha and Smuts in the First World War – this was the gap in the historiography that slowly started to crystallise in our minds. Of course, we do not presume that this topic has not been explored, at least in part by other historians, and let us add, by very good historians. But their works, brilliant in many cases, have often been on broader areas, and not completely focussed on the First World War. We found political, cultural and or social historical studies, with some military papers, mostly in the form of shorter academic articles or book chapters.[27] Other academic manuscripts and articles, many of excellent quality have some cross over, but often with a limited thematic focus for example, concentrating on a campaign such as East Africa, or a capability such as air power, or a particular discipline, such as political history.[28] The closest similar work we could find was that of Basil Williams, one of Milner's 'kindergarteners' and later a history professor. Williams had made use of the comparative element, but his focus was on a much wider remit, and included Botha's and Smuts's early lives, the Anglo-Boer

Brigade in the 1914–1918 War (Cape Town: Howard Timms, 1962). Further sources on the First World War and the role of the Union of South Africa include, E. Dane, *British Campaigns in Africa and the Pacific, 1914–1918* (London: Hodder & Stoughton, 1919); H. Strachan, *The First World War, Volume 1: To Arms* (Oxford: Oxford University Press, 2001); J.M. Brown and W.R. Louis (eds.), *The Oxford History of the British Empire, Volume 4: The Twentieth Century* (Oxford: Oxford University Press, 1999); H. Strachan, *The First World War in Africa* (Oxford: Oxford University Press, 2004); R.C. Warwick, 'The Battle of Sandfontein: The Role and Legacy of Major General Sir Henry Timson Lukin', *Scientia Militaria*, vol.34, no.2 (2006); I. van der Waag, 'Smuts's Generals: Towards a First Portrait of the South African High Command, 1912–1948', *War in History*, vol.18, no.1 (2011); I. van der Waag, 'The Battle of Sandfontein 26 September 1914: South African Military Reform and the German South-West Africa Campaign, 1914–1915', *First World War Studies*, vol.4, no.2 (2013); Grundlingh, *Participation and Remembrance: South African Black and Coloured Troops in the First World War*; T. Couzens, *The Great Silence* (Johannesburg: Sunday Times, 2014); B. Nasson, *World War 1 and the People of South Africa* (Cape Town: Tafelberg, 2014); and I. van der Waag, *A Military History of Modern South Africa* (Johannesburg: Jonathan Ball, 2015). And for a more recent campaign history, A. Cruise, *Louis Botha's War: The Campaign in South West Africa* (Cape Town: Zebra Press, 2015).

27 See for example, A.J. van Wyk, 'Botha en Smuts: Tweeling' in K. du Pisani, D. Kriek and C. de Jager (eds.), *Jan Smuts: Van Boerseun tot Wêreldverhoog, 'n Herwaardering* (Pretoria: Protea, 2017); S.B. Spies, 'The Outbreak of the First World War and the Botha Government', *South African Historical Journal*, vol.1, no.1 (1969).

28 E. Kleynhans, 'A Critical Analysis of the Impact of Water on the South African Campaign in German South West Africa, 1914–1915', *Historia*, vol.61, no.2, (2016). S. Dubow, South Africa's Racist Founding Father Was Also a Human Rights Pioneer, *New York Times* <https://www.nytimes.com/2019/05/18/opinion/jan-smuts-south-africa.html> accessed 25/09/2022; T. Dedering, '"Avenge the Lusitania": The Anti-German Riots in South Africa in 1915', *Immigrants & Minorities Historical Studies in Ethnicity, Migration and Diaspora*, vol.31, no.3 (2013).

War (South African War), through the First and Second World Wars.[29] This was the background that led to this work – a book length academic biographical study with a thematic focus on the First World War. By drawing on little used archival material the book highlights how our central characters interacted with people of all races, the mechanics of setting up the Union and the Union Defence Force, and how they overcame obstacles to achieve their objectives. The above exposition answers the second question, that yes something new can be added. Linked to the second question, is the critical subject of sources.

We assume that all or most academic historians and biographers ask themselves the question – do we have sufficient primary material to conduct our study? Our subjects Botha and Smuts were very different men. In some ways, Smuts wrote his life story while he was alive. He was educated at university and excelled at academics, he loved books, and wrote prolifically, on everything from military and political matters to philosophy and botany. Smuts's scholarship took different forms, and there exists an absolute treasure trove of published sources in libraries, bookstores, and online, as well as masses of archival materials in repositories in South Africa and the United Kingdom. In many ways the work on Smuts involved finding titbits from his colleagues and contemporaries, bringing out new ideas, thoughts, and motivations. This brings into focus the importance of official documentation, and the papers of his contemporaries.

This last point, the personal papers of colleagues, was important for Smuts, but was absolutely critical for the study of Botha, who, when it came to putting pen to paper, was the opposite of Smuts. Botha no doubt had a tremendous work ethic, but he did not keep diaries, and much of his correspondence is kept in the archival papers of his contemporaries, Gustav Preller, Sydney Buxton, Frans Engelenburg and Willem Leyds. Lack of primary sources is often a challenge for historians, and we would like to mention the obstacles faced by South African biographers looking to put forward new life sketches, of key Black, Coloured and Indian personalities, where there exist fewer primary sources.[30] Our work was dependent on the archivists who gathered Botha and Smuts's correspondence, official papers, and personal papers. In the case of Botha, Preller and Engelenburg, kept an incredible selection of newspaper articles often quoting the general. These proved critical.

At some points the two generals worked together, and at other points they served in different places – for the most part Botha and Smuts spent time apart during the Afrikaner Rebellion, GSWA campaign, the GEA campaign and during Smuts's time

29 B. Williams, *Botha, Smuts and South Africa* (London: Hodder & Stoughton, 1946), *passim*.

30 See B. Willan, *Sol Plaatje: A Life of Solomon Tshekisho Plaatje* (Johannesburg: Jacana, 2018); Pixley. Willan and Plaaje for a famous Black South African with a wealth of primary materials, and a well written biography. H. Hughes, *First President: A Life of John Dube, Founding President of the ANC* (Johannesburg: Jacana, 2011). There are a number of significant biographies of South African leaders – some examples include, *F.A. Mouton, Prophet Without Honour: F.S. Malan: Afrikaner, South African and Cape Liberal* (Pretoria: Protea, 2011); A. Grundlingh, *Slabbert: Man on a Mission* (Johannesburg: Jonathan Ball, 2021).

in London. Their correspondence provides insight into their relationship. Perhaps conversations that they would normally have had face to face are captured in letters that mostly were not intended for public consumption; but are now on record.

The final question asks whether we have an interest or fascination with Botha and Smuts. Historians and biographers allow themselves this luxury – a personal, professional, or quirky interest in their subject. This is important to keep up the motivation and perseverance, but again if we are completely honest, writers, historians and academic biographers know the truth – the need to learn and uncover more and get to the 'bottom of matters' provides a never-ending source of motivation.

The danger with a personal interest in a topic, is that it sometimes lends itself to bias. Going into this project we acknowledged this issue, and in order to mitigate it we have done our best to provide a balanced view of the two generals, and importantly our interpretations are supported by evidence. It is sometimes the case when one starts a book project that, despite telling oneself not to have preconceived notions, one finds some existing and sometimes well entrenched thoughts. In as much as the main characters of this story are flawed, so too are its authors; and biographers are limited by the selection and interpretation of the source material. This was true for us, and we tried as far as possible to use evidence to underpin our work.

After writing this book, we are not sure whether we 'like' the generals more or less; what we can say is that through the added research, their successes seem even more pronounced, and their failures, staggering. Although we must add that we are agreed, that if Botha and Smuts called us from the past, and asked us to go to a dinner party, we would undoubtably accept. The reasons for this thought experiment are threefold: firstly, it would be to continue the historical debate between the present and the past; secondly, in order to interview our subjects for the book; and thirdly, and almost most importantly, is the tantalising search for what we could not find in-between the words, the lines, and the books – what remained hidden despite processing reams of paper that hold the historical code of these figures. A quirk, a smile, an engaging anecdote about Smuts's farming that surprises Botha? Basil Williams claims that he was successful,[31] although Botha was clearly the master farmer – writing to Smuts in April 1918:

> Your farming is also doing well, except that I think Krige makes it unnecessarily difficult and hard for Mrs Smuts. I am sure it would be better if he were no longer your manager; and, from what I see, I think you should even cancel the contract for tree-planting and any other contract between you. Then the contract cannot be renewed at the end of the year. I do not much want to intrude upon your affairs, but as a friend, and in view of your absence, I have definitely come to this conclusion—put an end to it. For the rest things are going well there. My own

31 Williams, *Botha, Smuts and South Africa*, p.200.

> farming has also progressed beautifully, except that we have had far too much rain this year.[32]

Perhaps some further unexpected themes would be discussed. At the dinner Botha would perhaps surprise us and quote Spinoza while Smuts listens on. We found evidence of Botha making a note in the Transvaal Volksraad referencing Machiavelli and Spinoza.[33] Maybe Smuts would add some depth to Botha's quote or draw on classical sources. The two seem to have parts of the other. They were both brilliant and loved each other, they were like brothers.

We would ask them if the idea of a united British and Boer South Africa, was in fact Botha's, or if it was a practical consideration given the end of the Anglo-Boer War. Smuts saw to the legislative part, but Botha provided the vision; 'he was the heart of the movement, but Smuts was the brain.'[34]

At the dinner, we would look for evidence of the traditional conception of both men. Botha the loving, insecure, capable, and practical farmer, and commander, and Smuts, the intellectual, 'slim' (shrewd), confidant, philosopher warrior. Both romantic figures, the charming yet rugged Boer general, and the polished philosopher warrior – they inspired trust and captivated the Empire – would we be taken in?

But would a romanticised view of the past limit us, and ultimately disappoint the authors. Would we see Botha and Smuts through the eyes of their critics – an overweight, smiley, tubby cattle herder who by coincidence led a Boer force, and came to power; with his sidekick, a slight, scheming lawyer who condescendingly preached his lordly plans?

Our last question would be about oppression in modern South Africa, and if they had any way of knowing that things were going to go as bad as they did? Botha and Smuts's reshaping of South Africa's political system gave them the power to join and lead the Union in the First World War; but by giving this political power to Afrikaner constituents, it ultimately led to the National Party's victory in the 1920s, and the victory of extreme Afrikaner nationalists in the 1950s which formalised the Apartheid state.

The African National Congress, at the head of the liberation movements, fought for franchise for the second half of the twentieth century, which eventually led to free and fair elections in 1994. In a similar way questions will be asked about every South African government including those in the post 1994 landscape. The modern South Africa, the Rainbow Nation, is perhaps also due for historical re-examination, but this falls outside the scope of this book and will be on the shoulders of other contemporary and future historians and biographers.

32 Botha to Smuts, 26 February 1918, W. Hancock and J. van der Poel (eds.), *Selections from the Smuts Papers* (London: Cambridge University Press, 1966), vol. III, p.610.
33 Botha's notes in the First Volksraad, 4 May 1895, National Archives and Records Service of South Africa (NARSSA): Preller Collection, A 787, 11.
34 Hancock and Van der Poel (eds.), *Selections*, vol. III, p.3.

Botha and Smuts would of course never be able to answer these questions, it is also doubtful that they could understand the depth of our questions, as they, like us, are trapped in the confines of the norms of the times. The thought experiment excites the mind, but it is of course limited by the life and times we live in and the norms of the past – we could never completely understand their frame of reference, nor could we ask them to extrapolate the destruction and deprivation caused by their decisions. That being said, the passage of time does not absolve Botha and Smuts of their guilt, or their achievement.

They are historical figures who loom large on the South African historical landscape; with their colossal achievements and failures, we have laid out their narratives in the chapters of this book.

Volume Overview

The various chapters address different elements of the lives and experiences of Botha and Smuts. There is overlap. In equal measure the discussion is respectively based on the viewpoint of Botha and Smuts, from wherever they were at the time. For example, a few chapters overlap several years of the Great War; in 1916, Smuts had left to command the force in German East Africa, see Chapter 7, and Botha remained in South Africa, see Chapter 6. Botha writes to Smuts from South Africa, and likewise Smuts responds, Botha also visits Smuts in the field.

We have tried as far as possible to make sure that each chapter can be read as part of a cohesive narrative on the two generals, but also that the chapters can be read as standalone expositions – this may be of assistance to readers who have a particular interest.

At times historical words are used which are not intended to cause offense. For example, when the term 'native' is quoted, it is not meant as a pejorative term. It is only reflected as was written in the source. One final point on this, is that in South Africa, a number of racial groups, and Black, White, Coloured and Indian groupings remain official demographic categories. The term Coloured is not an offensive term in South Africa. The above-mentioned groupings are referred to throughout the book.

Chapter 1: The road to 1914, gives an overview of the context of the formation of the Union, and the road to the First World War, 1902–1914. It was a time where everything was in flux – a time of uncertainty. Botha's vision gave direction, a point marked on a future political map, while Smuts adapted the compass and put together the navigation plan.

Chapter 2: A bad beginning, 1914, addresses the landscape of the Union and the politics of war-time participation, in 1914. We explore the new moment, how Union brought together a range of different people with various interests – and the resulting conflict and cooperation. Lastly, we touch on Botha and Smuts's commitment to the First World War which brought matters to a head.

Chapter 3: Gambits and Crises, 1914, deals with the fall out over the decision to go to war, the 1914 Afrikaner Rebellion and the Battle of Sandfontein. We evaluate the

Union Defence Force's first military test, and the results, which led to the re-invasion of South West Africa.

Chapter 4: The conquest of German South West Africa, 1915, gives a detailed account of the GSWA campaign, in 1915. Botha and Smuts combined political and military roles, holding office, and commanding in the field. It was a quick campaign with considerable logistical challenges, but a good re-invasion plan that was well executed.

Chapter 5: Domestic Politics, 1915, proceeds with an account of the political campaign, which followed Botha's return from South West Africa, which culminated in the pivotal 1915 elections. The results, disappointing to Botha and Smuts, marked a change in the tide, but the two generals pushed back.

Chapter 6: Local polemics, Public Opinion and Foreign policy, 1915-1916, provides an overview of the local context in the Union from the viewpoint of Botha, and an interesting section on early attempts at forming an intelligence service in South Africa. It goes on to show Botha's mounting worries and frustrations, as Smuts took over command of the British force in East Africa.

Chapter 7: Campaigning in Africa and Europe in 1916, explores Smuts's strategic role in the German East Africa campaign. Taking over from a flailing British force, Smuts reinvigorated the campaign, his concept of operations and mobile attacks, drove the Germans into the field, liberating large swathes of territory. An overview of the South African operations in Europe is also provided.

Chapter 8: Not a serial fairy tale, 1916–1918, provides an analysis of the machinery and politics of war from the viewpoint of the Union. Addressing some broad and important themes, this chapter discusses matters of supply, disease, and recruitment 1916–1917.

Chapter 9: High Politics, 1917–1918, evaluates Smuts's role in London in the Imperial and British War Cabinets. He was uniquely placed to influence policy, he had the ear of Prime Minister Lloyd George, and was the star problem shooter. The chapter also provides a lens into Botha's experience in South Africa, during the challenging period, 1917–1918.

Chapter 10: A better ending? describes Botha and Smuts's role at the end of the war, and the Paris Peace Conference. This chapter deals with Botha's death in 1919, and some final thoughts on the legacy of the two generals.

Conclusion

Although lionised during the war by a British public hungry for heroes, there is a different side to Botha and Smuts. Shunned by Afrikaner nationalists at the time, they have remained divisive figures. Responsible for the enactment of the Land Act of 1913, which disadvantaged the majority of South Africans and shaped South Africa's socio-economic and political landscape, there are fresh calls (2015–2022 at the time of writing this book) for Botha and Smuts's statues to be removed. It is the unending dialogue between the present and the past that bring up these issues, and rightfully so.

The primary aim of this volume is to compare Botha and Smuts, in a biography focussed on the First World War. We seek to understand these two generals: Botha's charm, charisma, and magnetism; as well as Smuts's stoicism, and intellectualism – what was façade and were there two very human, imperfect, and sometimes inconsiderate, men? Together they provide a wonderful lens to understand South Africa's policy decisions which impacted twentieth century Southern African. They fought insurmountable odds, and achieved great victories, at home and abroad, but also made startling errors, and, ultimately, in classical fashion were crushed by the world they tried to create.

According to Sir James Rose-Innes, the Chief Justice of South Africa during the Great War, 'there has been a marked tendency for South African political leaders to run in couples, in an association so close as to be almost double-barrelled.'[35] This is an interesting observation. The pair has normally comprised a prime minister and a close colleague. Rose-Innes mentions several instances: Molteno and Saul Solomon, and their struggle to gain self-government for the Cape Colony; Sprigg and Upington, Rhodes and Hofmeyr, Merriman and Sauer, Botha and Smuts, and Hertzog and Havenga. But, of these duumvirates, Rose-Innes believed the Botha-Smuts consortium the most significant. Their political collaboration started at a crucial period in South African history and their governments – stretching from 1907 through to 1924 – dealt with significant problems: the weight, meaning, and spirit of the Treaty signed at Vereeniging that ended the Anglo-Boer War; the relationship between Dutch and English-speaking South Africans; and the bitter, persistently difficult legacies of the Anglo-Boer War and the wider political struggles in South Africa. Theirs was a David-Jonathan relationship.[36] It is difficult – even impossible – to understand the life of the one without an examination of the other. A 'double-barrelled' biography is the only course.

Botha died in 1919, shortly after the Paris Peace Conference – his heart gave in; a confluence of physical and emotional maladies. On the passing of Botha, and his legacy, Smuts observed:

> In time, no doubt, and with the lapse of years and the passing of this generation, the larger Botha will emerge… His colossal figure will then appear in its true historic proportions, and new biographers will arise to tell of the wonder of it all.[37]

35 B.A. Tindall (ed.), *James Rose Innes, Chief Justice of South Africa, 1914-27, Autobiography* (Cape Town: Oxford University Press, 1949), p.273.
36 A close, powerful intimate and platonic friendship often between soldiers.
37 Engelenburg, *Botha*, p.15.

Smuts earmarked a space for the telling of Botha's story, but he was not best placed to do it. J.X. Merriman suggested that Smuts write a fuller biography, but after taking office as the new prime minister, Smuts declined to do so because of his heavy workload. Smuts went on to suggest that Professor L. Fouché, who assisted him with the writing of the 'Report on the Outbreak of the Rebellion',[38] pen the biography on Botha.[39] He declined. A steady stream of biographers would volunteer to write Botha's story, not to mention that Harold Spender, an author and friend of Lloyd George, wrote Botha's story while the general was still alive – the book was published in 1916.[40]

Engelenburg, a contemporary and biographer, later wrote that that Botha was destined to have a niche in the national memory.[41] Smuts ensured that the memory of Botha was enshrined in statues, marking his place in South Africa's public spaces. Now former president Nelson Mandela's statue towers over the other effigies at the Union buildings in Pretoria, and King Dinizulu's bust is prominent in Durban – Botha's niche in the South African memory remains contested, but whether in open or closed public displays, the colossal figures of South Africa's past provides a mental and physical space for historical discussion.

Smuts too, was famous during his lifetime and Naphtali Levi wrote his biography, while the general was alive and even consulted with him. Although Smuts was not entirely encouraging of the book asking, 'I wonder what is in it because he really knows nothing of my life or private history!'[42] Smuts would come to terms with his fame; he received recognition in philosophic, political, military, and academic circles and the Smuts Memorial Committee would ensure his effigies remained present in South Africa. Winston Churchill, a contemporary and friend, paid respect to Smuts, reflecting on his, 'prolonged harmony of mind and body… healthy practical common sense, which guided him in daily action… his far-ranging outlook over the world scene….'[43] In recognition for his services Churchill advocated for a statue of Smuts in London – it still stands in Parliament Square.

Churchill went on to write a letter of condolence to Isie, Smuts's wife,

38 Request and acceptance correspondence from the Secretary of Defence and Prof. L. Fouché with regard to the writing of the history of the Afrikaner Rebellion, 16 March 1916 and 28 August 1916, DODA: Diverse 1, Box 1.

39 Smuts to Merriman, 14 October 1919, Hancock and Van der Poel (eds.), *Selections*, vol.III, p.15.

40 E.H. Spender, *General Botha: The Career and the Man* (London: Constable & Co., 1916).

41 Engelenburg, *Botha*, p.7. History writing as a discipline is also a form of public memory in the view of J. Tosh (ed.), *Historians on History* (London: Routledge, 2014), p.14. This volume may also be a form of public memory as interpreted by the worldview of the reader.

42 Smuts to Isie, 21 December 1916, Hancock and Van der Poel (eds.), *Selections*, vol. III, p.435.

43 P. H. Courtenay, 'Great Contemporaries: Jan Christian Smuts', *The Churchill Project, Hillsdale College* < https://winstonchurchill.hillsdale.edu/jan-smuts-churchills-great-contemporary/ > accessed 27/09/2022.

> Please accept my deepest sympathy in your sorrow and deprivation… a warrior-statesman and philosopher who was probably more fitted to guide struggling and blundering humanity through its sufferings and perils towards a better day than anyone who lived in any country during his epoch.[44]

In South Africa and the United Kingdom, statues of many South African heroes have emerged. Statues of Nelson Mandela and Mahatma Gandhi (an adopted Indian South African) are also present in Parliament Square London and allow for a broader historical discussion of change in South Africa.

They did not have social media, and followers in the modern sense, but statuettes of the two generals were created which promoted their image and built a narrative of their position in society – it was also used to comfort friends and family. While Smuts was in German East Africa, Botha wrote to Isie, keeping her abreast of events, and keeping up her spirits – he said he would, 'send you one of Jannie and my statuettes.'[45]

44 Courtenay, 'Great Contemporaries: Jan Christian Smuts', *The Churchill Project, Hillsdale College*.

45 Botha to Isie, 4 May 1917, Hancock and Van der Poel (eds.), *Selections*, vol. III, p.493.

1

The Road to War

The running of the Union is no easy task indeed!
Botha to Leyds[1]

Louis Botha's and Jan Smuts's commitment to Empire became a burden in 1914. The road to war started in 1902 – the year marked the milestone of complete British victory over Boer republicanism. Botha somehow managed to remain an optimist – his vision for a new White South Africa, comprised of Afrikaans and British societies. Accepted by some, it was limited, imperfect and racist, with the Black, Coloured and Indian majority ignored. Yet somehow and certainly in its time many thought it ingenious. Without holding power, he would mobilise Smuts.

Smuts was down and out and after becoming 'plain J.C Smuts', as he told his dear Isie, after the end of the Anglo-Boer War, a man of tremendous ability, he was soon to become General Smuts again. In the throes of a mild depression, Botha's vision gave Smuts an aim – this was all he needed to restart his powerhouse intellect. The second ingredient was an adversary – and Lord Milner became his nemesis, and that of the Boer people. Alfred Milner, once described as having Prussian efficiency, was a hard-boiled imperialist with a moustache too – smartly turned out, with dark features – his ample forehead held the contemplation of his policies for Southern Africa. It would take all Smuts's savvy and legal ability to fence with Milner – the first matter on the agenda was the case of the Cape Boer rebels. Botha wrote to Smuts, in September 1902, 'Stand fast, man, and keep up your courage. But if Lord Milner does not take care he will become the most hated man in the world.'[2] They would eventually find a way to save their Boer brothers in the Cape.

1 NARSSA: Leyds Archive, 262, Part II, Botha to Leyds, 18 August 1913.
2 Botha to Smuts, 25 September 1902 in Hancock and Van der Poel, *Selections*, vol.I, p.34.

The Road to Union

A modern wave of Afrikaner leadership emerged after the Second Anglo-Boer War – the pair of generals were at the helm in Pretoria.[3] Botha and Smuts – through *Het Volk*, created their first political platform for achieving their vision:

> The fundamental object of '*Het Volk*' is a policy of racial reconciliation, the avoidance of causes of distrust and division, the prevention of the ascendancy of one white race over the other, and the union of all white inhabitants of the State into a great South African nation, contented, prosperous and united, regarding South Africa with common patriotism and pride as its home, and working with united forces for its future greatness and glory.[4]

Later *Het Volk* would be reincarnated as the South African Party, mobilising voters in the Transvaal, the Cape, Free State and Natal. Botha and Smuts combined complementary personal skills. Botha, a man with a large heart, was sympathetic and human. His blue eyes were pensive and engaging – his moustache lifted when he deployed his disarming smile. A political player, he listened keenly, he was patient and could mobilise opinion – according to Jack Collyer, his chief of staff in South West Africa – he had a sixth sense of his opponent's intentions. Smuts was cut from very different cloth. His boyish face was hidden behind a moustache and beard, his eyes focussed intently at one subject at a time. Impatient and moody, he suffered fools lightly, and was dismissive when in thought – something that chimed with the upper classes of England. He was captivated by intellectual pursuits and in day-to-day tasks he was the epitome of competence. The two men had met before the outbreak of the Anglo-Boer War, but their mutual admiration developed over the years. After 1902, they combined personal ambition in a common drive to re-create South Africa. Louis Esselen, a close associate of Botha and then Smuts, warned a young Piet van der Byl never to leave with either man – whether by horse or vehicle – 'without a rifle and full magazine and iron rations in one's pocket, for one never knew what the old fellows would be up to; or on what job they would suddenly send you. Life was never dull when you were with them on active service.'[5] Botha and Smuts were men in a hurry.

Their concerns after the Anglo-Boer War were amnesty for the colonial rebels; the repatriation of internees of the concentration camps; and the absence of Afrikaans in the school curriculum. Botha communicated these concerns to Joseph Chamberlain in his 1903 visit, but the secretary of state for the colonies was satisfied with the

3 Ian van der Waag, 'Boer generalship and the politics of command', *War in History*, vol.12, no.1 (2005), pp.15-43.

4 University of South Africa (UNISA) Archives and Special Collections, Pretoria: Programme of the 'People's Union', 1907, United Party Archives, Transvaal Head Office.

5 Piet van der Byl, *From Playgrounds to Battlefields* (Cape Town: Howard Timmins, 1971), pp.186–187.

status quo. An imperialist, he had full confidence in Milner and his group of young, imperial-minded staffers that came to be known as Milner's 'Kindergarten'.[6] These bright young men were Oxbridge graduates and although intelligent, had relatively little experience. Milner groomed them to assist him with the growing administrative burdens.[7] Robert Brand, one of Lord Milner's kindergarten, described Transvaal Boers and British settlers as: 'two nations exist[ing] side by side … absolutely divided in language, customs, and ideals from the men governing them.'[8] The shapes did not match, the sizes were wrong, but Botha envisioned a united White South Africa. Perhaps an easy solution to a complex question.

Botha returned to South Africa from Europe in December 1902 after positioning himself strategically for the future and making friends and alliances. Smuts was also building his networks in England, and he and Botha were energised and brimming with ideas on uniting South Africa. At the heart of the issue Botha and Smuts believed that they could convince the White populations to live together – they had underestimated the anti-British sentiment of the Afrikaner people.[9]

Botha and Smuts evolved with the changing political situation, tackling the issues of resettlement (those who had been in the concentration camps and prisoners of war); Chinese labour in the Transvaal mines (engineered by Milner and having consequences in British politics); schooling; agriculture and economic development all of which fell under the umbrella of self-government. Botha's letter to Leyds in November 1903, gives the feeling of frustration, describing the sad state of prisoners of war who sacrificed so much and those who were still being held captive. Botha asked that De la Rey be sent to India to ensure the return of the prisoners – most of whom refused to acknowledge the peace settlement and swear allegiance to Britain.[10] The note was not in Botha's customary methodical style, sharing ideas or putting forward logistical or operational questions or answers in a logical manner. In this letter, he gives a flurry of emotion-filled phrases, painting the situation through the lens of a disenfranchised war leader. Smuts echoed Botha's disappointment in the lack of agency. In a note about dealing with Milner, Smuts discussed the difficulty in getting the necessary permissions for President Kruger's return – something that was not to be – Milner feared that Boer republicans would rally around the old stalwart.[11]

Paul Kruger, was the stubborn, and zealous leader of the Transvaal – with a face like a pile of rocks, outlined by a long beard, he embodied the tough Boer spirit.

6 Meintjes, *Botha*, p.121; Engelenburg, *Botha*, p.115.
7 Van der Waag, 'Hugh Archibald Wyndham: His Life and Times in South Africa,', pp.31–33.
8 Queen's University Archives, Kingston, Ontario (QUA): fonds 2110, box 1, correspondence general, John Buchan, Robert Brand to John Buchan, 18 December 1904.
9 Meintjes, *Botha*, p.121.
10 NARSSA: Leyds Archive, 262, Part I Botha to Leyds, 23 November 1903.
11 Smuts to Bredell, 15 August 1903 in Hancock and Van der Poel (eds.), *Selections*, vol.I, pp.123–124.

His death in 1904 signalled the end of a previous era and the coming of a new Boer moment – a moment of transition. It also allowed for the ascension of a new leader.

A large crowd gathered in Pretoria on 'Blood River Day' in 1904. They arrived for Kruger's state funeral. The Executive Council of the Transvaal Colony was present, together with a small detachment of Transvaal Police and the South African Constabulary. On closer inspection, initial impressions of British strength and magnanimity – the giving of a state funeral to the exiled former head of the Boer state – is belied by the circumstance. The crowd, picturesque if not impressive, was preponderantly Dutch, perhaps as many as 10,000 or 12,000, and controlled by what one British observer called an 'amateur Boer police'. Several Boer leaders, all former generals – Schalk Burger, Christiaan de Wet and Louis Botha – addressed the crowd.

His speech at the funeral of Kruger, was by way of the Transvaal's Mark Anthony oration to Julius Caesar. Olive Schreiner described the scene as something that she had never seen before, not even in Europe:

> The solemn rows of burghers in their old fighting clothes were very touching to me but the scene in the dim hall lit by electric lights, and the hundreds & hundreds of wreaths covering floor and walls to the far end where the old hero lay in his coffin, was moving beyond words. In the room behind were huge books in which all who came wrote their names.[12]

Smuts said that, 'Botha spoke with such feeling that I saw tears in many eyes. The Afrikaner people are going through deep waters, and he, to whom we all look up as our leader, speaks of himself as a worn-out horse. However, I have a feeling that, in spite of everything, we must go on clenching our teeth and persevering through everything until the dawn breaks.'[13] Engelenburg said Botha was the 'heart and soul' of Kruger's funeral procession – he transformed into the pre-eminent Transvaal leader.[14]

The death of Kruger passed the torch to Botha and by association to Smuts. Botha and Smuts held a series of meetings, rallying support for Boer interests in the Transvaal. Also reaching out to the governor of Natal, Botha thanked him for pardoning the colonial rebels and urged Leander Starr Jameson to do the same in the Cape. Jameson was a controversial figure, charismatic and inspirational to some, he also harboured delusions of military ability – soon dispelled by the commandos that put down his Raid – the Jameson Raid, an attempt in 1896, to inspire insurrection in the Transvaal. His large brow and big dark eyes carried the burden of the failed attempt – he now saw South Africa differently – Botha and Smuts were there to stay.

12 University of Cape Town Libraries, Cape Town (UCT): Olive Schreiner BC16/Box3, Olive Schreiner to Alice Greene, 24 December 1904.

13 Smuts to M.T. Steyn, 4 May 1906 in Hancock and Van der Poel (eds.), *Selections*, vol.II, p.270.

14 Engelenburg, *Botha*, pp.132–135.

Botha became the embodiment of Afrikaner republican interests and in 1904 at the *Volksstem* offices in Pretoria, *Het Volk* political party, was formed.[15] Pro-British contemporaries such as Abe Bailey criticised *Het Volk*, calling it no more than a 'military organisation' and suggesting that the Boer congress held to celebrate Afrikaner ideals was based on racial lines. A request was subsequently made for Botha to outline his political policies. Botha responded angrily to this suggestion calling it 'an insinuation so unworthy that it hardly merits serious attention'. He went on to explain that *Het Volk* aimed for mutual cooperation between the (White) people in the Transvaal.[16] *Het Volk* – an unofficial shadow government, existed alongside the Executive Council, no less powerful, supported by former Boer generals and commandants – the natural leaders of the late war. Milner, Bailey and others were correct – this was a Boer organisation, the commandos, in all but name. It was the political reincarnation of the forces who had lost the previous war, although it should be remembered that they were not defeated in the field.

Chamberlain and Milner had a similar vision for South Africa – Boer subjugation – one that was backed by Arthur James Balfour's (later Lord Balfour) conservative government.[17] On the Conservative Party Botha observed:

> Their general interference in the politics of South Africa from the days of the Jameson Raid up to the present constitutes one unbroken record of stupendous blundering and miscalculation, and we do not think that the destinies of the subcontinent ought to be entrusted to such people … I have no doubt that the government of this country is almost completely dictated by the mining magnates.[18]

The change in South Africa could therefore only come later, and thus the success of Botha's and Smuts's earlier trips to England bore fruit in 1906 with the election of a Liberal Party government. Milner left South Africa and Lord Selborne was appointed as high commissioner for Southern Africa. This ushered in a period of greater British and Boer cooperation – facilitated by Botha and Smuts.[19]

The leading Boer figures in the Transvaal worked towards putting together a proposal for self-governance. The initial concept for the design and form of governance was discussed between Botha and his colleagues in the Netherlands. Botha was careful to consult with leaders in the Orange Free State, and Abraham Fischer was

15 Engelenburg, *Botha*, p.128.
16 L. Phillips, *Transvaal Problems: Some Notes on Current Politics* (London: John Murray, 1907), pp.203–205.
17 See C. Headlam (ed.), *The Milner Papers: South Africa 1899–1905* (London: Cassell, 1933), vol.II.
18 NARSSA: Leyds Archive, 262, Part II Botha to Lord Courtney, 13 June 1903.
19 See D. George Boyce, *The Crisis of British Power: The Imperial and Naval Papers of the Second Earl of Selborne, 1895–1910* (London: The Historians Press, 1990).

selected as their leader.[20] The proposal that Botha refers to as the 'concept letter', went through a range of drafts and iterations, with a number of leaders, colleagues and professors in South Africa and the Netherlands.[21]

Following the Liberal Party victory in Britain, Botha sent Smuts to London to advocate for Boer interests and independence.[22] Smuts placed his considerable abilities and skills towards the creation of a proposal for the Transvaal constitution.[23] Smuts worked closely with Lord Selborne, ensuring that he kept his eye on British politics and elections – this had a critical impact on South African affairs.[24]

Ronald Hyam and Peter Henshaw argue that the Transvaal's self-government was decided by the Liberal and Tory parties, prior to Smuts's visit. They argue that Smuts placed himself at the centre of the narrative and that he convinced Prime Minister Campbell-Bannerman to allow Transvaal self-government. These historians argue that the Liberal British politicians did not act out of magnanimity, but of necessity. Not all British politicians trusted the Boer leaders and it made more sense to give them representative government as a reward, as opposed to slowly losing power and control.[25]

On 31 March 1906, the British authorities issued a letter indicating that the Transvaal was accorded representative government.[26] The Free State had to continue as a Crown Colony until they achieved independence in 1908. Despite certain old rivalries, the Transvaal constitution committee did put forward that the Free State (known as the Orange River Colony at the time) should also be given representative self-government 'in view of the past history of the people of this country and their behaviour since peace. This was duly agreed, they can legitimately lay claim to self-government'.[27]

The landslide victory of the Liberals over the Conservatives in the 1906 British general elections was in part based on public opposition to the Anglo-Boer War and a change in the political mood.[28] The fate of the Transvaal was thus aided by the political competition between conservatives and liberals in Britain with each espousing their values on the Empire's politics. With the Liberal Party now in power, Boer self-governance became a distinct possibility, and the Boer people were delighted.

20 NARSSA: Leyds Archive, 262, Part I, Buitendorp to Leyds, 24 August 1904.
21 NARSSA: Leyds Archive, 262, Part I, Botha to Leyds, 23 September 1904.
22 Engelenburg, *Botha*, p.138.
23 D. Reitz to Smuts, 29 October 1914 in Hancock and Van der Poel (eds.), *Selections*, vol.III, p.205.
24 NARSSA: Smuts Papers, Selborne to Smuts, 11 February 1904.
25 R. Hyam and P. Henshaw, *The Lion and the Springbok: Britain and South Africa Since the Boer War* (Cambridge: Cambridge University Press, 2003), pp.58–67.
26 Engelenburg, *Botha*, p.136; NARSSA: Leyds Archive, 262, Part II, Botha to West Ridgeway, 2 June 1906.
27 NARSSA: Leyds Archive, 262, Part II, Botha to West Ridgeway, 2 June 1906.
28 Engelenburg, *Botha*, pp.137–138.

Churchill, King Edward VII and Sir Henry Campbell-Bannerman all supported Transvaal self-goverment along with a large part of British society.[29]

Engelenburg claims that a Black politician (no name is given), sensing the change, went to see Botha in 1906, and that Botha did not personally oppose the colour bar as strongly as the Labour Party.[30] This point on Botha's stance about People of Colour in South Africa should be taken with a pinch of salt – evidence from the Colonial Papers show that Botha was clearly opposed to Black equality and franchise.[31] Smuts summarised the position:

> My dear Mr Merriman, Many thanks for your long and interesting letter and your comments on the memorandum. With much that you say I most cordially agree. In principle I am entirely at one with you on the Native question… But I don't believe in politics for them … I would therefore not give them the franchise.[32]

Botha wrote to Leyds, to tell him that *Het Volk* candidates had been put forward.[33] Confident of *Het Volk's* chances of winning the Transvaal elections, Botha philosophically wrote to Leyds, that sometimes 'one cannot be sure of the outcome of voting'.[34] This turned out to be prophetic – in 1910 Botha did not expect to lose against Fitzpatrick.

Botha claimed that Selborne's type of politics was very different to Milner's and that they would be able to work together.[35] Although perhaps more agreeable than Milner he was scathing of Afrikaner society. Lord Selborne, would go on to say that laziness, ignorance, and defiance and an 'undying hatred of England' were Dutch character traits.[36] Despite this, his politics was moderate – more moderate than Milner's at least.

Botha who had cut his teeth in the Boer politics of the New Republic and later the Transvaal, asked Selborne, whether the secret ballots were really secret, to which Selborne assured him that they most certainly were.[37] Although Selborne's perception of the Boers was initially influenced by Milner he later came to trust Botha, and commented, 'dear Botha, except when he attacks Milner, I do like him.'[38] Jameson,

29 Engelenburg, *Botha*, p.141; See also Hyam and Henshaw, *The Lion and the Springbok*.
30 Engelenburg, *Botha*, p.273; Meintjes, *Botha*, p.121.
31 See A. Odendaal, *The Founders: The Origins of the African National Congress* (Johannesburg: Jacana, 2012).
32 Smuts to Merriman, 13 March 1906 in Hancock and Van der Poel (eds.), *Selections*, vol.II, p.241.
33 NARSSA: Leyds Archive, 262, Part II, Botha to Leyds, 23 January 1907.
34 NARSSA: Leyds Archive, 262, Part II, Botha to Leyds, 9 June 1906.
35 NARSSA: Leyds Archive, 262, Botha to Leyds and De Haag, 25 September 1905.
36 William Cullen Library, University of the Witwatersrand, Johannesburg (Wits): A.881 Pim Papers, BL.1, Lord Selborne to Howard Pim, 18 January 1915.
37 NARSSA: Smuts Papers, A1, 5, Selborne to Botha, 5 February 1907.
38 Selborne to Lady Selborne, 23 August 1908 in Boyce, *Naval Papers of Selborne*, p.379.

commented to Selborne that Botha and Smuts were 'different' to any of the prominent Afrikaners with whom they had contact.[39]

Het Volk won 37 of the 67 seats and the Progressives won 21. Of the two minor parties, Labour took three seats and the Nationals won six.[40] Mr R. Solomons, the former lieutenant governor, who stood for the Nationals was comprehensively defeated. Following the elections, Smuts commented to John X. Merriman, prime minister of the Cape Colony, that he hoped Solomon would now join Botha's party.[41] Although Solomon declined to do so, he became an ally.[42]

Botha was elected as the Transvaal premier in 1907, while Smuts took on the dual position of colonial secretary and minister of education. Smuts wrote to Merriman, 'I might have been premier, but considered it would have been a mistake to take precedence over Botha, who is really one of the finest men South Africa has ever produced.'[43] In correspondence with President Steyn, Smuts took a more humble line and declared: 'We are following your suggestion and shall make Botha premier.'[44] In terms of Boer culture it was appropriate for Smuts to be humble and understated towards Steyn who was his senior. To Merriman, he could perhaps 'show off' a bit more adding, 'If he [Botha] had culture as he has chivalry and common sense, there would not be his equal in all South Africa. The varsity boys in the team will help him out most loyally…'.[45] Dr Bok, Smuts and H.C. Hull, among others, formed what a progressive leader referred to as 'the general's kindergarten'.[46]

Kitchener told Smuts in 1902, that when the Liberals took power in Britain, the Boers would most likely receive self-government. This proved to be true.[47] Botha went to London in 1907 to attend the Imperial Conference and was celebrated as the dashing general-cum-leader of the Transvaal.[48] It was fitting that Botha, the great horseman, would address the assembly and make a cavalry analogy. In his opening

39 Selborne to Lady Selborne, 21–22 October 1908 in Boyce, *Naval Papers of Selborne*, p.392.
40 Meintjes, *Botha*, pp.143–144; Engelenburg, *Botha*, p.144.
41 Smuts to Merriman, 2 June 1906 in Hancock and Van der Poel (eds.), *Selections*, vol.II, p.281.
42 NARSSA: Smuts Papers, A1, Solomon to Botha, 24 January 1908.
43 Smuts to Merriman, 4 March 1907 in Hancock and Van der Poel (eds.), *Selections*, vol.II, p.326.
44 Smuts to Steyn, 25 February 1907 in Hancock and Van der Poel (eds.), *Selections*, vol.II, p.325.
45 Smuts to Merriman, 4 March 1907 in Hancock and Van der Poel (eds.), *Selections*, vol.II, p.326.
46 NARSSA: Smuts Papers, A1, 7, Transvaal National Association to Smuts, 15 December 1909.
47 Smuts to Merriman, 25 February 1907 in Hancock and Van der Poel (eds.), *Selections*, vol. II, p.323; Engelenburg, *Botha*, p.139.
48 NARSSA: Preller Archives, A787, 96, Imperial Conference, *Sphere*, 13 April 1907; Preller Archives, A787, 96, 'General Louis Botha's Arrival', *Westminster Gazette*, 13 April 1907; Preller Archives, A787, 96, 'General Louis Botha: Prime Minister of the Transvaal', *Pall Mall Gazette*, 13 April 1907.

remarks he asked if he could speak in Dutch as he was a little unsure about his English. It was in fact Selborne who advised Botha that it would be best if he spoke in Dutch.[49] His interpreter was C.F. Beyers, a well turned-out flamboyant Boer general with a handlebar moustache and side parting that drew away from his sad eyes. Botha stated humbly, yet sincerely:

> The circumstances under which I am here this morning are somewhat different from those under which the other prime ministers are here. They have all been long in the saddle in the colonies which they represent. I have just gotten in the saddle and I am not firmly seated yet.[50]

Botha went on to assure the conference that the Dutch population would work towards the good of the Transvaal and the British Empire.[51] In practical terms, Botha and Smuts, embarked on a legislative mission – putting a number of Bills through parliament.

The Education Bill of 1907 allowed for affordable schooling for White children in the Transvaal. Smuts was instrumental in the formation of the education statute, while Botha made strides in terms of agriculture. He established the Land Bank, which provided credit to farmers, sent agricultural students abroad, and recommended writing-off previous agricultural debts. Botha met regularly with farmers in various districts to discuss politics and agriculture.[52] He also went on to oversee the formation of the Sheep Division, whereby South African wool became world renowned.[53] Ironic that the wool clip would lead to issues down the line.

The Selborne Memorandum put forward a formal request for a union to be formed of the Southern African colonies – there was interest in the Cape, as well as from the British government.[54] It was generally accepted that a central administration of the four different colonial governments was a good option. Smuts, with his incredible drive and capacity for work, dedicated himself to the creation of a framework for the Union of South Africa. He drew up the necessary plans which were presented at the

49 NARSSA: Preller Archives, A787, 96, 'Imperial Conference', *The Tribune*, 15 April 1907.
50 NARSSA: Preller Archives, A787, 94, Botha quoted in 'General Botha', *The Times*, 16 April 1907.
51 NARSSA: Preller Archives, A787, 94, Botha quoted in 'Points from the Speeches', *Daily Graphic*, 15 April 1907.
52 NARSSA: Preller Archives, A787, 92, Britstown municipality to Botha, 3 November 1911, Canarvaron community to Botha, 9 November 1911; 92, Afrikaner Bond to Botha, 9 November 1911; Willowmore district to Botha, 5 July 1912; Dutch Reformed Church of Kakamas to Botha, no date (possibly 1911–1912).
53 Engelenburg, *Botha*, p.159; NARSSA: Preller Archives, A787, 96, 'Imperial Conference, *Tribune*, 15 April 1907.
54 D.W. Krüger, *The Age of the Generals* (Johannesburg: Dagbreek, 1958), pp.29–32; See A.H. Marais, *Politieke Briewe, 1911–1912: Deel 2* (Cape Town: Tafelberg, 1973).

inter-colonial conference held in May 1908.[55] The findings of this conference were then reinforced and iterated at a meeting of key South African leaders in October 1908. At this conference the constitution for the union was drawn up. Whereas Smuts and Hull respectively advised on legal and transport matters, Botha put forward the human and business case for union.[56] Botha wavered on a 'native policy', but in terms of adding territories he hoped to include Basutoland, Swaziland and Zululand into South Africa. Selborne was keen to keep the proposed 'native policy' on the agenda at the Durban conference.[57]

At this conference Botha put his great diplomatic skill and charm on display, effectively removing blockages and allowing the various representatives to express their opinions and air their concerns. Jameson commented that 'Botha is a great factor and plays a capital game of bridge'. The motion to create a legislative union was passed by majority vote. Eminent South African historian Alex Mouton commented that Botha's role in in the formation of Union, was a political seduction.[58]

The British parliament in Westminster endorsed the proposal for the formation of the Union in August 1909.[59] A delighted Botha immediately wrote to Smuts, stating that the Bill had been approved.[60] In August 1909 a delegation of less impressed, Black, White and Coloured leaders, led by W.P. Schreiner went to London to oppose the Bill, but to no avail – many members of the delegation went on to become the founders of the African National Congress.[61] These leaders did good work in the background but never wielded any considerable influence – at least in their time.

The agreed date for the formation of the Union was the end of May 1910. Formal elections were scheduled for September and Botha and Merriman were in contention for the prime ministership. Botha admitted to considering a coalition as proposed by Jameson in 1909, however he realised that this would not suit the South African public – after consideration he informed Jameson that a coalition was completely off the table.[62] Botha and Smuts would be more open to collaboration in the 1915 elections. But in 1910, Botha opted for a party that was united and had leaders from all of the former colonies – a simple and seemly perfect solution to a highly complex and layered question. This took shape in the South African Party which subsumed *Het Volk*.[63]

55 Hancock and Van der Poel (eds.), *Selections*, vol.III, p.331.
56 Engelenburg, *Botha*, p.173.
57 Selborne to Crew, 24 August 1908 in Boyce, *Naval Papers of Selborne*, p.381.
58 Meintjes, *Botha*, p.163; Engelenburg, *Botha*, pp.174–175. Discussion with Alex Mouton took place during Antonio's PhD Viva in 2019.
59 NARSSA: Preller Archives, A787, 100, 'South African Union', *The Standard and Diggers News*, 19 August 1909; Engelenburg, *Botha*, p.184.
60 NARSSA: Smuts Papers, A1, 7, Botha to Smuts, August 1909.
61 See A. Odendaal, *Founders: The Origins of the ANC and the Struggle for Democracy in South Africa* (Aukland Park: Jacana, 2012).
62 NARSSA: Smuts Papers, A1, 7, Botha to Jameson, 4 November 1909.
63 Engelenburg, *Botha*, pp.191–192; NARSSA: Preller Archives, A787, 101, 'Dr Jameson's Change of Plans', *The Times*, 8 September 1909; Preller Archives, A787, 101, 'The First

Botha was appointed as interim prime minister and was overjoyed and overwhelmed with congratulations from all sides.[64] Botha, confident and in this moment, perhaps unintentionally insensitive, wrote to Merriman, who had been the frontrunner for the position, and asked him to join his cabinet – Merriman refused stating that he fully intended to run for the premiership. Abraham Fischer and Frederick Moor, the premiers of the Free State and Natal respectively, joined Botha's cabinet.[65]

An interim cabinet was put in place before the 1910 elections. Botha had made what some considered a political mistake in befriending Leander Jameson. Their friendship did not sit well with many Afrikaners who could not forgive Leander's actions in the Jameson Raid.[66] Botha's friendship with Jameson was also frowned upon by many English-South Africans.[67] Percy Molteno, an interesting figure, a humanitarian who supported the post Anglo-Boer War reconstruction as well as Black nationalist movements, commented that Botha had broken his confidence in befriending Jameson.[68] Merriman queried why Botha had befriended Jameson, writing to Steyn 'I cannot understand the sudden friendship'.[69] Botha's friendship with Jameson was a reflection of his policy of conciliation – but also a matter of practicality. Jameson was the leader of the Unionist Party, the official opposition, and politically he was in a position to support Botha.[70]

In line with the party-political system, Botha had to win a seat in a constituency. He stood in Pretoria East, which many considered surprising given that it was not his traditional support base – he went on to lose to Percy Fitzpatrick, known as Fitz, a politician and writer who famously authored *Jock of the Bushveld.* The Pretoria East constituency were largely Unionists, and although a closely run affair, Fitz came out on top. There is no doubt that Botha was motivated by hubris and the unwarranted confidence that by running against Fitz, he would limit Unionist influence in the Transvaal. Botha was incensed at the loss, blaming everyone but himself. R.H. Brand commented: 'I can hardly imagine there is anyone who would now not admit it was

Union Delegates Depart', *South Africa,* 4 September 1909; Preller Archives, A787, 102, 'Dr Jameson's Meeting', unidentified newspaper cutting, 1910. See G.J. Krause, 'Die Rol van Generaal Louis Botha in die Unifikasie van Suid-Afrika, 1902–1910 (Bloemfontein University of the Free State, 1953); and J.M.H. van Aart, 'Die Botha-bewind in die Transvaal, 1907 –1910', Potchefstroom. Potchefstroom University, 1958.

64 NARSSA: Leyds Archive, 262, Part II, Botha to Leyds, 4 July 1910.

65 NARSSA: Smuts Papers, A1, 9, Botha to Smuts, 3 January 1912; Engelenburg, *Botha*, p.201.

66 Widely seen as a precursor to the Second Anglo-Boer War. It was at once a statement of British imperialist intent, while also becoming one of the causes of the war.

67 Engelenburg, *Botha*, pp.193–194.

68 Molteno to Hertzog, 16 March 1911 in V. Solomon (ed.), *Selections from the Correspondence of Percy Alport Molteno, 1892–1914* (Cape Town: Van Riebeeck Society, 1981), pp.331–332.

69 Steyn to Merriman, 4 June 1911 in Marais, *Politieke Briewe*, p.13.

70 F.A. Mouton, '"The sacred tie": Sir Thomas Smartt, the Unionist Party and the British Empire, 1912–1920', *Historia*, vol.59. no.2 (2012), pp.8–10.

a mistake'.[71] Smuts said that the defeat 'came as a nasty knock'.[72] With a bruised ego, dejected and demoralised, Botha threatened to resign from politics. In a move that mirrored the great Kruger, Botha had childish moments – but once he gathered himself, Botha was elected in the safe seat of Losberg to the east of Potchefstroom.[73] Fitz went on to write a manuscript appealing for a Union – a book written in English and Afrikaans,[74] and Botha's initial reaction was to try and push Fitz out of politics,[75] he did not succeed and the two men went on to become bedfellows out of necessity. While Botha was magnanimous, he found any direct threat intolerable – in this regard he was as ruthless as Smuts.

Botha's attempts at premiership were firmly contested by J.X. Merriman, the well-established, older and successful Cape politician. President Steyn and Hertzog supported Merriman's candidacy – the old Free State vs Transvaal rivalry. However, the governor-general favoured Botha who also had many more supporters in London. The Westminster government needed a Boer leader who could be trusted to defend British interests in South Africa.[76] Botha used his charm attempting to weaken the Afrikaner Bond's support for Merriman.[77] The use of charisma, financial incentives, alliances and other means were within Botha and Smuts's arsenal. His reputation as a respected former general and capable premier of the Transvaal further empowered Botha,[78] while Smuts's intellectual abilities inspired confidence in the Union project – the combination was a partnership with finesse.

Botha went on to win the premiership in 1910. W. Carter, the archbishop of Cape Town, commented that he felt sympathy for Merriman but thought him erratic in his politics. Carter later said that he liked Botha and that he was 'perfectly sincere and wants to do the best he can for the country'.[79] It was a trying period, and it took Botha some time to find his feet as a constitutional statesman. Initially his parliamentary speeches came across as nervous and at times his statements on policy were shaky. But by mid-to-late November 1910 Botha's orations had gained confidence, something that the press picked up on.[80]

71 NARSSA: Smuts Papers, A1, 8, Brand to Smuts, 18 September 1910; Engelenburg, *Botha*, p.194.
72 NARSSA: Smuts Papers, A1, 8, Telegram by Smuts, 19 September 1910.
73 Engelenburg, *Botha*, pp.224–225.
74 Engelenburg, *Botha*, pp.224–225.
75 W.R. Guest, 'Fitzpatrick, Natal and the Unification of South Africa', *Natalia*, vol.11, 1981, p.54.
76 See N.G. Garson, *Louis Botha or John X. Merriman: The Choice of South Africa's First Prime Minister* (London: Institute for Commonwealth Studies, 1969).
77 For an alternate view on the appointment of the first prime minister, see P. Lewsen, *John X Merriman: Paradoxical South African Statesman* (Johannesburg: Ad Donker, 1982).
78 Meintjes, *Botha*, p.170; Engelenburg, *Botha*, p.197.
79 Wits: William Carter Papers, AB186, Carter to Algernon Lawley, 3 March 1907.
80 NARSSA: Preller Archives, A787, 102, 'Notes in the House', *The Cape Times*, 18 November 1910.

Botha, in one of his first acts as premier, released Dinizulu, who had been arrested in 1907.[81] This act of clemency endeared him to a large part of the population including People of Colour. Botha had a layered relationship with People of Colour but on the point of Dinizulu's arrest he was clear that the King was a scapegoat and was wrongly imprisoned. However, this act of kindness and fairness did not translate into franchise for Blacks, Coloureds or Indians – a matter captured in the British press.[82]

Botha's appointment of Hertzog to his cabinet did little to inspire his English-speaking supporters, and less to win over many English South Africans. Botha led a jealous and disunited cabinet.[83] Intrigue sparked up when he attempted to appoint Beyers as the speaker of the assembly. Beyers was an advocate and veteran Boer general who had good credentials but was an unlikely candidate. Merriman, supported by the Free State ministers, opposed the appointment. There was a broad feeling that all power should not be concentrated around Botha – Smuts had three portfolios (defence, finance, and interior) and Hull held the treasury. James Molteno, an accomplished politician, and advocate who defended the Boer rebels in the Cape Colony – the older brother of John Molteno Jr and Percy, was appointed as the first Speaker of Parliament in the stead of Beyers. This led to Beyers's disgruntlement. His disenchantment with the Botha-Smuts government affected his attitude and future rebellious acts.[84] In correspondence with Smuts, Botha revealed his true feelings, stating that Beyers was the greatest enemy to both Afrikaans and English South Africans.[85] It could be argued that if Botha really wanted a post for Beyers he would have given him one of the ministries such as agriculture, interior, defence or mines, but instead Botha concentrated those ministries between himself and Smuts.

Botha's policy of conciliation met its biggest obstacle in Hertzog who proposed a 'two-stream' policy in the face of Botha's 'one stream'. Botha suffered and tolerated a considerable amount of criticism from Hertzog and the nationalist part of the Afrikaner population. In May 1911, Hertzog, who represented the interests of a growing nationalist movement, told Steyn that he could no longer support Botha's policy of conciliation.[86] Steyn was also troubled by the way in which Botha was prosecuting his policy.[87] Hertzog threatened to leave Botha's cabinet but remained in

81 E.H. Spender, *General Botha: The Career and the Man* (London: Constable & Co., 1916), p.224; Engelenburg, *Botha*, p.273.
82 NARSSA: Preller Archives, A787, 100, 'How the Blacks are Handicapped', *The Labour Leader*, 13 August 1909.
83 NARSSA: Preller Archives, A787, 102, 'Dr Jameson's Meeting', unidentified newspaper cutting; Hyslop to Smuts, 24 July 1910; Engelenburg, *Botha*, p.225.
84 Meintjes, *Botha*, p.178; Engelenburg, *Botha*, pp.227–228.
85 NARSSA: Smuts Papers, A1, 9, Botha to Smuts, 4 July 1911.
86 Engelenburg, *Botha*, p.248.
87 Steyn to Merriman, 7 January 1911 & Merriman to Steyn, 16 January 1911 in Marais, *Politieke Briewe*, vol.4, p.5.

government when Botha conceded certain points, most of them related to his education policy.[88]

The rift between Hertzog and Botha, divided the newly formed Union cabinet and Colonel Leuchars threatened to resign if Hertzog continued his emotive and divisive speeches. Many Union ministers felt antagonised at Hertzog's continued orations. By late December 1912 the situation had reached breaking point and Botha, who had previously threatened to tender his resignation, in fact did so, dissolving the cabinet.[89]

The governor-general then asked Botha to form a new cabinet that same afternoon. Botha reappointed all his ministers with the exception of Hertzog – for all intents and purposes he was expelled.[90] This incident became the source of great intrigue and debate. In speaking about the split and Hertzog's speeches, Botha told Leyds that the whole situation was completely unnecessary. Botha wrote in desperation: 'I can't in heaven's name understand the futility, of raising suspicion with English-speaking South Africans regarding our relationship with Great Britain'.[91] Of course Botha missed Hertzog's point, that it was too soon after the trauma of the Anglo-Boer War to support Britain – and perhaps more importantly a strong nationalist movement was on the rise.

Brigadier General George Aston, chief of staff to Lord Methuen, viewed Mike du Toit – along with M.T. Steyn, and the Rusthof coterie – as the irreconcilables. Aston rapped Du Toit over the knuckles in 1913: for having – as a senior police official – expressed personal views against the government at the time of the cabinet reshuffle. Du Toit replied with a long letter of explanation: Botha's dismissal of Hertzog had 'spoilt his [Botha's] otherwise unblemished record irreparably'. Having an angry policeman, who 'implicitly believed' in Hertzog, was one thing; having senior, uniformed civil servants publicly object to the political process was quite another.[92] Du Toit, despite having served in the Transvaal State Artillery, was helped by Hertzog to get a post in the police. This was a harbinger for things to come.

To make matters worse, Hull voted with Hertzog against Botha and Smuts in a motion of no confidence, which devastated the prime minister.[93] Botha in correspondence with Preller, added that Hull had acted like a child. Although in principle he was right, he was not being loyal to the party when required.[94] Smuts echoed this sentiment, 'Hull is right on the merits of the case but has acted very wrongly in resigning

88 Engelenburg, *Botha*, p.250.
89 NARSSA: Engelenburg Archive, 6, Botha to Smart, 14 December 1912.
90 NARSSA: Smuts Papers, A1, 9, Letter to Smuts, 18 December 1912; Engelenburg, *Botha*, p.259.
91 NARSSA: Leyds Archive, 262, Part II, Botha to Leyds, 13 May 1913.
92 Royal Marines Archives, Southsea, UK (RMA): 1/6, 11/12/38 Maj Gen Sir George Aston Papers, M. du Toit to Aston, 3 September 1913.
93 NARSSA: Smuts Papers, A1, 11, Telegram by Smuts, 1913.
94 Botha to Preller, 7 June 1912, Marais, *Politieke Briewe*, pp.80–81.

at such a moment… General Botha's position has been much weakened by Hull's resignation.'[95]

Hertzog had out-manoeuvred Botha and continued a political guerrilla campaign against him. Botha came across as the attacker and Hertzog the victim.[96] Despite attempts by Steyn and others to plead with Hertzog and Botha to reconcile, it was not to be. Steyn asked Botha to reconsider Hertzog's expulsion but was met with a firm denial.[97] Botha wrote to Leyds in early May 1913 and said that the crisis led to a massive commotion in the South African Party. He thought that people would for the most part maintain their calm, see reason and not be swept away by emotion.[98] But this proved too much to ask. Afrikaner nationalism of the time was imbued with many ideas of Boer republicanism. To make matters worse, the clash between organised labour and the captains of industry was starting to boil over.

Botha, still a remnant of an older commando system, was slowly coming to terms with a changing society. He commented to Leyds that 15 years before, it would have been hard to believe that workers would be able to arrange an uprising of such a magnitude. Botha quipped: 'The running of the Union is no easy task indeed!'[99]

Matters of local politics came to a head in November 1913, when a party congress met to decide on the fate of the Botha government. The matter was put to a vote, and it was decided to continue with the government of the day – Botha won with 131 votes to 90. After the vote, De Wet stormed off and many of his Free State supporters followed him out of parliament.[100] After being removed from the South African Party, Hertzog formed the National Party in 1914, a new grouping which represented republican Afrikaners.[101] Botha wrote to Smuts from his farm Rusthof and discussed the difficulties of maintaining their policy of conciliation. He said that he wanted to keep the peace 'but without committing murder'.[102]

Smuts's responsibility as the minister of defence, interior and mines was onerous and by his own admission 'a terrible job'.[103] He put his cerebral powers on display and worked towards the Defence Act.[104] He aimed to create a modern military, somewhat different from the Boer armies in which he had served during the Anglo-Boer

95 Smuts to S.M. Smuts, 23 May 1912, Hancock and Van der Poel (eds.), *Selections*, vol.II, p.85.
96 Engelenburg, *Botha*, p.256; NARSSA: Smuts Papers, A1, 9, Letter to Smuts, 18 December 1912.
97 Engelenburg, *Botha*, p.259.
98 NARSSA: Leyds Archive, 262, Part II, Botha to Leyds, 8 May 1913.
99 NARSSA: Leyds Archive, 262, Part II, Botha to Leyds, 18 August 1913.
100 Spender, *General Botha*, p.255.
101 Meintjes, *Botha*, p.198.
102 NARSSA: Smuts Papers, A1, 11, Botha to Smuts, 23 December 1913.
103 NARSSA: Smuts Papers, A1, 8, Smuts telegram, 6 June 1910.
104 NARSSA: Preller Archives, A787, 102, 'Union Defence, Metheun's Views', *The Leader*, 11 May 1911.

War.[105] Firstly, at the imperial conference in 1907, Botha put forward the concept of a combined English and Boer armed force in a discussion with Haldane.[106]

Threat Perception and the Making of the Union Defence Force

Botha was of the opinion that the old commando system had value, but it needed a reorganisation – Smuts was the man for the job. From 1910 the generals started planning the re-design of the defence force. Botha wrote to the Canadian Prime Minister, Wilfred Laurier:

> In the earlier days of South Africa, however, the commando was especially suitable because every citizen had by the very conditions of his existence become an effective combatant requiring little to no training in the field. [With] the growth of a purely urban and industrial population without the habits and physical qualities naturally acquired in the course of a rough country life … rudimentary training … seems to be essential.[107]

Yet, increasingly, their most onerous task would be to convince others of the importance of their work. The heroes of the late war surrounded them and during the immediate post-war years, often supported Botha and Smuts. Koos De la Rey, the hero of the Western Transvaal, a towering figure with piercing eyes and Christiaan De Wet, the enigmatic pimpernel of the Free State ranked first in tactical ability. C.F. Beyers, the disenchanted, Jan Kemp, the formidable, Manie Maritz, the forceful, and lesser luminaries followed. All former generals, they remained in the public eye, but they were not statesmen. As Johannes Meintjes noted, 'their hold on the people was purely emotional, and for that reason it held an element of danger – as Botha and Smuts were fully aware.'[108] Botha and Smuts might trust some of them with responsible positions in the new state in the hope that new loyalties would develop. However, as they no doubt knew, they could not tame and harness everyone in the service of the new, modernising state.[109]

Several interlocking characteristics complicated South African security. While presumed far and relatively secure from the political discord of Europe and the Middle East, South Africa had its own fault lines that were vulnerable to geopolitical shifts in Europe. The German presence in South West Africa (Namibia) and the economic

105 Van der Waag, *A Military History*, pp.73–74.
106 NARSSA: Preller Archives, A787, 97, 'General Botha's Popularity', *Pall Mall Gazette,* 25 April 1907.
107 DODA: DC, Box 20, file 51/274 Botha to Laurier, 16 February 1910.
108 J. Meintjes, *De la Rey: Lion of the West* (Johannesburg: Keartland, 1969), p.318.
109 I. van der Waag, 'Re-Thinking South Africa's Military Past: The Curious Case of Brig Gen the Hon. C.F. Beyers', (Stellenbosch University: Professorial inaugural lecture, 2018), p.12.

ties and kinship they shared with a significant number of Afrikaners highlighted this. Moreover, the Second Anglo-Boer War cast long, historical shadows, and memories of European support at a time when the republics were forced into the British world. From 1902, as the likelihood of a war between the great powers increased, imperial rivalries and competition for resources – necessary to fuel European industry and manufacture the weapons of industrialised warfare – threatened to make the next war global and expensive. The possibility of British involvement in a European crisis would also affect South Africa's sense of relative geographic isolation and apparent strategic safety.

Defence planners in London and South Africa identified three broad security concerns in Southern Africa after 1902: seaborne assault, landward invasion, and internal unrest. The first two were remote and would involve a European power possessed of a navy or sharing land borders with South Africa – pointing to Germany, and less plausibly Portugal. But the primary focus fell on the third scenario of which there were various permutations: an African rising, shown by Bhambatha in 1906.

Industrial unrest on the mines of the Witwatersrand and Kimberley highlighted the internal security concern; and, until at least the concession in 1907 and 1908 of self-government to the two northern colonies, the possibility of an Afrikaner rebellion. Key in any of these situations was the holding of a heartland covering the intersections of the Transvaal, Orange River, and Natal colonies as well as the main railway connections between the Witwatersrand – and the goldmining and financial interests of Johannesburg – and the coast. A worst-case scenario as would threaten in September 1914 was a combination of three.[110]

As a means to bolster South Africa's defence, in 1907 the South African colonies set up an intercolonial conference to discuss greater cooperation in matters of defence.[111] When Botha visited London in 1909, prior to the formalisation of the Defence Act, he requested 20,000 rifles and several cannon from the British War Office.[112] Weapons and well trained personnel were needed – but the source of manpower stemmed from the divergent strands of the new Union – a mixed bag of forces, with different doctrinal approaches.

The Union was in many ways artificial. The four unifying colonies, themselves relatively new, differed markedly in geography, politics, and economic well-being and each territory – jealously guarding its identity – entered the Union with some hesitancy. As D.W. Krüger noted, the South Africans of 1910 had 'brought with them into Union not only their unified hopes for future political peace and happiness

110 For the broad strategy see Van der Waag, *A Military History*, pp.60–65. For its application to the Transvaal-Natal frontier, see I. van der Waag, 'Rural struggles and the politics of a colonial command: The Southern Mounted Rifles of the Transvaal Volunteers, 1905-1912' in Stephen Miller (ed.), *Soldiers and Settlers in Africa, 1850-1918* (Leiden: Brill, 2009), pp.251–285.

111 Van Der Waag, *A Military History*, p.63.

112 NARSSA: Smuts Papers, A1, 7, Botha to Smuts, August 1909.

after a war which had divided them as never before, but also their different memories of a separate past.'[113] The colonial politicians and civil servants – and the societies they represented – brought with them their own hopes and aspirations, and their fears and reservations. Inevitably, South African politics would remain conditioned by provincial interests, the ambitions of individual men, and their common, contested past.

The Union Defence Forces (UDF), which combined the Cape Colonial Forces, the Natal Militia, and the Transvaal Volunteers with the resurrected commandos of the former republics, was likewise a compromise between the determination of English-speakers to maintain the British military connection and the desire of Afrikaner nationalists for a restoration of Boer political and military traditions. While the new state required armed forces, it was less evident how the men from the armed forces of the four unifying colonies – speaking and protecting two languages and representing at least three military traditions – would integrate into the new defence structures. As the new minister of defence, Smuts faced this conundrum and tackled it head on. Unlike his early rivals, Hertzog and Beyers, Smuts recognised that the future lay not in the blind continuation of the republican forces but rather in a modern armed force based on Western doctrine.

Smuts required the inputs from carefully selected officers – many of whom were former enemies. They included South Africans like Tim Lukin, Roland Bourne, and Jack Collyer – colonial officers battle-hardened during the late war – and Imperials like Field Marshal Lord Methuen and Aston, who, at Smuts's request, remained in South Africa until the passage of the Defence Act.[114] The defence minister's easy erudition and his apparent association with British officials – who seemingly exerted undue influence and were seen to 'interfere' in the process of creating domestic armed forces – angered the more conversative Afrikaners.[115]

Smuts, however eager, had to move cautiously.[116] Former president of the Orange Free State, M.T. Steyn, vocalised widespread concern that the new force would introduce compulsory military service, create a spirit of militarism, and blur the lines between the Imperial and South African armed forces. From the Cape, elder statesman, Merriman, was wary that South Africa 'not be led into militarism and to any unwise pledges of sharing in the quarrels in [the] inciting [of] which we have not been consulted'.[117] Merriman's vision for a small force – well organised and well led but with 'not too much discipline' – was countered by the Unionists, who demanded

113 Krüger, *The Making of a Nation*, pp.3–4.
114 DODA: DC, Box 47, file 1063, South Africa Defence Bill.
115 See comments in Wits: AB186 Archbishop Carter Letters, William Carter to Algernon Lawley, 3 August 1919.
116 Rhodes House, Oxford (RHO): MSS Afr s.1250, Sir Herbert James Stanley papers, Herbert Stanley to Lord Gladstone, 7 Aug 1910. We are grateful to Kent Fedorowich for sharing this reference.
117 J.X. Merriman to M.T. Steyn, 16 January 1911 in Marais (ed.), *Politieke Briewe*, p.5.

a strong force able to meet local requirements but also deploy with British forces elsewhere in Africa when needed. An avalanche of criticism followed the introduction of the Defence Bill, which passed into law on 14 June 1912.[118] The Act satisfied the Unionists only. It not only stressed the importance of an interconnected imperial defence, and dependence on the Royal Navy to protect South Africa from foreign invasion, but the term 'South Africa' was used as a geographical expression. This Smuts left purposely undefined, although he had assured Lord Gladstone, the governor general, that 'it would surely cover any part of the continent of Africa South of the equator.'[119] But few thought the UDF would undertake operations beyond the Union's borders, and so the force remained for the moment a colonial constabulary with a coast-defence organisation. Few men shared Smuts's vision for a more balanced, modern force. The ambiguities would cause considerable confusion after the outbreak of war in August 1914.

Smuts now moved quickly to implement the provisions of the Act. He established the Department of Defence as a separate department of state on 1 July 1912 and, on the same day, the volunteer organisations of the former colonies were abolished and absorbed into the Union Defence Forces. In all, there were now six forces – the SA Permanent Force (SAPF), the Active Citizen Force (ACF), the Coast Garrison Force (CGF), the rifle associations (or resurrected commandos), the South Africa Division of the Royal Naval Volunteer Reserve (RNVR) and the Cadet Corps – falling under three new, separate and independent, executive commands: a Citizen Force Command, a Permanent Force Command, and a Cadet Command. These forces were organised in three lines of defence. The trained citizen force, of a size and so organised that a 'formidable and effective army can be put into the field', constituted the first line of defence. This had to be reinforced by trained citizen reserves, or the second line of defence. In an extreme emergency, all able-bodied citizens would be brought into service as a national reserve, which constituted the third line. As shown in table 1.1, the first line was supplemented in two important ways: by providing for a small nucleus of permanent forces – a special striking force for internal deployment – and by making special provision for the defence of South African ports.[120]

118 NARSSA: General C.F. Beyers Collection, col 1, ff. 45-47, M.T. Steyn to C.F. Beyers, 16 Feb 1912. See also the two petitions, Memorial of the Women of Nooitgedacht, undated (ff.104-7), and Memorial of the Women of Randjesfontein undated (ff.108-10). See also Petworth House Archives, West Sussex Record Office (WSRO): Hugh Wyndham to Lady Leconfield, 21 February and 27 February 1912.

119 Smuts did not consider the term 'South Africa' in any way limited by the Act of Union. DODA: DC, Box 47, file 1063 South Africa Defence Bill, Smuts to Gladstone, 16 Nov 1911.

120 UCT: BC 294 Duncan Papers, A49, Memorandum explanatory of the South African Defence Bill, pp.3–4.

Table 1.1: The threat perception and the design of the Union Defence Force, 1911.

Line of defence	Landward threat	Seaborne threat	Internal threat
1st Line	Active Citizen Force	Coast Garrison Force	Permanent Force (SAMR)
2nd Line	ACF Reserve, Class 'A' and Class 'B'		Field Reserve SAMR
3rd Line	The National Reserve		

The SAPF, which formed the standing army, fell under the Permanent Force Command. It comprised of five regiments of the South African Mounted Riflemen (SAMR) organised along the lines of the old Cape Mounted Riflemen (CMR) from which it had drawn substantial personnel. Like the old CMR it was earmarked for the suppression of internal unrest and as such had police and defence duties. Its five regiments were stationed in five SAMR districts, all old 'trouble spots'. Writing in 1914, the Secretary for Defence, Bourne, outlined the base-line expectation of the SAMR troopers; they were to be 'thoroughly good horsemen and riders, good shots, thoroughly dependable men; [and] men thoroughly fit for field service.'[121] Lukin, who had been Commandant of the Cape Militia, and had commanded the CMR earlier in his career, was appointed as Inspector General of the SAPF.

The ACF formed the backbone of the UDF. Earmarked primarily for external deployment, it comprised townsmen organised into infantry battalions and countrymen in mounted infantry regiments as well as several artillery regiments. Its 13 districts overlay the whole of Union territory. In the 18 months it took Smuts to set up and get the Bill through parliament, he had the various drafts reviewed by Steyn. The former president was frank:

> … everyone who is on our voters' roll must also be on the commando list—the disabled excepted. I do not want to see a repetition of men who had for years enjoyed full citizen rights slinking over the borders when war approaches… If you can think out an acceptable plan to bring the young Boer under discipline and to keep him in his own organization, then you can do much with him. Do not in any circumstances make an infantryman of him. Personally, I would rather be the commander of a lot of fowls than of a lot of Boers on foot. However bad he is on foot give him a horse and he is at once a true man.[122]

121 DODA: Archives of the Commandant General, SA Citizen Force, Box 4, file 61 SA Mounted Rifles, Secretary for Defence to Director War Recruiting, 1 October 1914.

122 Steyn to Smuts, 27 January 1911 in Hancock and Van der Poel (eds.), *Selections*, vol.II, p.23.

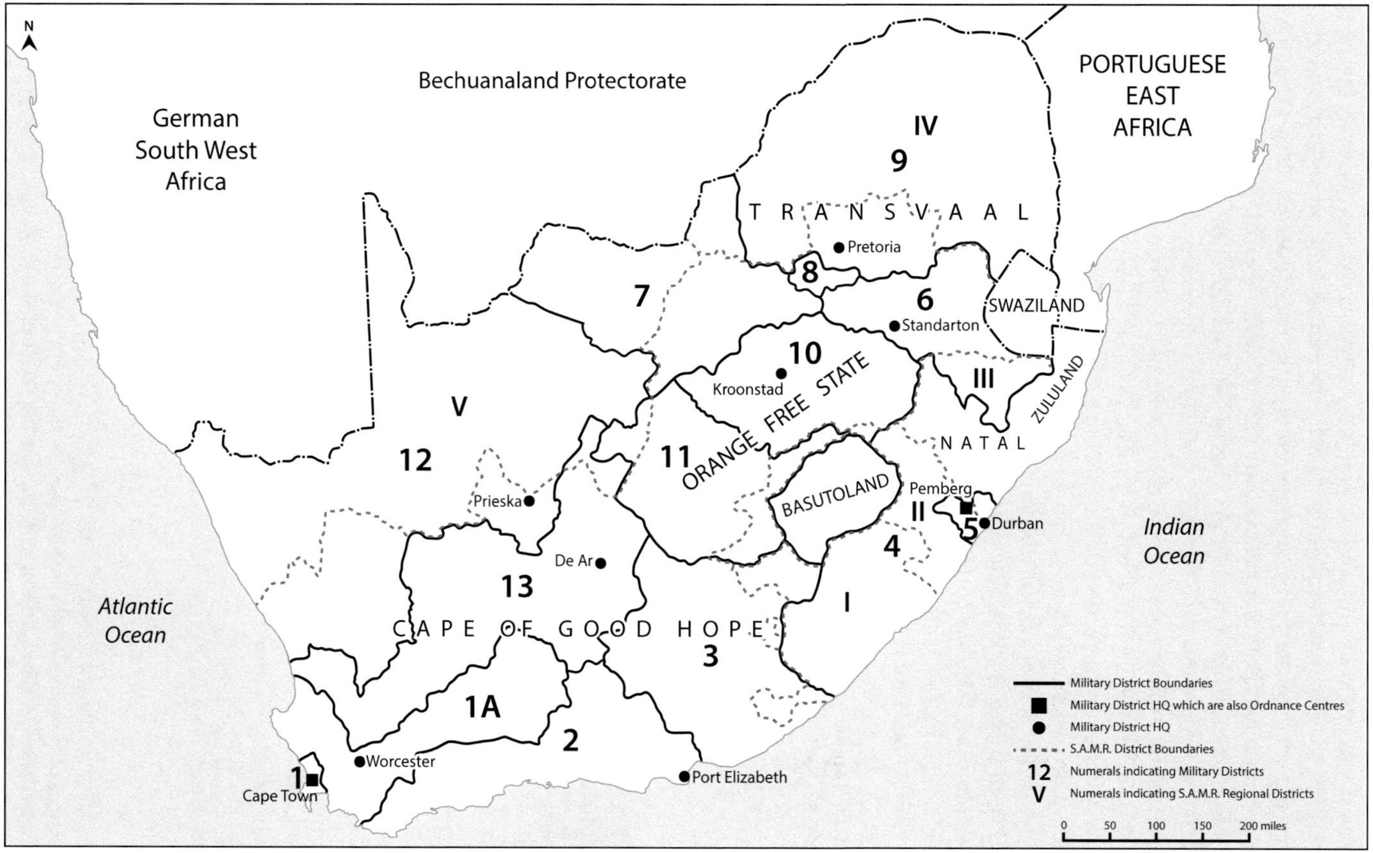

Map 1.1 South Africa and the 13 military districts of the Active Citizen Force and five districts of the SAMR.

This was the old type of thinking of which Smuts's had lived experience, but he was going to pull the commandos into the twentieth century, kicking and screaming.

A district staff officer (DSO) was appointed to each district, with a small staff to oversee training. The force was kept up to strength by qualified conscription and trained over four years, with 30 days continuous and non-continuous training each year. It became the receptacle for most of the old volunteer and militia regiments: of the total strength of the volunteers in the provinces (9,081) on 31 December 1912, 65 per cent signified their willingness to transfer to the ACF on its formation. As shown in Table 1.2, many remained with their 'old regiments', others taken into new or amalgamated units where a fiction of continuity was sometimes preserved. Commanded by 'gentlemen' – mostly landed and sometimes moneyed – these regiments drew their officers from South Africa's elite schools and their ranks from the burgeoning towns and surrounding farming communities. They looked up to the Permanent Force officers, to Lukin and Collyer for example, for their technical knowledge and their many years of military service.

Table 1.2: Numbers of militiamen and volunteers transferred from the colonial forces to the Active Citizen Force

Force	Strength on 31 December 1912	Transferred to Active Citizen Force					
		With old units		To new units		Total	
		Officers	Other ranks	Officers	Other ranks	Officers	Other ranks
Cape Volunteers	3,096	132	1,948	8	133	140	2,081
Natal Militia	2,449	121	1,285	21	176	142	1,461
Transvaal Volunteers	3,536	87	1,065	87	874	174	1,939
Total	9,081	340	4,298	116	1,183	456	5,481

(*Source:* U.G. 61 – 1913. Annual Reports, Department of Defence, 1913)

In the new UDF, a 'Boer' ring existed alongside this 'Colonial' ring. This comprised the former officers of the old republican forces, who – while lacking formal education and military training – had vast rural interests and enormous credibility in what others pejoratively termed 'the backveld'.[123] Here Botha had considerable influence, but also De Wet, Hertzog, Kemp and Maritz. They were drawn largely into the ACF and almost without exception dominated the rifle associations and included the men

123 The term 'backveld' was used by the English South Africans to refer to 'the rolling countryside of the two old republics'; see Arthur G. Barlow, *That We May Tread Safely* (Cape Town: Tafelberg, 1960), p.66. Barlow's definition, however, does not suggest the pejorative meaning that the term conveyed.

who rebelled in late 1914. Designed specifically to expose the male White population to military training, membership was largely rural and – in every sense the resurrected commando system, and chief symbol of Afrikaner nationalism – they provided the focus of the main controversy. Afrikaner Nationalists and some of the more nationalistic inclined members of Botha's governing party hoped to continue the old republican tradition of the commandos as a people's army. They even received support from unexpected quarters, including some Unionists.

The commandos had developed from the early eighteenth century to protect home and hearth, could easily be transformed into a third-line reserve, and were well-suited for internal security. Moreover, they presented an opportunity to instil musketry skills.[124] However, many realised, as no doubt did Smuts, that the rifle associations, with their early-modern structure, would have little ability to counter a large, sophisticated, external threat. The survival of the commando system in this form rankled some Unionists, much as the extension of the cadet system, from some English-medium schools to the education system nationally, rankled nationalists, who feared the regimentation of the Afrikaner youth and the fostering of 'an unhealthy kind of European militarism, an overbearing state culture alien to the personal loyalty traditions of Boer men'.[125] In December 1914, Wyndham, observing the compromises of 1912 at work, lamented the lack of military organisation. As he explained to his mother, 'We have at the present time two entirely different military organizations operating side by side in the field. One is the commando system, which in reality is no organization at all, & the other is a somewhat faint copy of the British system.'[126]

Predictably, several factors affecting the UDF undermined its reliability, organisation, and effectiveness. The matter of military culture is the most obvious and, for many years, the UDF remained an unhappy marriage between the British and Boer military value systems. A Defence Council – a safety mechanism to find consensus and, where necessary, protect language interests – met irregularly. It lacked real power, was foisted on Smuts at the insistence of the Natal and – for these reasons perhaps – convened on only 13 occasions between 1912 and July 1918.[127] Moreover, language and provincial interest were balanced even at the cost of military effectiveness. There were four defence councillors, two English and two Afrikaans, representing the four provinces. The high command, divided into three executives, comprised Lukin, an old colonial stalwart; Beyers, a staunchly republican former Boer general; and Beves, the former Inspector of the Transvaal Volunteers. The military 'rings' created before 1912, wrestled each other for power and position in the new structures and rushed the

124 UCT: BC 294, Duncan Papers, A49, Memorandum explanatory of the South African Defence Bill, p.2.
125 Bill Nasson, *Springboks on the Somme; South Africa in the Great War 1914–1918* (Penguin Johannesburg, 2007), p.38.
126 WSRO: Maxse Papers 455, Hugh Wyndham to Mary Maxse, 9 Dec 1914.
127 DODA: DC, Box 109, files 2270 and 2271, Defence Council Agenda of 1st and 2nd meetings.

available posts. Although remarkable 'racial' parity was achieved and at all levels, over the first four decades, without doubt, organisational fiefdoms stunted development and war planning, and fostered distrust and fission in the new structures.[128]

Notwithstanding, the UDF – far from being the 'middle ground' Smuts had envisioned – achieved a surprising, near-perfect balance between language and provincial interests. The 51 officers nominated for the first course at the newly established Military School in Bloemfontein, were drawn representatively from the integrating forces with near equal numbers in terms of language. Later dubbed the 'fathers' of the Union Defence Force, they included former Boer generals Manie Maritz, Ben Bouwer and Jan Kemp, W.E.C. Tanner from Natal, E.T. Thackwray from the Transvaal Volunteers, and half a dozen officers of the CMR. Posted to the new headquarters in Pretoria and as the district staff officers of the 13 military districts, they became – in theory at least – the defence minister's 'missionaries', sent out to explain the working of the new defence legislation, and register, attest, and train the men in their districts. This was the politics of consensus and 'representation' seemingly at its best. However, as Aston, the commandant at the Military School, noted 'they all came with a sort of official veneer of goodwill to each other but were really like a lot of dogs smelling round each other and ready to snarl and bite at the first chance.'[129] For some men, including Maritz and Kemp, integration into the UDF promised opportunity to strike a future, well-timed blow against the British Empire.[130]

Beyers is a fascinating figure in this regard. All high-ranking officers no doubt influenced appointments and satisfied requests made by their political superiors or former-force underlings. But Beyers – who had sat on the head committee of *Het Volk*, alongside Botha and Smuts – took more extreme steps. Hugh Wyndham, a Unionist MP, who 'lost' his command of the integrating Southern Mounted Rifles – noted in late 1910 that Beyers was 'a very violent Boer', capable of making 'very racial speeches' and that if he were made 'Minister of Defence, or Commandant General, [this] would lead to the dismemberment of any defence force that we may possess at present or in the future'.[131] Wyndham's words later proved prescient. In the meantime, Beyers cajoled Bourne regarding appointments, promotions, and seniority, and removed the more 'British' officers from the new ACF regiments, while his opponents finding easy cause accused him of fostering 'racialism' and a reactionary Boer stance. Moreover,

128 I. van der Waag, 'Smuts' Generals: Towards a first portrait of the South African high command, 1912-48', *War in History* vol.18(1) January 2011, pp.1–29.

129 RMA: Major General Sir George Aston Papers, General Sir George Aston's Diary, 7 December 1912. I. van der Waag, 'South Africa and the making of military officers, 1902-1948' in Douglas E. Delaney, Robert C. Engen, and Meghan Fitzpatrick (eds.), *Military Education and the British Empire, 1815-1949* (Vancouver: University of British Columbia Press, 2017), pp.85–107.

130 J.C.G. Kemp, *Die Pad van die Verowеraar* (Kaapstad: Nasionale Pers, 1946), pp.107–108.

131 WSRO: Petworth House Archives, Hugh Wyndham to Lady Leconfield, 2 November 1910.

Beyers was preoccupied with status and position and found himself increasingly at odds with the defence minister over matters ranging from his eccentric departures from the regulation uniform, and his public commentary on the application of the language policy in the UDF, to his persistent politicking at a national level.[132] He was the proverbial square peg in a round hole.

Naval defence inevitably triggered heated debate. All political parties recognised the need for a naval presence in South African waters, but they could not agree on its form or character – whether an embryonic South African navy be formed, or a continued reliance on the Royal Navy. Bourne, who held the defence purse strings, argued that a South African navy would for many years be beyond the resources of the Union. He supported the idea of continued contribution – as the coastal colonies had done – to maintain the Royal Navy presence.[133] Merriman agreed. The naval contribution was nothing other than an insurance premium for South Africa's seaborne trade and any move to create an independent navy, as was happening in other dominions, would bring disruption and spell disaster.[134] On the other hand, the nationalists viewed any naval contribution as a form of imperial tribute and an emblem of ultra-Jingoism, although Merriman's idea of an insurance premium made the matter more palatable. This former-president Steyn argued was at least 'a more business-like proposal than a blind contribution.'[135] Even Smuts did not like the idea of having a South African government meet in Cape Town under the shadow of British naval guns.

The presence of two British commands in South Africa – the South African Military Command, headquartered at The Castle in Cape Town, and the Royal Navy's Simon's Town station – caused political mischief from both sides. The Africa Station was small, insular, and decidedly patrician, and a frustrating posting for higher-ranking personnel. Many of the admirals and their senior staffs were aristocrats or noble sprigs and, while at times limited attempts were made to reach out to the local community, many of their set 'hated Simon's Town.'[136] British officials professed difficulty in dealing with South Africans, while local officials found their British counterparts pretentious, and fostering old-world, class distinctions. None of this endeared the British set to broader South African society, of whom even the English-speakers, as John Darwin noted, had 'generally little sympathy for what they regarded as an over-rigid class system at home.'[137] Required for the adequate defence of South Africa, the

132 I. van der Waag, 'Re-Thinking South Africa's Military Past: The Curious Case of Brig. Gen. the Hon. C.F. Beyers' (Stellenbosch University: Professorial inaugural lecture, 2018), pp.14–18.
133 DODA: Diverse Group 1, Box 15, file 199, Colonial Defence Committee Memoranda on General Defence Matters, Bourne to Smuts, 8 September 1910.
134 J.X. Merriman to M.T. Steyn, 16 January 1911 in Marais (ed.), *Politieke Briewe*, pp.5–6.
135 M.T. Steyn to J.X. Merriman, 10 February 1911 in Marais (ed.), *Politieke Briewe*, p.8.
136 WSRO: Petworth House Archives, Mrs Fitzroy – wife of Goodenough's staff captain – quoted in Maud Wyndham to Lady Leconfield, 21 September 1920.
137 D. Cannadine, *Ornamentalism: How the British Saw their Empire* (Oxford: Oxford University Press, 1950), p.137.

British military and naval presence were very visible signs of South Africa's constitutional subordination and military dependence on Britain.

Whilst universal conscription on the Swiss model formed the basis for recruitment into the UDF, military service was confined to men classified as 'white'. The compromises made in the making of the Union enabled the two northern provinces – the former republics – to imbue wider South Africa with their republican ideals and practices of racial inequality. Black South Africans were precluded from service in terms of the Defence Act, although in times of emergency they could be attested by special parliamentary authorisation.[138] The district staff officers, responsible for recruitment and training in their respective districts, adopted specific procedures regarding the registration and attestation of citizens deemed to be not 'of European descent'. They entered separate structures, served largely in auxiliary roles, and did not enjoy the benefits given to White service personnel. As discussed in chapter 8, this unfair, discriminatory practice was ventilated in 1917 when recruiting officers, facing manpower shortages for the Western Front, attested 'coloured' men for service with the Brigade in France. In practice thousands of Black, Coloured and Indian soldiers, assistants, drivers and labourers served in all the South African theatres of the First World War.

Within a year of its founding, the UDF faced its first test. This came in the form of the first of several internal deployments that would take place over the next decade – on this occasion to quell industrial unrest. A strong miners' organisation had been established on the Witwatersrand soon after the resumption of mining in 1901. A strike in May 1907, to resist changes in working conditions, was suppressed by Smuts – then Colonial Secretary of the Transvaal – using imperial troops to protect scab labour and mining property.[139] But, in July 1913, labour discontent on the mines led to a general strike, which spread rapidly from New Kleinfontein on the East Rand. Botha and Smuts were forced to broker a settlement. Loathe to rely on imperial troops, Smuts would not be caught off guard again.

Another strike started on 7 January 1914. Smuts mobilised the defence force, placing troops at all key points, and special constables – across party lines – were sworn in. Botha remarked that he was surprised that 'Afrikaners were poisoned with socialism'.[140] But he and Smuts made sure they took the necessary precautions. Men of the commandos, under De la Rey's command, guarded the mines and homes of mine owners: the irony was not missed. The strike ended on 15 January at the Johannesburg trades hall, where the executive of the Transvaal Federation of Trades

138 DODA: Archives of the Adjutant General 1914-1921, Box 189, file 489, Coloured Men in Overseas Brigade, Staff Officer General Staff Duties to District Staff Officers, 18 Febraury 1913. See also Ian Gleeson, *The Unknown Force: Black indian and Coloured Soldiers Through Two World Wars* (Rivonia: Ashanti, 1994), p.9.

139 I.L. Walker and B. Weinbren, *2000 Casualties. A History of the Trade Unions and the Labour Movement in the Union of South Africa* (Johannesburg: SAUTC, 1961), pp.23–24.

140 NARSSA: Leyds Archive, 262, Part II, Botha to Leyds, 18 August 1913.

and their diehard supporters had barricaded themselves. They surrendered. The UDF had seemingly passed its first test. However, during the night of 26 January, the nine strike leaders who were not of South African birth were embarked at the point of a bayonet and deported to Britain.[141]

Smuts's action sparked an outcry on the point of civil liberties. The government introduced a bill to indemnify its actions during the strike and legalise the deportations, which split the House of Assembly across party lines. Merriman considered it 'a fatal error.'[142] Having been born in Britain, Wyndham told his wife that 'he might be deported himself on Smuts's ruling at any time.'[143] The editors of the *Pretoria News* and the *Daily News* supported the government's action, although it had been high-handed. The Bill passed into law and the crisis – everyone thought – was over. Lord Gladstone, the outgoing governor general, told his successor that he would have a good reception in South Africa and, with the Rand Crisis over, possibly a quiet time to deal with the 'big issue' for the next five years: 'the Native Question itself, and its economic relation to White labour'.[144] A quiet time indeed and with the looming war, the Native Land Act of 1913 remained the set piece – this oppressive legislation shaped the South African socio-economic landscape, and prevented the Black people from owning land.

Conclusion

As Bill Nasson has argued, the political exclusion of the Black majority was easily shrugged off, for the Union 'would serve Britain's long-term economic, political and strategic needs by stimulating more rapid economic development and by nurturing Anglo-Afrikaner reconciliation and accommodation'.[145] Botha and Smuts's vision was idealistic and in of itself highly limited.

They believed their policy and plan to be the best course of action – that of conciliation. This proved to be a tenuous middle-ground for a modernising South Africa – the joining of British and Boer cultures turned out to be an almost impossible task. The split between Botha and Hertzog represented the wider division. The break that came in 1913 would lead to a sequence of dramatic events – including rebellion. Wyndham,

141 Jonathan Hyslop, *Notorious Syndicalist. J.T. Bain: A Scottish Rebel in Colonial South Africa* (Johannesburg: Jacana, 2004).

142 Mary Drew to Dorothy Parish, 31 January 1914 in L. Masterman (ed.), *Mary Gladstone (Mrs Drew): Her Diaries and Letters* (London: Methuen & Co, 1930), p.475.

143 Hagley Hall Archives (HHA): 2/36/35, Maud Wyndham to Lady Cobham, 6 February 1914.

144 The British Library, London (BL): Add MS 86947 Buxton Papers, Gladstone to Buxton, 12 June 1914.

145 Bill Nasson, *Springboks on the Somme: South Africa and the Great War, 1914–1918* (Penguin Johannesburg, 2007), p.1.

then the Union shadow Minister of Defence, noted that 'wars, whether industrial or civil [were then] quite the fashion'.[146] The Union was ultimately governed by two generals, Botha and Smuts, and as military men they needed a suitable defence force – the UDF gave them the military means to execute their foreign and domestic policies within the framework of the British Empire but pushing South African interests all the while.

146 WSRO: Petworth House Archives, Hugh Wyndham to Lady Leconfield, 9 July 1914.

2

A Bad Beginning, 1914

I have to do my duty.
Botha to Leyds[1]

Botha tried to exude confidence. This was not always easy, but the one thing that Botha had in abundance was charisma. He could find an interest, angle or opportunity, and shape conversations placing participants at the centre. But he had taken on a massive task – the new South African experiment – it was after all his vision, a nation for Boer and Briton.

Smuts was not imbued with the charisma of Botha. His was a steely focus – he demonstrated that through force of will and intellect, backed up by hard work, a new South African system could be realised. However, not all their compatriots would share in their vision – doubtlessly it was a vision realised on an uneven platform. As a result a number of crude comments were directed at Botha – the ultimate "King's Boer".

Botha's Vision in Practice

Any slight, or comment affected the general. He was so very sensitive – in 1913, Gillet mentioned to Smuts that, 'General Botha expressed himself as very sore and hurt because the Free Staters had not consulted him'. On the reverse side, Botha was sensitive to the feelings of others, and in 1911, Botha wrote to Smuts, 'I am afraid their feelings will be hurt and that we must as far as possible avoid, for it is always the little and not the much that gives one trouble'.[2] Smuts, who deeply admired Botha's strength, could never understand why he paid any attention to the jibes. In Engelenburg's 1929 English biography on Botha, for which Smuts wrote the introduction, he said that Botha had

1 NARSSA: Leyds Archive, 262, Part II: Botha to Leyds, 6 October 1914.
2 Gillet to Smuts, 30 July 1913, and Botha to Smuts, 3 March 1915, Hancock and Van der Poel (eds.), *Selections*, Vol. III, p.41.

'sympathetic power [that] not only meant great power but also great pain to him… he was abnormally sensitive'.[3] He understood that it was Botha's great heart – his compassion – that equally made him an excellent judge of character and emotionally vulnerable. Smuts went on to reminisce that Botha was made of such emotional intensity that he often could not sleep when a bad comment was directed at him – in this sense Smuts said Botha 'was like a woman'.[4] To the reader, this statement may seem odd and sexist, but by the norms of the day, it was a way for Smuts to explain that Botha was emotionally intelligent. Smuts was probably also sexist when compared to contemporary norms. Botha often welled up and was certainly not the only famous leader to break down in tears –the towering Winston Churchill often cried, even in parliament, when facing the tough challenges of the Second World War – who could blame him.

Botha and Smuts had put in practice through a fortunate coincidence of political, military, and economic factors, as well as good leadership, compromise and charm, an assortment of former colonies, a disparate cultural mix, held together by personal and historical debts, entitlements and ambitions – this was the foundation of the 1910 Union of South Africa. Despite his love for his people, Botha had committed himself to the ideals of the British Empire – and the difference between the two was stark. Smuts too was committed to a South Africa within Empire. Both were men of war, perhaps a product of their times – Smuts, an accidental Boer general, and Botha who fell into the role of commander only to become the Transvaal commandant-general – they proved themselves through their ability and had a clear understanding of what was to be done. Botha's reasonableness was backed up by force; only to be used when the force of Smuts's reasoning failed. Their path led them into direct conflict with other Boer leaders, many either republican or disgruntled.

For the most part Boer frustration was localised in the Free State and the northern Cape, with a peppering of Transvaal generals stirring under the noses of Botha and Smuts. The hesitant general Beyers was a case in point and a complex man – little trusted, with a chip on his shoulder, which was only counterbalanced by his larger-than-life persona, extravagant uniforms and ego. He was a misunderstood, sometimes unlucky and ultimately tragic figure who would die after pulling some Transvaalers into the rebellion. For many, the straw that broke Afrikanerdom's back was South Africa's involvement in the First World War.

In July 1914, Botha and Annie took a trip to Rhodesia (now Zimbabwe), with the intention of travelling as far north as the Congo. During this time Winston Churchill, then First Lord of the Admiralty, telegraphed Pretoria to say that war with Germany was imminent. Botha returned home immediately.[5] Desperate to get back to South Africa, Botha almost boarded a German ship, and if it was not for a last-minute intervention the prime minister would have become a prisoner of war. One can almost

3 J.C. Smuts who wrote the introduction to Engelenburg, *Botha*, p.17.
4 Engelenburg, *Botha*, p.17.
5 Meintjes, *Botha*, p.207.

imagine his insecurity, with Smuts by his side, considering potential, economic, social, military and political issues. But with it came a hint of opportunity, and they set about tackling what would become the most serious challenge of their lives.

In 1910, with the formation of the Union, Smuts took three ministerial portfolios, mines, defence and interior, a colossal workload, even for Oom Jannie. Eventually forced to let a few go, he was no doubt one of the busiest men in South Africa at the outbreak of the First World War. Smuts in characteristic fashion was prodigiously putting pen to paper when he heard about the war. He was sure to maintain communications with a range of key role players and friends in South Africa and the United Kingdom – he ensured that the 'correct' South African narrative was put forward; and that their logistical needs were considered.

Without consulting parliament, Botha confirmed that the Union would support the British geo-strategy with an invasion of German South West Africa. The British Imperial Defence Offensive Committee stated that the capture of German South West Africa was essential to the domination of the seas.[6] Sea routes through the Mediterranean and Middle-East to the Indian Ocean were compromised and sea navigation around Cape Point, was of even greater strategic importance.

Needless to say, the German South West African campaign played a small if important part in the British global maritime strategy. The secretary of state for the colonies, Lewis Vernon Harcourt, confirmed that it was 'a great and urgent imperial service'.[7] The objectives included the control of the ports of Lüderitzbucht and Swakopmund which aimed at limiting German maritime operations.[8] A further objective was the wireless stations in Windhoek, Lüderitzbucht and Swakopmund, which provided communication functions to the German war effort.[9] The wireless stations were used to provide links to German warships as well as land-based forces through wireless stations in Togoland, Cameroon and Tanganyika. Through the use of relay stations, and with favourable weather conditions, messages could be transmitted from Windhoek to Berlin.[10] A final purpose to the invasion of German South West Africa, which was similar to the other British colonial conquests, the captured territories would be made available to the Crown upon the cessation of hostilities.[11]

6 TNA CAB 45/112: The Campaign in GSWA, Narrative of Events, 4 August 1914.
7 J.J. Collyer, *The Campaign in German South West Africa, 1914–1915* (Pretoria: Government Printer, 1937), p.6.
8 D.W. Krüger, *The Age of the Generals* (Johannesburg: Dagbreek, 1958), p.81.
9 G. L'ange, *Urgent Imperial Service* (Rivonia: Ashanti, 1991), p.7.
10 Van der Waag, *A Military History*, p.93; Krüger, *Age of the Generals*, p.81; L'ange, *Urgent Imperial Service*, p.7; Anon., *Union of South Africa and the Great War, 1914–1918, Official History* (Pretoria: Government Printer, 1924), p.10; H. Paterson, 'First Allied Victory: The South African Campaign in German South-West Africa, 1914–1915', *Military History Journal*, vol.13, no.2 (2004), p.1; A. Lentin*Jan Smuts; Man of Courage and Vision* (Johannesburg, Jonathan Ball, 2010), p.31
11 S.B. Spies, 'The Outbreak of the First World War and the Botha Government', *South African Historical Journal*, vol.1, no.1 (1969), p.48.

Smuts, in a letter to Deneys Reitz, summarised their intent, 'when all is over and German South West Africa again forms a part of our Afrikaner heritage, feeling will quickly swing round and our action be generally approved.'[12] Botha and Smuts were betting that the results of their military victory would lead to territorial acquisition, and that would gain them political favour in the 1915 elections – they were right about military victory, and acquiring territory, but wrong about gaining votes.

Not all Afrikaners bought into the idea that the invasion of German South West Africa was necessary, or in South Africa's best interests. Many held the historical view that it was in fact the British who invaded the Boer republics, most recently in 1899, and the invasion of German South West Africa was a further expression of British jingoism.

Botha and Smuts were in a difficult position. They had to contribute to the war effort as the leaders of a British Dominion, but at home they faced a growing backlash from many Boers who felt no loyalty to the King. Many were scarred by the trauma of the Anglo-Boer War, an ordeal, Botha and Smuts knew all too well. Botha was lucky to have sent his family to the Netherlands in 1900, while others were not as fortunate. It was a tightrope, that they balanced with tension, force, and little tact. Charming, intelligent, and unreasonable to a fault, they had taken their position and would not be moved.

Botha was strongly opposed to the idea of optional neutrality, an idea that had currency in certain South African circles at the time.[13] The only question Botha and Smuts entertained was the extent of South Africa's involvement; and the type of participation in the war effort.[14] Botha and Smuts stood firm in their conviction that the Union of South Africa was an integral part of the Empire and as such was automatically at war because of its status as a dominion of the British Empire.[15] Their duty, at least in their mind was clear, they were to take an active role, conquer what they could and take new land.

It is interesting to note that despite Botha's strong stance on South African neutrality, he took a more lenient approach towards the Netherlands. In writing to Leyds, Botha indicated, 'we wholeheartedly hope that the Netherlands will be able to stay out of the war...'[16] Leyds wrote back explaining that although the Netherlands remained neutral, approximately 300,000 troops were mobilised to protect their borders.[17] Botha and Smuts were practical men, and they had committed themselves to the Crown. Unlike the Netherlands that was geographically closer to the conflict

12 Smuts to Reitz, 22 September 1914, Hancock and Van der Poel (eds.), *Selections*, Vol. III, p.198.
13 Botha to Steyn, 8 September 1911 in Marais, *Politieke Briewe*, p.23.
14 N.G. Garson, 'South Africa and World War I', *The Journal of Imperial and Commonwealth History*, vol.8, no.1 (1979), p.1.
15 NARSSA: Preller Archive, 90, 'Generaal Botha in Losberg', *De Volksstem*, 29 September 1914; Meintjes, *Botha*, p.208.
16 NARSSA: Leyds Archive, 262, Part II, Botha to Leyds, 14 October 1914.
17 NARSSA: Leyds Archive, 262, Part II, Leyds to Botha, 4 September 1914.

and risked destruction, the Union was far away and would not be exposed to the high intensity war and deprivations of mainland Europe. Botha and Smuts could not abandon Britain in its time of need.

The Politics of Participation

Botha's South Africanism did not succeed in uniting the majority of Afrikaner and British South Africans, and by 1914, more than ever, the Union was bitterly divided. Botha hoped to turn the war into an opportunity to unite Boer and Briton – an early attempt at nation building, at least for the White populations.[18] The historian D.W. Krüger commented that the outbreak of the First World War came too soon as the people of South Africa were not yet united or ready for such a conflict. It was too strong a test for a new Union. It came too soon after the Anglo-Boer War and too soon after the breaks in the ranks of Afrikanerdom.[19]

Botha and Smuts faced a complex situation. There was a growing wave of Afrikaner nationalism that was on a collision course with the well-connected and strongly pro-war Unionist and South African parties. This manifested in a constitutional dilemma which came at a difficult time, and not long after the ministerial crises of 1912 and 1913, that saw J.B.M. Hertzog ousted from the South African Party. Hertzog went on to form the National Party, supported by a majority of republican-minded Afrikaners, and they soon became the official parliametnary oppostion. The South African Party was a broad church, and by the outbreak of the war, Botha and Smuts were managing so many competing interests, that politically, it became untenable.

Although appreciating South Africa's political and military difficulties, London pushed Pretoria towards an early expedition.[20] However, broad-based public opinion stood in sharp contrast to the parliamentary division approving the war plans. Botha and Smuts, egged on by the English-speaking community, embraced the comfortable notion that their Afrikaner compatriots welcomed the opportunities for nation building and patriotism.[21] Hugh Wyndham, a prominent Unionist and shadow defence minister, misreading the situation entirely, reported that 'the feeling amongst the Boers out here is excellent'[22]; while his wife, a Lyttelton, was sure that

18 Van der Waag, *A Military History*, pp.91–92.

19 Krüger, *Age of the Generals*, p.80.

20 NARSSA: PM 1/1/32, file 4/97/1914 War, German South West Expedition & Supply of Ammunition & Guns, Lord Harcourt to Lord de Villiers, 8 August 1914 and 23 August 1914.

21 WCARS: A.583 F.S. Malan Collection, vol.22, 'De Britse-Duitse Oorlog' (The Anglo-German War), diary of F.S. Malan, 7–10 August 1914; and Spies, 'The Outbreak of WW1', p.47.

22 WSRO: Petworth House Archives, Hugh Wyndham to Lady Leconfield, 13 August 1914,. These sentiments were also held by Carter. See Wits: AB186 Archbishop Carter Letters, William Carter to Algernon Lawley, 13 August 1914.

'the feeling can never go back to what it was before that's certain.'[23] Yet, far from nation-building and creating some common 'feeling', the war presented for what Bill Nasson has termed 'the non-loyalist strata of Afrikaner society' unique opportunities for party-politicking.[24]

The initial cable from London requested that all British troops in South Africa be freed for service in France. A second cable requested the invasion of German South West Africa.[25] Botha approached the latter cable with caution, perhaps realising the danger it posed to the delicate political balance. He knew the thoughts of many of the hardened burghers, the bitter-enders who fought tooth and nail against the British – how would he convince them that this was the right thing to do? His task was now to persuade his Boer compatriots that the invasion of German South West Africa was in their best interests. A difficult task, with many burghers still praying for a return to the republics of old,[26] but for Botha, his only option was loyalty to the Crown.[27] The pro-British Boers were not the only ones who would support the war effort, and representatives of the Zulu, Tembu and other African groupings, as well as Coloureds, and Indians, all joined in to support the war effort, hoping to gain political capital and economic opportunities as a reward for their loyalty.

Pixley Seme one of the founders of the African National Congress (ANC) cited political expediency as a fundamental reason for supporting the war effort. He was educated at Columbia and Oxford universities, graduating with a degree in law, and like Smuts and Hertzog he was an attorney and was admitted to the bar in Britain. Along with other African intellectuals, including but not limited to Richard Msimang, George Montsioa, Solomon (Sol) Tshekisho Plaatje and Alfred Mangena, they set up the South African Native National Congress (SANNC), the predecessor to the ANC. The SANNC raised troops for the First World War as did many other political and community-based organisations. In contemporary times, the ANC has taken a lukewarm approach to remembering the First World War, casting it as an imperialist war. To some extent they viewed the Black servicemen as agents of the White state. This is perhaps too strong a judgement on the earlier version of their political party. In the defence of the motivations of People of Colour who served in the First World War – without wanting to oversimplify it, their intent was broadly to gain a platform for political power. At the time the Black, Indian and Coloured politicians made use of

23 HHA: 2/36/45, Maud Wyndham to Lord Cobham, 11 August 1914.
24 B. Nasson, 'A great divide: popular responses to the Great War in South Africa', *War & Society*, vol.XII (1994), p.50. See also N.G. Garson, 'South Africa and World War 1', pp.69–70. On the rebellion generally and the often difficult position of the Loyal Afrikaners, see K. Fedorowich, 'Sleeping with the Lion? The Loyal Afrikaners and the South African Rebellion of 1914-15', *South African Historical Journal*, vol.49 (2003), pp.71–95.
25 TNA CAB 45/112: Campaign in GSWA, 1914-1918, Narrative of Events, 6–9 August 1914.
26 Meintjes, *Botha*, pp.214–215.
27 Engelenburg, *Botha*, pp.279–281.

the means available. Although the modern ANC is critical of the war, Seme similarly critiqued the early ANC movement, even if for different reasons. As an advisor to the Zulu King, he went on to recommend that the Zulu nation be proactive in supporting the British war effort. His hope was to gain a position of influence and to gain political advantage for the Zulu people.[28]

At this point the Zulu kingdom was only a monarchy in name and the king received an allowance from the Botha and Smuts government. Botha who had a complex relationship with King Dinizulu, freed him from prison after he was falsely found guilty of complicity and crimes in the Bhambatha Rebellion. This was one of Botha's first acts as prime minister of the Union in 1910. They had an understanding, and built a relationship over time, but their friendship was certainly not one of equals, and Botha and Smuts, were paternalistic and racist in their belief and approach. Bongani Ngqulunga's recent work on Seme, shows how Botha's office delayed in approving travel permits for Dinizulu to get much needed medical treatment.[29]

Botha's life and history brought him in contact with Dinizulu and the Zulu nation. He took his cattle to Zululand for grazing in his earlier years and cut his teeth fighting against a Zulu faction with Meyer's commando in the 1880s. Botha respected African nations but made significant mistakes too. Smuts had a different relationship with Africans, and although he was strong and paternalistic in his approach, he was not cruel – he ultimately enjoyed intellectual exchanges and would become friends with Gandhi, who was also a racist. Smuts would later face tremendous critique from the then newly formed United Nations, for his colonial approach to South-West Africa.

Botha and Seme exchanged letters, although many were in fact written by Dr Bok, Botha's private secretary. Botha had little time for Seme, and the prime minister questioned his standing as advisor to Solomon the Zulu King.[30] Botha's relationship with Africans was only good as long as it was on his terms. He expressed disappointment in having to ask for Zulu assistance in the war and said that they should have offered their support of their own accord. Botha and Smuts wanted Africans to be at once co-operative and submissive.

Seme was not of that mould – he was smart, driven and educated, although not without his flaws and vices, he saw a vision for African franchise and freedom. It was the Native Land Act of 1913, that electrified him into action and solidified many African leaders and intellectuals to form the ANC. They sounded their disappointment in the new oppressive legislation through protest and formal grievances to British politicians. Liberal voices in the United States and Britain were horrified at the Land Act. The ANC joined international voices, in condemning the Land Act

28 See B. Ngqulunga, *The Man Who Founded the ANC: A Biography of Pixley ka Isaka Seme* (Cape Town: Zebra, 2017).
29 Ngqulunga, *The Man*, p.119.
30 Ngqulunga, *The Man*, p.119.

and started the earliest of attempts at what would come to be known as Wilsonian self-determination.

The concept of African liberation was foreign to Botha and Smuts – raised in the tradition of White superiority, framed in hundreds of years of history and the founding *Voortrekker* narrative; they were happy to receive support from Blacks, Indians, and Coloureds, but full political franchise was not an option. In 1914 partial Indian franchise was granted, and in the Cape, Coloureds were granted some historic political rights – but this was a small concession, and the overall picture, was still outlined in the spirit of the Treaty of Vereeniging; Whites at the top table. Most White South Africans at the time believed in a White only central government, and this was reinforced by the economic limitations imposed on the Black population, codified in the Land Act of 1913.

Most African peoples likened the War to buying political favours that could be traded in later on, and the Thembu King, Dalindyebo amaThembu, wrote a letter that underpinned the views of many African nations, 'I have learned with great concern that there is a great war in Europe … His Most Gracious Majesty … may be ever victorious both upon land and upon sea … I desire to declare that I and the people over whom I am placed will be faithful and true, and loyal in our service to His Most Gracious Majesty … and we will be ever ready to assist the Government of His Majesty "God Save the King".'[31] This was the type of letter that Botha and Smuts wanted. A voluntary commitment to support the war.

Sol Plaatje, the intellectual, writer, one of the founding members of the SANNC, and journalist, held a similar position, one that supported the war. Botha and Plaatje had different political positions, but personally they got on, largely because they could converse in Dutch. Plaatje was a British interpreter during the siege of Mafikeng during the Anglo-Boer War and spoke seven languages. His Dutch gave him an insight into the Boer people and something that Botha appreciated. Plaatje lived a life of activism and he wrote a book in response to the 1913 Land Act: *Native Life in South Africa*, which was eventually published in Britain after struggling to raise funds for its publication.[32] The book evolved and he would later add his lived experience to the manuscript. In 1914 Plaatje found himself in England at the start of the First World War, adapting and re-writing his book; during the initial phases he went on to strongly support the war effort.[33] But from late 1916 onwards he voiced his opposition to recruiting Blacks for the war effort.

Abdullah Abdurahman was a politician and leader of the African People's Organisation (APO). A charismatic leader, and orator he served as the first Coloured Cape Town Councillor, a post he held for most of his political career. The APO tried

31 BL: Add MS 86947 Viscount Buxton Papers, King Dalindyebo, Umtata, to Chief Magistrate of the Transkeian Territories, 19 August 1914.

32 S. Plaatje, *Native Life in South Africa* (London: P. S. King and Son Ltd.,1916), *passim*.

33 For a comprehensive account of Plaatje's life, see B. Willan, *Sol Plaatje: A Life of Solomon Tshekisho Plaatje* (Johannesburg: Jacana, 2018).

to gain political capital by supporting the war effort and Abdurahman personally led a recruitment drive. Indian troops and auxiliaries were also raised, especially in Natal, and so Black, Coloured, and Indian troops, stood with the British Empire.[34] Colonel Sir Charles Crewe, the Unionist polician and former Cape defence minister, summarised the paternalistic position, 'the most magnificent thing is the way all parties have stood together throughout the Empire when we as a people were assailed.[35]

Mahatma Gandhi, lawyer, anti-colonial leader, politician and civil rights activist had left South Africa and returned to India in 1914 at the start of the First World War. He had won partial franchise for Indian South Africans and was on a quest to bring greater freedoms to India. Gandhi supported the war effort and had previously come out in support of the British in the Anglo-Boer War, helped establish the Natal Indian Ambulance Corps, and served in a non-combat role as a stretcher bearer. Interestingly during the Anglo-Boer War, Gandhi, Winston Churchill, and Botha were all present at the Battle of Spion Kop. It was Botha's baptism of fire – he had some of his first experiences as a commander in this battle, while Gandhi was a stretcher bearer in the service of the British, and Churchill had made his famous escape from Boer captivity and allegedly swam across the Apies River, a non-perennial stream. Churchill later re-joined the British forces. Commissioned as a lieutenant in the South African Light Horse Regiment, he was a courier carrying orders to and from the front as Gandhi carried away the dead and wounded. So it was that these three men would be present at the same place, an aspirant republican commander, an imperialist courier, and a colonial stretcher bearer – the future prime minister of the Union of South Africa, the future prime minister of Britain, and the prominent anti-colonial leader in India's struggle for independence.

Gandhi and Botha did not get along. Botha in his paternalistic attitude saw Gandhi as an upstart. Gandhi was effective and his 1913 protests won freedoms for Indian South Africans – a momentous achievement for the time. Botha was frustrated and outplayed by Gandhi. Writing to Smuts the prime minister said, 'Dear Jannie, this morning I telegraphed you about Gandhi and others—whether we cannot arrest them again. I felt so irritated at their attitude, now again in Natal, that really one could take them by the throat.'[36] Churchill came to strongly dislike Gandhi in the 1920s and 1930s, and the rivalry and tension between the two leaders had a considerable impact on the Indian sub-continent, Britain, and its colonies.[37]

Smuts had a different type of relationship with Gandhi, both lawyers, and shrewd operators, they developed a mutual respect. They settled the issue of Indian migration

34 See Nasson, *Springboks*, pp.19–21.
35 Wiltshire and Swindon History Centre (WSHC): Viscount Long Papers, 947/469, Crewe to Long, 15 September 1914.
36 Botha to Smuts, 23 December 1913, Hancock and Van der Poel (eds.), *Selections*, Vol. III, p.151.
37 See A. Herman, *Gandhi and Churchill: The Rivalry That Destroyed an Empire and Forged Our Age* (London: Arrow, 2009).

in January 1914. Gandhi gifted Smuts a pair of sandals that he had made, and Smuts would later go on to write, that he was not worthy of wearing the sandals of such a great man. All of them were great men, with great flaws, and history would indeed judge them harshly.[38]

The Union Enters the War

Botha and Smuts made a political calculation and imagined that Afrikaans and English South Africans would see things from their viewpoint. Despite Botha's earlier commitment to London to pursue a campaign against German South West Africa, with Smuts's beavering away at early plans of conquest in August 1914 – the overzealous pair required parliamentary approval.[39] The Defence Act of 1912 stated that the Union's forces could be used in matters of defence only.[40]

Smuts regarded South Africa as a geographic expression, such as Central or East Africa, and in effect that was also the view of the Botha government. The Defence Act of 1912 had intended the term 'South Africa' to refer to the entire region of Southern Africa.[41] Botha and Smuts applied their convenient spatial understanding to justify the invasion of German South West Africa. Botha addressed the House of Assembly and said that the Union had an obligation to serve the British Empire and that it was a matter of honour. Botha went on to state that a German force had entrenched itself in Nakob and had crossed the border into South Africa.[42] In reality a handful of German soldiers were reconnoitring a border post in and around Nakob, and this act was exaggerated for political expediency. An account from the time, a Reuters telegram that stated that the

38 Smuts's statue at the University of Cape Town was vandalised in 2016 and his bust in Cambridge was removed in 2018. All part of the decolonisation of education movement, and current responses to the contested history of South Africa – they were an expression of modern feeling towards the past. Gandhi would also not go unscathed, with his statues vandalised in Johannesburg in 2015 in Manchester in 2021, and also in the US state of California in 2021. The University of Ghana removed Gandhi's statue in 2018 for his racist views. Botha's statues were vandalised in 2015 and 2016 in Cape Town, Durban and Pretoria and in 2020 a lobby group has petitioned to have his statue removed from in front of parliament in Cape Town.

39 DODA: Pretoria, Diverse 1, Box 2, Rebellion Commission of Enquiry, vol.1, Testimony by Louis Botha, 29 June 1916; Testimony by Coenraad Jacobus Brits, 15 March 1916; DC, Box 252, 17138, Reports of Force Commanders in GSWA, Operations in and around Sandfontein 25, 26 and 27 September 1914, 19 August 1915.

40 W.A. Dorning, 'A Concise History of the South African Defence Force 1912–1987', *Militaria, South African Journal for Military Studies*, vol.17, no.2 (1987), p.4.

41 Krüger, *Age of the Generals*, p.82.

42 NARSSA: Preller Archive, 90, 'The Prime Minister's Speech', *Pretoria News*, 10 September 1914.

Germans had invaded the Union at Nakob caused 'nervous unrest in Upington, Kenhardt, Keimoes and Kakamas.' But the German activity 'can hardly be called an invasion.'[43]

There was also a minor incident in which a farmer was shot. The point was well captured by Crewe in a letter to Viscount Long, the conservative politician, 'they finally agreed to defend the country from attack and since then the Germans have been considerate enough to invade us; although they have come only a mile or two over our border and have not the remotest intention of coming any further, it is enough for the Boers and Botha may well be trusted to make the most of this impudent and aggressive invasion.'[44] At a time when the politics between the South African Party and the National Party was heated, a minor shoot-out between German soldiers and South African farmers became part of the narrative for invasion.[45]

J.B.M. Hertzog, the leader of the National Party, fierce opponent of Botha, and a former Free State Boer general, took a very different line. He felt strongly that the people of South Africa were not obliged to fight in a 'British' war – his approach was one of non-participation. Hertzog, a lawyer who followed a similar path to Smuts having studied at Victoria College – modern Stellenbosch University – went on to be awarded a PhD in law at the University of Amsterdam. He conceded that South Africa was at war because Britain declared war on Germany, however, he felt that active participation was not a requirement, and that it was not in the best interests of the Union.[46]

Botha's motion for the invasion of German South West Africa was seconded by Sir Thomas Smartt, the leader of the Unionist Party.[47] Smartt, an Irish born, Cape politician serving under Rhodes had taken over from Leander Jameson, of Jameson Raid fame. Botha had developed a friendship with Jameson, much to the dismay of many republican Afrikaners.[48] To many Afrikaners, Jameson was the epitome of British imperialism. Botha was charming and demonstrated his policy of conciliation in practice, and it was through his link and personal bond with Jameson that Botha managed to exert influence on Smartt – conciliation and pragmatism. Jameson implored Smartt to cooperate with the Botha-Smuts government, something Smartt did out of necessity and common interest. Later on, Botha would lament to Smuts about the division 'Smartt and other Unionists... would support us only while the war lasts.'[49] Botha and Smuts's policy of reconciliation involved reaching out to and working with former enemies, whether Boer, or British. Emily Hobhouse, raised a

43 DODA: SAMR, box 1046, file 516/33, Nervous unrest amongst the Public of the North West, Captain E.M. Fisher, SAMR, OC 'C' Squadron 5th Regiment, to the Adjutant 5th Regiment SAMR, 22 August 1914.
44 WSHC: Viscount Long Papers, 947/469, Crewe to Long, 15 September 1914.
45 WSHC: Viscount Long Papers, 947/469, Crewe to Long, 15 September 1914.
46 Krüger, *Age of the Generals*, p.84.
47 NARSSA: Preller Archive, 90, 'The Prime Minister's Speech', *Pretoria News*, 10 September 1914.
48 F.A. Mouton, '"The sacred tie": Sir Thomas Smartt, the Unionist Party and the British Empire, 1912–1920', *Historia*, vol.57, no.2 (2012), p.5.
49 Botha to Smuts, 13 April 1916, Hancock and Van der Poel (eds.), *Selections*, vol. III, p.357.

stark point to her friend and confidant Smuts: 'the opportunity has come again for Botha to practise his conciliatory policy, and it would be a change for once to show conciliation to his own people.'[50]

Smuts and Hobhouse developed a close friendship. Botha on the other hand respected Hobhouse but kept her at a distance. The pretty and kind Hobhouse enthralled Smuts, who with his experience in England understood her and could relate. Hobhouse was a critic of British jingoism and a firm opponent of the concentration camps set up during the Anglo-Boer War. She was a humanitarian, and gave Smuts access to her networks, something that facilitated his early political work, advocacy and lobbying.

The impact and influence of Hobhouse should not be taken lightly – she was a critical voice during and after the Anglo-Boer War, and how the Afrikaners loved her, both old and young. She returned to South Africa in 1903 with Helen, Botha's daughter, and President Steyn (former president of the Free State). Later on, Hobhouse was asked by Steyn to unveil the Boer War Women's Memorial in Bloemfontein. Eventually the honour would go to Mrs Steyn who unveiled the memorial – a way to remember the Boer women and children who died in the concentration camps. The tremendous efforts of Hobhouse in support of the Afrikaner people during and after the Anglo-Boer War did not go unnoticed. Although she could not attend on account of her health Hobhouse's letter was read out at the ceremony.[51]

Jameson and Smartt were different to Hobhouse, they were firmly on the side of the British in the Anglo Boer War, did not critique army tactics, and had lived experience of the conflict – they were if nothing else pro-British and imperialist. The British colonial heritage competed with Afrikaner republican ideals. A moment of stark realisation was at the Women's Memorial which saw Steyn, Botha, De Wet and De La Rey speak. Afrikaner culture, identity, and nationality were being re-awakened – Botha and Smuts's policy was in danger.

Botha had to find a bridge to cross the divide with British politicians. Smuts and Botha found support in the Liberal Party and placated the more conservative voices by leveraging the gold mines in the Transvaal, a central interest of the British. Their approach ticked the boxes of British colonial officials as well as politicians in England – Botha was a man they could work with, and Smuts was… well Smuts was almost one of their own. There could not have been a sharper and plainer divide between Hertzog and the nationalists who were anything but imperialist, jingoist and pro-British. The clash of two systems, two cultures, and two civilisations was reflected in the war debate in South Africa.

Hertzog welcomed the parliamentary and legal debate, and he countered the motion for invasion explaining that the people of South Africa knew all too well the meaning of such a war. He proposed a delay, claiming that the motion had come as a surprise. Smuts and Botha, who had already made a commitment to the British

50 Hobhouse to Smuts, 30 July 1913, Hancock and Van der Poel (eds.), *Selections*, Vol. III, p.128.
51 Meintjes, *Botha*, p.198.

felt immense pressure. Botha rejected the option of an adjournment and the House decided by 85 votes to 12 that the motion should not be delayed. The prime minister made an emotional plea. It was a point of honour, he said, and any attempt to avoid supporting the war effort would stain South Africa's proud history. In putting forward the case Botha assured the House that South Africa had no hidden agenda about acquiring territorial possessions – perhaps intended to appease the nationalists, but this turned out to be untrue.

In his speech Botha walked a fine line and referenced the schism in Afrikanerdom in speaking about Afrikaners loyal to the Crown and those opposed. Referring to the loyal 'English Afrikaners', he also spoke of the 'Dutch Afrikaners', who he said were not disloyal at heart, and asked them (the British) for further patience.[52] Botha's statement made some key assumptions. For one it assumed that all Afrikaners would at some stage come over to his point of view, and secondly that he was right. His speech also left out Black, Coloured, and Indian voices, who he assumed would follow the government's direction – on that point he was correct. The offensiveness of asking all peoples to fight on the side of the White elite, after passing the Land Act a year prior is startling and highlights the paternalistic attitudes of the day.

Smuts relied on the prime minister's 'enormous influence' to sway others.[53] This Botha often did at a great personal cost, as he would always take home the insults, sneers, muffled comments, and rumours. It was Botha's ability to convince others that gave him power – he achieved this through his emotional intelligence, pulling on levers of trust, favours, affection, loyalty, and love.

Tactically he was effective, and after considerable deliberation in a divided cabinet, South Africa acquiesced on 10 August – sanctioning the German South West African campaign[54] – the motion passed, with 91 votes to 10.[55] Botha would later announce the formal entrance to the war in September 1914 after the meeting of Parliament.

For his efforts in uniting the different colonies into the Union of South Africa, Smartt was awarded a knighthood, on Botha's recommendation.[56] It was the making of allies that allowed Botha and Smuts to push forward their agenda.[57] Smuts and

52 NARSSA: Preller Archive, 90, 'The Prime Minister's Speech', *Pretoria News*, 10 September 1914.

53 Smuts to Crewe, 18 December 1914, Hancock and Van der Poel (eds.), *Selections*, Vol. III, p.219.

54 NARSSA: PM 1/1/32, file 4/97/1914, War German South West Expedition & Supply of Ammunition & Guns, Lord Harcourt to Lord de Villiers, 8 August and 23 August 1914. See also NASAC: A.583 F.S. Malan Collection, vol 22, Diary of F.S. Malan, 7–10 August 1914.

55 H. Strachan, *The First World War, Vol. 1: To Arms* (Oxford: Oxford University Press, 2001), p.546. L'ange gives the final votes as 92 to 12 in favour of Botha: L'ange, *Urgent Imperial Service*, p.17.

56 Mouton, 'Sir Thomas Smartt, the Unionist Party and the British Empire', p.5.

57 See D. du Bois, 'Appraising Louis Botha's Award of a Knighthood for Frank Reynolds in 1916', *South African Journal of Cultural History*, vol. 30, no.2 (2016); *Supplement to the*

Botha gave posts, loans and opportunities to friends and colleagues accruing political capital, debts and favours. This worked for people of the same worldview: the Unionists, Labour and moderate Afrikaners; however, the Afrikaner nationalists were a different story altogether.

D.W. Krüger , the prominent South African historian and professor, suggests that the outbreak of the First World War, bridged the gap between the Botha government and Labour, however, the schism between with Afrikaner nationalists was irreconcilable.[58] With the majority of Free Staters opposed to Botha, G.D. Scholtz, the historian and newspaper editor, claims that the Transvaal and Orange Free State were brought into direct conflict by the move to Union.[59] A large part of the Boer public regarded Botha as having become more British than he was Dutch, whereas Smuts's Britishness was always more prominent. Hertzog took full advantage of Botha and Smuts's 'Britishness' and claimed that it was anti-South African.[60] Although Botha struggled with Hertzog, Smuts and Hertzog were to have moments of competition and cooperation following the death of Botha in 1919, and then again in the 1940s.

Botha and Smuts regarded the motion for war, the legislative basis, as important but academic – more fundamentally they tackled a couple of critical questions: firstly, one of increased Boer unhappiness, especially at the prospect of war. Of course, the death and losses from the Anglo-Boer War were still fresh in the minds of a large part of Afrikaner society. The loss of economic opportunity and prosperity remained a reality and worst of all, the impact of the dreadful concentration camps and the loss of family members had forever scarred much of South African society. Most of the lives lost were those of women and children. To convince the family members of victims to fight for the British Empire, who had in fact set up those camps, was a big ask, although, strange as it may seem, it was no clearcut issue. Many 'British Afrikaners' suffered terrible losses in the Anglo-Boer War. Smuts had lost children in the concentration camps, while Botha had managed to send his family abroad. The impact of these camps impacted all of South African society not only the White communities; Africans too had suffered greatly, even more – serving both Boer and Briton, and receiving little for their sacrifices.

The second question Botha and Smuts faced was a practical one – how to invade German South West Africa. The military means was the UDF – perhaps not a perfect tool, certainly not in mid-1914, but one that was to be honed and refined – it was a journey from a tough but ragtag bunch of colonial and commando units, with no staff system, to something approaching an effective planning and fighting force.

A critical concern to Botha and Smuts was that the UDF was an untested force, at least in its new amalgamated form, despite the previous individual combat experience

London Gazette, no.28542, 2 January 1911; Cannadine, *Ornamentalism*.

58 Krüger, *Age of the Generals*, p.10.

59 G.D. Scholtz, *Die Rebellie 1914–1915* (Pretoria: Protea, 2013), p.22.

60 O. Pirow, *James Barry Munnik Hertzog* (Cape Town: Howard Timmins, 1958), p.55.

of the commandos and regular units. Besides training and doctrine, the UDF was also not short of logistical issues. In a note to General Sir A.J. Murray, Smuts complained of the War Office's position, not allowing the UDF access to British materiel stored in the dominion at the outbreak of war. These were to be redirected to Britain for use elsewhere. Smuts put up a number of points, that supplies would be needed for the invasion of German South West Africa, and that these stores would be cheaper to replace in Britain and could be expensed to South Africa.[61] Nonetheless supplies would remain a challenge throughout the invasion.[62]

Smuts consulted senior officers in South Africa and Britain about establishing the structures, units, and leadership cadre for the campaign. Botha and Smuts raised volunteer units to ensure that they had the required personnel, both in number and motivation. Reaching out to Crewe, then war-time director of recruitment, Smuts asked him about potential commanders. Crewe responded that commanding officers could be recruited from the ranks of the South African Mounted Rifles (SAMR).[63] In private, Botha was not afraid to share his feelings about Crewe, and told Smuts, 'I always thought that Crewe would be your fifth wheel of the coach. He is a trying man who wants to climb up on your shoulders.'[64] Nonetheless, Botha and Smuts took his advice, but many Boer commanders were also appointed to lead the commandos. Crewe was a Unionist party MLA, and although critical of the governor general Lord Buxton, proved a war-time ally of Smuts and Botha.[65] Botha got on well with Lord Buxton, and it was only at the start of their professional relationship during the campaign in German South West, that he felt some frustration. This was because Buxton involved himself in operational affairs. But this was to soon pass and the two went on to become great friends, with Botha confiding in him during the difficult years of 1915–1919.

Smuts involved Duncan McKenzie, the former commandant of the Natal Militia, in the invasion, stating, 'we think it our duty to organise and mobilise a fighting force in case of eventualities.'[66] McKenzie had previously served on the side of the British in the Anglo-Boer War and prior to that had played a key role in quashing the Bhambatha Rebellion. It was initially planned for him to remain in South Africa in case of a local uprising in Natal. Crewe summarises the thinking at the time, 'be it remembered that there are 5,000,000 natives … apt to be restless in war time always… '[67] McKenzie was eventually appointed to lead one of the columns of advance in the German South West African campaign. Only when Botha and Smuts pushed him,

61 Smuts to Murray, 17 August 1914, Hancock and Van der Poel (eds.), *Selections*, Vol. III, p.189.
62 TNA CAB 45/112: Campaign in GSWA, Narrative of Events, August–December 1914.
63 Smuts to Crewe, Hancock and Van der Poel (eds.), *Selections*, Vol. III, p.188.
64 Botha to Smuts, 13 April 1916, Hancock and Van der Poel (eds.), *Selections*, Vol. III, p.359.
65 See WSHC: Viscount Long Papers, 947/469.
66 Smuts to McKenzie, Hancock and Van der Poel (eds.), *Selections*, Vol. III, p.189.
67 WSHC: Viscount Long Papers, 947/469, Crewe to Long, 25 August 1914.

did he spring into action. Whereas some would portray McKenzie as a dashing and dynamic cavalry officer, his brutality in the Bhambatha Rebellion, and sluggishness in the south of German South West Africa, showed different sides to the same man.

In recent times his exploits in the Bhambatha Rebellion have received considerable critique and a street named after him in Pietermaritzburg has recently been renamed.[68] These were of course all complex and layered characters – all playing a role in the re-shaping of modern South Africa, with their biases, good and bad points, interests, faults and ego – much like Smuts and Botha.

The Botha government declared its intention to provide for its own defence. This allowed for British forces stationed in South Africa to be deployed to other theatres of the war.[69] Botha and Smuts were prisoners of geography – the shared border between the Union and German South West Africa. Their enemy was the German colonial protection force, the *Schutztruppe*, who posed at best a limited threat to South Africa – the only credible risk would be an attack supported by Afrikaner rebels.[70] However, on the defensive facing an invading force, things would be slightly different, and with the help of the desolate terrain, the German forces proved a tricky opponent, at least during the initial stages of the conflict.[71] Botha and Smuts managed to satisfy the British war requirement of releasing British forces for service in France much to the delight of hard-line Afrikaners. But any joy was most certainly overshadowed by being asked to support the British invasion of German South West Africa. With that in mind, and renewed talk of Boer republicanism and independence, little more was needed to spark rebellion.

The Politics and Personalities of the Afrikaner Rebellion

The split between Botha and Hertzog on South Africa's entry into the First World War personified the split in Afrikanerdom. Several prominent leaders, who became the leaders of the Afrikaner Rebellion, opposed the Botha government. They included, Major J. Kemp, a dashing, and brave Boer general, Brigadier General C.F. Beyers, the uncertain and pensive Boer commander, General C.R. de Wet, the formidable and tactically brilliant former chief commandant of the Free State and Lieutenant Colonel M. Maritz, the tough talking, extremist Boer republican; all of whom had served in the Anglo-Boer War. Most of the rebels, disgruntled in one form or another, were firm supporters of an Afrikaner republic and they took to the field against the Botha

68 See'When being 'a man of his time' is not a good enough excuse', Witness (news24.com); J. Guy, *Remembering the Rebellion* (Durban: University Kwazulu Natal Press, 2006).
69 Van der Waag, *A Military History*, p.93.
70 Krüger, *Age of the Generals*, pp.80–81.
71 See A. Garcia, *First Campaign Victory of Great War: South Africa, Manoeuvre Warfare, the Afrikaner Rebellion and the German South West African Campaign* (Warwick: Helion, 2019).

government. Although the German force posed little threat of invasion, by fomenting rebellion in the Union, they added an additional layer – an attack by proxy.[72]

The initial attempt at invading German South West Africa was planned using 'A' and 'B' Forces, commanded respectively by Colonel H. Lukin[73] and by Lieutenant Colonel M. Maritz, as well as limited sea landings. Lukin's forces were representative of the Afrikaner and English split which in turn mirrored the new Defence Force and the broader Union. Lukin had a long and distinguished career, serving in a range of conflicts including the Anglo-Zulu War in 1879 where he was seriously wounded, the Anglo-Boer War 1899–1902, where he was recognised for gallantry; he also held additional staff and command positions. He went on to serve on the Western Front and was knighted for his efforts. Botha, although publicly encouraging, was not impressed by his performance in the German South West African campaign.[74] Maritz was a different figure to Lukin, a hard-boiled Boer republican who had illusions of Afrikaner independence, that harped back to the pre-Anglo-Boer War era. He was not trusted by Smuts or Botha.

The initial plan for invasion comprised of a cross-border incursion into the German colony with amphibious landings at key ports. The only trouble with the cross-border invasion was that Maritz had defected and was determined to launch an Afrikaner rebellion.[75] The German administration was well aware of the delicate political situation in South Africa,[76] and several accounts claim that the Kaiser held a meeting with Beyers in 1913.[77] The British imperial defence council was cognisant of the potential for Germany to foment rebellion in South Africa, however, prior to 1914 the understanding was that this option was neither practicable nor necessary.[78] This all changed on 2 August 1914, with the pressures of the First World War mounting, the German Chief of the General Staff, decided to go on the offensive, and ordered his forces to incite an uprising in South Africa.[79] By supporting and encouraging rebellion, the

72 Collyer, *The Campaign in German South West Africa*, p.5; B. Farwell, *The Great War in Africa 1914–1918* (New York: Norton, 1986), p.75.
73 Later Major General Sir Henry Lukin.
74 Botha to Smuts, 2 June 1915, Hancock and Van der Poel (eds.), *Selections*, Vol. III, p.293. Lukin's statue remains in the Company's Garden in Cape Town and for the moment out of public critique – it remains to be seen how the re-evaluation of the general will play out in the contemporary statue debate.
75 Nasson, *Springboks*, pp.43–44; R.C. Warwick, 'The Battle of Sandfontein: The Role and Legacy of Major General Sir Henry Timson Lukin', *Scientia Militaria, South African Journal of Military Studies*, vol.34, no.2 (2006), p.74. See also, DODA: Diverse 1, Box 2, Evidence given in the Rebellion Commission of Enquiry.
76 DODA: World War 1 Diverse (hereafter WW1 D), Box 8 instructions from Headquarters, 20 August 1910,; Anon., *Official History*, p.9.
77 DODA: Diverse 1, Box 2, Rebellion Commission of Enquiry Vol 1, 117–119, Testimony by Colonel Barend Daniel Bouwer, 2 March 1916; H.F.B. Walker, *A Doctor's Diary in Damaraland* (London: Edward Arnold, 1917), p.158.
78 DODA: D, Box 8, 37 instructions from Headquarters, 20 August 1910.
79 Spies, 'The Outbreak of WW1', p.48

Germans hoped to delay the Union's invasion plans.[80] Their strategy was based on the assumption that an Afrikaner uprising would not only delay the invasion but could potentially compromise the combat cohesion of the Union Defence Force.[81]

The Afrikaner Rebellion was the result of simmering tensions in the country which dated as far back as the Anglo-Boer War which saw the loss of many Afrikaner women and children, in the most dreadful of circumstances – the now infamous concentration camps. Above all, the loss of Boer independence was a sore point and with the memory of the war still fresh, De Wet, Beyers and other Afrikaners harboured a deep resentment towards the British.[82]

Beyers was of a different ilk to De Wet, Kemp and Maritz. He did not hold strong views in terms of defeating Botha's forces in the field but saw the rebellion as a protest to the German South West African campaign.[83] He lacked the determination of the other military leaders and he was seen to be wavering and undecided. Kemp and Maritz were former Boer generals who received positions in the Union Defence Force after 1910. Attending the first staff course at Bloemfontein Military School, Kemp and Maritz exchanged covert ideas of how it might be possible to exact revenge on the British. Kemp was strong willed and had a reputation for resisting authority and being disruptive.[84] Known to be fiercely courageous, bordering on reckless, especially under the command of the legendary De La Rey, Kemp was tactically brilliant, and his exploits were almost unbelievable. His feats could be mistaken for those of the nemesis of a Victorian hero – a horse shot out from under him, leading mounted charges over flat terrain, and eventually pursued across a desert, and escaping into German South West Africa. Kemp thought that rebellion was a military option to establish an independent republic, which would replace Botha and Smuts's British looking Union.[85]

It was the division of leaders, those for and those against Botha and Smuts, who shaped the landscape of the Afrikaner Rebellion. The Union, still a new experiment, was divided. In broad terms, Natal and the Cape were in favour of participation in the First World War on behalf of Britain; the Transvaal was split; and much of the Free State and the Northern Cape was opposed to taking an active role. Afrikaner nationalists no matter where, were strongly opposed to the war.[86]

Smuts and Botha found many prominent Boer leaders undecided on rebellion. Perhaps the most important was General de la Rey, and Botha used all his influence

80 Collyer, *Campaign in German South West Africa,* p.5; Farwell, *The Great War in Africa,* p.75; Garcia, *First Campaign Victory*, p.31.
81 Collyer, *Campaign in German South West Africa,* p.5; Farwell, *The Great War in Africa,* p.75.
82 Krüger, *Age of the Generals*, p.82.
83 Scholtz, *Die Rebellie*, p.135.
84 Van der Waag, *A Military History*, pp.69, 80, 100.
85 J.C.G. Kemp, *Die Pad van die Veroweraar* (Cape Town: Nationale Pers, 1942), pp.296–297.
86 Meintjes, *Botha*, pp.206, 209.

to sway him.[87] The history remains contested as to De la Rey's intention to rebel, but it is generally believed that he was in favour of creating a Boer republic.[88] Whether he ultimately would have opposed the Botha government remains unclear due to his untimely death just prior to the outbreak of hostilities. D.W. Krüger maintains that it is almost certain that despite Botha's efforts to convince De la Rey, he had indeed planned to rebel.[89] De La Rey and Botha were distant cousins, but Oom Koos, as he was known, was with Beyers on the evening he was accidentally shot – they were on their way to Potchefstroom, and some say they were intending to incite rebellion while others disagree – the jury is still out. De La Rey's brother had rebelled, and his wife appealed to Smuts to have him released.[90] It was a divisive affair, where brothers fought on opposite sides, similar to the Anglo-Boer War. Smuts had a very close relationship with the De La Reys, he served under Oom Koos in the Anglo-Boer War and remained a confidant and family friend. After De la Rey's death Botha lamented the loss of his friend confiding in Leyds, 'the tragic death of General de la Rey is a tremendous blow'.[91]

In many ways, the battle for a united White South Africa was a battle for loyalties. Those faithful to Botha versus those loyal to Hertzog, De Wet and Beyers.[92] The devotion of *burghers* to a commandant, leader or general was an integral part of the commando system and imbedded in the fabric of Afrikaner identity. The personal and political rift between Hertzog and Botha and their respective political approaches was an underlying cause of the Afrikaner Rebellion.[93]

Despite the surge of Afrikaner nationalism Botha and Smuts were confident that they had the support of the majority of Afrikaners in the Free State.[94] This proved incorrect and a strong republican trend was evidenced in the 1915 elections. Reitz commented that almost half of the population was not on speaking terms.[95]

The political divide in Afrikaner ranks represented the different attitudes and beliefs of the 'bitterenders' of the Anglo-Boer War and those who signed the

87 Meintjes, *Botha*, p.209.
88 Engelenburg, *Botha*, p.282; Meintjes, *Botha*, pp.214–215.
89 Krüger, *The Age of the Generals*, p.83.
90 De La Rey (Mrs) to Smuts, 9 November 1913, Hancock and Van der Poel (eds.), *Selections*, Vol. III, p.213.
91 NARSSA: Leyds Archive, 262, Part II, Botha to Leyds, 6 October 1914.
92 D.E. Reitz, *Trekking On* (London: Travel Book Club, 1947), p.10.
93 DODA: Diverse 1, Box 2, Rebellion Commission of Enquiry, Testimony by Deneys Reitz, 28 February 1916; Anon., *The Times History of the War* (London: *The Times*, 1915), pp.484–485; Fedorowich, 'Sleeping with the Lion?', p.74; A. Grundlingh and S. Swart, *Radelose Rebellie, Dinamika van die 1914–1915 Afrikanerrebellie* (Pretoria: Protea, 2009), p.45; S. Swart, '"A Boer and his Gun and his Wife are Three Things always Together": Republican Masculinity and the 1914 Rebellion', *Journal of Southern African Studies*, vol.24, no.4 (2008), p.741.
94 NARSSA: Leyds Archive, 262, Part II, Botha to Leyds, 6 October 1914.
95 Reitz, *Trekking On*, p.48.

peace treaty. Whereas Botha, Smuts and De la Rey who were Transvaalers, advocated a peace deal, Steyn, De Wet and Hertzog from the Free State, represented the dogged Boer resistance that demanded independence at all costs.[96] Although there were exceptions – many Free State leaders signed the Peace of Vereeniging, while not all Transvaalers did, Jan Kemp being a case in point. The two broad camps, the Free State and the Transvaal, had separate followers and the 1914 Rebellion was framed by the leaders and their spheres of influence. The rebel leadership made use of *burghers* and commandos who had remained loyal to them and their hard-line republican outlook.[97] The commando system was patriarchal and incorporated social and economic issues imbedded in a military rank system. Thus, the same *burghers* who were dependent on their leaders for work would be called up for service by the field cornet or commandant. The authority of the commandant, the leader, was absolute and was very much a part of an older Boer masculine culture. As such, the patriarch was the dominant decision maker and the community leader.[98]

Botha and Smuts's South Africanism did not meet the personal, social, economic and/or political needs of the rebel leaders.[99] The change in society brought about by imperialism, mineral exploitation and a modernising South Africa led many poverty-stricken Afrikaners to believe that their identity was being threatened. In the past being a landless farmer who worked on someone else's farm (being a *bywoner*), was not frowned upon. However, in the new Union many deprived Afrikaners felt that their livelihood was being compromised by Black sharecroppers.[100] Poor Afrikaners came looking to Botha and Smuts for answers – they claimed that Black sharecroppers were given opportunities while they, indigent White families working on farms, were being neglected.[101] Seme the dynamic and controversial founder of the ANC created a Black owned cooperative that bought up farms. When his business encroached on the eastern Transvaal, Botha's constituency, it is almost certain that the prime minister felt the pressure. The success of Black sharecroppers impacted the poor, but Black business ventures impacted the elite Boers too, and Botha was not having it.

Botha and Smuts responded with a statute, largely pushed by Afrikaner nationalists, that would forever shape modern South Africa, the 1913 Natives' Land Act. This oppressive legislation was passed in an attempt to curb Black agrarian competition and came to represent the Botha government's response to the *bywoner* grievance

96 Krüger, *Age of the Generals*, p.23.
97 Krüger, *Age of the Generals*, pp.90–91.
98 S. Swart, 'The Five Shilling Rebellion', *South African Historical Journal*, vol. 56, no.1 (2006), p.98; Grundlingh and Swart, *Radelose Rebellie*, p.46; Swart, 'A Boer and his Gun', p.739.
99 Grundlingh and Swart, *Radelose Rebellie*, pp.75–76.
100 Swart, 'A Boer and his Gun', p.741; Swart, 'The Five Shilling Rebellion', p.96.
101 Swart, 'The Five Shilling Rebellion', p.96.

and the proposed solution to the growing 'poor white' situation.[102] The Land Act also aimed to protect the wealthy South African Whites. Plaatjie castigated Botha and Smuts for their lack of strength and conceding the Land Act, to the Afrikaner nationalists. He went on to lead a strong campaign against the statute. Plaatje would only pause in his advocacy efforts at the start of the First World War, when he assisted in the recruitment for the war effort. He was savvy in his approach, tying Black participation into party politics. He used the recruitment drive as a lever, to position Black rights between Botha and Smuts's attempts at White unity.[103]

Botha, acutely aware of the mounting tensions, economic despair, and the outbreak of the First World War, put on his general's cap, and invited his senior military officers to a conference which he chaired on 14 August 1914.[104] Major J. Kemp, Lieutenant Colonel Maritz and Brigadier General C.F. Beyers opposed the idea of invading German South West Africa.[105] Botha addressed the conference and informed the officers present that their responsibility was to the higher command and to the government. He made it clear that their personal feelings should not have an impact in the invasion of the German colony.[106] The rebel leadership was not convinced and while in Pretoria, they held their own meeting.[107] They questioned Botha and Smuts's legitimacy – 12 years earlier they were fighting on the same side against the British – now they found themselves fighting for the British in a war not of their choosing. Maritz took the opportunity to show his fellow rebel leaders letters from the German government which promised them military support if they staged a rebellion. However, Maritz pointed out that this support would be limited to arms and ammunition, of which they were admittedly in short supply.[108]

Conclusion

Botha and Smuts had misread the situation completely. They hoped that the war would provide the platform for nation building and promote a united Boer and British

102 Swart, 'Desperate Men', p.162; E.J. Bottomley, 'The South African Rebellion of 1914, The Influence of Industrialisation, Poverty and "Poor-Whitism"', *African Studies Seminar Paper*, University of Witwatersrand, June 1980, p.9.

103 See Willan, *Sol Plaatje*.

104 DODA: Diverse 1, Box 2, Rebellion Commission of Enquiry vol.1, Testimony by General Louis Botha, 29 June 1916; Testimony by General Coenraad Jacobus Brits, 15 March 1916.

105 DODA: Diverse 1, Box 2, Rebellion Commission of Enquiry vol.1, Testimony by General Louis Botha, 29 June 1916.

106 DODA: Diverse 1, Box 2, Rebellion Commission of Enquiry vol.1, 144, Testimony by General Coenraad Jacobus Brits, 15 March 1916; 958, Testimony by General Louis Botha, 29 June 1916.

107 DODA: Diverse 1, Box 2, Rebellion Commission of Enquiry vol.1, 144, Testimony by General Coenraad Jacobus Brits, 15 March 1916.

108 Krüger, *Age of the Generals*, p.86; Anon., *The Times History of the War*, p.498.

patriotism.[109] They were wrong, and this became increasingly evident when, in mid-September, Beyers made it known publicly that he was resigning from the Defence Force.[110] The nationalists published Beyer's resignation in their newspaper before Smuts and Botha were officially informed. Smuts and Botha, seething, responded immediately attempting to control the narrative, publishing their version of events in the *Volksblad,* the government's mouthpiece, in which Botha and Smuts owned shares. Sir Roderick Jones, the colourful owner and general manager of Reuters, as well as a firm supporter of Botha and Smuts assisted in putting out their version of events.[111] He co-bought Reuters with money loaned from Jameson – it was a game of loyalties and influence where power and media was bought and used to control national narratives. Crewe a keen supporter of Botha and Smuts, was the chief director of the *Daily Dispatch*, based in East London, and voiced the South African Party's opinion to an English South African readership.[112]

Upon the resignation of Beyers, Botha decided to take command of the Union forces in the field. Botha had never completely trusted Beyers and in his correspondence with Leyds, said that 'the deplorable, for lack of a harsher word, resignation of Beyers has caused considerable concern'.[113] In a brave and bold move Botha took on the task of suppressing unrest in the Union himself – he was appointed as the commander-in-chief of the South African military, under Section 81 of the Defence Act of 1912,[114] and formally appointed on 23 September 1914.[115] Smuts remained his capable second in command and chief of staff – roles he carried out with staggering efficiency. Smuts to Botha was Louis-Alexandre Berthier to Napoleon – chief organiser and first of his marshals. About Berthier, Napoleon commented, that he 'has served me longest and has never failed me.'[116] Smuts never failed Botha. In almost quixotic fashion Botha would mount his horse and take charge. He explained to Leyds, 'under the circumstances, I have to do my duty and lead our troops in the field.'[117]

109 Van der Waag, *A Military History*, p.94; Spies, 'The Outbreak of WWI', p.50.
110 Krüger, *Age of the Generals*, pp.86–87.
111 Roderick to Smuts, September 1914, Hancock and Van der Poel (eds.), *Selections*, Vol. III, p.199.
112 Crewe to Smuts, 22 December 1914, Hancock and Van der Poel (eds.), *Selections*, Vol. III, p.221.
113 NARSSA: Leyds Archive, 262, Part II, Botha to Leyds, 6 October 1914.
114 DODA: AG 1914–1921, Box 8, Commander-in-chief, Government notice for the next issue of the *Union Gazette*, 18 October 1914.
115 TNA CAB 45/112: Campaign in GSWA, Narrative of Events, 23 September 1914.
116 'Louis-Alexandre Berthier, prince de Wagram', *Britannica* <https://www.britannica.com/biography/Louis-Alexandre-Berthier-prince-de-Wagram> (accessed 17 October 2021).
117 NARSSA: Leyds Archive, 262, Part II, Botha to Leyds, 6 October 1914.

3

Gambits and Crises, 1914-1915

You English will never understand how hard this is for me.

Botha[1]

Botha and Smuts had not intended to lead troops in the field especially against their fellow countrymen. The outbreak of rebellion and the fractures in government shocked them into action. The memory of a handsome Louis Botha, with a trimmed beard, and bandolier commanding forces in the Anglo-Boer War, seemed a distant memory. His dash in leading raids into Natal and the defence of the Tugela Line were well known, but his skill and leadership were to be tested again. Smuts's sharp mind, bravery and strategic ability were also to be put to the test. At first, the attorney general of the Transvaal, he transformed himself by sheer force of will into a capable guerrilla general – although commanding a small tactical unit, Smuts's concepts were always strategic – and the invasion of the Cape was a case in point.

Smuts as a young man, although of poor origins, would fast become part of the intellectual elite. A scholar and lawyer, he instantly made his mark on South Africa firstly in Rhodes's and then in Kruger's administrations, but he struggled to empathise with the plight of the common man. Smuts read Greco-Roman history and literature, perhaps not something to which his contemporaries from the Free State and Transvaal could easily relate. His adventure came when Pretoria fell during the Anglo-Boer War, and he would frame his narrative like an odyssey similar to the 'barbarians' invading Greece where the Greeks were the Boers and the Persians the British. He was keen to demonstrate that he was not a coward, and although not the best soldier, he would become a general.[2]

1 Botha lamented in tears following the Battle of Mushroom Valley. See H.F. Trew, *Botha Treks* (London: Blackie & Son, 1936), p.32.

2 In his letter to De La Rey, discussing the invasion of the Cape Colony, during the Anglo-Boer War Smuts claimed that some generals were better soldiers than he, but he was best placed to lead such a mission because he possessed the political acuity and the necessary

Smuts joined the Victoria College Volunteer Rifle Corps, at the beginning of his second year of studies.[3] He was competent, at times ingenious and certainly brave, but he would never hold a command of any substantial size during the Anglo-Boer War, and he certainly did not hold a strategic choke point such as Thermopylae.

That honour would be left to Botha, whose feats on the Tugela Line temporarily halted the British and laid the foundation for his career. If there was to be a Boer Leonidas, of the two it would be Botha. Contemporaries debated the greatest Boer commanders, and historians long after still continue the discussion, but regardless of the order of the top three, Botha would be up there with Koos de la Rey, and Christiaan de Wet. Perhaps operationally De La Rey was better, and tactically De Wet may have been top, however it was Botha's conventional command that provided the Boer victories and Britain's Black Week. His guerrilla raids into Natal were pivotal; he inspired the commandos to dream, and he bolstered the flagging Boer resolve. There is also a lower rung of Boer commanders, and Smuts's name most certainly features, along with Hertzog and other capable leaders. Smuts showed guts and swagger – brave to a fault – and he evaded British forces, invaded and raided the Cape, becoming a fine Boer commander. Botha stood head and shoulders above Smuts, rising to the highest military rank in the Transvaal: Commandant General. This in turn gave him the political platform. But Botha's career could not be understood in isolation without considering the life and times of his primary lieutenant, Smuts. From their exploits on the veld, they now led a Dominion of the British Empire. With their training from small Boer republican politics and hard fighting in war, but no formal study at military and staff colleges, the pair balanced international economic interests, local political and socio-economic issues and at the sharp end – world conflict. If nothing else these were both men of action.

Botha and Smuts Take Charge

The threat of General De Wet, one of the best Boer generals of the Anglo-Boer War, necessitated a drastic response. Botha and Smuts knew that victory was dependent on battlefield success but also winning the battle for influence and legitimacy.[4] There was no one better suited on both fronts, and like his role models before him, Lucas Meyer and Piet Joubert, emulating the commandant generals of old, Botha, took to the field. His secret weapon was Smuts, not workshy and with a brilliant mind he managed the

training from De La Rey: Smuts to De La Rey, 16 February 1901, Hancock and van der Poel (eds.), *Selections*, vol. II, p.376.

3 H. Paterson, 'Jan Christiaan Smuts as a General in East Africa, 1916: An Appraisal', *Military History Journal*, vol.15, no.2, 2010.

4 See A. Garcia, and E.P. Kleynhans, 'Counterinsurgency in South Africa: the Afrikaner Rebellion, 1914–1915', *Small Wars & Insurgencies*, vol.32, no.1, 2021; Van der Waag, *A Military History*.

resources of state; controlling logistics, troop movements and monitoring the intelligence picture.

Under the leadership of Botha, Smuts put his mental prowess on display running the headquarters in Pretoria with little help, except for H.R.M Bourne and a few key aids and clerks. In practice he was Botha's second-in-command and chief administration officer. It would be easy to imagine how the two generals thought back to their experience in war, to the tales on which they were raised, of great exploits of battle and adventure – the *Voortrekkers* crossing inhospitable terrain and fighting for their future. Perhaps the two considered how they would craft the historical narrative for future historians.

It was these two fascinating characters who would lead the campaign. A perfect pair as if scripted by the author of a novel – one bigger, the other slight – the bigger one more emotional; Botha once got angry at Annie for denying him his preserved ginger.[5] The slimmer one always smarter than the rest – Smuts once successfully argued for the deportation of strike leaders on the most dubious of legal claims.[6] Equally determined, equally loyal – they formed a bond and together told a story about the future of South Africa. They proposed a Union – Botha was the primary narrator and put together a creative high-level plot – of course he had lived experience in marrying an English-speaking South African. Smuts crafted the detail with broad strokes. His knowledge of the classics gave him the depth. They attempted to weave a new society with only white thread: British and Boer. Black, Indian and Coloured strands were on the periphery, not a part of their story, just the dressing. The UDF was the instrument that was to manufacture loyalty to empire.

The First World War tested the machinery of the Union and its new Defence Force – both mirroring the Afrikaner-British marriage – it was a new experiment. The Union's compromise was between English speakers trying to maintain the 'British connection' and Afrikaner nationalists longing to restore Boer political and military traditions. Barely two years old and notwithstanding the initial blunders and mistakes, the Union Defence Force, was pulled together in no small measure as a result of the ability and determination of Smuts (see Chapter 1).[7] Using their imperfect military means they pushed for an early advance. In the dusty, desolate, deserts the expeditionary UDF would experience its first reversal.

Botha and Smuts wanted action on the front. Lukin's forced marched up to Sandfontein was one of the first moves. With operations already under way in

5 Meintjes, *Botha*, p.293.
6 Meintjes, *Botha*, p.203.
7 These blunders are thoroughly recounted in Strachan, *The First World War in Africa*, p.64. They include Smuts' overconfidence and the lapsing of a month before parliament was called; the lack of ammunition in South Africa and poor cooperation with the Royal Navy; speculation and the dualities of the South Africa Defence Act; and, genuine confusion resulting from the absence of a central staff and command organisation, and contingency plans, and all these were exacerbated by an initial intelligence failure.

September 1914, defence headquarters ordered Maritz to advance north – on this route was Sandfontein.[8] This was a part of the broader invasion attempt that included landings at Port Nolloth and Lüderitzbucht. Maritz refused to support the operation. With or without support, Lukin's advance group, led by Lieutenant Colonel Grant, were exposed and became a vulnerable target for the Germans.

The first iteration of the invasion plan incorporated what came to be known as A, B and C Force. Lukin led A Force across the German South West African border. This coincided with C Force making an amphibious landing at Lüderitzbucht, on 18 September. Advancing through arid terrain, Lukin's vanguard, approximately 200 soldiers from the 4th and 5th Regiments of the South African Mounted Rifles pressed forward eventually occupying Sandfontein on 19 September.[9]

Lukin's forces included the Witwatersrand Rifles, SAMR units: the 4th Permanent Battery Transvaal Horse Artillery, and the 1st, 4th and 5th Regiments. These units were supported by an Ammunition Column, Signal Section, South African Engineer Corps section, and Water Boring section, Railway Regiment, Post Corps and Ordinance components. The invasion was a complicated logistical operation, and the forces including their supplies were sent by ship from Cape Town and Durban.[10]

'B' Force commander, Manie Maritz, was a stubborn, tough and raging republican who defected to the German side. He provided valuable intelligence to the Germans and weakened Lukin's advance.[11] The desertion and changing of sides of many key Afrikaner leaders created the 1914 Afrikaner Rebellion – it had the flavour of an anti-colonial war. It was at its core a people seeking their identity and coming to terms with a changing world, one where they no longer controlled their political and economic future.

Botha and Smuts juggled the important tasks of tackling the emerging rebellion while continuing the invasion. The two operations were complex, resource dependent, and had to be completed piecemeal, they required separate actions, considerable personnel, and different strategies. Botha and Smuts processed the impending domestic crisis, never imagining that the political experiment of Union was the cause. To them it was the disloyal Boers, the ones who refused to see reason – their reason. The campaign was important to ensure the British were content, but the threat of a

8 I. van der Waag, 'The Battle of Sandfontein26 September 1914: South African Military Reform and the German South-West Africa Campaign, 1914–1915', *First World War Studies*, vol.4, no.2 (2013); R.C. Warwick, 'The Battle of Sandfontein: The Role and Legacy of Major General Sir Henry Timson Lukin', *Scientia Militaria, South African Journal of Military Studies*, vol.34, no.2 (2006).

9 DODA: AG 14, Box 13, 7, Report on the Battle of Sandfontein 26 September 1914; Van der Waag, 'The Battle of Sandfontein26 September 1914', p.9.

10 DODA: DC, Box 252, 17138, Reports of Force Commanders in German South West Africa, 'A' Force operations during the initial stages of the German South West African campaign, 19 August 1915; Paterson, 'First Allied Victory', p.1.

11 See DODA: Diverse 1, Box 2, Evidence given in the Rebellion Commission of Enquiry; Warwick, 'The Role and Legacy of Major General Sir Henry Timson Lukin', p.74.

burning South Africa was also a threat. They divided their focus. At the same time as considering the treacherous resignation of Beyers and Kemp, Smuts knew Lukin had to continue his advance searching for water sources in German South West Africa. Unbeknownst to Lukin, while he was advancing on Raman's Drift, a German force was heading in his direction.[12]

Meantime, C Force commander Lieutenant Colonel Beves landed at Lüderitzbucht. The Germans had withdrawn, destroyed the railway to slow down his advance, and concentrated their forces for an attack on Sandfontein. In a coordinated action the German forces at Sandfontein made a tactical withdrawal only to join up with other units and attack Lukin's vanguard, led by Grant, on 26 September.[13]

Lukin found himself in a precarious situation. He was not in favour of advancing without the necessary logistical support, but defence headquarters insisted, adding that they would send up additional supplies as soon as possible. The military aim was to protect the forces that landed at Lüderitzbucht, by drawing attention to Lukin's force.[14] Lieutenant Colonel Von Heydebreck led the German operation – a competent and daring commander, with the dubious record of having served in the violent Hererro and Nama genocides, he had also created the Camel Corps. Von Heydebreck centralised his forces including those of Major D. von Rapport, Major H. Ritter and Major Viktor Frank who each commanded a column.[15]

The location of Sandfontein could not have been worse, surrounded by high ground and without sufficient time to prepare defensive positions, the South African forces were vulnerable.[16] With a clear intelligence picture Von Heydebreck was in control. He brought his approximately 2,000 men, with artillery and machine guns to bear.[17] Grant was caught by surprise, out gunned, and out played. To his credit he commanded the South African forces as best he could. Lukin tried his utmost to relieve Grant's position but was again checked by the forward planning of Von Heydebreck who had anticipated the move and placed blocking forces en route. After about 10 hours

12 DODA: DC, Box 252, Report by Lukin on 'A' Force operations during the initial stages of the German South West African campaign, 19 August 1915; L'ange, *Urgent Imperial Service*, p.21; Collyer, *The Campaign in German South West Africa*, p.31.
13 DODA: DC, Box 252, 17138, Reports of Force Commanders in German South West Africa, Operations in and around Sandfontein 25–27 September 1914, 19 August 1915; Simpkins, *Rand Light Infantry*, p.17.
14 DODA: DC, Box 252, General Staff to General Lukin23 September 1914; Anon., *Official History*, p.14. See Garcia, *First Campaign Victory*.
15 Anon., *Official History*, p.14.
16 DODA: AG 14, Box 13, 7, Report on the Battle of Sandfontein 26 September 1914.
17 E. Dane, *British Campaigns in Africa and the Pacific 1914-1918* (London: Hodder & Stoughton, 1919), p.36. Van der Waag, 'The Battle of Sandfontein26 September 1914', p.10; DODA: DC, Box 252, 17138 IO, Historical Record of the Campaign in German South West Africa, 4 November 1919, General Botha's Despatch (GOC MC GSW Campaign) 9 July to 28 October 1920.

of fighting, Grant raised the white flag.[18] Grant's force sustained 18 killed and 42 wounded including Black, and Coloured troops and assistants before capitulating; whilst the German casualties numbered 23 killed, including Von Rapport. Injured in battle, for the remainder of the war Grant's fate was one of internment and suffering.[19]

The cause of the South African defeat, simply put, was that the Germans had performed better – they had a better plan, and it was well executed; whereas the South Africans were caught off guard and had lost the initiative – it was ultimately an intelligence failure. However, the Battle of Sandfontein, did not compromise the UDF's fighting strength. The operational reality was that Lukin's force was limited in the distance it could advance with the logistical support available. It was used to distract from the landing at Lüderitzbucht – but was also part of an advance along multiple fronts. Historians allocate varying amounts of blame to Maritz, largely for betraying his government. One version, based on official sources, states that Maritz's force had the objective of holding the Orange River line to stave off a potential German raid.[20] This was perhaps only a small part of the story, and based on a vague understanding in the moment.

The operational picture was that the German forces were divided with around 3,000 in the north and approximately 2,000 soldiers in the south.[21] The internal lines of communication in German South West Africa made the massing of forces for potential raids into Union territory a real possibility. It is possible that Maritz had different objectives at different times. What is certain is that when he was supposed to have supported Lukin, Botha and Smuts had a clear idea that he had already defected.[22]

D.W. Krüger posits that Botha and Smuts knew that Maritz had rebelled, and despite ordering him to support Lukin, they knew he would disobey the command.[23] In the official enquiry into the rebellion Botha covered himself. He testified that given Maritz's geographical position he would not have been able to support Lukin.[24] Reports from September 1914 show a similar understanding and state that Maritz's force was too far away and too disorganised to support the advance.[25] By mid-September 1914 Botha had confirmation that Beyers and Maritz were in cahoots, and Beyers's and

18 DODA: DC, Box 252, 17138, Reports of Force Commanders in German South West Africa, Operations in and around Sandfontein 25–27 September 1914, 19 August 1915; Report by LukinAnnexure B: List of Killed, Wounded and Captured at and about SandfonteinAugust 1915.
19 DODA: DC, Box 252, 17138, Report by Lukin Annexure B: List of Killed, Wounded and Captured at and about SandfonteinAugust 1915.
20 TNA CAB 45/112: Campaign in GSWA, Narrative of Events, September 1914.
21 TNA CAB 45/112: Campaign in GSWA, Narrative of Events, September 1914.
22 Nasson, *Springboks*, p.67; Dane, *British Campaigns in Africa and the Pacific*, p.35; Meintjes, *Botha*, p.233; Paterson, 'First Allied Victory', p.2.
23 Krüger, *Age of the Generals*, p.81.
24 DODA: Diverse 1, Box 2, Rebellion Commission of Enquiry Volume 1, Testimony by General Louis Botha, June 1916,
25 TNA CAB 45/112: Campaign in GSWA, Narrative of Events, September 1914.

Kemp's resignations were splashed over the front pages of nationalist newspapers. With the available sources of information, and Botha's emotional insight, it is almost certain that he knew that Maritz would not support Lukin. It is also certain that Botha would have had a limited interest in the detail of Lukin's deployment, as he employed a decentralised approach, one which required commanders on the ground to make decisions. Smuts was not present at the inquiry. His absence in 1916 was due to his responsibilities commanding the forces in East Africa.

Contemporary historians such as Warwick, allocate a fair share of the blame to Smuts, the Minister of Defence, and this rhymes with Collyer who over 80 years ago apportions some of the fault to defence headquarters for pressurising Lukin to advance despite his concerns about logistics. Collyer believed that the invasion would have been risky with or without the support of Maritz.[26] Smuts, was clear – he wanted to reaffirm the political objective in support of the British Empire, and that required operational results as well as to protect the landing at Lüderitzbucht.[27] Lukin defended his decision to capture Sandfontein, by doing so he would have captured the only water source on his route of advance.[28] Smuts, went on to blame Lukin for leaving too small a force at Sandfontein. The determined minister of defence continued encouraging Lukin to maintain control of the Orange River line, offering additional reinforcements. The lack of naval support for the deployment of forces to Swakopmund, the internal Rebellion, and the need to concentrate forces on the border became a further motivation to postpone the northern invasions and amphibious landing at Swakopmund.[29] The naval situation was a dependency. Botha observed:

> … Ministers have the honour to say, in reply to the Secretary of State, that the delay is not due to larger numbers of Union Force being sent to coast of German West Africa. All preparations are complete for force to sail from Cape Town on 5th September, but Ministers have just been advised that the Admiral is not ready to provide a naval escort for the expedition before the 12th September. Ministers regret that the departure of the force will have to be postponed to that date, though, if an escort is available, the expedition will start before.[30]

The threat of rebellion overshadowed the action at Sandfontein and a number of competing considerations came to the fore, including, the evacuation of the South African territory of Walvis Bay which was raided on 26 September. Although Walvis Bay posed no military threat to the Germans, the evacuation of British citizens was

26 Warwick, 'The Role and Legacy of Major General Sir Henry Timson Lukin', p.65; Collyer, *The Campaign in German South West Africa*, p.47.
27 Warwick, 'The Role and Legacy', p.74.
28 DODA: DC, Box 252, 17138, Reports of Force Commanders in GSWA, Operations in and around Sandfontein 25–27 September 1914, 19 August 1915.
29 TNA CAB 45/112: Campaign in GSWA, Narrative of Events, 26 September 1914.
30 NARSA: PM 1/1/32, file 4/97/1914, Botha to Governor General, 24 Aug 1914.

an important consideration. The issues around transport for delivering troops, evacuations, and war ships to protect them; in combination with logistical challenges pushed Botha and Smuts to the limit.[31]

September 1914 was a complicated time, and the fog of war kept matters suitably vague. Botha and Smuts were on the ropes, facing an internal uprising, and suffering a conventional defeat. With the advantage of hindsight, it is easy to forget the difficulty faced in that moment – it was their darkest hour. They responded by making use of their extensive intelligence networks, comprised of old commando structures, the UDF, South African Party constituents, and magistrates as well as loyal supporters. An isolated case, although one which had almost prophetic attributes, occurred around two weeks before the Battle of Sandfontein when Wakkerstroom magistrate, C. Griffith, wrote of a meeting with a local resident. Griffith was told, 'that if the Forces meet with a reverse and the Germans invade the Union the majority of the Citizen Forces would refuse to take up arms against the invaders', the contention being that the Government had needlessly brought about a state of war in the Union. Griffith was careful to add that his informant was from the anti-Botha section and that this was not his opinion, or that of the majority in his district.[32] Maritz put forward a similar story, and claimed that if his force was obliged to invade German South West Africa, then all Active Citizen Force soldiers would resign. They had a point, and whereas it was not all Citizen Force soldiers that rebelled, there were many that did.

Despite the threats of mass revolt, this was not to be. In practice the defeat at Sandfontein did not have a significant negative impact on the campaign. If anything, it gave the UDF, Smuts and Botha an opportunity to regroup, resupply, replan and launch a fresh offensive. The reverse rattled the British government who became more receptive to supplying additional artillery and allowing a group of bombadiers previously earmarked to be deployed elsewhere, to remain in country to support the campaign.[33] Most importantly the Battle of Sandfontein happened in the shadow of the rebellion, which consumed Botha and Smuts. At its core, the rebellion questioned their legitimacy and if it was indeed an anti-colonial uprising, it begged the question if Smuts and Botha were more British than Boer.

Botha and Smuts fought a war on two fronts. They adopted a piecemeal approach, concentrating forces on separate objectives, using different strategies; the rebellion, a domestic war was to be fought on internal lines as a fight for legitimacy and supremacy, whereas the invasion would use external lines and be expansionist. The limitations of ships and logistics led to the plan of invasion being adapted and the northern invasion force was postponed. The mobilised forces on the Union's northern border comprised those which planned to invade across the Kalahari and Namaqualand. In addition,

31 See TNA CAB 45/112: Campaign in GSWA, Narrative of Events, August–October 1914.
32 NARSSA: A78 C.T. Te Water Papers, Magistrate Wakkerstroom to Secretary of Justice, 10 September 1914.
33 TNA CAB 45/112: Campaign in GSWA, Narrative of Events, October 1914.

a military force at Lüderitzbucht, remained in place. Additional units were sent to reinforce Lukin's position and bolster the Orange River line, to respond to potential threats from the *schutztruppe* and German backed Afrikaner rebels.[34]

Suppressing the Rebellion

When Maritz refused the order to support Lukin, the die was cast. Maritz's attacks on Union positions and his declaration of a republic in early October 1914 effectively negated the opportunity for a negotiated settlement.[35] The only practicable option was limited offensive action to quell the uprising. Maritz's actions caused considerable concern, and intelligence reports confirmed Beyers with a commando in the Transvaal. Initially Botha had hoped that Beyers's resignation and suspicious movements in the field were a protest, part of a political ploy to oppose the South African Party rather than a military operation aimed at overthrowing the government.[36] Never entirely convinced about Beyers, Botha knew he would have to oppose his old colleague in combat while trying not to inflame an already tense political situation between English and Afrikaner South Africans.

Botha was committed to using volunteers, and he called a meeting with his commandants and generals requesting their assistance in the campaign.[37] There were 35 commandants and Afrikaans officers in attendance and only 15 positions available. Those loyal to Botha including, Brits, Alberts, Van Deventer, Manie Botha, Myburgh, as well as Collins, Bezuidenhout and others, went on to serve with him on the campaign. Those who did not receive positions of command agreed to serve in a lower capacity.[38] The loyal colleagues of the Standerton district, those of the Transvaal, and the connections of the Anglo-Boer War stood in support of Botha. Smuts did not command the same loyalty, but he had many supporters; Deneys Reitz and other friends came rushing forward.

Reitz, clearly worried about Hertzog's inflammatory speeches following Botha's announcement of the Union's intention to invade, wrote to Smuts from the Free State district of Heilbron 'If they are called up I feel sure that serious disturbances will take place … against the Government and even the Commandant declares that he will support the burghers in resisting any commandeering orders.'[39] Smuts in a calm

34 See TNA CAB 45/112: Campaign in GSWA, Narrative of Events, August – October 1914.
35 Van der Waag, *A Military History*, pp.98–99.
36 Reitz, *Trekking On*, p.19.
37 NARSSA: Preller Archive, 90, 'Generaal Botha in Losberg' *De Volksstem*, 29 September 1914.
38 TNA CAB 45/112: Campaign in GSWA, Narrative of Events, August–September 1914; DODA: Diverse 1, Box 2, Rebellion Commission of Enquiry Volume 1, 967, 968, Testimony by General Louis Botha, 29 June 1916. See also Reitz, *Trekking On*.
39 Reitz to Smuts, 12 September 1914 in Hancock and Van der Poel (eds.), *Selections*, vol.III, p.197.

and measured tone responded that the campaign was continuing and that volunteers would be used. A steely Smuts added defiantly, 'There is much, very much, talk. Some are afraid of a revolution or civil war. I am not. Nevertheless, I shall be glad if you will keep your ears and eyes open and keep me informed of what goes on.'[40]

Botha remained in contact with President Steyn, the former leader of the Free State, and they exchanged generally friendly and cordial letters. Botha used this contact to seek approval for his policies but also to try and exert control over Hertzog and the Free Staters, or at least as a back channel to get across his point of view. Steyn did not necessarily agree with Botha, nor did he particularly like Botha's approach. Steyn and Botha had disagreements in the past – a case in point was around the Anglo-Boer Women's memorial. Besides Botha feeling 'hurt' by the project being led by the Free Staters, Botha also wrote to Steyn about another monument project. Botha had asked Steyn to consider a *Voortrekker* monument, while the Women's memorial was not yet completed. Botha went further adding that prominent British officials should take part in the *Voortrekker* monument project. Steyn rejected the idea on two grounds, firstly it was not practicable to do two monument projects simultaneously and secondly that in his view the British policies were the cause of the *Voortrekkers*' migration.[41] After reading Steyn's response, Botha who was concerned that the Women's monument would stir emotion against the British which in turn would compromise his conciliation policy, dropped the subject. Again during the rebellion in 1914, Botha reached out to Steyn asking him to intervene and calm the rising tension. Steyn refused to do so, which left Botha aggrieved. Steyn claimed that he preferred to use his influence in an indirect way because he disagreed with the government's decision to enter the war. Steyn supported Hertzog and claimed that the ongoing clash between Hertzog and Botha caused him great pain.[42] Botha and Smuts focussed on the task at hand.

With the key loyal commanders and trusted soldiers in place, Smuts applied his keen mind to suppressing the rebellion. He declared martial law in October 1914, making use of the military districts to manage logistics and gather intelligence on the rebel leaders and their forces.[43] Botha concentrated his forces in and around Pretoria and using the strategy of the central position, deployed on internal lines to the various flashpoints.[44] Botha's concept of operations was dependent on intelligence and mobility.[45] The rebel leaders targeted included Maritz in the Northern Cape, Beyers and Kemp in the Transvaal and De Wet in the Free State.

40 Smuts to Reitz to Reitz, 22 September 1914 in Hancock and Van der Poel (eds.), *Selections*, vol.III, p.198.
41 Botha to Steyn, 1908 in Meintjes, *Botha*, p.159.
42 Engelenburg, *Botha*, pp.213–216; Meintjes, *Botha*, pp.174–175.
43 Meintjes, *Botha*, p.239; Fedorowich, 'Sleeping with the Lion?', p.80. M.E. Ritchie, *With Botha in the Field* (London: Longmans, 1915), p.4.
44 Trew, *Botha Treks*, p.29.
45 Garcia, *The First Campaign Victory*, p.94.

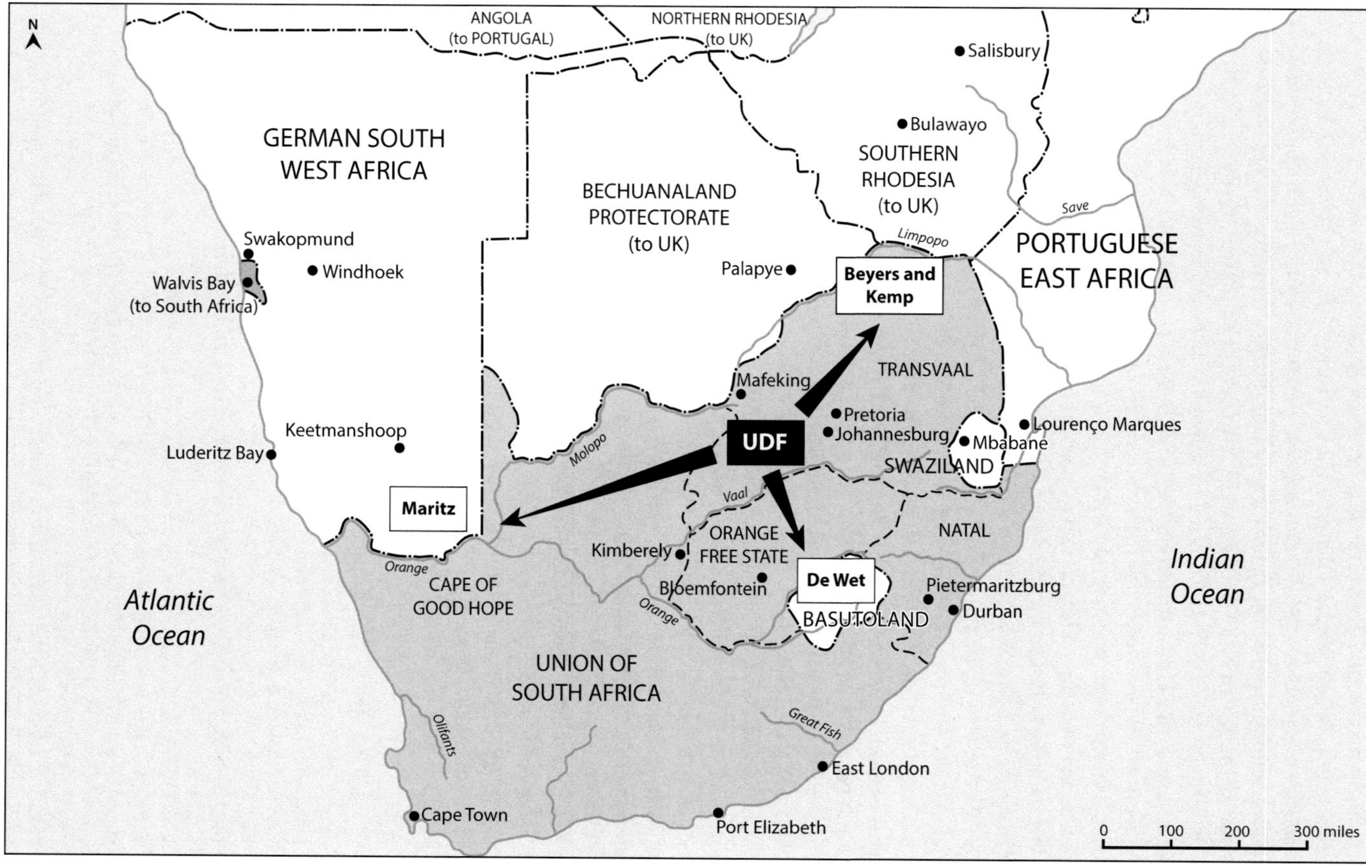

Map 3.1 Afrikaner Rebellion: Strategy of the central position.

Botha and Smuts's intelligence net was based on loyalties, the military districts, police and magistrates, as well as various rifle associations.[46] Using these sources to inform their intelligence picture, the next steps were dependent on the ability to manoeuvre, reach the enemy quickly and defeat them. The Union Defence Forces' mobility was facilitated through the use of motor cars, horses and armoured trains. Infrastructure projects in the form of 227 kilometres of railway construction between Upington and Prieska allowed the Union to project its military power into the Northern Cape and by extension to the border of German South West Africa.[47] Colonel C. Brits (later a brigadier general) who was fiercely loyal to Botha, was deployed to Upington to deal with the threat posed by Maritz. It was said that Botha saved Brits's life in the Anglo-Boer War – he would forever after be a Botha man.

A circular from the Secretary of Defence soon confirmed Brits's appointment to include 'all the Union Defence Forces in No.12 District, including the forces under Colonel Maritz's command …'. He was also authorized to convene and confirm general courts martials.[48] Botha, not taking chances, selected a friend, and one with a powerful personality, to take charge in the Northern Cape and deal with the difficult situation created by Maritz's treason.

Whilst all this was happening Union forces in German South West Africa were in a holding pattern, with key units being redeployed. Adding considerable strength, Botha reinforced the Northern Cape with Enslin's Horse Regiment, the Durban Light Infantry, the Imperial Light Horse, and a heavy battery of artillery. They were concerned, Smuts confided in his mother, that Maritz would potentially attack Union positions in the north.[49] The strengthened Union force served the dual role of defending against a rebel attack and mobilising for a cross border invasion of German South West Africa.[50]

Botha's aim was to extinguish the rebellion before it transformed into civil war.[51] He requested Colonel J.J. Alberts, Collins, Mentz, Cilliers and Brigadier General M.W. Myburgh to speak to their followers and each raise approximately 1,000 *burghers*.[52] Smuts managed the ministry of defence, and his immense capacity for work was brought to bear in supporting Botha by providing a staff, planning, intelligence and

46 Fedorowich, 'Sleeping with the Lion?', p.83.
47 Fedorowich, 'Sleeping with the Lion?', p.83.
48 DODA: SAMR, box 1044, file 516/69 Colonel Brits, Circular from Secretary for Defence, 2 Oct 1914.
49 Smuts to S.M. Smuts, 10 October 1914 in Hancock and Van der Poel (eds.), *Selection*s, vol. III, p.203.
50 DODA: Diverse 1, Box 57, General Botha's Operations against the Rebels, Order from Defence Headquarters, 21 November 1914; Diverse 1, Box 2, Rebellion Commission of Enquiry Volume 1, Testimony by General Louis Botha, 968, 29 June 1916; Testimony by General Barend Gottfried Leopold Enslin403, 17 April 1916.
51 Krüger, *Age of the Generals*, p.91.
52 DODA: Diverse 1, Box 2, Rebellion Commission of Enquiry Volume 1, Testimony by General Louis Botha, 968, 29 June 1916.

logistical function. With a firm administrative base, the key to the success of military operations was Botha's leadership, his military credentials and his influence.[53]

Botha took to the field after 12 years – he would lead from the front. Confiding in Leyds, Botha declared, 'I must do my duty'.[54] He had last taken up arms during the Anglo-Boer War but was prepared to do so again. Upon his departure, fighting back tears, he said to Annie: 'I have said goodbye to you in many difficult circumstances, but never on such a painful occasion as this. God give me strength to do my duty.'[55] He believed that the majority of Afrikaners supported him or could be convinced to support him.[56]

This was of course not entirely accurate – many opposed the war, and even Smuts's dear Emily Hobhouse wrote to him in October 1914 lamenting the conflict and appealing to his sense of mercy. She felt for the *burghers* who were 'called upon to invade a country against which they have no quarrel to uphold a country which only fourteen years ago was treating them as the Germans are now treating Belgium. I cannot bear to think that dear de Wet and Beyers and Kemp will meet a rebel's death. You have asked too much of human nature…'.[57] Indeed Botha and Smuts asked for the impossible – they tried to bend the world to suit an untested political idea – it was and remained an experiment. Reitz wrote to Smuts. He had argued with his father, the former Orange Free State president and prominent cultural icon F.W. Reitz, about the Botha-Smuts government's invasion plan, and Steyn's position on the matter. After their fight, Reitz felt that his father started seeing Botha and Smuts's point of view – it was layered, and the senior Nationalist echelons remained unconvinced.[58]

Botha's first objective was Beyers, who was reported to be outside Rustenburg. Although D.W. Krüger claims that Beyers rebelled half-heartedly, Deneys Reitz maintains that Beyers, who led the Transvaal rebellion was heading towards Pretoria.[59] Botha confided in Smuts that he did not trust Beyers[60] – deplorable Beyers.[61] The choice of operations which Botha led is telling. He took command of the operations against Beyers and De Wet and used loyal commanders to pursue Kemp and Maritz. Beyers and De Wet did indeed pose the biggest political threat with De la Rey out of the picture. There is also a feeling that on a more personal level, Botha and Smuts did not like Beyers. He was perpetually unsatisfied, a wavering uncertain character who always felt hard done by. A case in point was when he was appointed as

53 Van der Waag, *A Military History*, p.99.
54 NARSSA: Leyds Archive, 262, Part II, Botha to Leyds, 6 October 1914.
55 Trew, *Botha Treks*, p.29.
56 NARSSA: Leyds Archive, 262, Part II, Botha to Leyds, 6 October 1914.
57 Hobhouse to Smuts, 29 October 1914 in Hancock and Van der Poel (eds.), *Selections*, vol. III, p.206.
58 Reitz to Smuts, 20 October 1914 in Hancock and Van der Poel (eds.), *Selections*, vol. III, p.206.
59 Reitz, *Trekking On*, p.26.
60 NARSSA: Smuts Papers, A1, 9, Botha to Smuts, 4 July 1911.
61 NARSSA: Leyds Archive, 262, Part II, Botha to Leyds, 6 October 1914.

commandant-general of the Citizen Force and Beyers wrote to Smuts that he would accept the position subject to a £50 increase in salary.[62]

With his trusted bodyguard Botha entrained to Rustenburg on 25 October 1914 in pursuit of Beyers who was accompanied by approximately 4,000 rebels.[63] Botha led from the front with a bodyguard that represented his politics of 'conciliation'; a joint complement of English-speaking and Afrikaans-speaking soldiers. The bodyguard, commanded by Major H.F. Trew, was comprised of 100 men.[64] The combat was limited and Beyers's forces were dispersed without much heavy fighting.

Botha's operations against Beyers, would later become the source of a false allegation. Senator A.D.W. Wolmarans claimed that Botha had 'blood on his hands' and said that the general had ordered his soldiers to 'shoot down' Beyers's rebels *en masse*. Botha categorially denied this. He had given the order for the rebels to be captured and not shot. These accusations weighed heavily on Botha, and it would become the scene of a future battle in the courts. However, matters on the battlefield were not Black and White, and the government troops bore some resentment after the rebels conducted an ungentlemanly action. Botha explained that in a ruse to confuse his men, some of Beyers's rebels had used white arm bands, the insignia of government forces, to then attack his soldiers.[65] An outraged Botha thought them 'cowards'.[66] The commandos were still in plain clothes, like the style of old. Following this encounter Botha's men engaged and dispersed Beyers's rebels in and around Olifantsnek. Soon afterwards the majority of Beyers's rebels surrendered.[67]

Botha deployed Alberts against Kemp's force who were forced to retreat from Treurfontein.[68] With Kemp on the run and his initial victory against Beyers, the prime minister returned to Pretoria and started planning his deployment to the Free State.[69] Initially Botha mobilised his men in Vereeniging on the Transvaal side of the Vaal River. This was their forming up position and the base from which Botha launched his

62 Botha to Leyds, 6 October 1914, Beyers to Smuts, 11 June 1912 in Hancock and Van der Poel (eds.), *Selections*, vol. III, p.96.

63 DODA: Diverse 1, Box 57, Botha's Operations against Rebels, Telegram to Defence Headquarters, 26 October 1914; AG 1914–1921, Box 8, Rebellion, Report by post office official at Millvale, 25 October 1914.

64 DODA: DC, Box 632, General Botha Defence Headquarters to Quartermaster General, 3 October 1914. See also Trew, *Botha Treks*.

65 NARSSA: Preller Archive, 106, De Botha-Wolmaranszaak', *Ons Vaderland*, 21 September 1917.

66 DODA: Diverse 1, Box 57, General Botha's Operations against the Rebels Telegram Botha to Smuts, 13 November 1914.

67 DODA: Diverse 1, Box 57, General Botha's Operations against the Rebels, Telegram to Defence Headquarters, 27 October 1914; Anon., *Official History*, pp.16, 23; Meintjes, *Botha*, p.241; Ritchie, *With Botha*, p.29.

68 DODA: AG 1914–1921, Box 8, Armoured Trains, Colonel Alberts report to General Smuts after the action at Treurfontein19 October 1914.

69 DODA: Diverse 1, Box 57, General Botha's Operations against the Rebels, Telegram from Quartermaster General to Defence Headquarters, 12 November 1914.

operations into the Free State. Lukin had returned from the failed invasion attempt and the reverse at Sandfontein. Lukin had good military experience, and despite the loss at the Battle of Sandfontein, he held a key position in the operations against De Wet.

Botha trekked with his force. Brits, having come down from the Northern Cape via Pretoria, arrived at Winburg on 11 November.[70] After receiving intelligence about the location of De Wet, who was at Mushroom Valley, Botha put forward the plan of operations.[71] The strategy involved the encirclement of De Wet's forces and Myburgh, Lukin, Brits and Colonel G. Brand played key roles.[72] The attack commenced at daybreak on 12 November, and the initial shots of cannon fire dispersed the rebel force. Myburgh attacked through the centre, but a wily De Wet managed to make his escape.[73] Botha, who was accustomed to commanding from the front, encountered some resistance from Trew who attempted, often unsuccessfully, to keep Botha away from the firing line.[74]

Botha had positioned matters so that the cut-off force would capture the retreating rebels. However, the heliograph message did not reach Lukin and as a result many of the rebels escaped. 'That wretched miscommunication that was the cause of the delay', exclaimed an exasperated Botha.[75] The end of the battle brought on a wave of emotion for the saddened prime minister. Looking at the fallen *burghers* he said, 'you English will never understand how hard this is for me'.[76]

At pains Botha lamented, '... instead of being able to go to German South West Africa, I have been in the field fighting small groups of misguided men of my own race. It is a sad day indeed for me in which this duty has fallen to my lot.' But, Botha acknowledged, he had 'the cordial support of the great majority of my countrymen and that the spirit of the commandos which I have in the field in the Transvaal and Free State, consisting predominantly of Dutch farmers, leaves nothing to be desired.'[77]

The Battle of Mushroom Valley was a significant engagement in the rebellion that claimed the lives of 22 rebels[78] and the capture of approximately 300 more.[79] The rebel-

70 DODA: Diverse 1, Box 57, General Botha's Operations Against the Rebels, Telegram from Quartermaster General to Defence Headquarters, 12 November 1914.
71 Meintjes, *Botha*, p.242; Trew, *Botha Treks,* p.29.
72 Trew, *Botha Treks,* p.31.
73 Ritchie, *With Botha*, p.9; DODA: Diverse 1, Box 57, General Botha's Operations Against the Rebels, Telegram Botha to Smuts, 13 November 1914.
74 Trew, *Botha Treks,* p.32.
75 DODA: Diverse 1, Box 57, General Botha's Operations Against the Rebels, Telegram Botha to Smuts, 13 November 1914; P.J. Sampson, *The Capture of De Wet: The South African Rebellion, 1914* (Cape Town: Wentworth Press, 1915), p.172; Trew, *Botha Treks,* p.32; E.W. Nortier, 'Major General Sir Henry Timson Lukin (1860–1925): The Making of a South African Hero', M Mil, Military Academy, Stellenbosch University, 2005, p.23.
76 Trew, *Botha Treks,* p.32.
77 WSHC: Viscount Long Papers, 947/466, Botha to Long, 7 November 1914.
78 L'ange, *Urgent Imperial Service*, p.68.
79 DODA: Diverse 1, Box 57, General Botha's Operations Against the Rebels, Telegram Botha to Smuts, 13 November 1914.

lion in the Free State had been dealt a severe blow. Botha and Smuts coordinated the actions of the forces, operating throughout the Union. Kemp, who was in full retreat, embarked on a herculean trek through the Kalahari to link up with Maritz in German South West Africa. De Wet, who was also on the run tried to reach German South West Africa but was eventually captured by Brits in the Northern Cape.[80] Botha and Smuts made good use of intelligence and mobility; they operated on internal lines using a strategy of the central position, and ensured that government forces were deployed at the right time to the correct place to neutralise the rebel threat.[81]

The tragic death of Beyers, who drowned in the Vaal River, while on the run from government forces, and the defeat of De Wet signalled the end of the uprising and the rebellion gradually petered out.[82] In early 1915 there were occasional flashes of successful resistance and the German backed rebel attack at the Battle of Nydesputs is one such example. On this occasion 170 Union soldiers were taken prisoner, nine killed, and 20 injured.[83] It was nearly impossible for the German backed rebels to maintain the offensive given their general lack of logistical support, and the strong position of the UDF. A bedraggled Maritz and Kemp arrived in the German colony only to be pressured to return to attack the Union's forces in Upington. Their attempt was firmly repulsed by Van Deventer's force and the remainder of the rebels surrendered on 30 January 1915.[84] The table below shows the statistics for the total number of rebels captured and surrendered.

Table 3.1: Rebels captured and surrendered[85]

Province	**Captured**	**Surrendered**	**Total**
Orange Free State	3,138	3,985	7,123
Transvaal	2,350	648	2,998
Cape	398	192	590
Totals	5,886	4,825	10,711

80 Reitz, *Trekking On*, p.63.
81 Garcia, *First Campaign Victory*, p.111.
82 Krüger, *Age of the Generals*, p.93.
83 See DODA: DC, Box 252, Telegram from Colonel Van Deventer to General Smuts, 18 and 20 January 1915: DODA: AG 14-21, Box 166, Casualty List, February 1915; Other statistics for the battle are given as 10 killed and 18 wounded: DC, Box 252, Telegram from Colonel Van Deventer to General Smuts, 20 January 1915; Diverse 1, Box 2, Rebellion Commission of Enquiry Volume 1, Testimony by Mr Pieter de Wet, 222, 28 March 1916.
84 Nasson, *Springboks*, pp.48–50.
85 DODA: Diverse, Box 1, Treason trials, Rebels captured and surrendered. Excluding the Battle of Upington.

The Rebel Narrative and Botha and Smuts's Counter-narrative

At the trials that followed the rebels faced charges of treason, but Botha and Smuts focused on the leadership as opposed to the rank and file. Of the rebel leadership, 12 Union Defence Force officers were court-martialled, but only one, Jopie Fourie, was sentenced to death. He became a martyr and the stuff of legend, allegedly singing a patriotic Boer song while facing the firing squad. The implications of Fourie's execution would come back to haunt Botha and Smuts – many Boers could never forgive what would be interpreted as the harshest of acts. Smuts and Botha had to make a point. It was more Smuts than Botha, and the prime minister struggled to fight back tears.[86] Schalk Burger, the former acting president of the Transvaal, writing to Smuts in December 1914, summarised the situation: 'The drama played by Fourie is terrible. Well, he has had his punishment—he is dead! But what feelings that leaves among our people! And yet it was the only thing you could do.'[87] Smuts, a month earlier wrote to John X. Merriman, acknowledging the impossibility of the situation, 'it is a dirty, miserable business which will be a blot on our fair name for ever, in whatever way we get out of it now.'[88] Botha would never live down the experience of the Afrikaner rebellion – his heart was broken, and although he put up a brave front, and even eventually accepted responsibility for the execution Jopie Fourie, many compatriots never forgave him. Their loyalty could never be to the British Empire.

In 1914, Plaatje reworked his book *A Native Life in South Africa*. With the outbreak of the Afrikaner Rebellion, he was keen to highlight the theme of 'African loyalty' versus 'Boer disloyalty'. Initially focussed on the Land Act of 1913, it became increasingly autobiographical, including aspects of his sea journey to Britain.[89] This book would only see publication in 1916, it drew attention to the discrimination of the Land Act, and gave ammunition to the liberal voices in Britain, America, and South Africa. In practice, however, it had little impact, but now the work forms a key historical source, showcasing Plaatje's writing, his political advocacy, and scholarship. The volume also shows the roots of African nationalism in South Africa. Botha and other Afrikaner leaders struggled to hide their contempt for Plaatje's work.[90]

In December 1914, Botha addressed a group at a press event at his residence in Pretoria. He said that the rebellion was over and that personally it was one of the most difficult times of his life. He mentioned that he was inclined towards giving the leaders of the rebellion a lenient sentence, but this would ultimately have to be decided

86 Meintjes, *Botha*, p.198.
87 Burger to Smuts, 22 December 1914 in Hancock and Van der Poel (eds.), *Selections*, vol. III, p.223.
88 Reitz to Merriman, 3 November 1914 in Hancock and Van der Poel (eds.), *Selections*, vol. III, p.203.
89 B. Willan, *Sol Plaatje: A Life of Solomon Tshekisho Plaatje* (Johannesburg: Jacana, 2018), p.281.
90 Willan, *Sol Plaatje*, pp.308–310

by the courts.[91] Smuts gave kudos, 'General Botha deserves all praise and gratitude for his work and the way he has used his enormous influence in the right direction. The collapse of the rebellion came sooner than he had ventured.'[92] The courts did in fact hand down lenient sentences; but that became a problem in itself. Botha's influence, as big as it was, could not sway the republicans, and many of his supporters were also not happy. Burger voiced his concerns to Smuts, 'Then, what about the ringleaders who are now still at large? Why are A. D. Wolmarans, Rev. de Klerk, Tielman Roos and others not arrested? Zwart Wolmarans is the biggest and first rebel since August, at Treurfontein. He committed the first and greatest treason by turning round with his Commando'.[93]

A year later, in December 1915 the impact of the political compromise and disdain for the lenient sentences, was palpable. A thoroughly disgusted Reitz complained to Smuts, 'I must tell you plainly that in these parts we have now done with the Government—they have grossly broken their word to us and shown us a hundred times less consideration than to the rebels. Life here is now really intolerable thanks to the way in which the Government has protected us. We have had a hasty executive meeting here and the whole branch (South African Party) has decided to resign from the Party. Of course we are not going to join the Nationalist trash but we are now done with the present Government.'[94] A telling indictment from a diehard and loyal Smuts and Botha supporter. He worshipped Smuts and Botha, and his exploits with Smuts in the Anglo-Boer War was the subject of his first semi-autobiographical work, *On Commando*. His service in the German South West African campaign is captured in another autobiographical account, *Trekking On*. His frustration in December 1915, was far removed from the victorious spirit, evident a year earlier – the result was that both sides felt hard done by.

Professor Leo Fouché, a prominent historian, and friend of Smuts, was requested to conduct the investigation into the causes of the outbreak of the rebellion and the government's action to supress it.[95] On completion of the work, Meintjes claims that he took some time to reflect, and felt that his assessment was not entirely objective.[96] This is contrasted by more recent historical scholarship which suggests that Fouché believed his work to be objective but regretted doing it because the investigation had estranged him from a large part of Afrikanerdom. Alex Mouton, a prominent South

91 NARSSA: Preller Archive, 90, Botha quoted in 'Horses for Botha', *Pretoria News,* 18 December 1916.
92 Smuts to Crewe, 18 December 1914 in Hancock and Van der Poel (eds.), *Selections*, vol. III, p.219.
93 Burger to Smuts, 22 December 1914 in Hancock and Van der Poel (eds.), *Selections*, vol. III, p.223.
94 Reitz to Smuts, 11 December 1915 in Hancock and Van der Poel (eds.), *Selections*, vol.III, p.328.
95 F.A. Mouton, 'Professor Leo Fouche, the History Department and the Afrikanerisation of the University of Pretoria', *Historia*, vol.38, no.1 (1993), p.2.
96 Meintjes, *Botha*, p.286.

African historian, claims that there is evidence in the British records (the published Blue Books) that, despite Fouché's attempts at objectivity, the investigation was indeed biased and intended as a justification of the Botha-Smuts government's actions while not addressing the rebels' motivations.[97]

In attempting to comprehend the complex causes of the rebellion, the theme of competition between the two sides of Afrikanerdom comes through. Deneys Reitz, the soldier, writer and confidant of Smuts, put forward his view declaring that 'every member of the South African Party stood by Botha, and while not every Nationalist was a rebel, it is literally true that every rebel, without a single exception, was a Nationalist'.[98] Buxton confirmed the divide stating: 'The political position here is by no means satisfactory. There is intense bitterness between the two sections of the Dutch, which is being utilised by the disloyal section for the purpose of racial antipathy.'[99] Understanding the power of influence, Botha simply referred to the rebels as 'misguided men of my own race.'[100] Then too, the political divide was framed by the different respective economies of the Transvaal and Free State. Without trying to oversimplify it, the Free State, had for the most part a homogenous White Afrikaner population, that was strongly reliant on agriculture, and the Transvaal had a White population comprised of British, Afrikaans, Jewish and other South Africans, as well as a thriving mining sector.[101] Fuelled by historical schisms, there was a stark division between hard-line republican Afrikaners, mostly in the Free State and northern regions of the Cape Province who longed for an independent republic and those in the Transvaal and the historical British colonies, the Cape and Natal, who sought to create a new South Africa within the British Empire.

Some scholars regard the government's inability to provide gainful employment for the growing ranks of poor Whites as a further cause of the rebellion.[102] Whereas the economic situation coupled with politicised anger may have been the cause, there was also an element of opportunism. Many of the young poor Whites or *bywoners* had substantial debts and were more interested in achieving financial independence than political objectives.[103]

The stereotype was a poor male Afrikaner, without work or opportunities who saw certain farmers and politicians doing well, while they remained working in positions

97 Mouton, 'Professor Leo Fouche', p.2.
98 Reitz, *Trekking On*, p.40. Gurr, a political theorist, suggests that political violence in the form of rebellion almost always has a political objective: T.R. Gurr, *Why Men Rebel 40th Anniversary Edition* (New York: Routledge, 2016), p.4.
99 BL: Add. MS 87096, Buxton Papers, 1915–1924, Buxton to Grey, 21 July 1915.
100 WSHC: Viscount Long Papers, 947/466, Botha to Long, 7 November 1914.
101 Garcia, *First Campaign Victory*, p.84.
102 S. Swart, '"Desperate Men": The 1914 Rebellion and the Polities of Poverty', *South African Historical Journal*, vol.42, no.1 (2000), p.169. For the 1914 Rebellion, see Fedorowich, 'Sleeping with the Lion?'; Van der Waag, *A Military History*; and Krüger, *Age of the Generals*, p.51.
103 Swart, 'Desperate Men', p.167.

that they regarded as beneath them. The backdrop of growing Afrikaner nationalism collided with increasing economic and individual Boer leader dissatisfaction. They were influenced by prominent leaders, who tied in a foggy nostalgia to the old republics, an independence they could not remember and the hope of a better future – the result was a poor rebel.[104]

Patrick Duncan, once part of Milner's Kindergarten, a group of young, well-educated and determined British civil servants who came to support Milner following the Anglo-Boer War, served on the parliamentary select committee on the Rebellion. In his investigation of the uprising Duncan declared, that 'in the long drought many of these people have lost what little they had, and rebellion does not seem such a serious thing to desperate men.'[105] The initial parliamentary committee was unable to complete its report due to the unavailability of certain key witnesses. Later, a judicial commission was set up and published its findings as the *Report of the Judicial Commission into the Causes of and Circumstances Relating to the Recent Rebellion in South Africa, December 1916*. Those involved in the inquiry were Justice Johannes Henricus Lange (chairperson), Justice Malcolm William Searle, and Justice Frederick Augustus Hutton. They were later responsible for sentencing the rebels in the specially appointed treason trials. Generally, the rebellion commission, committee and trial were poorly executed, and Buxton commented that there handling was 'unfortunate'.[106]

Conclusion

The military victory did not translate into any sort of substantial political capital. The rebel trials and commission were loaded and attempted to whitewash the past. The result was widespread frustration that for the most part went untreated. Botha and Smuts could not see past their vision of a united White South Africa.

Smuts carried much of the administrative burden for both operations; suppressing the rebellion and the invasion. Botha relied on Smuts to handle the Union's financial matters. Following the resignation of H.C. Hull as minister of finance in 1912, Botha was seething, but asked Smuts to help. He was confident, but cautious of the increased expenditure, and was keen to cut superfluous spending – the invasion and the broader South African economy had to be based on a sound fiscal plan. Smuts enlisted the support of John. X. Merriman. Botha had initially asked Merriman to be the minister of finance in the 1910 cabinet, but Merriman took this as an insult. Smuts wrote to Merriman, 'estimates and other financial questions could be informally discussed by

104 See S. Swart, 'Desperate Men': The 1914 Rebellion and the Polities of Poverty', *South African Historical Journal*, vol.42, no.1 (2000).

105 Grundlingh and Swart, *Radelose Rebellie*, p.26. Duncan's son by the same name would go on to become a well-known anti-Apartheid activist which in itself is interesting and formed part of a later chapter of South African history.

106 BL: Add MS 87052, 1914–1918, Buxton to Bonar Law, 27 November 1915.

us. Do you look upon the idea favourably? I feel sure that such an informal talk will be for the good of the country, which is faced with very heavy extraordinary expenditure and a falling revenue in these strange times. I have never posed as a financial expert and as you know I am half dead with my efforts in quite another direction. So you must be good and help.'[107]

In December 1914, with the mechanics of logistical supply, weaponry, and materiel ticking away in the background, many South Africans and Britons trusted that Botha would go on and effectively lead the campaign – a sentiment echoed by Crewe who said that, 'I have great faith in Botha as Commander-in-Chief and I think somehow all will go well.'[108] Crewe as the director of the newspaper the *Daily Despatch* , used it to promote the pro-government message. With much of the Union behind them, Botha and Smuts faced their biggest military test since the Anglo-Boer War. Armed with the fledgling UDF, the end of the Rebellion allowed for the re-invasion of German South West Africa.[109]

107 Smuts to Merriman, 19 December 1915 in Hancock and Van der Poel (eds.), *Selections*, vol. III, p.221.

108 Smuts to Crewe, 22 December 1914 in Hancock and Van der Poel (eds.), *Selections*, vol. III, p.222.

109 W.A. Dorning, 'A Concise History of the South African Defence Force 1912–1987', *Militaria, South African Journal for Military Studies*, vol.17, no.2 (1987), p.4.

4

Conquest of German South West Africa, 1914–1915

I shall outmanoeuvre him with flank movements.

Botha to Smuts[1]

The suppression of the rebellion had gone better than Botha and Smuts had anticipated. Botha wrote to Smuts: 'Through loyalty to each other we have so far been successful in the biggest difficulty [rebellion], and why should we now assume that we shall no longer have the Lord's blessing? Far from it; we have every reason to persevere in our policy and to hold more strongly and firmly to our faith.'[2]

Assuming command of the invasion force in German South West Africa, Botha arrived at Walvis Bay in February 1915. Colonel P.C.B. Skinner, on loan from the British Army, was the commander who took Walvis Bay before Botha assumed direct command of the Northern Force.[3] The Northern Force was the final piece needed, and complemented the advance of the Southern Army which was composed of the Central, Southern and Eastern forces (see Map 4.1).[4] The Northern Force advanced on Windhoek. The initial phases involved clearing positions with a token German defence. Botha correctly anticipated that the first substantive German defensive positions would be at Riet, Pforte and Jakkalsfontein.[5]

1 Botha to Smuts, 27 February 1915 in Hancock and Van der Poel (eds.), *Selections*, vol. III, p.243.
2 Botha to Smuts, 1 February 1915 in Hancock and Van der Poel (eds.), *Selections*, vol. III, p.236.
3 L'ange, *Urgent Imperial Service,* pp.138–139; DODA: AG 1914–1921, Box 8, G5/305/9199, Commander-in-chief, Goverment notice for the next issue of the *Union Gazette*, 18 October 1914.
4 Garcia, *First Campaign Victory*, p.130.
5 DODA: DC, Box 252, 17138, Historical Record of the Campaign in GSWA, 4 November 1919; Botha to Smuts, 27 February 1915 in Hancock and Van der Poel (eds.), *Selections*, vol. III, p.243.

Second Invasion of German South West Africa

Colonel P.S. Beves led the initial force which landed at Lüderitzbucht, named 'C' Force, on 18 September 1914. Beves was the inspector of cadets following the establishment of the Union Defence Force. During the re-invasion Brigadier General D. McKenzie took command of Beves's force which was renamed the Central Force.[6] Botha, showing confidence, told Smuts, that the infantry under Beves, 'will fight well'.[7] A keen student of military affairs, Botha and Smuts's staff college was a practical one, the Anglo-Boer War.

McKenzie, the previous commander of the Natal Colonial Forces, led the Central Force. He was slow and lethargic and tried Botha's patience. Conscious of the sensitivity, Botha tried not to push McKenzie too far, but could not hide his frustration stating plainly that he, 'no longer has the confidence that he should have of his army… he does not understand infantry.'[8] With Botha in the north, and McKenzie at Lüderitzbucht, there were two additional cross-border invasion forces in play.

These were the Southern and Eastern forces. The Southern Force was led by Colonel Van Deventer who commanded the force in Upington which repelled Maritz and Kemp. Colonel C.A.L. Berrange, had served previously with Lukin during the first invasion attempt, and now held his own command, the Eastern Force, which deployed from Kakamas.[9] Botha who relied on a decentralised form of command, trusted his commanders.[10]

The senior officers in command were representative of Botha's experiment, bringing together the Afrikaner and British sides of the South African coin. There was also a large contingent of Black, Coloured and Indian soldiers as well as local Namibian guides and scouts that facilitated and enabled combat operations. Although absent from most of the older historiography, modern historians have provided considerable evidence to indicate the crucial combat support role of People of Colour in German South West Africa, East Africa, and other First World War theatres.[11] Despite this

6 Paterson, 'First Allied Victory, p.2; Nasson, *Springboks*, p.68.
7 Botha to Smuts, 27 February 1915 in Hancock and Van der Poel (eds.), *Selections*, vol. III, p.243.
8 Botha to Smuts, 30 March 1915 in Hancock and Van der Poel (eds.), *Selections*, vol. III, pp.269–270.
9 DODA: AG 1914–1921, Box 150, Strengths, General Summary, Southern Force, 4 April 1915.
10 Botha and Smuts would also provide opportunities to gain favour. This is why Lord Selborne referred to Botha as a 'jobber', Selborne to Lady Selborne, 23 August 1908 in Boyce, *Naval Papers of Selborne*, p.379.
11 See for example, A. Grundlingh, *War and Society:Participation and Remembrance, South African Black and Coloured Troops in the First World War, 1914-1918* (Stellenbosch, Sun Press, 2014); Gleeson, *The Unknown Force: Black indian and Coloured Soldiers through Two World Wars* (Rivonia: Ashanti, 1994); W.M. Bisset, 'Unexplored Aspects of South Africa's First World War History', *Scientia Militaria*, vol.6, no.3 (1976). B. Nasson, *World War 1*

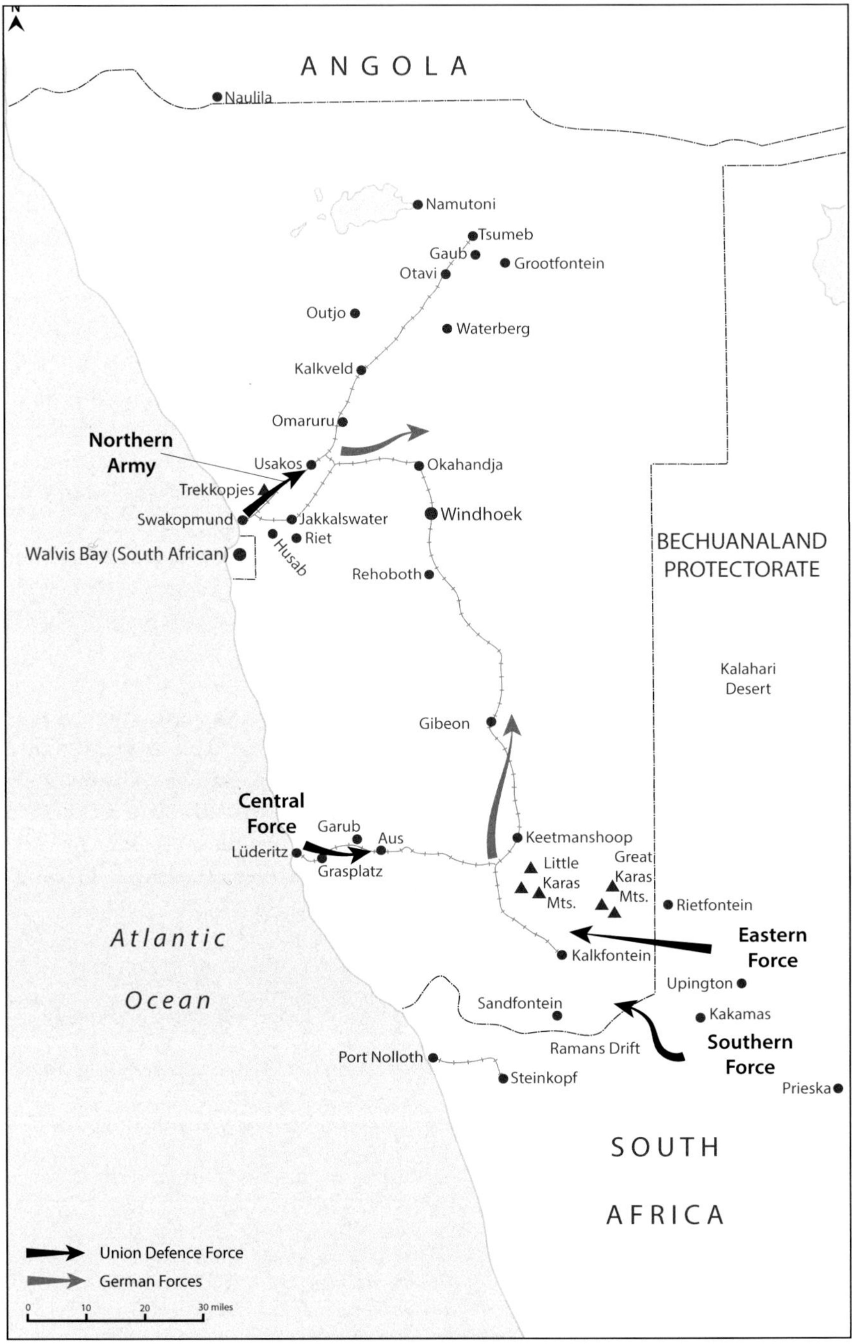

Map 4.1 Advance of South African forces in German South West Africa.

important role, some contemporary South African politicians were scathing of Black support of the Botha government. The entire subject requires careful consideration, keeping in mind the period in question and the norms of the day. The Black, Coloured and Indian soldiers were largely forgotten by the new and old South African governments – it is the writers, historians, families, sociologists, journalists, anthropologists and academics who keep their names alive.

With a massive numerical superiority, the Union forces faced Lieutenant Colonel Franke, who succeeded Von Heydebreck after his death in November 1914.[12] Franke commanded approximately 5,000 *schutztruppe*. His aim was simple – to maximise the use of terrain while operating on internal lines and delay the Union forces for as long as possible in order to hamper the British geo-strategy of redeploying troops in the colonies to other theatres of conflict.[13] Franke, who was highly rated by South African intelligence, was thought to be more competent than Von Heydebreck. The events of the campaign would later dispel this idea.[14] Von Heydebreck had the military credentials, and savvy. The only thing he shared with Franke was their brutal participation in the Namibian genocides – Franke, although brave, proved to be the most average of commanders.

The terrain was a neutral factor, because both sides had to overcome the same hazards, however the *schutzruppe* had the advantage of being on the defensive and using internal lines of communication. Rapid internal deployment was a force multiplier – the results could be seen in the German victory at Sandfontein. The terrain in German South West Africa included large expanses of desert and an acute lack of water.[15] Botha said, 'water remains our greatest enemy' adding, that German South West Africa was a 'natural fortress on a huge scale'.[16] He had previously been on the other side, using the natural fortress of the Tugela against the invading British Army. The German colony was marked by a lack of infrastructure. With no formal roads there was a railway system which connected the coastal towns of Lüderitzbucht and Swakopmund to the interior where Windhoek, Karibib and Kalkfontein were the main towns.[17] The railway outlined the contours of the port towns, which were at sea level, and which were buffered by a

and the People of South Africa (Cape Town: Tafelberg, 2014); Van der Waag, *A Military History*; A. Samson, *World War I in Africa: The Forgotten Conflict among European Powers* (London: I.B. Taurus, 2013); A. Grundlingh, *Fighting their own war. South African Blacks and the First World War* (Johannesburg: Ravan Press, 1987); Garcia provides evidence of the crucial combat support role that Black, Coloured and Indian South Africans provided in ensuring a rapid victory in South West Africa – Garcia, *First Campaign Victory*.

12 Some sources give his death as January 1915.

13 Van der Waag, 'The Battle of Sandfonte in' p.3.

14 Anon., *Official History*, p.14; Van der Waag, *A Military History*, p.95.

15 See Van der Waag, *A Military History*, p.104; and E. Kleynhans, 'A Critical Analysis of the Impact of Water on the South African Campaign in German South West Africa, 1914-1915', *Historia*, vol.61, no.2 (2016).

16 Botha to Smuts, 7 March 1915 in Hancock and Van der Poel (eds.), *Selections*, vol. III, p.255.

17 S.C. Buxton, *General Botha* (London: Hazel, Watson & Viney, 1924), p.94; DODA: DC, Box 252, 17138, Historical Record of the Campaign in GSWA, 4 November 1919.

desert belt that then rose to the interior plateau at 1,060 metres above sea level. The dusty desert belt was an arid, narrow strip which spanned 60 to 160 kilometres. The railway was a key means to overcome the barrier of the desert.[18]

Botha wrote to Smuts, 'lack of transport is my chief obstacle.'[19] Force projection was dependent upon horses, ox and mule drawn waggons, as well as motor cars but one of the most critical features was the rail system. In turn the provision of labour for the construction and maintenance of the communication lines was contingent on Black, Coloured and Indian assistance. General Thompson reported a group of 500 'Coloured boys' who constructed the railway, and a team of 200 'Natives' who were required at all times, to clear the railway lines of sand from the moving dunes.[20] Besides the supporting role as a force enabler of Botha and Smuts's war of manoeuvre, People of Colour also held additional positions. Abraham Morris, a proud and capable Bondelswarts fighter, served in a key role as a scout. Serving with the Union forces in the south of the German colony and having previous experience fighting the Germans in the early 1900s, with an intimate knowledge of the terrain, he proved a brilliant scout and was mentioned in dispatches.[21]

The arid nature of the terrain was a critical consideration in the conduct of the campaign. Excavation of boreholes was one of the methods used to overcome the thirsty terrain but also exposed some of the day-to-day squabbles. Botha was alarmed that Lieutenant Colonel Hawksley wanted six months to dig the boreholes – the entire duration of the second invasion! Botha annoyed at the pedant, wrote to Smuts, 'I am sending you a telegram today to recall Lieutenant Colonel Hawksley. He is a hopelessly unsuitable man and quite unfitted for our work. He must first have six months to bore for water because he will do nothing which is not in King's Regulations. Meanwhile boring is going on and I shall not wait for that. When he has gone, Muller [C. H.] and others can help. He writes dozens of letters a day to vilify everybody and

18 DODA: DC, Box 252, 17138, Historical Record of the Campaign in GSWA, 4 November 1919; Collyer, *The Campaign in German South West Africa*, pp.6–7; Anon., *Official History,* p.11; Van der Waag, *A Military History*, p.95; DODA: DC, Box 252, 17138, Reports of Force Commanders in GSWA, Despatch no. 4 by General Botha, 15 May to 18 July 1915.

19 Botha to Smuts, 3 March 1915 in Hancock and Van der Poel (eds.), *Selections*, vol. III, p.247.

20 NARSSA: Smuts Papers, Box 112, Major General Thompson: Report on a visit to German South West Africa, 20–27 March 1915.

21 See G.L.M, Lewis, 'The Bondelswarts Rebellion of 1922', MA thesis, Rhodes University, 1977; A.M Fokkens, 'The Role and Application of the Union Defence Force in the Suppression of Internal Unrest, 1912–1945', MMil thesis, Stellenbosch University, 2006; A.M. Fokkens, 'The Suppression of Internal Unrest in South West Africa (Namibia) 1921–1933' in *Scientia Militaria*, vol.40 no.3, 2012; E. Kleynhans and A. Garcia, 'The Union Defence Force and the suppression of the Bondelswarts Rebellion, 1922', *Small Wars and Insurgencies*, 2022.

find fault. Personally, I think he is mad and that there must be something wrong with him. Yours, Louis.'[22]

Botha's frustration stemmed from the fact that it required time and resources to get his forces into play. This was made worse by the fact that the invasion routes were fundamentally influenced by the availability of water.[23] In order to overcome the lack of potable water a combination of methods was used. On the northern advance, and where possible water was accessed from the bed of the Swakop River. Pumping, desalination, and condensation plants offered limited supplies of water, and the filtration and pumping systems often experienced technical problems.[24] Additional water was shipped from Cape Town, to supplement the local supply, and clean water was often mixed with the brackish local water to make it more potable. Lastly, the Engineer Corps sunk boreholes which provided additional water. This proved invaluable. A particular sore point was that the German forces systematically poisoned the water wells as they retreated. Botha complained about this ungentlemanly act and said that it was against the rules of war.[25]

Balancing practical concerns, a frustrated Botha wrote to Smuts:

> I have received a letter from Buxton with regard to the two portfolios for which you are responsible. I must say I was disappointed when I read the letter and it is clear to me that he has no grasp of our difficulty … I am waiting for his arrival personally to indicate the dangers to him … I can agree to Graaff … as regards Hull, I feel that to take him into the Cabinet will be the quickest way to break up our party… So, Jannie, you will have much toil and trouble but it will be in a mitigated form and with a little tact you will come through … to give Burton Finance has my approval, but there are serious objections to giving him Railways as well, and to give Railways to Natal will again immediately encourage provincial jealousy. Is it not best to keep a stiff upper lip and struggle through … I am sorry to say that our officers get on very badly with Captain [W.F.S.] Edwards and Lt.-Col. [A.R.] Hoskins, and I feel this so strongly that I have now given instructions that our officers must under no circumstances come into direct contact with these people but get everything through Jooste [J.P.]. Jooste is an amazing help to us; he and Louis Esselen deserve much thanks—day and night they advance everything in the right direction … Some of the rifles are not good, but they will serve; but the ammunition is very bad—the cartridge-case is cracked … bigger Howitzers—we must be provided with these and second, you must consider seriously whether it is not desirable to buy 300 camels to carry … if you can speed up the aeroplanes, do so.[26]

22 Botha to Smuts, 2 June 1915 in Hancock and Van der Poel (eds.), *Selection*, vol. III, p.293.
23 Garcia, *First Campaign Victory*, p.59.
24 TNA CAB 45/112: Campaign in GSWA, Narrative of Events, February–April 1915.
25 W. Whittal, *With Botha and Smuts in Africa* (London: Cassell, 1917), p.137.
26 Botha to Smuts, 1 February 1915 in Hancock and Van der Poel (eds.), *Selections*, vol. III, pp.236–238.

The first decisive point on Botha's advance was the Riet defensive line. Botha wrote that he was worried about drinking water for the horses and was forced to follow the water sources on the bed of the Swakop River. [27] Lieutenant Colonel Hugh Wyndham was of the opinion, and he was most likely correct, that the Union Defence Force did not have a solid plan in place for the First World War.[28] An exercise in improvisation with good leadership was the only answer. To overcome the challenges posed by the geography, Botha made efficient use of logistic systems; to move forward in tactical bounds in accordance with the operational picture, the availability of supplies, and the state of his forces.

Botha looked at a number of key matters including the sloppy organisation of remounts and the slow pace of the railway construction. He was focussed and determined to pull all the forces under his command into a new direction: 'The other stations are supplied by rail from Usakos, ... for eighty miles and then struggle to get water. So the march in that direction without a railway is out of the question ... I hope to leave in a week's time ... give the Germans a good fright and, by this flank movement, to threaten their capital and cut their communications... help McKenzie and possibly cut off the Usakos bunch. I am sending the 2nd Brigade to Jakhalswater from Husab. If there is enough water I shall leave 500 men there ... I shall myself go with the 1st Brigade via Riet'.[29]

In his advance on Riet, Botha placed a depot at Husab, which became a forward supply base on the advance to Riet.[30] Water access and logistics to support the mobile operations. Botha centralised the supply of the Northern Army so as to advance on Riet and by mid-March he had at his disposal five and a half days of supplies.[31] This included, among other ordnance and logistics, 110 supply and transport wagons, 59 ammunition wagons, and 51 water carts to carry water and mitigate the aridity of the desert.[32]

Botha wrote to Smuts:

> Here all goes well but slowly, and Collyer and I exert ourselves day and night to pull things straight. Believe me, when we got here things were in a bad mess. Now the off-loading is so much improved that we off-loaded and disembarked Brits with his right wing and all their kit in one day; and, imagine it, 1,440 animals and 500 tons of fodder and food in ten days. ...the officers are informed in Cape Town that they can get all other transport here. Now this is wilfully

27 Botha to Smuts, 17 February 1915 in Hancock and Van der Poel (eds.), *Selections*, vol. III, p.242; Meintjes, *Botha*, p.261; NARSSA: Smuts Papers, A1, 112, Major General Thompson: Report on a visit to GSWA, 20–27 March 1915.
28 Van der Waag, 'Smuts's Generals', p.43.
29 Botha to Smuts, 7 March 1915 in Hancock and Van der Poel (eds.), *Selections*, vol. III, p.256.
30 DODA: DC, Box 252, 17138, Historical Record of Campaign in GSWA, 4 November 1919.
31 Collyer, *The Campaign in German South West Africa*, p.62.
32 DODA: AG 1914–1921, Box 182, Mounted Strengths, Field state, 12 April 1915.

> misleading… Alberts's right wing is now at Goanikontes and at Haigamkob; this is 24 and 30 miles … Frames has taken all the infantry Brigades' wagons, but these supply them all as I now have Skinner at Nonidas. Our advance posts should be at Rossing any day and 10 miles east of Alberts, so that we now control about 35 miles inland. We have had heavy mist here each night for the last few weeks and it gets so dark that one can hardly find one's way … The enemy is concentrating at two places—at Usakos and Jakhalswater … Wehle, according to all information, is their best man, but I shall outmanoeuvre him with flank movements. I shall begin as soon as Myburgh is here, that is, when his horses are ready... You must not address our political telegrams to 'Hoofd,' or every clerk will read them. Send them to 'General Botha' then Bok opens them; or use the private code word 'Country'.[33]

Botha displayed tremendous energy in the first substantive operations of the campaign. In a march reminiscent of the Anglo-Boer War, he advanced with his forces on Riet, departing at 1430 hours on 18 March and arriving in Riet in the early morning of 20 March, where Botha immediately engaged in battle. Botha gained the respect of his soldiers as he marched in the same conditions, enduring the same sacrifices.[34] An account of Botha's exploits tells us that he always slept with his boots on when advancing and when the command: 'Opsaal! Saddle up!' was given he was often among the very first men to be mounted on his horse.[35]

Botha was a pragmatist, who displayed keen attention to detail. For example, he deployed his mobile forces in two parallel columns to prevent too much dust being created. He also forbade smoking during the all-night march so as not to be spotted by the enemy's scouts.[36] Additionally Botha requested Smuts to provide night readable compasses to ensure accurate navigation and to reduce the dependency on scouts.[37]

Once the initial transport difficulties, for the first phase, were overcome, largely through Smuts's administrative ability, a confident Botha observed:

> I am very eager to move forward as quickly as possible and you may depend on me that this will be done … I send you a copy of a telegram (No. 506) which I sent you as from me personally and not from 'Hoofd', also copy of a reply to it, about which I must admit I feel a little hurt. I cannot believe that you have yourself drawn up the wording of your answer. I shall always be the last to take

33 Botha to Smuts, 27 February 1915 in Hancock and Van der Poel (eds.), *Selections*, vol. III, pp.242–243.
34 Trew, *Botha Treks*, pp.95–96
35 NARSSA: Preller Archive, 105, 'General Louis Botha', *De Brandwag*, August 1919.
36 Trew, *Botha Treks*, 97; Meintjes, *Botha*, pp.261–262.
37 Botha to Smuts, 27 February 1915 in Hancock and Van der Poel (eds.), *Selections*, vol. III, pp.242–243.

> it amiss if you, with all your worries, become a little impatient, but Jannie, if you want to rap me over the knuckles, do not let it go via all the clerks at both ends.[38]

The emotion was soon to pass and Botha focussed on the matter at hand. Arriving in Riet on 20 March Botha's forces continued with operations against the Germans who were holding out in a defensive position. The engagement began with an artillery exchange.[39] Botha and Brits force faced the defensive position directly. The commander-in-chief planned to commit forces to each of the positions in the defensive line. He was determined to attack and simultaneously neutralise any attempt at counterattack or reinforcement. Utilising the 1st and 2nd Mounted Brigades Botha proceeded with a broad envelopment and an in-depth attack on the defensive position.'[40]

Botha took command of the operations and had Brits attack the position at Riet in and around the Langer Heinrich hills, where the German entrenchments and a counter-attack stifled the South African assault.[41] Commandant Bezuidenhout was sent to envelop the German position but was unsuccessful due to a perceived topographical error.[42] While the direct attack on Riet commenced, Alberts and his forces (which included the Standerton and Ermelo commandos) attacked the German forces at Pforte. Alberts, under Botha's command, effectively cut off the German force at Pforte by deploying an enveloping force comprising three commandos through the gap between Hussabberg and Pforteberg.[43] The outcome was that the Germans at Pforte surrendered.[44]

Despite the surrender at Pforte, the situation at Riet ended in a stalemate. Botha's forces were forced to look for water by digging in the dry-looking Swakop Riverbed eventually finding it. The forces at Riet were forced to retreat when their lines of communication to the rear were cut.[45] Trew again struggled to keep Botha away from the firing line. After all he did this on the Tugela Line during the Anglo-Boer War but he insisted to remain close to the action.[46] Botha and Smuts achieved the first substantial victory of the invasion.

38 Botha to Smuts, 3 March 1915 in Hancock and Van der Poel (eds.), *Selections*, vol. III, p.246.
39 Trew, *Botha Treks*, pp.97–102; Ritchie, *With Botha*, pp.34–35.
40 Nasson, *Springboks*, p.70; H.F.B. Walker, *A Doctor's Diary in Damaraland* (London: Edward Arnold, 1917), p.42.
41 DODA: WW1 GSWA, Box 23a, Citations, GSWA, Northern Army 1st Mounted Brigade Potchefstroom 'B' Commando, 17 February 1918.
42 DODA: DC, Box 252, 17138, Historical Record of Campaign in GSWA, 4 November 1919; Anon., *Official History*, p.40.
43 DODA: DC, Box 252, 17138, Historical Record of Campaign in GSWA, 4 November 1919; L'ange, *Urgent Imperial Service*, p.186.
44 Trew, *Botha Treks*, p.114; Paterson, 'First Allied Victory', p.5.
45 Ritchie, *With Botha*, p.36; Trew, *Botha Treks*, pp.105–109.
46 Trew, *Botha Treks*, p.103.

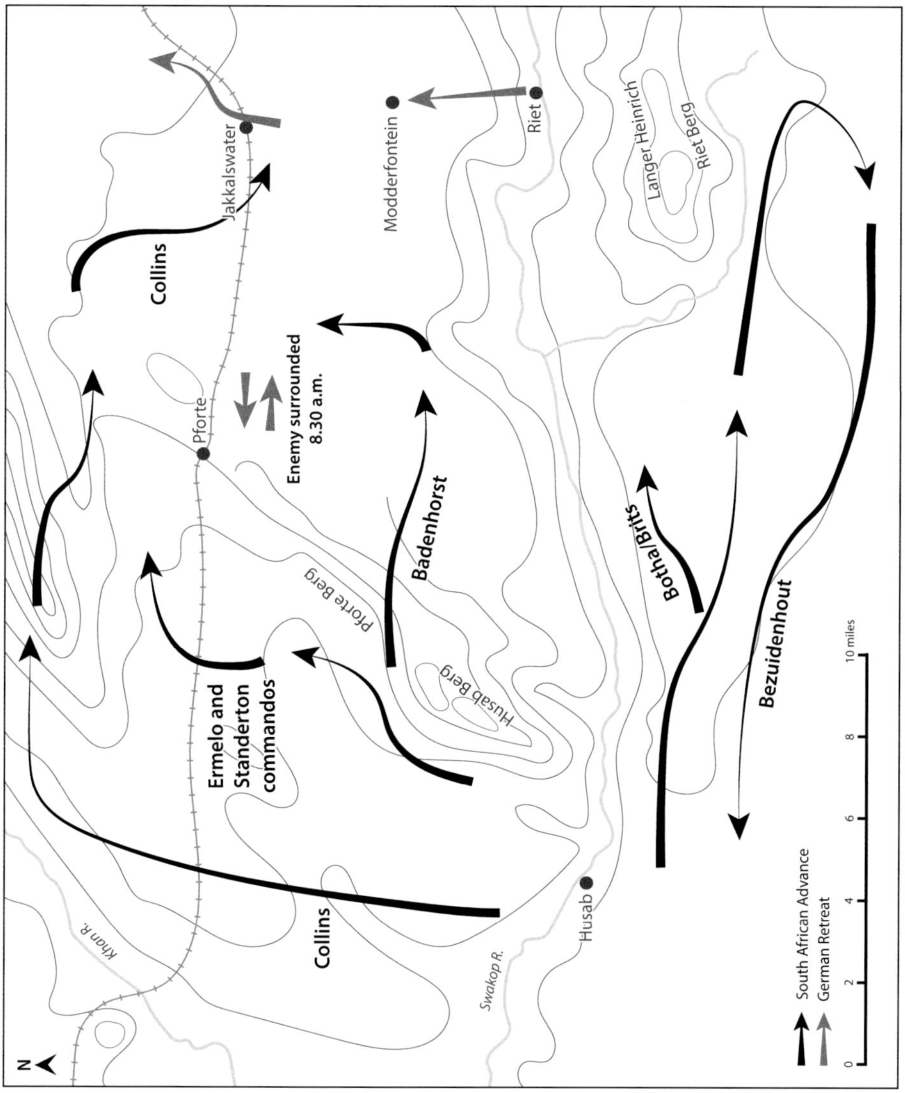

Map 4.2 Battle at the Riet defensive line.

Closing in on the Objective

While Botha advanced with the Northern Army, the Central, Southern and Eastern forces operated in the south of German South West Africa. Following the progress in the north, Botha was anxious for an advance in the south. He spoke to General McKenzie in late March 1915 to encourage him to proceed with operations.[47] Emboldened by his recent victory, Botha became the generalissimo, lecturing and showing his understanding of the theatre of operations:

> I have told him [McKenzie]very plainly that there can be no more waiting and that he must do more with such a big, costly army… I am even inclined, if he wishes it, to take command and attack Aus. I cannot say more because … were I to go further, he would resign … I admit that McKenzie is much too small for this work; he also no longer has the confidence that he should have of his army. Between ourselves, I am sure the enemy has left Aus. Over 300 explosions were heard east of Aus facts and the further fact that my commandos now threaten Windhuk show clearly that the enemy would be mad still to hold Aus. They have a small army—why should they run the risk of having a considerable part of it cut off 400 miles from their capital? No, Jannie, I feel that Aus lies empty … I have told McKenzie to move out this evening, or not later than tomorrow, and to take the northern ridges first and capture Aus along the ridges, while a mounted commando must work round south with the infantry in the centre.[48]

Smuts took command of the Southern Army, but before his arrival Botha made it clear that his initial plan for deployment was wrong. Again wearing the general's cap and as a master strategist, Botha had strong words regarding Buxton's involvement, and made this known in a telegram – Botha summarised the matter 'he pokes his fingers into things which have nothing to do with him … our business is too grave and he had better leave the operations in our hands, for he is definitely not in a position to understand them properly.' Botha went on to advise Smuts about his invasion plan:

> Jannie, this is an amazingly big country in which to wage war. I have given much attention to all the plans of invasion and attack and especially your plan to advance in the south to Seeheim. May I hope that you will allow me to give you a little advice. Allow me first to assure you warmly of my delight that you are coming to take command in the south… Now, as regards your plan—it is definitely wrong. Where you want to go in, smaller commando groups should go in—it will cost too much in transport, and van Deventer and Celliers are

47 Trew, *Botha Treks*, pp.103, 79.
48 Botha to Smuts, 30 March 1915 in Hancock and Van der Poel (eds.), *Selections*, vol. III, p.269.

> sufficient for that. You should come direct to Lüderitzbucht, form two wings out of the cavalry now under McKenzie in one brigade, and let McKenzie take command of them alone. He does not understand infantry and should be head of a smaller mounted force only. You then take command over him and the others in the south and after Aus is occupied you will have a big open country for operations … after such a movement Seeheim, Kalkfontein, Warmbad and the outlying places must fall of themselves, and then you are in a position to do a great deal of important work. It will help me tremendously, for if the enemy is really concentrating near me, I shall soon be in very serious fighting. You must telegraph me your final invasion plan.[49]

Botha was straight forward and critical, and it is certain that where he was in command, everyone knew who was the historic commandant-general – but Botha did love and trust Smuts as a commander. Their private correspondence was the sharing of ideas between brilliant friends, one an organisational specialist, and the other the master strategist. Botha added, 'supposing something were to happen to me, you would be near and would then be obliged to come and take command there.'[50] Trew went on to support that the two worked in partnership and Botha would often soundboard his ideas off Smuts.[51]

Botha was right, and the South African forces eventually took Aus unopposed – the *Official History*, summarised Botha's explanation stating that withdrawal was a result of the overall operational conditions in German South West Africa. Botha's strategic envelopment forced the Germans to abandon their position and head northwards.[52] Botha understood and said, 'I am convinced that the heaviest work lies north.'[53]

In April, Botha received information that the German forces were planning to attack a position on the railway line. They attacked the South African position at Trekkoppies on the precise day the advance on Karibib and Windhoek was to begin.[54] The South African force repulsed the German attack and sent a report of the story to *The Cape Times*.[55] While sending updates through the newspapers, Botha was concerned about the wellbeing of the soldiers and their families. Sensitive to the difficulties of being away from home – he wrote to Smuts,

49 Botha to Smuts, 30 March 1915 in Hancock and Van der Poel (eds.), *Selections*, vol. III, p.270.
50 Botha to Smuts, 30 March 1915 in Hancock and Van der Poel (eds.), *Selections*, vol. III, p.270.
51 See Trew, *Botha Treks*.
52 Anon., *Official History*, p.47; Collyer, *The Campaign in German South West Africa*, p.92.
53 Botha to Smuts, 30 March 1915 in Hancock and Van der Poel (eds.), *Selections*, vol. III, p.270.
54 TNA CAB 45/112: Campaign in GSWA, Narrative of Events, 27 April 1915.
55 TNA CAB 45/112: Campaign in GSWA, Narrative of Events, 28 April 1915.

> … you know we decided long ago that the commandos could post letters free, but the wives or people in the Union were to use stamps. The result is that the wives don't understand this—they post free and then the letters are not delivered, and the men do not hear from them. Do allow the wives to post free as well; the men are making great sacrifices for land and people, and they deserve it. Also see Roland (H.R.M. Bourne) and have his censorship instructions modified; they are entirely based on European conditions and letters are censored for all kinds of nonsense.[56]

On 24 April 1915, a short period after his arrival, Smuts wrote that the Germans were retreating at a rapid pace and he doubted whether the Southern Army would be able to catch up. He wrote to his mother, 'Perhaps I shall overtake them at Gibeon where I hope to be within two weeks'.[57] The Union's Southern and Eastern forces had pushed the Germans out of the southern part of their colony. Smuts was partially right that he would meet them at Gibeon, but he was not able to rout them. After a failed attempt to cut the German retreat, McKenzie seized Gibeon on 27 April, thereby neutralising the German threat in the south. Following the victory Smuts, disbanded much of the Southern Army and reported that Botha was planning to push forward with great energy to capture Karibib and Windhoek.[58]

Smuts visited Botha on the northern line of advance on 1 May 1915, where they discussed the future planning of the campaign.[59] Botha was convinced that he would take the German capital unless it was strongly defended – he was correct.[60] Karibib and Windhoek were captured by 12 May 1915 without a shot fired in anger, and at Windhoek the final wireless station was found disassembled.[61] The aim of the rapid advance on Windhoek was to prevent the amalgamation of German forces.[62] In this the UDF was unsuccessful and the combined German force, still mostly intact retreated. With the changing operational situation, Botha and Smuts reduced the size of the invasion force, which lessened the logistics and materiel required, but was sufficient to complete the mission.[63]

56 Botha to Smuts, 7 March 1915 in Hancock and Van der Poel (eds.), *Selections*, vol. III, p.256.
57 Smuts to Isie, 24 April 1915 in Hancock and Van der Poel (eds.), *Selections*, vol. III, p.272.
58 TNA CAB 45/112: Campaign in GSWA, Narrative of Events, 3 and 9 May 1915.
59 TNA CAB 45/112: Campaign in GSWA, Narrative of Events, 1 May 1915.
60 TNA CAB 45/112: Campaign in GSWA, Narrative of Events, 7 May 1915; Collyer, *Campaign in German South West Africa,* p.95; DODA: DC, Box 252, 17138, Historical Record of Campaign in GSWA, 4 November 1919; Anon., *Official History,* p.29.
61 Nasson, *Springboks*, p.74; Anon., *Official History,* p.40; Whittal, *With Botha and Smuts in Africa*, p.62.
62 Trew, *Botha Treks,* p.121; DODA: DC, Box 252, 17138, Historical Record of Campaign in GSWA, 4 November 1919.
63 TNA CAB 45/112, Campaign in GSWA, Narrative of Events, 10 May 1915.

In early May Botha wrote to the Rehoboth Baster leader Captain Van Wyk. They had initially held a meeting on 1 April where Botha had declined their offer of military assistance. Early in May Botha received a message from Van Wyk repeating the offer but Botha reiterated his point that People of Colour should not participate in the war. Botha also requested that Van Wyk and his people, for their own protection, place themselves behind the South African troops.[64]

One can only imagine that Van Wyk must have been surprised to hear that it was a 'White man's war', especially given the number of local scouts, Black labourers, drivers, guides and assistants. Not to mention the local groups who had lived in Southern Africa for thousands of years. Botha and Smuts used People of Colour in the UDF for their objectives, and there was a historical precedent. It was the same in the Anglo-Boer War, where both the British and Boers made use of Black people in support and combat roles, but at the same time were keen to claim that the conflict was a 'White man's war'. [65] They did not want to share the fruits of their conquest. The Rehoboth Basters fought their own war which took the form of a rebellion against the *schutz-truppe*. Their efforts provided some assistance to the Southern Army, tying up a few German units. The Rehoboth dug in at Sam Kubis to which the Germans responded with a direct attack killing and injuring many Basters. The ill-prepared Baster forces were eventually saved by the advance of the Southern Army. The Basters interpreted this as divine intervention and Sam Kubis day is still celebrated today. Following the Battle of Sam Kubis, many Basters conducted reprisal attacks murdering farmers and steeling livestock. Once Botha had taken Windhoek he was keen to re-establish control and ordered Colonel H. Mentz to stabilise the situation and discuss the return of Basters to their reserve. Later on Botha's son-in-law Lieutenant Colonel De Waal wrote the report on the Rehoboth Rebellion of 1915 and placed the blame on the Germans for their treatment of the Baster people.[66]

Checkmate

From the time of the capture of Windhoek in May 1915 until mid-June 1915, Botha took an operational pause to gather the necessary logistics for the continuation of mobile operations.[67] Furthermore, Botha reached out to Smuts, now back in South

64 TNA CAB 45/112, Campaign in GSWA, Narrative of Events, 3 May 1915; G.J.J. Oosthuizen, 'The Military Role of the Rehoboth Basters during the South African Invasion of German South West Africa, 1914–1915', *Scientia Militaria*, vol.28, no.1 (1998), p.98.

65 Oosthuizen, 'The Military Role of the Rehoboth Basters', p.98.

66 Oosthuizen, 'The Military Role of the Rehoboth Basters', pp.105–107.

67 TNA: CAB 45/112, Campaign in GSWA, Narrative of Events, 27 May 1915; 19 June 1915; Anon., *Official History*, p.32.

Africa, to help resolve the logistical issues around roads, bridges and railways.[68] Smuts focussed his mind to help solve their 'most difficult question', that of transport.[69] On his first day back from the campaign, on 14 May, Smuts wrote to Wolstenholme from Cape Town, lamenting that,

> …wild mobs are (as I write) surging through the streets around me to destroy property of German subjects as a reply to the sinking of the Lusitania. But effective measures have been taken to cope with this rioting. It has however been very bad these last few days in various parts of South Africa. Public indignation has been at white heat over the torpedoing of the Lusitania.[70]

Incensed at the anti-German riots, Botha declared to Trew: 'I hate mob law, it is always cruel, cowardly and unjust. What have the unfortunate German citizens in the Union to do with the policy of the German Government on the High Seas. If the cowards want to show their disgust at the sinking of the steamer let them enlist and go to France.'[71]

Botha worked out the supply and infrastructure equation while preparing for the final advance. He reduced the size of the mounted brigades from 2,500 to 1,500.[72] In considering the sandy terrain, he recommended that the waggons be pulled by 12 mules, as opposed to the earlier planned 11, to provide more power.[73] Botha inspected the railway reconstruction himself because he felt this was an essential component of infrastructure for the final advance. The gauge of the railway line had to be changed. The two-foot gauge was replaced by one of three-foot six inches, and Botha set the construction target of 3.2 kilometres per day.[74] The construction of the railway was one of the mission critical tasks done by People of Colour.[75] Botha, brimming with confidence, wrote Smuts:

68 DODA: DC, Box 252, 17138, Historical Record of the Campaign in GSWA, 4 November 1919; TNA: CAB 45/112, Campaign in GSWA, Narrative of Events, 27 May 1915.
69 Smuts to Wolstenholme, 14 May 1915 in Hancock and Van der Poel (eds.), *Selections*, vol. III, p.274.
70 Botha to Smuts, 7 March 1915 in Hancock and Van der Poel (eds.), *Selections*, vol. III, p.255.
71 Botha, cited in Trew, *Botha Treks*, p.134.
72 TNA CAB 45/112: Campaign in GSWA, Narrative of Events, 27 May 1915.
73 Botha and Smuts, 28 February 1915 in Hancock and Van der Poel (eds.), *Selections*, vol. III, p.249.
74 Botha to Smuts, 7 March 1915 in Hancock and Van der Poel (eds.), *Selections*, vol. III, p.255.
75 NARSSA: Smuts Papers, A1, 112, Major General Thompson, Report on visit to GSWA, 20-27 March 1915.

> I reckon that I shall have finished within a month … and should be very disappointed … if I were not on the way home within a month of my setting out. I shall have little or no time for writing during this period, and so I now bring a few points to your notice. You and our colleagues must now seriously begin to consider how we shall administer this territory until the future of this country is finally decided at the peace in Europe.[76]

In mid-June Botha indicated 'the chances of early success are dependent on whether the enemy mean to fight or retire'.[77] He added that if the Germans decided to retreat 'the nature of the country will prevent me stopping him from doing so unless he commits to an engagement in which case I hope to achieve good results if all goes well'.[78] At this point in the campaign Botha faced the Germans in the northeast of the colony. In the final advance he explained that they were in a strong defensive position at Kalkveld. He added that German preparation was not directly proportional to their will to fight and exclaimed, 'of course the enemy has already evacuated laboriously prepared defensive positions without fighting.'[79]

Botha prepared a central advance and a double envelopment to capture the final German positions. The envelopments were executed by Botha's trusted commanders, Brits and Myburgh. They were deployed on incredibly long and arduous marches to encircle and cut the retreat of the German forces. Not all commanders were happy with the manoeuvres – Botha struggled to hide his frustration, and wrote to Smuts, 'I am sorry to tell you that Lukin is already beginning to say that he cannot make the long marches … Collyer is his brother-in-law and is busy gingering him up so that he may still possibly get through. These people have so little courage.'[80]

Myburgh's force was deployed in a north-easterly direction towards Tsumeb and Brits's force in a northerly direction to take Namutoni.[81] This movement was planned to outmanoeuvre the German forces. Botha understood that he would lose contact with Brits and Myburgh as he sent them on their deployments to envelop the German position. One of the key parts of Botha and Smuts's style of war was that the

76 Botha and Smuts, 2 June 1915 in Hancock and Van der Poel (eds.), *Selections*, vol. III, p.291.
77 TNA CAB 45/112: Campaign in GSWA, Narrative of Events, 17 June 1915; DODA: DC, Box 252, 17138, Reports of Force Commanders in GSWA, Despatch No. 4 by General Botha, 15 May to 18 July 1915.
78 TNA CAB 45/112: Campaign in GSWA Narrative of Events, 17 June 1915.
79 DODA: DC, Box 252, 17138, Reports of Force Commanders in GSWA, Despatch 4 by General Botha 15 May to 18 July 1915; TNA CAB 45/112: Campaign in GSWA, Narrative of Events, 17 June 1915.
80 Botha and Smuts, 2 June 1915 in Hancock and Van der Poel (eds.), *Selections*, vol. III, p.291.
81 DODA: DC, Box 252, 17138, Reports of Force Commanders in GSWA, Despatch 4 by Botha 15 May to 18 July 1915.

subordinate commanders understood their intent and were allowed to use their initiative in achieving the objective.[82]

In order to secure victory, Botha had to prevent a retreat of the German forces through the Caprivi Strip to link up with the *schutztruppe* of Lettow-Vorbek in German East Africa. Reitz commented that Botha was apprehensive about the possibility that the German forces would retreat northwards and commence a guerrilla campaign. That would have extended the war considerably and have had a significant influence on Union politics as the National Party continued their line of severely criticising the expedition.[83] The divide in the Union reflected that in the UDF. Botha encapsulated this in a note to Smuts, 'I am sorry to have to say so, but you can have no idea how strong racial feeling still is here on both sides among our troops, and it is a fact with which we shall have to reckon.'[84]

Myburgh defeated the German force at Gaub on 2 July 1915 and then moved to Tsumeb.[85] The force under Brits advanced on Outjo. Brits and his men then proceeded to Namutoni towards the end of June 1915. The Germans at Namutoni surrendered to Brits on 8 July,[86] and the remaining German forces in the field had at this stage moved to Khorab where the final stand occurred.[87]

Botha planned a classic encirclement. He had the central force positioned at Otavifontein, while Myburgh and Brits had provided the double envelopment which had effectively isolated and encircled the German force. Botha and Seitz entered into negotiations for the surrender of the Germans. In previous discussions Botha had found Franke in a poor state of health and commented that his hands shook terribly. At the end, the fragile state of Franke's mind due to his alcohol and opium addiction,[88] was most likely transferred, in some part, to that of his psychologically debilitated force. Seitz, the German governor, accepted Botha's offer of unconditional surrender via letter at 0200 hours on 9 July 1915.[89]

82 DODA: DC, Box 252, 17138, Reports of Force Commanders in GSWA, Despatch 4 by General Botha 15 May to 18 July 1915; Collyer, *Campaign in German South West Africa*, p.133; Trew, *Botha Treks*, p.153; See A. Garcia, 'A Manouevre Warfare Analysis of South Africa's 1914–1915 German South West African Campaign', *Scientia Militaria*, vol.45, no.1 (2017).

83 Reitz, *Trekking On*, p.49. In terms of the practicality of this type of guerrilla operations, Botha opined that certain terrain types in South West Africa were well suited for rapid hit and run tactics: DODA: DC, Box 252, Despatch No. 4 by Botha, 15 May to 18 July 1915.

84 Botha and Smuts, 2 June 1915 in Hancock and Van der Poel (eds.), *Selections*, vol. III, p.291.

85 Trew, *Botha Treks*, p.159.

86 Meintjes, *Botha*, 269. On the military theory of the campaign, see A. Garcia, 'Manoeuvre Warfare in the South African Campaign in German South West Africa during the First World War', MA thesis, University of South Africa, 2015.

87 Anon., *Official History*, p.46.

88 Van der Waag, *A Military History*, p.95.

89 Trew, *Botha Treks*, p.175; DODA: DC, Box 252, 17138, Reports of Force Commanders in GSWA, Despatch No. 4 by General Botha covering the period 15 May to 18 July 1915.

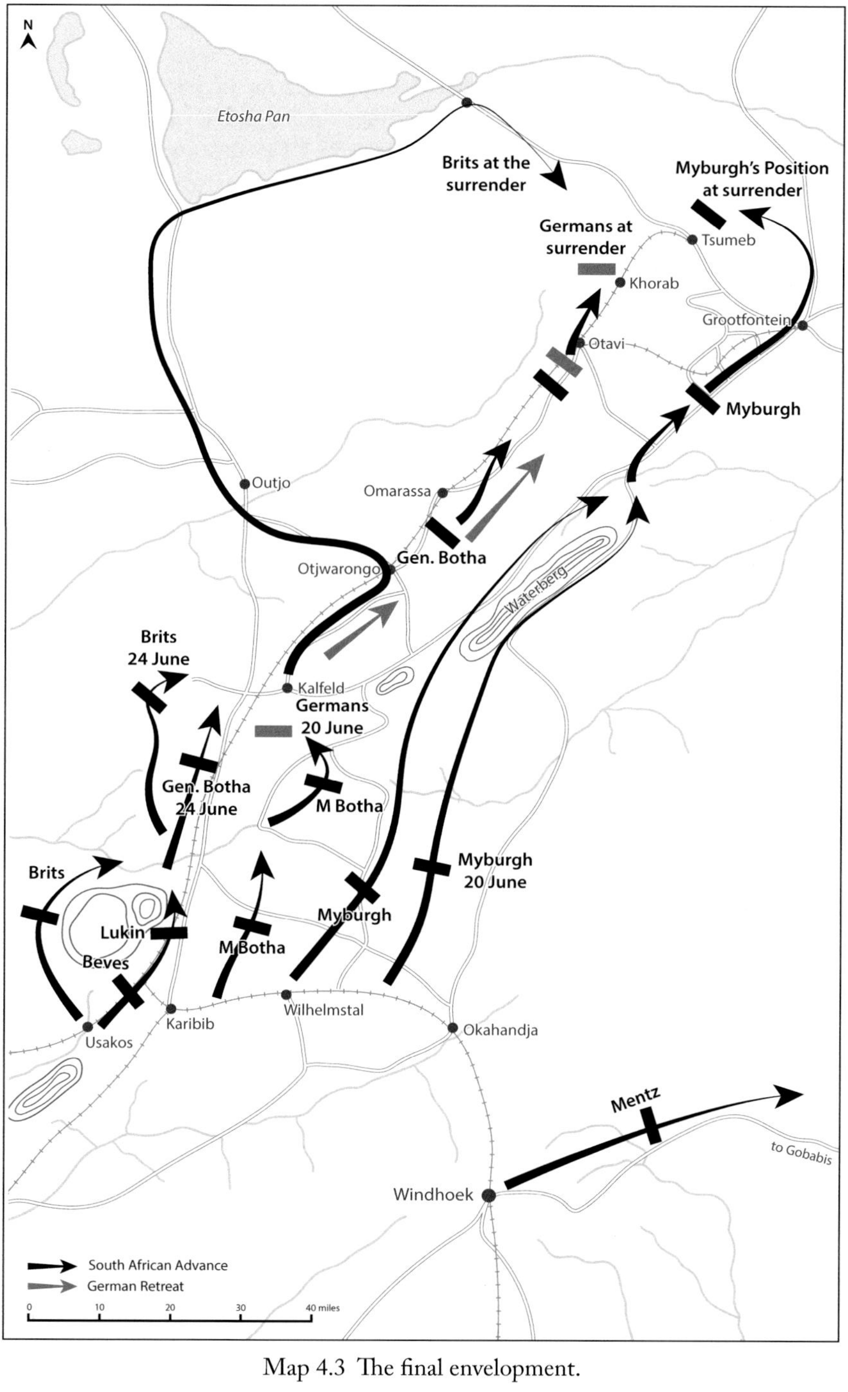

Map 4.3 The final envelopment.

Botha met with Colonel Franke to discuss the terms. An armistice was arranged prior to the final surrender. Botha claims to have specifically excluded the movements of Brits and Myburgh.[90] Franke contested this and claimed that the armistice was for all forces including those under Brits and Myburgh. There may have been some sort of deception on the part of Botha who claimed that the agreed armistice did not include the enveloping forces.[91] There is no evidence to suggest he intentionally deceived Franke, however, the logic does not ring true that an armistice would have included certain forces whilst excluding others. It seems more feasible that Botha was unable to contact his mobile enveloping forces prior to their engagement with the *schutztruppe* based at Tsumeb and Namutoni. It was also in Botha's favour to have the German forces surrounded and cut off so as to ensure a decisive victory.

The German capitulation included approximately 4,000 officers and men with 30 artillery pieces.[92] Botha later claimed that 5,995 German soldiers surrendered throughout the campaign of which 1,225 were captured prior to the final surrender, and 4,740 put down their arms at the last stand.[93] Directly after the campaign, messages of congratulation flooded in from all over the Union.[94] The peace terms were lenient and he allowed all reservists to return home.[95] Many were farmers and this chimed with Botha and Smuts's experience. Botha and Smuts's leniency may have derived from their experiences at the Peace of Vereeniging, but no doubt also reflected Botha's gentleness. German South West Africa became a protectorate under South Africa, which was run initially by a military governor and later an administrator.[96]

Botha did not want to damage the territory and intended to adopt the German colonists as Union subjects. Botha and Smuts were also sensitive to the humanitarian needs of the Ovambo people who faced a food shortage after the cessation of hostilities. The Botha administration created a relief programme that provided food in return for labour and through these efforts, pioneered largely by Smuts, many lives were saved. Furthermore, as a way to alleviate economic suffering, the Botha-Smuts government relocated poor Afrikaner families to South West Africa.[97]

Botha and Smuts had the Union and South West Africa linked by a railway network as an operational requirement of the invasion. The technical detail of the

90 DODA: DC, Box 252, 17138, Reports of Force Commanders in GSWA, Despatch No. 4 by General Botha covering the period 15 May to 18 July 1915.
91 DODA: DC, Box 252Correspondence between General Botha and Lieutenant Colonel Franke on the subject of a breach of armistice by Union troops at Tsumeb, 6 July 1915.
92 Trew, *Botha Treks*, p.169.
93 NARSSA: Preller Archive, 90, 606, Article, *Rand Daily Mail*, 14 March 1916.
94 TNA CAB 45/112: Campaign in GSWA 1914-1918, Narrative of Events, July 1915.
95 Smuts to Merriman, 10 July 1915 in Hancock and Van der Poel (eds.), *Selections*, vol. III, p.304.
96 TNA CAB 45/112: Campaign in GSWA 1914-1918, Narrative of Events, 30 October 1915.
97 Nasson, *World War 1 and the People of South Africa*, pp.83–85.

railway project is discussed at length by Major A.J. Beaton.[98] The rail system represented a political move at territorial acquisition and allowed access to the hinterland of its new 'administrative area'.[99]

The German South West African campaign and the Afrikaner Rebellion solidified Botha's reputation as a general of great skill and Smuts as a supreme administrator. Botha had previously declined all imperial honours and an offer of a peerage. The only tribute that appealed to him was the title general. In 1907, after being named as premier of the Transvaal, Lord Selborne asked Botha if he would like to be officially recognised as 'general' in the British press. Botha gladly accepted Selborne's offer.[100] Initially the British were opposed to considering the Boer generals as 'real' generals. The title was formalised in 1911, when Botha accepted an honorary generalship – he said it was the one title his people would understand and he believed this solidified his position as 'the general'.[101] Botha lived up to this title, and Smuts gave a fine display.

Botha's skill in generalship was based on the tradition of the commando system.[102] He had a clear vision of what it took to gain a victory and in his reports and citations he states the campaign met with success because of the speed and surprise of the encircling actions of Brits and Myburgh.[103] Botha was conscious of the need to allow his subordinate commanders to operate in a decentralised manner, using their own initiative within the framework of his overall intent.[104] Whittal, the commander of the Royal Naval Armoured Car Squadron suggests that it was in fact Botha's 'elastic' military training (a reference to the Anglo-Boer War), which gave him the insight to complete the campaign in a rapid and efficient manner.[105] The campaign, drew wide interest, not only from observers, commentators and military historians but also from participants in the campaign. Authors such as Whittal, Trew, Ritchie and Collyer were present on the battlefield and have captured the motivations of all those involved.[106]

98 A.J. Beaton, 'Notes on Railway Construction during the Campaign in German South West Africa', *Civil Engineering*, vol.14, no.1 (1916).
99 G. Miescher, 'Arteries of Empire: On the Geographical Imagination of South Africa's Railway War, 1914/1915', *Kronos*, vol.38, no.1 (2012), p.24.
100 Selborne to Lady Selboure, 21 March 1907 in Boyce, *Naval Papers of Selborne*, p.317.
101 Meintjes, *Botha*, p.183.
102 Van der Waag, 'Boer Generalship', *passim.*
103 DODA: WW1 GSWA, Box 23a, Citations GSWA, Northern Army, Commander of the 1st Mounted Brigade Special Appointments, 17 February 1918; Reports of Force Commanders in GSWA, Despatch No. 4 by General Botha covering the period 15 May to 18 July 1915; Collyer, *Campaign in German South West Africa*, p.114.
104 DODA: DC, Box 252, 1713, General Botha's Despatch (GOC MC GSW Campaign) 9 July to 28 October 1920, Historical Record of the Campaign in GSWA, 4 November 1919; DODA: DC, Box 252, 17138, IO.
105 Whittal, *With Botha and Smuts in Africa*, p.4.
106 Collyer, *Campaign in German South West Africa*; Whittal, *With Botha and Smuts in Africa*; Trew, *Botha Treks*; Ritchie, *With Botha in the Field*; Walker, *A Doctor's Diary in Damaraland*; Reitz, *Trekking On*; P.K.J. Robinson, *With Botha's Army* (London: Allen &

The commander of Botha's bodyguard, Trew, was of the opinion that Botha showed skills equal to the great captains of war and demonstrated genius in his campaign.[107] Where Trew may have had a definite bias towards Botha, Collyer puts forward what is perhaps a more logical insight, that Botha combined strategic and tactical abilities in a way that many generals could not.[108] Trew asks whether historians would regard Botha as a great captain of war.[109] In reaction to this the current authors agree that there is a strong argument that Botha does indeed meet the requirements of a great historical commander. He certainly demonstrated qualities such as leadership, ingenuity, decisiveness, power of personality and charisma, as well as an understanding of his forces and those of the enemy, as well as how to deploy them.[110]

Botha's success was underpinned by Smuts – his unofficial chief of staff, his second in command and master administrator: he led the ministry of defence, he was a staff system embodied in a single man, he pulled together logistic and planning threads integrating a number of workstreams; he commanded the Southern Army, was a sounding board to Botha; served a communication function, linking with the governor general, British, and South African (White) society. Smuts learned some lessons in strategy and tactics, through his experience in South West Africa – these underpinned his experience in the Anglo Boer War. But perhaps some of the learning in an 'easier' campaign, created a false expectation.

During the campaign, Botha made use of the embryonic Aviation Corps, which conducted forward reconnaissance and rudimentary bombing. The aerial reconnaissance helped shape Botha's intelligence picture.[111] Smuts would go on to write a key

Unw in 1916); W.W. O'Shaughnessy and W.S. Rayner, *How Botha and Smuts Conquered German South West* (London: Simpk in 1916); L'ange, *Urgent Imperial Service*; H. Strachan, *The First World War, Vol. 1: To Arms* (Oxford: Oxford University Press, 2001), T.R. Ungleich, 'The Defence of German South West Africa during World War I', MA thesis, University of Miami, 1974; A. Cruise, *Louis Botha's War: The Campaign in German South West Africa, 1914–1915* (Johannesburg: Zebra, 2015); Van der Waag, *A Military History*; A. Delport, ''Boks and Bullets, Coffins and Crutches': An Exploration of the Body, Mind and Places of 'Springbok' South African Soldiers in the First World War', MA thesis, Stellenbosch University, 2015; Nasson, *World War 1 and the People of South Africa*; A. Samson, *World War I in Africa: The Forgotten Conflict among European Powers* (London: I.B. Taurus, 2013).

107 Trew, *Botha Treks*, p.vi.

108 Collyer, *Campaign in German South West Africa*, p.168.

109 Trew, *Botha Treks*, p.vi.

110 Garcia, *First Campaign Victory*, p.195.

111 DODA: WW1 WD, Box 2, Air/1/1247/204/7/4, Historical record of No. 26 (SA) Squadron South African Aviation Corps and Historical record of the South Africa unit of the Royal Flying Corps; WW1 WD, Box 1, Air 1/1247/204/7/1, Report by Major Wallace on the campaign in GSWA, 1915, 21 July 1916; Air 1/1247/204/7/1 vol.2, Aviation report on GSWA, April 1915–1916, Report of Transport Officer. See A. Garcia, 'Airpower in the Union of South Africa's First World War Campaign in German South West Africa', *Historia*, vol. 62, no. 2 (2017).

report which was critical to the establishment of the Royal Air Force.[112] In the area of international and organisational strategy, Smuts was almost unrivalled.

It is also true to say that Botha and Smuts, although at different levels, had experience of holding a defensive position against an advancing force. This was the case on the Tugela Line, and although Botha put up a splendid defence, which gave him a platform for his military career, eventually the position was turned. Botha's position in the German South West African campaign, was the reverse of his previous experience – he now invaded with the stronger force while his enemy was on the defensive. Smuts's role in the Anglo-Boer War involved mobile operations, largely with a company sized force of around 400 *burghers*, showing dash, and valour. The command of a much larger force in the suppression of the Afrikaner Rebellion and the invasion of German South West Africa taught Smuts about the logistical challenges of supply and the organisational requirements of a large army. Botha's critical note to Smuts showed some of the limitations in his operational thinking, but this should not detract from his overall ability and performance. Rather this should be seen as two generals advising each other. The application of the South African forces allowed for the execution of a rapid campaign, which can be compared to manoeuvre warfare.[113] The successful speedy completion of the campaign had the additional benefit of saving money. Buxton, a proud governor-general, commented that the cost of the campaign had been £15 million, which equated to the approximate cost of three days total warfare expense for the British Empire.[114]

Buxton congratulated Botha and Smuts on their achievement, and while he congratulated Botha 'very heartily on the admirable conduct and success of the whole campaign'[115], he enthused more when writing to Smuts three days later:

> I want to send you a personal line of congratulations on the ending – the very successful ending – of the G.S.W. affair. It has been a very big job and one fraught with special difficulties. Your share in the whole affair has been splendid. The organisation has been wonderfully good – especially as so much of the machinery had to be improvised.[116]

The governor general recognised the different roles the two former Boer generals had played. Botha, the large, personable magnet, the general and commander had drawn his followers together, while Smuts, the *éminence grise* – with the assistance of Roland Bourne, and others – had refashioned the defence force as a useful instrument of government and imperial policy, even if an exercise in improvisation. The

112 Royal Air Force Museum Archive (RAFMA): Report by General Smuts on Air Organisation and the Direction of Aerial Operations, August 1917.
113 See Garcia, 'Manoeuvre Warfare'.
114 BL: Add. MS 87042, Buxton Papers 1915-1924, Report on GSWA, 1919.
115 BL: Add MS 86963, Buxton Papers, Buxton to Botha, 6 July 1915.
116 BL: Add MS 86963, Buxton to Smuts, 9 July 1915.

strain, as Buxton noted, had indeed been tremendous, but Botha and Smuts – and perhaps the country – had withstood it. It secured Botha's credentials as a man of action and a competent and respected general, and Smuts as a supreme military and civil administrator.

Botha – the romantic general of 1907 who first represented the Transvaal as its prime minister in London – appeared to have been re-invented.[117] But with the success of the German South West African campaign, he became the romantic general of the British Commonwealth of Nations.[118] Smuts was even closer to the British Empire, and they soon came knocking on his door with requests for his service in other theatres and London. Smuts became the bridge to the Empire at war. Their popularity in the British Empire, did not necessarily translate into the same in South Africa.

Conclusion

The divide between the Botha-Smuts government and Hertzog split the Afrikaans-speaking South African population down the middle, and where many supported the government, there were also many who opposed it. The Afrikaner Rebellion of 1914 was a result of underlying issues in South African society, including poverty, relative deprivation, diverging goals and dissatisfied leaders – issues that were triggered by the Union's entry into the First World War.[119] There was a price for a united Boer and British South Africa, and this included a war, on both military and political fronts.

F.S. Malan, a member of Botha's cabinet, was at first reluctant to become involved in the First World War on Britain's behalf and said that by committing South Africa to the war, Botha risked losing the sentiment of the Afrikaner people.[120] Malan was proved correct. Botha and Smuts, took possession of German South West Africa in the interests of the Union. They hoped that their military victory would build the relationship between Boer and Briton. In respect to Botha's previous experience, the invasion and conquest of German South West Africa reflected his exploits with Meyer's commando in Zululand where the reward for their efforts was The New Republic: a long-standing legacy of Boer and African war and politics. In 1907 Sir W. Hely-Hutchinson wrote to Lord Selborne saying that Botha committed himself as an imperialist and would not be able to extricate himself if he tried.[121] If Botha

117 NARSSA: Preller Archives, 96, *Westminster Gazette*, 13 April 1907, 'Imperial Conference', *Sphere*, 13 April 1907, 'General Louis Botha's Arrival'.
118 Western Cape Archives (WCA), Kilpin Collection, A1456, 'Empire's most Romantic Figure', *Cape Times*, 30 August 1919.
119 Reitz, *Trekking On*, p.48.
120 I. van der Waag, 'All Splendid, but Horrible: The Politics of South Africa's Second 'Little Bit' and the War on the Western Front, 1915–1918', *Scientia Militaria: South African Journal of Military Studies*, vol.40 no.3 (2012), p.76.
121 Hely-Hutchinson to Selborne, 18 April 1907 in Boyce, *Naval Papers of Selborne*, p.319.

was an imperialist, in the view of Hely-Hutchison, then Smuts certainly would be one too. Spies argues that territorial aggrandisement was the primary motivating factor for Botha.[122] Most Botha and Smuts biographers agree that the campaign in German South-West Africa added to the territorial acquisitions of the Union. An earlier example, which is perhaps indicative of a trend was that in 1908 when Botha and Smuts tried to exert control over Swaziland and Basutoland, however this proved unsuccessful.[123] Reitz said that Botha was 'fighting for a territory which he regarded as part of his own territory'.[124] The capture of the German colonies was a part of the British imperial strategy and placed conquered territories at the disposal of the Crown.[125]

The conquest of German South West Africa was criticised and proved to be a recurring motif for the National Party, all of which put great strain on Botha's emotional endurance. Smuts wrote to Merriman, 'The German surrender has already had a marked effect on our local Hertzogites. Poor things! They seem to have been looking all the time for some serious reverse to come!'[126] But the political war was still ongoing, and the 1915 election was the next hurdle.

122 Spies, 'The Outbreak of WWI', p.52.
123 Selborne to Lady Selborne, 23 August 1908 in Boyce, *Naval Papers of Selborne*, p.379.
124 Reitz, *Trekking On*, p.48.
125 Spies, 'The Outbreak of WW1', p.48.
126 Smuts to Merriman, 10 July 1915 in Hancock and Van der Poel (eds.), *Selections*, vol. III, p.304.

5

Domestic Politics, 1915

Are you the General Botha of the Tugela? … Yes. Botha.[1]

Botha returned as the conquering hero from the German South West Africa campaign in July 1915, he joined Smuts who was keeping the administrative machine well oiled; and together they planned and fought a tough election campaign. It was an uphill battle, fending off attacks from the National Party on the one hand and dealing with Unionist demands on the other. Botha and Smuts faced the stark reality of flagging support for their party.

The Botha–Smuts government was nearing the end of its life. They were convinced that they would win, but the election was to be contested with much bitterness. The National Party, established in January 1914, had used the intervening years to organise itself and its offensive was targeted directly at Botha and Smuts.[2] Of course with the recent history of the Anglo-Boer War and the horrendous concentration camps, it did not take much to convince the Boers that the British did not have their best interests at heart. By late 1916, Botha saw a caption of a cartoon in the newspapers and identifying with the words wrote to Smuts that in South Africa it was 'always one damn thing after another.'[3] Those 'damned things' were what embittered Botha in his last term as prime minister of the Union, from 1915 until his passing.

From Battlefield to Electoral Campaign

Botha, who was the face of the South African Party, started a non-stop election campaign which took him to public meetings, military parades, and other events.

1 NARSSA: Preller Archive, 93, Botha quoted in 'General Botha's Tour', *The Star*, 3 September 1915.
2 Meintjes, *Botha*, p.274.
3 Botha to Smuts, 2 June 1916 in Hancock and Van der Poel (eds), *Selections*, vol. III, pp.370–372.

He opened the Pretoria agricultural show in August 1915 and told the crowd that it made him happy to be close to his profession. He went on to say that there was no profession, in his opinion, as fine and noble as that of the farmer, adding that 'the farmer was in effect a small king in his own domain'.[4] Lord Selborne, the trim well turned-out High Commissioner to South Africa, claimed that Botha was a true farmer at heart and an efficient one at that. Sir Walter Hely-Hutchinson, the colonial administrator, and former Governor to the Cape Colony, agreed with Selborne, adding that in 1907 Botha was the appropriate choice for premier and minister of agriculture.[5] In his address at the SAP congress of 1915, Botha made special mention of the Irrigation and Conservation of Waters Act, 1912, the Hartebeespoort Irrigation Scheme Act, 1914 (on the Crocodile River), and the Land Bank Act of 1912. These were key additions to the body of legislation as far as the agricultural industry of South Africa was concerned.[6] Selborne adding, that in terms of agriculture, Botha was a progressive.[7]

Botha maintained a close eye on matters of farming, and in fact in later years it was an agricultural issue, the question of the wool clip, that landed Botha in deep water with South African farmers. See Chapter 9 for further discussion. The wool clip was one extra weight added to Botha's heavy load – in despair and downtrodden from years of political haranguing, failing health and constant criticism, he exclaimed to Buxton: 'I am worried to death about the wool question. I might have to resign.'[8] The voice of this weary and despondent Botha was very different from the triumphant conquering hero who returned from German South West Africa in 1915.

Much of Botha's electioneering was based on his military prowess and the success of the recent campaign. Botha and Smuts attended a public meeting attended by some 4,000 people in Johannesburg, where Botha praised those who had served in the campaign for their valour. Botha thanked those who were part of the military parade and went on to say that the infantry had faced the hardest task of all – collectively they had been required to take 300 million steps in a dry and desolate terrain.[9] On a separate occasion and in keeping with support to the military, Botha addressed the men of the 2nd Brigade in early August and denigrated those who tried to lead the UDF men astray calling them 'Khaki Tommies'. He added that despite these false

4 NARSSA: Preller Archive, 90, Botha quoted in 'the Agricultural Show', *Transvaal Chronicle*, 2 August 1915.
5 Hely-Hutchinson to Selborne, 18 April 1907 in Boyce, *Naval Papers of Selborne*, p.319.
6 UNISA: United Party Archives, South African Party Central Congress, 1911–1923, 2, Address by General Botha, August 1915. See also BL: Add MS 86963, Buxton Papers, Secret note, Durban, 4 July 1915.
7 UCT: Duncan Papers, Box 95, File BC 694, D 6.3.4, Selborne to Duncan, 8 July 1907.
8 BL: Add MS 87052, Buxton Papers, 1914–1918, Botha to Buxton, 21 December 1917.
9 NARSSA: Preller Archive, 90, Botha quoted in 'Generaal Botha te Johannesburg', *De Volksstem*, 6 August 1915.

claims, 'thank God we have done our duty and our conscience is clear. We have saved the honour of our people'.[10]

This was Botha and Smuts the men of principle who believed that South Africans had done their duty in German South West Africa; they had promoted nation building, by fighting a common enemy. They stressed that the Defence Force had 'gained a territory' which added status, economic opportunity and pride to the Union of South Africa.[11] In preparation for the elections and readjusting to the evolving political landscape, Botha addressed the SAP conference in August 1915. He took stock of the recent history of South Africa, its complex problems, and its valuable achievements:

> I think that I can say without fear of contradiction that in South Africa, in any case, no administration has taken the reins of government under more difficult conditions than my colleagues and myself (cheers). To bring into being the Union and to unify into one administration the four different governments was a gigantic task. Prejudices and provincial feelings became stronger … twice over this period ministerial crises broke out … industrial problems which led to rioting … the greatest calamity came with the outbreak of the war and the rebellion … we have had challenges … but I believe everyone will agree the Union has been a decided success.[12]

Botha's final statement could have been rephrased in the form of a question. The cheers of his party may have helped him in the moment, but perhaps Botha was attempting to convince himself that things were not as bad as they were. He had previously suffered the effects of hubris in running and losing to Percy Fitzpatrick in Pretoria East. Smuts knew that they were walking a tightrope but all they could do was push forward – they had already staked so much in their policy. Smuts conveyed his concern to Merriman in May 1915, 'It is a great pity that we shall have to hold a general election at a time when the currents of passionate, poisoned feeling are running so high.'[13] Roderick Jones, the Reuters man in Cape Town, was 'glad to see that Smuts, contrary to the general belief regarding himself, quite realises the force and extent of this Hertzog wave through the Union'.[14] A 'decided success' was perhaps an overstatement, as Botha and Smuts's problems within Afrikanerdom were mirrored in the capitalist and mining sector.

10 NARSSA: Preller Archive, 90, Botha quoted in 'Our Mushroom Christians', *Rand Daily Mail*, 7 August 1915.
11 NARSSA: Preller Archive, 93, Botha quoted in 'Coming Elections', *The Star*, 3 September 1915.
12 UNISA: South African Party Central Congress, 1911–1923, 2, Address by General Botha, August 1915.
13 Smuts to Merriman, 25 May 1915 in Hancock and Van der Poel (eds), *Selections*, vol. III, p.285.
14 BL: Add MS 86963, Buxton Papers, Roderick Jones to Buxton, 2 July 1915.

At the conference, Botha, in a roundabout way, addressed the matter of the miners' strikes in 1913 and the railway strike of 1914. The miners' strikes had been a serious cause of concern for the Botha-Smuts government. The first time this occurred Botha and Smuts were perhaps not fully aware of the power of militant labour. They signed a deal with labour which tilted the balance of power in favour of the worker. This did not sit well with Botha but even less so with an indignant Smuts. On the second occasion, during the coal mining and railway strike which took place towards the end of 1913 and the early months of 1914, Botha and Smuts took decisive action, suppressing any strike action through the deployment of the Active Citizen Force, a new form of the commandos, British imperial forces, and the trusted commandants of old led by the indomitable General de la Rey. Smuts then proceeded to deport the ringleaders on the most dubious of legal basis.

Legalities were the least of Botha and Smuts's worries, and they had a tendency to manage the legal frameworks to suit their needs.[15] Olive Schreiner, the South African author and anti-war campaigner, criticised Botha's use of British military units to quell the strike, saying it was an attempt to shift the blame from the Boer to the English forces.[16] This was most likely not the case. It was probable that Botha and Smuts wanted the strikes quashed with the least amount of political backlash and the deployment of commandos and British forces served the purpose of providing a strong and racially 'balanced' force.[17] South Africa depended heavily on mining, and it was within a milieu of industrialisation and capitalisation that Botha held power. Although the macroeconomic interests of the Botha-Smuts government were non-negotiable, the prime minister always had space for human needs, and this too applied to the health concerns of miners.

The rank and file of the strike were largely British immigrants who were frustrated by the taxing conditions and high likelihood of death from miners' phthisis.[18] In response the government passed sound legislation such as the promulgation of the Workmen's Compensation Act and the Miner's Phthisis Act. These statutes were aimed at assisting the workers.[19] The Phthisis Act, was first promulgated in 1912, following a report from a Commission on Miners' Phthisis and Pulmonary Tuberculosis and aimed to prevent the disease through the control of harmful dust entering the airways of the miners. Benefits were paid out to sufferers. This was

15 Krüger, *Age of the Generals*, pp.75–76.
16 UCT: Olive Schreiner, BC16 Box 5, Olive Schreiner to William Schreiner, 17 July 1913.
17 Racially balanced in the context of the time and from the viewpoint of Botha and Smuts, having Boer and British forces.
18 B. Freund, 'South Africa: The Union Years' in R. Ross, A.K. Mager and B. Nasson (eds), *The Cambridge History of South Africa, Vol.2, 1885–1994* (Cambridge: Cambridge University Press, 2012), p.212.
19 UNISA: South African Party Central Congress, 1911–1923, 2, Address by General Botha, August 1915. See also TNA CO 632: Colonial Dominion Office (hereafter CDO), Union of South Africa Acts, 1910–1925.

coupled with the Workmen's Compensation Act which between 1912 and 1916, paid out funds to 6,472 workers who had been forced into retirement from mining. The lessons learned from South Africa informed British studies in occupational health and mining.[20]

While Botha and Smuts's efforts in farming and the mining industry were progressive, their politics was defined by compromise and racial paternalism. In some ways it may have been forward thinking for its time, but it was also traditional in many ways – a case in point was the appalling 1913 Native Land Act, a legislative decision that reshaped South Africa. The Land Act redrew the lines of power and opportunity, and the impact on Blacks, Coloureds, and Indians was devastating although it varied in severity depending on the province. The Free State was the worst hit, and Blacks who had previously owned land, or had a position of power, even if limited, were reduced to servants and labourers – it was a form of indenture.[21] Sol Plaatje was devastated by what he witnessed in the Free State – 'the great rural spasm' something vividly illustrated in his book.[22]

In his address to the South African Party, Botha said that the passing of the Native Land Act of 1913, was a 'statesmanlike' way of addressing rising tensions between People of Colour and Whites.[23] A rather curious way to refer to the side-lining and oppression of the majority of people in South Africa. The Land Act elicited strong opposition from the founders, and members of the SANNC including John Dube, Pixley Seme, Sol Plaatje and Richard Thema, who had initially held off critiquing the statute in order to stand in solidarity with the war effort.[24] Merriman considering the practicalities stated that he hoped that the Land Act would not result in a Black uprising.[25] Botha's so called 'statesmanlike' approach to People of Colour was widely criticised by liberal voices; indicting him for taking decisions of political expediency without principle – Olive Schreiner thought it 'shameful'.[26]

An earlier version of the Native Land Act was put forward at the Inter-Colonial Conference of 1903–1905 which was set up by Lord Milner.[27] The final product the Land Act of 1913 was monumental – for the first time in South African history,

20 A. Meiklejohn, 'The Development of Compensation for Occupational Diseases of the Lungs in Great Britain', *British Journal of Industrial Medicine*, vol.11 (1954), pp.199–200.
21 Willan, *Sol Plaatje*, p.330.
22 H. Hughes, *First President: A Life of John Dube, Founding President of the ANC* (Johannesburg: Jacana, 2011), p.180.
23 UNISA: South African Party Central Congress, 1911–1923, 2, Address by General Botha, August 1915.
24 Willan, *Sol Plaatje*, p.324.
25 Merriman to Smuts, 22 February 1917 in Hancock and Van der Poel (eds), *Selections*, vol. III, p.452.
26 Harry Ransom Center, University of Texas, Austin (HRC): Olive Schreiner Letters Schreiner to John Hodgson, 5 April 1917.
27 E.H. Brookes, 'General Louis Botha', *Theoria: A Journal of Social and Political Theory*, vol.13 (1959), p.6.

land was divided on a racial basis. Plaatje and John Dube, a founding member of the SANNC, educator, essayist, linguist and scholar, were far from happy. They were told that the Land Act was not intended to be the final say on the matter but was a temporary solution to be revisited. Botha referred to this caveat in correspondence with the Inter Denominational Conference of Native Ministers and Christians of South Africa, stating that the Land Act was not envisaged as the conclusion of the matter. It was a temporary solution, subject to further amendment.[28] The eminent historian D.W. Krüger postulates that the outbreak of the First World War led to the Land Act being kept as is, and the matter was never revisited.[29] This was more than likely a delaying tactic, kicking the issue down the road with no intention of changing it.

To some extent Plaatje believed Botha was forced into passing the legislation by the republican Afrikaner section. The truth is that Botha and Smuts held the belief of racial superiority – they were not going to fight for equality – they were after all traditional and paternalistic Afrikaners even though one was kind and charming, and the other smart and decisive, they were men of their time. Buxton was of the opinion that, 'Botha was trusted by the natives'[30], but neither Botha nor Smuts acted in their best interests, but rather used any trust and influence for their interests. A case in point and also demonstrating the power dynamic was where Botha told Plaatje that he should focus on recruitment for the war effort as 'this would help the native people better than any propaganda work (against the Land Act)'.[31]

Botha and Smuts were racists, at least by the standards of modern times. Botha had sanctioned attacks, although indirectly, on African groupings during the Anglo-Boer War; he was opposed to Black political franchise and was paternalistic. The Natives Land Act formalised the views of the majority of Whites in South Africa, and where there were voices in opposition, they were too few. Dube put a petition to Botha citing their grievances with the Land Act. Dube had toured the country finding evidence of the destruction and poverty caused by the legislation. He wrote to Botha stating that he preferred to resolve the matter in the Union, but if needed the SANNC would take the issue to London.[32] Botha and Smuts held all the cards and when the SANNC met with the Secretary of State for Colonies, Lewis Harcourt, a colleague of Botha it was clear that he would run interference. Harcourt held the line of the SAP government, denying every request of the SANNC – he had no intention of putting Botha in a difficult or embarrassing position. When the SANNC deputation asked to meet with the King Botha intervened again. He blocked Plaatje and other SANNC representatives from meeting the King, stating that 'no useful purpose

28 NARSSA: Preller Archive, 106, Botha quoted in Fair Play and Justice', *Rand Daily Mail*, 29 July 1919.
29 Krüger, *Age of the Generals*, p.63.
30 BL: Add MS 87085: Buxton Papers, Buxton on Botha, Notes, undated.
31 Botha quoted in Willan, *Sol Plaatje*, p.331.
32 Hughes, *First President*, pp.180–182.

will be served... the result might be an inconvenient precedent for the future.'[33] The Land Act was destined to have devastating consequences for the future of People of Colour in South Africa, and the statute would forever remain the legacy of Botha and Smuts. In 1915 the SANNC and Plaatje held back from strong and vocal attacks on the Botha-Smuts government – they believed the tactical move was to support the war effort. Hoping for franchise and opportunity they held off, but their efforts went unrewarded. In 1915, Botha and Smuts were given a reprieve and focussed on the election. But from late 1916 onwards Plaatje, Dube and other would become more and more vocal on the government's policies.

Meintjes suggests that in his election campaign Botha held over 30 meetings between 21 August and 21 September, addressing a range of different crowds.[34] In fact Botha's election campaign continued into October with political gatherings taking place in Kroonstad and Ladybrand amongst other places.[35] In an attempt to rally support, he spoke of all that had been achieved by the Union.[36] The prime minister spoke of the duty to the Crown; of Maritz's complicity with the Germans from 1913 onwards, and the duty and honour of South Africans to the war. Botha was at pains to refute National Party accusations that he commandeered forces to suppress the rebellion.[37] Botha and Smuts counted on their military victory to gain votes, and the Nationalists questioned the validity and necessity of the campaign – they pushed back against the war effort from the start.

A case in point was the commission of inquiry into war stores which took place during the last week of March 1915. Materials had been bought for the German South West African campaign and the quashing of the Rebellion – this bolstered the materiel provided by the War Office. The Nationalists refused to cooperate during parliamentary recess, spending their time on the organisation of their Party.[38] Politically it was fair play, and they made political capital.[39] The Nationalists would later become the voice piece of anyone who felt hard done by the war effort. A poor administrative system was mostly to blame but the government could not get away from the point that they had not paid all of their bills. Henry Dickson, a wagoner from Paarl, supplied the Department of Defence with wagons at the request of the

33 Botha quoted in Willan, *Sol Plaatje*, p.268.
34 Botha quoted in Meintjes, *Botha*, p.276.
35 NARSSA: Preller Archive, 93, General Botha at Ladybrand', *Rand Daily Mail*, 30 September 1915; 'We shall Win', *Rand Daily Mail*, 1 October 1915; 'Generaal Botha te Potchefstroom', *De Burger*, 4 October 1915; 'Noisy Meeting at Bloemhof', *Rand Daily Mail*, 13 October 1915.
36 Botha quoted in Meintjes, *Botha*, p.276.
37 Botha quoted in NARSSA: Preller Archive, 90. 'A Straight Lead', *The Sunday Times*, 21 August 1915.
38 DODA: DC, Box 1, file 12, Members who took part in debate in Parliament Carel Britz to Secretary, War Stores Commission, 26 Jun 1915.
39 DODA: DC, Box 1, file 12, Members who took part in debate in Parliament Henry Dickson to Secretary, War Stores Commission, 18 Sep 1915.

Director of Transport, but, despite his claims, never received a reply. By September 1915 he threatened, unless he received immediate satisfaction, to furnish all of the information about the wrongs he had suffered 'through your action' to the National Party members of parliament.[40] There were significant allegations of mismanagement, financial irregularities and bribery against the Director of Transport and Remounts of the Permanent Force Colonel C.V. Hosken.[41]

These accusations of corruption were brought up in the initial draft of the war stores official report. When the report was internally circulated in 1916, H.R.M. Bourne the secretary for defence was outraged and voiced his feeling to Botha and Smuts, 'The report, however, adopts a disgraceful line in mentioning names of officers against whom "there are reasonable suspicions of bribery" but no evidence. I do not think the Government can make that portion public.'[42]

A Changing Political Landscape

Botha and Smuts, cast one eye on the internal running of the UDF, but maintained their focus on the election – their narrative of duty and honour played to the British ear, and suited the Unionists and elements of Labour as well as many Blacks, Coloureds, and Indians. Try as he may, Botha and Smuts's retelling of history did not sit well with republican-minded Afrikaners. They received taunts and insults from Nationalist audiences. They were blamed for the deaths of De la Rey, Beyers, Fourie and other rebel leaders. Botha was tested to the limit. It was to the advantage of the Nationalist narrative to place the deaths of all three leaders at the feet of Botha and Smuts. De la Rey was a stalwart of the old system, a leader, a general and a man of considerable influence. Botha always spoke highly of him, and Buxton quotes the prime minister as saying, 'He [De la Rey] was the best soldier I had ever met, and the bravest man'.[43] His death although tragic, and according to Botha a 'tremendous blow',[44] most likely saved the Botha government from a wider-scale uprising at a time when the Afrikaner Rebellion was gathering momentum.[45]

40 DODA: DC, box 1, file 12 Members who took part in debate in Parliament, Henry Dickson, Wagon Builder, Paarl, to the Secretary of the War Stores Commission, 18 September 1915.
41 Bourne to Smuts, 14 April 1916 in Hancock and Van der Poel (eds), *Selections*, vol. III, p.360.
42 Botha to Smuts, 23 March 1916 and Bourne to Smuts, 14 April 1916 in Hancock and Van der Poel (eds), *Selections*, vol. III, pp.360–361.
43 Botha quoted in S.C. Buxton, *General Botha*, (London: Hazel, Watson & Viney, 1924), p.234.
44 NARSSA: Leyds Archive, 262, Part II, Botha to Leyds, 6 October 1914.
45 Krüger, *Age of the Generals*, p.87.

Beyers's mutinous act was termed 'deplorable' by Botha[46] and Merriman called his actions 'a very curious sense of military duty'.[47] Botha and Beyers had a layered and complicated relationship that stemmed from the Anglo-Boer War when Botha was his commander. Smuts was not a fan and had fallen out with Beyers during the Anglo-Boer War; at one point, he was Beyers's subordinate. In the aftermath of hostilities, finding a position for Beyers in the Union had been a complicated matter.[48] Beyers added his personal grievances to wider political frustrations and led an armed protest.

Although the suppression of the rebellion and the campaign hinged on Botha's influence,[49] offensive action was only one option and the prime minister attempted to mediate a peace settlement through Steyn.[50] Nothing came of this, and government forces pursued Beyers while on the run. Beyers was as uncommitted in his rebellion as he was to the Union; tragic and uncertain, he drowned while crossing the Vaal River in late 1914.[51] He had taken the decision to rebel and remain on the run. Surrendering was an option, although one he chose not to explore. Jessie Innes, the wife of Sir James Rose Innes, a former chief justice wrote, 'It was a great shock to everyone to discover how he (Beyers) had betrayed his country & being drowned makes everything much easier for Botha, who has had a terrible task in having to fight against his very own people.'[52] Despite her frank and callous reference to Beyers's death, it did in fact make Botha's life easier, as did the unfortunate passing of De La Rey.

The death of Jopie Fourie was a different matter altogether and was also blamed on Botha and Smuts. On this count, Botha and Smuts had more responsibility. The case of Fourie was a complicated one. He had rebelled without resigning his commission, although not the only rebel to do so, this was the legal basis for his execution.[53] Botha and Smuts needed to make an example of one rebel. This had unintended consequences for the SAP as his death and memory was constructed as one of martyrdom for Afrikaner nationalism.[54] Smuts argued that Fourie was sentenced to death because he and his band of followers had committed murder. Botha went on to state that it was not only Smuts who took the decision to execute Fourie – that it was a government pronouncement.[55] These words no doubt cut into his soul.

In trying to defend a tough position that came across more and more pro-British, Botha insisted that it was very difficult to fight his own people, but he was forced to

46 NARSSA: Leyds Archive, 262, Part II, Botha to Leyds, 6 October 1914.
47 Van der Waag, *A Military History*, pp.98–100.
48 Botha to Smuts, 4 July 1911 in Hancock and Van der Poel (eds), *Selections*, vol. III, p.45.
49 Van der Waag, *A Military History*, p.101.
50 Krüger, *Age of the Generals*, p.92.
51 Krüger, *Age of the Generals*, p.92.
52 National Library of South Africa, Special Collections (NLSA): Dorothy von Moltke MSC 26/2.7/12, Jessie Innes to Dr Jacobs, 11 December 1918.
53 Van der Waag, *A Military History*, p.100.
54 Krüger, *Age of the Generals,* p.93.
55 NARSSA: Preller Archive, 90: Botha quoted in 'SAP Conference', *Rand Daily Mail,* August 1915 & SAP, *Volksstem*, 21 August 1915.

do so out of duty.[56] Olive Schreiner wrote, 'Jan Smuts is a man of blood. It breaks my heart that he should have come to this. Botha while ignorant and un-educated is a far more human man'.[57] Smuts was certainly conscious of the gravity of the situation and the Union was by no means the only dominion, colony, country, or Empire to sentence rebels to jail terms or have them executed. Smuts lamented, 'It (the rebellion and consequences) is a dirty, miserable business which will be a blot on our fair name for ever, in whatever way we get out of it now.'[58]

Bruised and battered, Botha's sensitivity, proved to be a weakness on which his enemies capitalised.[59] The opposition to Botha was considerable and in 1915 the pamphlet entitled *Louis Botha contra Generaal Christiaan De Wet* was written by M.P.C. Valter, editor of the monthly magazine of the pro-Boer Nederlansche Zuid-Afrikaansche Vereeniging (Dutch South African Society, or NZAV). This manuscript insulted Botha and criticised his conduct in the rebellion and during the Anglo-Boer War.[60] Professor H.D.J. Bodenstein, wrote a book in response to the criticism, *Was General Botha a Traitor?*, defending the prime minister's name.[61]

The 1915 elections reflected a changing political moment in South Africa. Merriman, who had lost out to Botha in becoming the first Union prime minister in 1910, now sent his greetings and 'all good wishes for your success'.[62] This message from Merriman, although short and formal, was sincere and represented a political realignment, facilitated by South Africa's entry into the First World War. On some level Merriman was also a man of Empire, an identity married to one of a patriotic South African, forward thinking, and a leading politician and parliamentarian. In the war effort he supported Botha, who counter-balanced the extreme views of both the Nationalists and the Unionists. In correspondence with Smuts, Botha said, 'Merriman is at present my best friend – he is at my office almost every day' and in keeping with his sensitive and possibly also practical side, Botha added: 'I think it would be a good thing, if you have time for it, to send him a letter now and then.'[63]

Support for Botha and Smuts was not a foregone conclusion in 1915. Olive Schreiner commented that whereas Botha was the favourite to win, the question about coalition

56 NARSSA: Preller Archive, 90, Botha quoted in 'General Botha', *The Star*, 21 August 1915.

57 HRC: Olive Schreiner Letters, Olive Schreiner to John Hodgson, 19 October 1915.

58 Smuts to Merriman, 3 November 1914 in Hancock and Van der Poel (eds), *Selections*, vol. III, p.208.

59 Meintjes, *Botha*, p.276.

60 NARSSA: Preller Archive, 93, M.P.C. Valter, C.L. van Langenhuysen, 'Louis Botha contra Generaal Christiaan De Wet', no date.

61 H.D.J. Bodenstein *Was Generaal Botha n Verader*? (Johannesburg: De Busy, 1916) – a draft was also found in thr Preller Archive; NARSSA: Preller Archive, 93, 'De Verwording van Generaal Botha', *De Burger*, 31 December 1915.

62 NARSSA: Preller Archive, 86, Merriman to Botha, 20 October 1915.

63 Botha to Smuts in Hancock and Van der Poel (eds), *Selections*, vol. III, p.358.

with the Unionists was a concern.[64] The Unionists in Natal were keen for the Unionist Party leadership to pronounce on their policy in the forthcoming election. There was considerable uncertainty. Some urged a coalition and suggested that negotiations had already taken place. Duncan not comfortable with the unofficial alliance with the SAP, said, that men who otherwise were in sympathy with the Unionists, were 'being got hold of by so-called independent candidates whose only programme is to support Botha'.[65]

Duncan explained the position in his meetings in Pietermaritzburg and Durban: 'it would be a great mistake for the party at present to rush unconditionally into an alliance with Botha simply because of what he has done in regard to the rebellion and the G.S.W. expedition'. Yet there were many strongly of the opinion that some public pronouncement should be made before the so-called independent candidates got into the field – the feeling being that it was not wise to go about offering unconditional support to Botha.[66] Duncan wrote to Smartt and suggested that the matter be addressed in a speech, 'Natal has been too much left alone in the past …'[67]

Smartt showed the letter to Alfred Hennessey – who was also the Unionist party organiser, and according to Buxton a 'very intelligent fellow'.[68] The trouble was with the Natal Unionists, who the party elders felt had succumbed to 'the Botha wave of enthusiasm', which Botha was using for all it was worth. Some felt they were going over 'to the winning side', but the party seniors argued that, if they were 'to have no consideration or connection with the Rand seats we would have to see what we could do in such places as Namaqualand, Somerset East, Aliwal North, etc.'.[69] They tried to shore up a strong position at the end of August; a powerful Unionist Party was necessary to support the war policy but also be a force should they and Botha part ways after the war.

Hennessey saw Buxton in Durban in early July 1915. Hennessey was touring the country ahead of the coming general election. Politics in Natal – where the 'British' were divided clearly between those who 'disliked and distrusted all Boers and wanted to have nothing to do with them', and those that would give full support to Botha – was particularly vexing. Unlike in the Cape and Transvaal provinces, where the Unionists might accept compromises, in Natal there was no middle ground.[70] The Unionists scrambled to find suitable candidates, there being a shortage of young men seeking a political career.[71]

64 Free State Archives Repository (FSAR): CC de Villiers A64/93, Schreiner to Mrs De Villiers, 17 October 1915.
65 UCT: BC294 Duncan Papers, D.1.34.6, Duncan to Smartt, 10 May 1915.
66 UCT: BC294 Duncan Papers, D.1.34.6, Duncan to Smartt, 10 May 1915.
67 UCT: BC294 Duncan Papers, D.1.34.6, Duncan to Smartt, 10 May 1915.
68 BL: Add MS 86963, Buxton Papers, Buxton to Bonar Law, 6 July 1915.
69 UCT: BC294 Duncan Papers, D.1.34.7, Smartt to Duncan, 22 August 1915.
70 BL: Add MS 86963 Buxton Papers, Secret note, Durban, 4 July 1915.
71 BL: Add MS 86963 Buxton Papers, Secret note, Durban, 4 July 1915.

Thomas Smartt, in a rare moment of absolute clarity, saw the situation for what it was. Many men were swept up in the spirit of the times and the immediate need to win the war. They did not want political parties and fiercely contested elections; instead, they had only one thing to do and there could be only one leader. Smartt would therefore 'not be surprised to find many members of our Party carried off their feet by their splendid enthusiasm in the great cause and their generous appreciation of General Botha's work'.[72]

Smartt was of the opinion that the Unionist electorate could not abandon,

> … all safeguards and leave to chance all that we have stood for in the past. In our hearts we and the loyalists of all parties feel deeply grieved and humiliated that our country alone in the Empire – alone among the Allies who are fighting for liberty and for civilization, is divided in spirit and is given over to a wretched struggle of party politics. South Africa alone in this world crisis was unable to present a united front.[73]

Hugh Wyndham, a Unionist MP, shared the sentiment, 'It is very striking to feel how remote the War is out here compared to London. Everything seems to be going on as usual, and the war is by no means the constant topic'.[74] Smartt concluded, that the Unionists had no choice, but to give the government, who were loyal, their 'unwavering and unstinted support until the final victory is won'.[75]

However, Smartt argued, supporting the SAP involved two appeals: 'for the wholehearted support of the government's war policy; and for a freehand in anything else they will propose in Parliament during the following five years. Every loyal South African could respond to the first, but, to the Unionists, a blank cheque was just as unnecessary, as it would be unwise'.[76] At his party congress, Botha appealed for support to see the war through and promised that the government would implement no programme or policy until the war was over.

Smartt reflected:

> This Parliament was being elected not for the war alone; there would be many questions that would arise during its existence. There were the questions of paying for the war, the raising of new taxes, the settlement of South West Africa, in addition to the routine matters based on important principles. This crisis has been met in different ways in different countries – Coalition, National Governments, truces, Unanimous Parliaments etc., but I know of no instance where the extinction of exiting parties sincerely holding different principles

72 UCT: BC294 Duncan Papers, D.1.34.8, Smartt to Duncan, 28 August 1915.
73 UCT: BC294 Duncan Papers, D.1.34.8, Smartt to Duncan, 28 August 1915.
74 WSRO: Petworth House Archives, Hugh Wyndham to Lady Leconfield, 22 Sep 1915.
75 UCT: BC294 Duncan Papers, D.1.34.8, Smartt to Duncan, 28 August 1915.
76 UCT: BC294 Duncan Papers, D.1.34.8, Smartt to Duncan, 28 August 1915.

> in domestic policy has been demanded as proof of patriotism or as a necessary condition for national effort.[77]

Principle gave way to pragmatism and Smartt and Smuts entered negotiations into how to put the SAP and Unionists into the best position. The interplay of negotiations was fraught with complexity. Hennessey and Sir David Graaff, a businessman and politician, were the two main negotiators, and both referred back to their principals. Hennessey enjoyed a frank discussion with Smartt and Duncan and was able to convey their position openly. Graaff was in a very different situation; he spoke to Smuts, who concealed a very difficult game. Sometimes Smuts hustled with Duncan, which upset Hennessey. Smuts argued they were putting up men of straw, that if the government lost, the Unionist would have to form their own ministry. Hennessey was not bothered, and Smuts approached Duncan. He wanted a deal, and not have to address the seats piecemeal, as Smuts would take full advantage of the Unionists' difficulties on the Rand. Hennessey wanted Duncan to make it clear to Smuts that the only seats the Unionists would not contest were Randfontein, Krugersdorp, Vrededorp and possibly Commissioner Street, and that they meant what they said about contesting one of the SAP seats on the Rand.[78]

Hennessey saw Graaff to discuss the mechanics of the arrangement of their two parties not contesting the same seats, which would prevent a Nationalist or Labour victory. Buxton correctly commented that such an arrangement would have to be handled very carefully; while a coalition would probably follow the election, 'any idea of a coalition before the election would probably very much damage Botha politically'.[79] An arrangement could not be too obvious. Smuts told Hennessey that 'it was necessary for the SAP to be able to point to some contests between Bothaites and Unionists in order to show that they maintained their independence'.[80]

The agreement drew criticism. Drummond Chaplin said, 'Botha cannot expect to get more than 60 seats (Crewe says 50) out of 130, and all his talk of getting a majority over all other parties is bluff. His people, I hear, first promised not to contest Unionists seats: then they disregarded this promise and put up candidates against safe Unionists.[81] The SAP would eventually go back to the original position of not challenging Unionist seats. Hugh Wyndham put it clearly, 'The Hertzog party is undoubtedly exceedingly strong, and I don't think there is the smallest chance of Botha getting a majority over all parties, and he will only be able to retain office with our (Unionist) assistance. He has now recognized this and consequently our two parties are not opposing one another in constituencies where to do so would be

77 UCT: BC294 Duncan Papers, D.1.34.8, Smartt to Duncan, 28 August 1915.
78 UCT: BC294 Duncan Papers, D.1.18.1, A.T. Hennessey to Duncan, 29 August 1915.
79 BL: Add MS 86963 Buxton Papers, Secret note, Durban, 4 July 1915.
80 BL: Add MS 86963, Buxton Papers, Hennessey cited in Secret note, Durban, 4 July 1915.
81 WSHC: 947/468, Viscount Long Papers, Chaplin to Long, 14 September 1915.

to hand over the representation to a Hertzogite or a Labour man.'[82] Not challenging for seats was most likely a mistake for the SAP, as the Unionists were in poor shape. George Farrar was dead, after an unfortunate accident in German South West Africa – he would have been the heart and soul of the Unionist campaign; the party had lost 'the only inspiring leader we've got'.[83]

Chaplin wrote, 'Poor George Farrar's death is very sad. Lady Farrar is coming out and my wife is perhaps going down to help her at the funeral. It seemed so unlucky that he should have been killed in that way, when the campaign there was practically over.'[84] To make matters worse for the Unionists, Drummond Chaplin took the post of administrator of Southern Rhodesia and the resignation from Parliament of Sir Lionel Phillips, the lean, energetic mining magnet, saw the Unionists lose their strongest and most popular leaders.[85]

Fighting for Influence

Botha and Smuts tussled to retain political influence, trying to win back support in the Free State, and consolidate their position with British South Africans. Schreiner commented to F.S. Malan, referring to Botha's dual language policy, that when Botha spoke English it was that of 'silly imperialism' and when he spoke Dutch it was 'narrow back veldism'.[86] Maud Wyndham continued the theme writing that, 'Hertzog's party is the old backveld Boer, and a number of the young men too who think its heroic to try and get back to the old republics and be a Dutch speaking and Dutch governing country again.'[87] It was in fact the so called 'backveld' that would change the shape of the South African political landscape. The Afrikaner Rebellion of 1914 was an indication of political dissatisfaction and the result of not having the platform to advocate for their interests – but the elections gave them the constitutional mechanism to vote for change.

Botha toured the Free State and *De Volksstem* published a special edition, 'Botha's peaceful Free State campaign', an ironic comment on his exploits in the suppression of the rebellion.[88] Claims of peace needed a pinch of salt, as there certainly were a few heated discussions and moments where it came to blows. Wyndham added some

82 WSRO: Petworth House Archives, Hugh Wyndham to Lady Leconfield, 22 September 1915.
83 WSRO: Petworth House Archives, Maud Wyndham to Lady Leconfield, 14 September 1915.
84 WSHC: 947/468, Viscount Long Papers, Chaplin to Long, 30 May 1915.
85 BL: Add MS 86963, Buxton Papers, Secret note, Durban, 4 July 1915.
86 National English Literary Museum (NELM): Olive Schreiner to F.S. Malan, 16 October 1913.
87 WSRO: Petworth House Archives, Maud Wyndham to Lady Leconfield, 29 September 1915.
88 NARSSA: Preller Archive, 92, 'Generaal Botha's vreedzame Vrijstaatse veldtocht', *De Volksstem*, 23 August 1915.

context, 'The large cities were comparatively quiet. However, in the country districts where the Dutch were divided, the meetings were rowdy and in the Free State some blood was shed.'[89] His wife Maud Wyndham, added a story which may have had a flavour of gossip, about a stormy meeting in George, 'a small town … very peaceful and sleepy and English and picturesque. It ended with a fight and apparently, four sets of false teeth were swept up in the street the following morning.'[90] Perhaps one of the most serious to be reported was a meeting in late September that ended in a tumult and, almost unbelievably, an attempt on Smuts's life. Maud went on: 'His friends restrained him, or he would have tackled the 'rabble' himself. This did Botha and Smartt a great deal of good. Labour people wrote to the papers disowning any dealing in the scrummages.'[91]

Botha's presence was not welcome in many of the towns, and in Vredefort a fight broke out at a rally between SAP and Nationalist supporters.[92] Tempers ran high and it was alleged that the nationalists instigated a fight at a meeting in Winburg,[93] where insults such as 'traitor, bloodhound, Judas, and murderer' were hurled at the sensitive prime minister.[94] Botha's emotional intelligence failed him – he could not or did not want to understand how his decisions affected his people. But Botha pushed ahead and remained a man of action. On one occasion when the prime minister met with Hennessey toward the end of September it was reported that he arrived 'in a heated and breathless state – having been tackled by one of his own followers and Botha pushed him out of the Club.'[95]

Buxton did his own tour of the Orange Free State, where he had met 'rebels' and loyalists alike; the former looked to the general election for a great accession of strength – and they were sanguine about the number of seats they expected to win – to enable them to deal with their grievances and 'pay off old scores'. For the moment at least, Buxton felt, 'they were prepared to act on constitutional lines. In Senekal, the 'rebels' told Buxton that: 'They had been goaded into their action by their grievances, and the way in which they considered the Botha Government had treated them and ignored them and their interests in every way'.[96] They disclaimed any hostility to the

89 WSRO: Petworth House Archives, Hugh Wyndham to Lady Leconfield, 22 September 1915.
90 WSRO: Petworth House Archives, Maud Wyndham to Lady Leconfield, 23 September 1915.
91 WSRO: Petworth House Archives, Maud Wyndham to Lady Leconfield, 29 September 1915.
92 NARSSA: Preller Archive, 92, 'Generaal Botha's Vrijstaatse Reis', *De Volksstem*, 25 August 1915.
93 NARSSA: Preller Archive, 93, 'Hertzogite Tactics, *Rand Daily Mail*, 29 September 1915.
94 Krüger, *Age of the Generals*, p.102.
95 WSRO: Petworth House Archives, Maud Wyndham to Lady Leconfield, 29 September 1915.
96 BL: Add MS 86963 Buxton Papers, Secret note, Durban, 4 July 1915. See, Garcia, *The First Campaign Victory*, for a discussion on relative deprivation.

imperial connection however it would be reasonable to assume that there was a mixed economy of interests; but regardless of politics, Buxton was received with great courtesy across the countryside.

It was clear that Botha had lost significant support – pushing and shoving, trading blows. The Afrikaner population, especially in the Free State were not happy and their voice would be heard in the election.[97] Botha with all his gravitas struggled to convince the Boers to support his party. Hennessey told Smuts not to tour the country as he was more likely to do harm than any good. Buxton supported the idea adding that Smuts disliked electioneering. Hennessey added, 'it would be impossible now for him to cover more than a tithe of the country before the elections, as the towns are so numerous and the distances are so great, – as I know to my own cost'.[98]

At an election campaign meeting in Bethulie in early September, Botha spoke about the rebellion. He gave his version of events as to why certain Boers had supported the uprising. He said that Maritz and other leaders had deceived their followers stating that the prime minister and Smuts supported the uprising. Botha phrased it in a way that suited his narrative. Maritz and other leaders had emotionally extorted the Boers saying that if they did not fight, they would be sent to Germany.[99] Keen to capitalise on the territorial growth of the Union, Botha claimed that when Britain won the war, of which he was certain, then German South West Africa would become part of the Union.[100] He was right, although, this was contrary to his previous statements in parliament in 1914, where he declared that the Union had no territorial ambitions.[101] In some ways Botha's statement confirms Hely-Hutchinson's view that Botha had 'become an imperialist' and favoured expansionism.[102] Olive Schreiner commented, 'I believe we shall in years to come pay a heavy price for it (the invasion of GSWA)'.[103] It would be convenient to imagine that Olive Schreiner somehow divined the issues of modern South Africa, and the independence struggle of Namibia. In many ways Botha, through his premiership, shaped the modern Southern African agenda.

With the split in Afrikanerdom, Botha relied on his power of personality and influence. He cast a long shadow, one that connected a modernising South Africa, with the older Boer world, one of Kruger, Joubert, Steyn, and many more who pulled on historical and emotional formation stories of the Voortrekkers. At a meeting, Botha

97 Krüger, *Age of the Generals*, p.102.

98 BL: Add MS 86963 Buxton Papers, Secret note, Durban, 4 July 1915.

99 NARSSA: Preller Archive, 93, Botha quoted in 'Coming Elections', *The Star*, 3 September 1915.

100 NARSSA: Preller Archive, 93, Botha quoted in 'Coming Elections', *The Star*, 3 September 1915.

101 NARSSA: Preller Archive, 90, Botha quoted in 'The Prime Minister's Speech', *Pretoria News*, 10 September 1914.

102 Hely-Hutchinson to Selborne, 18 April 1907 in Boyce, *Naval Papers of Selborne*, p.319.

103 FSAR: CC de Villiers A64/93, Schreiner to Mrs De Villiers, 17 October 1915.

was asked by a certain Mr Visser, 'Are you the General Botha of the Tugela?', Botha answered 'Yes', to which Visser replied, 'that is enough for me.'[104] It was apparent that Botha, the man and general, was becoming a legend in his time, but even this was not enough to claw back sufficient support. The situation was made worse by the alliance of the National Party and Labour. It was this alliance in 1910 that saw Frederick Creswell enter parliament as a Labour MP.

Creswell had served with the Rand Rifles as their second-in-command and saw service in the German South West African campaign. With the campaign nearing its end and with his regiment on lines of communications duties, he asked Buxton whether it was not more expedient for him to return to resume his role as leader of the Labour Party. Creswell, recognising that there were much bigger questions, hoped to bring his party together and that it should take its share in 'assisting in the success of the war in any way they could'. Creswell believed his party were 'more or less together'. Buxton countered that while 'the more sane and sensible were gaining the upper hand', there remained 'a considerable and vocal "war on war" section'.[105]

Buxton reported that Creswell, 'issued a Manifesto to the Labour Party, taking the National view, practically on the lines he indicated to me in the talk which I sent home in 'notes' last week. As far as I can yet judge he is receiving the support of the great bulk of the Labour Party. He received a unanimous vote of confidence from his constituents at a meeting he held a day or two ago [early to-mid-July 1915] since issue of the Manifesto.'[106]

The Labour Party had weakened since the war; especially with the tension created between the 'war on war' section and the others. Hennessey felt Labour would get about 12 seats on the Rand.[107] This proved to be ambitious. Labour supporters had boycotted the meeting in Johannesburg in favour of the European Contingents; Creswell, who according to Buxton, might have taken a stronger line in favour of a Contingent, was quiet following his return and Bill Andrews, chairman of the Labour Party, was steadily finding converts for his 'war on war' policy.[108] Andrews would go on to lose his seat in the 1915 elections.

Creswell believed that the war's end would usher in enormous socio-economic change.[109] He was right, and he was the voice of White worker rights, complaining that the burden of additional taxation fell too heavily on the working classes and that the mines and landlords ought to have drawn a heavier burden. Notwithstanding, he was not positive about Labour's potential success at the coming election. He told Buxton that, before the outbreak of war, he expected to come back with 35 seats, but

104 NARSSA: Preller Archive, 93, Botha quoted in 'General Botha's Tour', *The Star*, 3 September 1915.
105 BL: Add MS 86963, Buxton Papers, Secret note, 2 July 1915.
106 BL: Add MS 86963, Buxton Papers, Buxton to Bonar Law, 13 July 1915.
107 BL: Add MS 86963, Buxton Papers, Secret note, Durban, 4 July 1915.
108 BL: Add MS 86963, Buxton Papers, Secret note, Durban, 4 July 1915.
109 BL: Add MS 86963, Buxton Papers, Secret note, 2 July 1915.

that this would now probably number 20. Buxton, equally frank and a supporter of Botha, told him that their voting in Parliament – always with the Hertzogites – had done great harm. Creswell agreed. The wartime leadership showed himself a patriot and in practice they had no views in common with the Nationalists, except 'to turn out the Government'.[110]

Archbishop Carter said, 'the opposition as a party is not very strong – and will probably be weaker after the next Election – if, it is expected, the Labour party increases.'[111] Labour would not increase, but at the time Creswell accurately predicted that there would be no majority for any party in the new parliament, leading to some amount of political instability.[112] Creswell argued that the primary opposition to the government came from the view that it was unrepresentative. He thought – and to Buxton's surprise this view coincided with Steyn's – that the government ought to have dissolved two years earlier (during the crisis of 1913) when they would probably have received a commanding majority and would be in a very strong position as a wartime government. 'But now day by day they were weakening.'[113]

In 1915, five years after the official formation of the Union, it was still an experiment with all its historical divides. There was no South African nation, no consensus on the war. Even the nomenclature differed. For English South Africans, following the British trend, it was the Great War.[114] For the clerks in the South African defence department it was 'the European Crisis'; for their counterparts in the prime minister's office in 1914, it was 'the German South West Expedition', almost as if these two events could be separated.[115] For many of the African nations supporting the Union government with the promise of a better future, the conflict was referred to as the 'great war', or the 'the great war in Europe'.[116] For F.S. Malan, who served in Botha's cabinet, it was, in August 1914, 'die Brits-Duitse-oorlog' (the Anglo-German War),[117] a description supported by M.T. Steyn, the former Boer president, who, writing to Smuts on 31 July 1914, reckoned that, 'the troubles in England are the

110 BL: Add MS 86963, Buxton Papers, Secret note, 2 July 1915.
111 UCT: AB186 Archbishop Carter Letters, William Carter to Algernon Lawley, 27 February 1915.
112 BL: Add MS 86963 Buxton Papers, Secret note, 2 July 1915.
113 BL: Add MS 86963 Buxton Papers, Secret note, 2 July 1915.
114 M. Howard, 'The First World War Reconsidered' in J. Winter, G. Parker and M.R. Habeck (eds), *The Great War and the Twentieth Century* (New Haven and London, 2000), p.14. *De Burger*, taking a surprisingly neutral line, described it too as 'De Grote Volkerenstrijd'. See, for example, *De Burger*, 29 February 1916, 20 March 1916 and 17 July 1916.
115 See, for example, NASAP: PM 1/1/32, file 4/97/1914 War German South West Expedition & Supply of Ammunition & Guns; and DODA: DC, Box 573, file D.9199 European Crisis General, vol.7.
116 See for example, BL: Add MS 86947 Buxton Papers, King Dalindyebo, Umtata, to Chief Magistrate of the Transkeian Territories, 19 August 1914.
117 NASAC: A583 F.S. Malan Collection, vol.22, 'De Britse-Duitse Oorlog' (The Anglo-German War), diary of F.S. Malan, 7 to 10 August 1914.

result of the South African War. One sees still more. This war has driven England out of her "splendid isolation" into her "ententes" and her yellow alliances and today she has fallen foul of Continental entanglements. The mills of Providence grind slowly indeed!'[118]

Many had hoped for this in 1899/1900. Now 14 years later it had happened and there was, to the mind of the Afrikaner nationalist, no reason whatsoever to help Britain. They might, as Steyn was suggesting, rather seize the moment offered by providence.

Botha, perhaps naively, had hoped to unite the country behind the war effort. This was, as Frans Malan noted, 'wonderful politics' and Botha succeeded to a surprising degree in quietening the voice of radical labour and nationalistic Afrikaners. However, as Malan predicted, Botha, by committing South Africa to the war, would run 'the danger of losing the sentiment of the [Afrikaner] people.'[119] The war and the questions it opened fuelled Afrikaner nationalism.

Unsurprisingly therefore, Botha, and Smuts battled to achieve and then maintain consensus in their cabinet. Faced with potential defections and the growing rift in Afrikanerdom, his first wartime ministry was unstable and his second ministry, formed after the October 1915 election, could only govern with Unionist support, though not in formal coalition. The state of the parties was as depicted in Table 5.1.

Table 5.1: The position of parties in South Africa, The House of Assembly, 1910 and 1915.[120]

	1910			1915		
Party	**Seats won**	**No. of votes**	**Percent**	**Seats won**	**No. of votes**	**Percent**
Labour	3	11,549	10.9	4	25,690	9.8
Labour – GM				-	802	0.3
Independent	12	19,563	18.5	5	10,911	4.2
Independent – Lab	1	815	0.8			
Independent – SAP	1	3,430	3.2			
Independent – UP	2	*				
National Party				27	78,184	29.9
SAP	66	30,052	28.4	54	93,482	35.8
Socialist	-	448	0.4			
Unionist	36	39,766	37.6	40	48,034	18.4

* The Independent Unionists were uncontested in two seats in the Cape Province.

118 M.T. Steyn to J.C. Smuts, 31 Jul 1914 in Hancock and Van der Poel (eds), *Selections*, vol. III, p.184.
119 NASAC: A583 F.S. Malan Collection, vol 22, Diary of F.S. Malan, 9 August 1914.
120 B.M. Schoeman, *Parlementêre verkiesings in Suid-Afrika, 1910-1976* (Pretoria: Aktuele, 1977), pp.33, 66–67.

The election results were disappointing for Botha and Smuts. They had won 54 seats of the 130 in the House. The Unionists remained the official opposition with 40 seats. A disheartened F.S. Malan, said it was clear that the other party 'bigwigs', with few exceptions, remained steadfast. The big change was with the Nationalists who enjoyed considerable support: their candidates drew approximately 78,000 votes, although this translated to only 27 seats – 16 in the Orange Free State, seven in the Cape, and four in the Transvaal.[121] The remaining four seats went to the Labour Party. Three of Botha's ministers lost their seats and perhaps as many as 40 per cent of Afrikaners had turned their backs on him. The Free State voted almost solidly for Hertzog. Botha was over confident thinking that he would gain five seats in the Free State,[122] but this was not to be; the South African Party ended up only winning one seat there.[123] Moreover, the National Party had gained significant ground in the Transvaal and the Cape. Dr D.F. Malan was the new provincial leader, of, as Buxton called it, the 'Cape-Malan party', who with others had established *Die Burger* as the Cape Town based mouthpiece of the Nationalists. Malan's party in the earlier days: 'professed not to be Hertzogite but to be only anti-Botha'. Buxton added that 'it might bring in a certain number who do not care to be labelled Hertzogites. For this reason, it was dangerous.'[124]

Finding a Way Forward

The 1915 election saw the complete defeat of Labour, at least for the moment, and a significant blow to SAP support. Smuts had predicted the SAP's poor showing putting forward 'that Labour and the National Party would get 40 seats, Unionists 30 and the South African Party 60, adding that he would be 'much surprised if we do worse than that'.[125] The election results stunned Botha. The hubris was striking as he sent off a brigade to the war effort, losing their votes, or at least a portion thereof, during a difficult and contested election.[126] Perhaps learning the lesson, a pensive Botha, wrote to Smuts in 1916 informing him that the Fauresmith constituency was being contested in local elections, but 'unfortunately I understand that a few hundred of our voters are with you on commando.'[127] The SAP had experienced a significant

121 WCARS: A.583 F.S. Malan Collection, vol.23, Diary of F.S. Malan, undated, pp.14–15.

122 NARSSA: Preller Archive, 93, Botha quoted in 'A Talk with the Prime Minister', *Pretoria News*, 18 October 1915.

123 Krüger, *Age of the Generals*, p.102.

124 BL: Add MS 86963 Buxton Papers, Secret note, Durban, 4 July 1915.

125 Smuts to Merriman, 30 August, Hancock and Van der Poel (eds), *Selections*, vol. III, p.311.

126 Hugh Wyndham hints at the fact that Botha was sufficiently confident not to keep the brigade in South Africa for the election that October. Unwisely, he had thought he could afford to lose their votes: WSRO: Petworth House Archives, Hugh Wyndham to Lady Leconfield, 9 September 1915.

127 Botha to Smuts, 21 March 1916 in Hancock and Van der Poel (eds), *Selections*, vol III, p.348.

decrease in popularity. Buxton comments that although Botha did not live to see the 1920 election, had he been alive his influence may have made a slight difference, but it is unlikely that it would have drastically changed the result.[128]

The Nationalists had gained ground in the Cape, not only in terms of a small number of seats, but more worryingly in terms of the number of votes polled in constituencies where they were beaten.[129] Botha and Smuts had lost their majority but remained in power with the parliamentary backing of the official opposition. The Unionists wholeheartedly supported Botha and Smuts's war policy, and their 40 seats gave the SAP a working majority. However, as the governing party and the official opposition realised, any attempt at coalition would drive more Dutch speakers into Hertzog's arms. The government would as a result continue as it had, only, as Crewe noted: 'in future entirely dependent on us [Unionists] every day for help and support which will be given ungrudgingly.'[130] Botha first thought to resign. He had previously threatened to do so, but Drummond Chaplin, did not 'for a moment suppose he will do it.'[131] It was perhaps a Krugerian offer of resignation, and more an emotional response.[132] But he had little choice, as D.W. Krüger argued, 'He had to carry on because there was no other Party strong enough to form a government and somehow the war had to be seen through'.[133]

Botha's agreement with the Unionist Party to not compete for seats in each other's constituencies was a mistake as many British-South Africans would probably have voted for the South African Party over the Unionists, at least with Smartt as leader. Frustrated with himself and the result, Botha had to face a new period with an uncomfortable partnership with the Unionists.[134] Botha's relationship with Smartt, the Unionist leader, was layered with many moments of tension. Smartt had fumbled a number of times, showing poor leadership. When Jameson and Botha became friends, many Afrikaners were alienated, and this had lost Botha votes. Smartt and Botha were never to become friends, but Buxton attempted to bridge the gap and befriended Smartt in the hopes of tempering his politics. This was a step up from Gladstone's relationship with Sir Thomas, who had nothing but disdain for him.[135] Even towards the end, when Botha invited Smartt to the Peace Treaty in Versailles, Smartt replied that it was only the governor-general who could invite him on behalf of the imperial British government.[136]

128 Buxton, *General Botha*, p.179.
129 WSHC: 947/469, Viscount Long of Wraxall Papers, Crewe to Long, 23 October 1915.
130 WSHC: 947/469, Viscount Long of Wraxall Papers, Crewe to Long, 23 October 1915.
131 WSHC: 947/468, Viscount Long of Wraxall Papers, Chaplin to Long, 14 September 1915.
132 Paul Kruger would often threaten resignation, then plead, order, shout and brow bash to get his way.
133 Krüger, *The Making of a Nation*, p.103.
134 Mouton, 'The sacred tie', p.15.
135 Mouton, 'The sacred tie', p.15.
136 Buxton, *General Botha*, 171.

Botha was far from comfortable with the 'horse trading' but was forced to accept the reality of the situation.[137] The Unionists, although giving Botha a majority in the house, felt excluded from real government. They were drawn, in some degree, into wartime decision support and even military office, but there was no war government or government of national unity. What is more, the Nationalists would have no part in the war effort and on this matter, they were joined at times by what remained of the Labour Party. Yet, Botha, like the official opposition, believed that good war news would solidify the country, undermine the belief in nationalist quarters that Britain was going to be defeated, and so build a larger measure of national unity. Wyndham noted that the Afrikaner, recognising potential post-war rewards, had 'a healthy desire to be on the winning side.'[138] At its core Botha refused to accept a final break between himself and the Afrikaner far-right, and continued to hope for rapprochement. An almost unbelievably delicate position negotiating Boer republican and Unionist interests – but this was his vision after all, an almost impossible political experiment.

Despite the disappointing results and a decline in confidence from the electorate, Botha remained popular to many Afrikaans and English-speaking South Africans. Many loyal supporters wrote to Botha, praising his efforts, complimenting him on his campaign victory in German South West Africa, and congratulating him on his election victory. These letters came in from all over the country and were sent from people of stature as well as from ordinary citizens.[139] Samuel Marks, the industrialist, Kruger's former confidante now a Union senator wrote to Botha, 'Heartiest congratulations on your great victory... hoping the coming term will be more peaceful than the last'.[140] Abe Bailey also sent his 'heartiest congratulations'.[141] General Viljoen, with whom Botha had served in the Anglo-Boer War, congratulated him, adding 'our gratitude soars'.[142] A letter from a certain Mr Percy Jallot in the Cape province wrote, 'congratulations on your latest glorious victory. Wishing you long life and happiness to rule over us on behalf of his Majesty'.[143] Botha also received letters of congratulation from the Free State. One such letter from A. Joubert, congratulated him and said that although there was not overwhelming support for Botha in the Free State there was still a strong support base.[144] These letters must have lifted Botha's spirits.

137 NARSSA: Preller Archive, 93, Botha quoted in 'Warning to Nationalists', *Rand Daily Mail*, 4 November 1915, and Meintjes, *Botha*, p.277.
138 WSRO: Petworth House Archives, Hugh Wyndham to Lady Leconfield, 30 September 1915.
139 NARSSA: Preller Archive, 86, Lamb to Botha, 19 October 1915; Letter to Botha, 10 October 1915; Letter to Botha, 21 October 1915; Letter to Botha, 21 October 1915.
140 NARSSA: Preller Archive, 92, Marks to Botha, 21 October 1915.
141 NARSSA: Preller Archive, 92, Marks to Botha, 21 October 1915.
142 NARSSA: Preller Archive, 92, Marks to Botha, 21 October 1915.
143 NARSSA: Preller Archive, 86, Jallot to Botha, 22 October 1915.
144 NARSSA: Preller Archive, 86, Joubert to Botha, 23 October 1915.

A further victory for Botha was the conviction of a Mr Munnik, who made false claims that Botha was involved in the taking of gold during the Anglo-Boer War. The accusation was made at the time of the 1915 elections and created added strain for Botha.[145] Personal and political attacks took their toll on his health, and he reached out to his friends to unburden himself.

It was during the First World War, that Botha and Lord Sydney Buxton developed a deep friendship. Buxton, Botha's future biographer provided an outlet for Botha to destress and became a sounding board for his ideas. Their friendship was one of mutual respect, and Botha would unburden himself when with Buxton.[146] Charmed and inspired, Buxton later told Botha's life story, adding great insight into Botha's experience during the First World War. Buxton was himself an interesting man. He was a liberal politician, intelligent, soft, and kind, the type of man that got along easily with Botha. Upon Buxton's arrival, he came face to face with the troubles of the Union, the Afrikaner Rebellion, the German South West African campaign, and then the national elections.

Conclusion

The years, 1915 to 1919, involved political, military and economic issues which stretched Botha's resolve to the limit. In many ways the electoral results of the 1915 elections were the start of his decline, when signs of depression first started to emerge. It was not the first time that Botha approached elections with confidence bordering on hubris. In 1910, he challenged Percy Fitzpatrick for his constituency, Pretoria East, losing by the narrowest of margins – Botha was devastated. Buxton recorded Botha's response to the 1915 elections in his diary, and personal papers, and they eventually became the basis of his biography on Botha.[147]

With the military campaign in German South West Africa over and the elections a thing of the past, Botha and Smuts faced a complicated moment. Military questions regarding the German East African campaign and the Western Front remained in flux and domestic politics was rife with division. The intricacies of the situation were not apparent to everyone. After the elections, Lady Leuchars, the wife of Sir George Leuchars the former minister from Natal who had initially fallen out and resigned over Hertzog's speeches, wrote to Annie Botha 'I rejoice with you, anxiety now over'.[148] This was premature; with Smuts on campaign Botha still had to deal with local issues of pay for the contingents, recruitment and the political fallout of the elections – these issues are discussed in Chapter 6 as well as early attempts at creating a formal South African intelligence service.

145 NARSSA: Preller Archive, 106, 'Premier's Honour Vindicated', *Cape Times*, 30 October 1915.
146 Meintjes, *Botha*, p.278.
147 BL: Add MS 87093, Buxton Papers, Botha to Buxton, 21 December 1917.
148 NARSSA: Preller Archive, 86, Lady Leuchars to Mrs Botha, 21 October 1915.

6

Local Polemics, Public Opinion and Foreign Policy, 1915–1916

Extremists on both sides are the difficulty and the danger.

Botha[1]

In 1915, when Smuts was first asked to assume command in German East Africa, Botha replied, 'your duty is here'. When Smuts was asked a second time Botha obliged and agreed to let Smuts leave.[2] Oom Jannie remained in command until 1917 at which time he was transferred to London to attend the Imperial War Conference. When his friend left to go on campaign, Botha, in a thoughtful note brimming with emotion wrote: 'My heart and soul are with you and I shall do everything to help you, be assured of that … God bring you back safely to us will always be my prayer.'[3] Smuts departed to take command of the German East African campaign from February 1916 until January 1917 and then served in London until 1919 – the detail of these experiences are captured in Chapters 7, 8 and 9. This Chapter deals with Botha's difficulties, challenges and opportunities in the Union, 1915–1916.

Ross Anderson, a preeminent scholar on Africa in the First World War, suggests that the campaign in German East Africa had imperialist and South African expansionist interests. The campaign in German South West Africa, considering the norms of the day, made some amount of sense logistically and geographically, but it was fundamentally aimed at territorial aggrandisement; German East Africa was removed in time and space and also conceptually. Smuts, never very far from an ingenious and sometimes far-fetched idea, believed that a territorial claim on German East Africa could be used as a bargaining chip with the Portuguese to trade for Mozambique. He suggested it might be prudent to consolidate the territories

1 Botha quoted in Buxton, *General Botha*, p.170.
2 NARSSA: Preller Archive, 92, Botha quoted in De Volksraad', *De Volksstem*, 2 February 1916.
3 Botha to Smuts, 23 February 1916 in Hancock and Van der Poel (eds.), *Selections*, Vol. III, p.336.

south of the Zambesi.[4] The full extent of Smuts's ability to argue for his and Botha's interests, especially regarding making German South West Africa a colony in all but name, was put on full display during the mandate question at the Paris Peace conference in 1919. Balancing Wilsonian principles of self-determination, a paternalistic outlook, and South Africa's political interests he massaged the system, panel beating it until it suited his needs, and shoehorned South West Africa as a Class C Mandate under Pretoria's control.[5]

The lead up to Smuts's odyssey was littered with political and military issues. Botha remained behind to face the consequences of an apparent failure in the Union experiment. Local politics were flavoured with partisan divide and framed within the British Empire.

War Recruitment and Issues of Payment

South Africa's willingness to contribute to the war effort was important to Botha and Smuts. Bonar Law, who was asked in the House of Commons whether London had invited South Africa to send an official contingent to France, approached Pretoria for approval of a pre-drafted text. Before the conclusion of the German South West Africa campaign, Botha's government had expressed a readiness to send a contingent to Europe.[6] Botha had postponed committing to the detail until the victory in German South West Africa. Buxton later summarised the campaign as, 'was well thought out, well planned, well handled, short and clean cut.'[7] With the victory in hand, Smuts and Botha started to raise volunteers to serve in Europe and German East Africa.[8]

By July 1915, the Union prepared for the possibility of sending contingents to other war theatres. Some town councils sought to use the opportunity. The Town Clerk for Grahamstown, for example, offered to provide a camouflage training ground – 'wooded and otherwise'. And by August 1915, men were applying for positions in the expeditionary force that was to leave for Europe. Some requested special appointments, such as R.M. Dunbar, who hoped to find a position with the 'Divisional Supply Train'. Louis Matthews, expressing perhaps a common concern, was 'afraid

4 R. Anderson, 'World War 1 in East Africa, 1916–1918', PhD thesis, Glasgow University, 2001, 18; Smuts to Merriman, 30 August 1915 in Hancock and Van der Poel (eds.), *Selections*, Vol. III, p.310.
5 See C. Heyns and W. Gravett, 'Smuts se bydrae tot internasionale reg en organisasie' in K. Du Pisani, D. Kriek, and C. De Jager, (eds.), *Jan Smuts: Van Boerseun tot Wêreldverhoog, 'n Herwaardering* (Pretoria: Protea, 2017).
6 NARSSA: War 1914-15: Army, Imperial, GG 668, file 9/93/24, Bonar Law to Buxton, 8 November 1915.
7 BL: Add MS 87042, Buxton Papers 1915-1919, Buxton's Report on German South West Africa, 1919.
8 Van der Waag, *A Military History*, pp.108–109. See DODA: DC, Box 765, Correspondence between Botha and Van Deventer, June 1917.

of being left in the cold.'[9] One man offered to run the army post office on the lines of the Canadian model. He was told in no uncertain terms that, unlike the Canadians and their several divisions, South Africa was sending 'a solitary brigade' and that the brigade's establishment of one corporal and two privates for the postal service was more than adequate.[10]

Smuts, who now took on the role of field commander, believed that South African military training and experience was better suited for the African terrain – this fit the narrative of his recruitment campaign for German East Africa.[11] Buchan suggested that Afrikaners, renowned as light cavalrymen and having enhanced this reputation in German South West Africa, were not expected to be attracted to British-style infantry and so they were by preference destined for Tanganyika.[12] Botha made a similar argument, adding that although he was convinced of the need to send forces to the Western Front, he was strongly of the opinion that 'a campaign in German East Africa is more in our line than is a European campaign'.[13] Despite this, Smuts added that the European theatre seemed more appealing to some soldiers, apparently because German East Africa was seen as a 'minor theatre'.[14] The campaigns supported the Empire, and were part of Smuts and Botha's ideas of South African expansion; they were aligned in thought and they echoed British imperialist ideas.

The Botha government put forward a proposal to further support the war effort and an eager British government was 'grateful for the offer of a South African contingent as well as a heavy artillery contingent – details to be settled.'[15] However, Smuts was to be disappointed. The recruitment drive opened on 21 July 1915, in time to draw the troops returning victorious from German South West Africa.[16] A call was made both for heavy artillery as well as infantry,[17] although the War Office had asked specifically

9 DODA: DC Group2, box 690, file DC 128/958/9199 Applications for Overseas Contingent, Louis Matthews to Nicholson, Quartermaster General's Office, 25 November 1915.

10 DODA: DC Group 2, box 689, file 958/9199 Overseas Contingent, Quartermaster General to E. Sturman, 11 August 1915.

11 BL: Add MS 87052, Buxton Papers, 1914-1918, Smuts' speech on German East Africa, *Cape Times*, 23 November 1915.

12 J. Buchan, *The History of the South African Forces in France* (London: Nelson, 1920), p.15.

13 Graaff to Smuts, 8 June 1915, Hancock and Van der Poel (eds.), *Selections*, Vol. III, p.296.

14 BL: Add MS 87052, Buxton Papers, 1914-1918, Smuts quoted in the *Cape Times*, 29 November 1915.

15 BL: Add MS 86963 Buxton Papers, Secretary of State to Governor General, 5 July 1915.

16 NARSSA: GG 667, file 9/93/7 War 1914-16: Imperial Army, South African Overseas Expeditionary Force, Smuts to Buxton, 14 July 1915. It was also decided, to settle public uneasiness, to publish official correspondence relating to the raising and deployment of the South African contingents. See NARSSA: GG 668, file 9/93/26.

17 'Fresh Call for Volunteers; Union's Second "Little Bit"; Mostly Infantry Wanted; Details of Terms of Service', *Rand Daily Mail*, 21 July 1915; 'Heavy Artillery in Flanders; General Terms of Service', *Rand Daily Mail*, 22 July 1915; and 'Wanted in Europe; Call for Heavy Artillery, Opening for South Africans', *Rand Daily Mail*, 22 July 1915.

for infantry. As expected, there was a flurry of interest, particularly from inhabitants of British blood.[18] Men rushed again to the colours.

While starting the recruitment campaign, a new request was sent – one for assistance from the Dominions to increase the number of tunnelling companies in France. Each new company was to comprise 200 expert facemen and 100 less-skilled assistants for the making and timbering of shaft and tunnels. Smuts responded on behalf of the government. His answer was unhelpful. He noted the scarcity of skilled miners in South Africa's goldmines. Eight-one were already serving with the South African expeditionary force and a further 93 men of De Beers and other diamond mining companies were employed on garrison duty in South Africa and South West Africa. He raised several objections – some practical, but largely political – to allowing these men to from a tunnelling company for trench warfare in France: the 'white' miners were unaccustomed to the manual labour left to 'black' miners; and shaft and drives in South Africa were made with explosives, through rock, whereas in France timbering was essential for military tunnelling through loose ground near the surface. While few South African miners may have had experience with such carpentry and timbering, Smuts stressed the political argument and the deep-seated racial prejudices of the time: namely, that Black South Africans would not stand the climatic conditions in Europe or 'the severe strain of modern warfare.'[19] Smuts's assumption would be disproven. London did not pursue the suggestion of a composite company officered and NCO'd by South Africans.

Sir Abe Baily offered to raise 100 sharpshooters for service in France. The Army Council accepted the offer and Pretoria approved. They left South Africa on 22 April 1916 and trained at Bordon and were paid as British infantry, although, for pay and accounting purposes, the small detachment became part of the South African Continent. Bailey met the cost of the detachment in addition he paid each man an allowance of one shilling a day for the whole period of service with an additional two shillings per day to the men with dependants.[20]

Despite Sir Abe's good efforts, rich beneficiaries, the small White population as well as the complexity of South Africa's other tasks, including the pending deployment to Tanganyika, it was agreed that South Africa could not raise and maintain much more than a brigade in France.[21] On August 10, 1915, Botha informed Buxton

18 See the applications and expressions of interest in the series of files under reference DC 128/958/9199 and titled 'Applications for Overseas Contingent' in DODA: DC, Boxes 689, 690 and 691. At the first rumours, the town clerk of Grahamstown offered his 'commonage, both wooded and otherwise for a training ground' for the overseas contingent. Town Clerk, Grahamstown to Minister of Defence, 13 July 1915, DC, Box 690, file DC 128/958/9199 Applications for Overseas Contingent.
19 NARSSA: GG 668, file 9/93/19 War 1914-15: Army, Imperial, Ministers' Minute 1316, 30 September 1915.
20 NARSSA: GG 668, file 9/93/43 War 1914-15: Army, Imperial.
21 Buchan has suggested that Botha, not wanting to 'denude the country of too many of her most loyal and vigilant citizens', could send no more than a brigade of infantry to Europe. Buchan, *South African Forces in France*, p.14.

that the South African contingent would comprise one infantry brigade, one signalling company, one field ambulance and one general hospital, in addition to five batteries of heavy artillery and some, if not the whole, of the personnel for five four-gun batteries of field artillery and some aviation personnel, together with aeroplanes and accessories.[22] Botha, however, noted rather ominously that reinforcement 'may prove difficult.'[23]

In July 1915, Smuts, fully aware of the importance of the European Contingent commented:

> The present proposal is to start with one brigade of four thousand at once, and if enough men volunteer to form a second brigade of four thousand … both here and in GSW that the names of men who are anxious to serve in Europe are to be given in … he proposed to instruct Commanding Officers privately to make some enquiry into the cases, and if they thought the question of a wife, or children, or dependents likely to be a serious one, to put some decent difficulties in the way of the man volunteering.[24]

This proved ambitious and the four battalions recruited, became the 1st South African Infantry Brigade. They were, 'designed to represent the main divisions of the Union, and recruits were given the option of joining the regiment affiliated to their own province.'[25] This formed part of a difficult, but broad-fronted attempt to gain language equity and balance sectarian interests. As it transpired, the two main military efforts were to be East Africa and France, where Smuts, himself, and Brigadier General H.T. (Tim) Lukin were to command respectively, the former representing the Afrikaans sector, the latter the English. Moreover, with only about 15 percent of the original brigade being Afrikaans, the bulk of the contingent that went to France was of British descent .[26] Further detail about recruitment, supply, and medical issues is explored in Chapter 8.

Tied up with recruiting was fear of a second rebellion which turned out to be a red herring. Charles Crewe, Director of Recruitment, and Hugh Wyndham agreed that the second Rebellion was a non-starter, but for different reasons. Wyndham explained his position:

22 NARSSA: GG 667, file 9/93/7 War 1914-16: Imperial Army. South African Overseas Expeditionary Force, Bonar Law to Buxton, 24 Jul 1915, and Botha to Buxton, 10 Aug 1915.
23 NARSSA: GG 667, file 9/93/7 War 1914-16: Imperial Army. South African Overseas Expeditionary Force, Botha to Buxton, 10 Aug 1915.
24 BL: Add MS 86963, Buxton Papers, Note, Thursday, 8 July 1915.
25 Buchan, *South African Forces in France*, p.16.
26 As Ian Uys has shown, by the end of the war, 'the portion of Afrikaners had increased from 15 to 30 per cent.' I. Uys, *Rollcall; The Delville Wood Story* (Johannesburg: Uys Publishers, 1991), p.5.

> The air here has been thick with rumours during the last few days on the subject of reported risings of Boers in various parts of the country – but there is happily no truth in them, though there can be no doubt that the spirit is willing enough – only the absence of arms and ammunition being the impediment. I understand Botha is having a conference of various Boer commandants, whom he can trust, to discuss the situation. I don't think it will come to a rising, owing to the lack of arms, and the absence of anyone to give the lead, but it is all very disturbing. Meanwhile Smuts is going on like a house on fire in German East, and if he really succeeds in finishing that off, by the end of the August, all the loyal troops return from there, we shall be as right as rain.[27]

Crewe writing to Buxton put the discussion into perspective:

> I also certainly concur in what you say about the numerical strength of the European Contingent, two brigades is 8,000 men, – if possible? – kept up to strength would be as many as it would be wise or safe to send, until as you say we see more clearly what the future probabilities in S. Africa are. I see a good many well to do farmers here from the Southern Free State and what they say is that there is not likely to be any recrudescence of rebellion and that the anti-Botha party are very busy politically, trying to get their own back this time in a constitutional manner. After all I do not think any rebellion would be really dangerous, the Cape Dutchman is on the whole scarcely a bellicose individual, the Transvaal or Free State usually take opposite views or sides, and last time the Englishman was scarcely called upon to help suppress and we could of course turn out many thousands if and when required. So I cannot help thinking 8,000 men can be spared… [if the election] were postponed the rebels would possibly give up constitutional methods for unconstitutional.[28]

Crewe was probably closer to the truth. In 1913 the formation of the National Party, signalled a divide and breakaway from the broad-church SAP policy – a hodgepodge for everyone. It was a response to the constitutional crisis. This was part of the schism that contributed to the Rebellion. The complex reasons for uprising include a range of personal issues, poverty, societal concerns, and political jealousies – these were politicised by the rebel leaders and supported by the Germans. The tactical result spoke for itself – a decisive defeat. But a year later in 1915 with lenient sentences, a divided White society and a dominion at war, the National Party faced a new reality. They realised that in Botha and Smuts's Union, they had the all the rights, they had popular support, constituencies, and the mechanism to achieve political change – the elections.

27 WSRO: Petworth House Archives, Hugh Wyndham to Lady Leconfield, 28 June 1916.
28 BL: Add MS 86963, Buxton Papers, Charles Crewe to Buxton, 4 July 1915.

In 1946, at the time of the unveiling of the Botha equestrian statue, Smuts proclaimed that Botha's memory was 'the shared heritage of all South Africans'. The vandalisation of the Botha statue, and Smuts's own at the University of Cape Town, in 2015 and 2016 reflected instead a divided, contested memory of both men.
(T. Zwane, 'EFF and ANC at odds over "offensive statues"', *Mail and Guardian* and L. Hess, 'Louis Botha statue outside parliament defaced', *News 24*)

Botha's first cabinet (1910) reflected the fragile politics of Union consensus. Trouble was already brewing. Front: J.W. Sauer, L. Botha, and A. Fischer. Back: J.B.M. Hertzog, Henry Burton, F.R. Moor, C. O'Grady Gubbins, J.C. Smuts (in scholarly repose), H.C. Hull, F.S. Malan, and D. Graaff. (NARSSA: Botha's first cabinet, 1910)

The defeat of the vanguard of Lukin's column at Sandfontein (September 1914) surprised an overconfident leadership, while the adversities faced by the prisoners shocked the South African public. (DOD Archives, Photographic Selection, Prisoners at Sandfontein, 1914)

Military service in South Africa and on campaign reinforced the hierarchies of power and privilege. (DOD Archives, Photographic Collection)

The campaign in German South West Africa - allowing rapid advance and broad, sweeping movement, suited the South African approach to warfare. The experience in East Africa was a remarkably different affair. (DOD Archives, Photographic Selection, South African forces on horseback, 1915)

"General Officers of World War I" by John Singer Sargent. Rendered following Botha's death in 1922, it was donated to the National Portrait Gallery by Sir Abe Bailey. Smuts and Botha stand at two and three from the left. (© National Portrait Gallery, NPG 1954)

Botha and Smuts are feted in Cape Town. As Reitz later noted: they 'had added to the Union a territory larger than Germany, and they had done it with fewer casualties than the cost of an average trench raid in France'. (DOD Archives, Photographic Selection, Botha and Smuts in Cape Town, 1915)

The East Africa campaign was predominantly an infantry affair, dependent on vulnerable lines of communication that remained constantly on the verge of breakdown. (DOD Archives, Photographic Collection)

1st South African General Hospital, France. The South African casualties on the Western Front dwarfed those of the other Union campaigns. (DOD Archives, Photographic Collection, South African General Hospital in France)

Botha and Smuts in East Africa. (DOD Archives, Photographic Collection, Botha and Smuts in East Africa, 1916)

A hospital ship at the Cape Town docks, c.1916. The casualties sustained in East Africa, first at Salaita, were controversial and Botha had to rely on Smartt, leader of the official parliamentary opposition, to help him avoid a debate Hertzog's nationalists would demand in Parliament. (DOD, Archives, Photographic Collection, DOD Archives, a Ship docked in Cape Town)

Botha and Smuts on campaign. (DOD Archives, Photographic Collection, 1916, Botha and Smuts on campaign)

Imperial War Cabinet members, Lieutenant General Jan Smuts and Major General H.H. Ganga Singh Maharajah of Bikaner, inspecting troops in London, 1917. Their perspectives in Cabinet sometimes aligned although for very different reasons. (Open source)

Imperial War Cabinet, 25 June 1918. (National Portrait Gallery, PG X32127)

Botha and Smuts at Versailles. Both men sought to mitigate the sentence passed against Germany - believing the harsh terms would lead to another war. (Open source)

Botha returned from Versailles a tired and dangerously ill man. He died on 26 August 1919. (NARSSA, Botha and Smuts returned to South Africa, 1919)

Recruitment for the forthcoming campaign, and the protection of the Union were two sides of the same coin, and with less concern of an uprising, it facilitated deploying men outside South Africa. At the beginning of October, Crewe was hard at work getting the last drafts of the Brigade away to Britain and mobilising the forces for East Africa. He hoped to reinforce the contingents after the October 1915 election.[29] By late October with the general election over, pushed hard to recruit troops for East Africa. Crewe commented that in global terms, the South African contribution would remain small when compared with the other Dominions, but he added a counterpoint that they did not have South Africa's difficulties.[30]

An example of this was how the strategic and tactical concerns of warfighting were soon overshadowed by questions of recruitment and pay. These would divide the South African Party and drive a deeper wedge between the Unionists and Botha. Botha to his credit stood firm on opposing conscription, an initiative that the Unionists pushed strongly.[31] Botha knew that anything besides voluntary service would collapse the fragile balance.

Although Botha mostly focussed on the political intent rather than the detailed military planning, he could not help himself but have an initial look at the campaign plans for German East Africa. Buxton comments that he, with Botha and Smuts poured over maps discussing possible options for the campaign.[32] Once the planning was done, for once he did not saddle up and lead his troops – no, on this occasion it would be Oom Jannie in command.

With Smuts away, Botha held his position as prime minister and managed the ministry of defence on a temporary basis.[33] His workload was increased drastically but he managed to keep his head above water.[34] Buxton, writing on Smuts's departure, said that 'it was to Botha a prodigious gap and accentuated the sense of pressure and responsibility.'[35] It was also in Buxton that Botha found a friend; they trusted one another implicitly. According to Buxton they almost always agreed.[36]

Botha had other valued confidantes, including his friend, and former private secretary, Dr W.E. Bok, who had left his immediate service for a post in justice. Bok had always translated for the prime minister, and Botha would sometimes complain of Bok's flowery language claiming it was 'more Bok than Botha'.[37] He was always at Botha's side and Lord Sandhurst recalled an embarrassing incident where Bok, who

29 WSHC: 947/469, Viscount Long of Wraxall Papers, Crewe to Long, 9 October 1915.
30 WSHC: 947/469, Viscount Long of Wraxall Papers, Crewe to Long, 23 October 1915.
31 Meintjes, *Botha*, p.279.
32 Buxton, *General Botha*, p.226.
33 Meintjes, *Botha*, p.283.
34 Engelenburg, *Botha*, p.312.
35 Buxton, *General Botha*, p.197.
36 Buxton, *General Botha*, pp.223–225. See BL: Add MS 87052, Buxton Papers, 1914-1918, notes on Botha, 4 January 1917.
37 Botha quoted in Meintjes, *Botha,* p.182.

was translating for Botha was misidentified and ushered out of a dinner party by a pair of nervous stewards. He was admitted later on when his identity had been established, and one can only imagine the sigh of relief blown by Botha.[38] It was on these key team members that Botha came to depend. Smuts had commented to Merriman that Botha had perhaps not had the best formal education, 'if he had culture as he has chivalry and common-sense, there would not be his equal in South Africa. The varsity boys in the team will help him most loyally'.[39] Besides the academically gifted allies of the 'General's Kindergarten', Botha also relied on his politically astute and wealthy connections. One example was Sir David Graaff.

A Botha confidante, Graaff was a businessman who had built immense wealth in pioneering the cold storage industry in South Africa, and later became a politician and attended the 1911 Imperial Conference with the prime minister. Appointed as the minister of posts and telegraphs, although he suffered from ill health, Graaff provided a pillar of political support while Botha and Smuts were in the field invading German South West Africa. Of Graaff, Botha said, 'He is so loyal, upright and able'.[40] Upon the resignation of Hull, and Smuts's deployment to German South West Africa, Graaff took over the finance portfolio, from 1915 to 1916. On this and the finance ministry, Buxton lamented, 'since Union there has not been anyone with any financial knowledge in the Cabinet'.[41] But Buxton realised what a good friend Graaff was to Botha and admitted: 'he guides him [Botha] with a silken thread.'[42] It may have been a result of his uprightness, ability and loyalty, and perhaps some guiding with a silken thread, that Botha requested Buxton to put forward Graaff's name for the Knight Commander of the Order of St Michael and St George. Graaff's financial support for the war effort no doubt did little to hurt his case. Buxton initially opposed this request but eventually gave in to the old general, stating, 'Botha is always so reasonable in his requests that it is a pleasure to meet them'.[43] Botha required all the assistance he could muster in addressing issues of recruitment and pay during the First World War.

Botha was careful that matters linked to pay did not to get out of hand after the hotly contested October 1915 elections.[44] He made use of the *Volksstem* to respond to the motion for an increase in pay for the Union's soldiers serving in East Africa.[45] Try as he may he could not get ahead of the problems linked to the mustering and payment of soldiers – they became a political liability, especially the European theatre.[46]

38 Viscount Sandhurst, *From Day to Day, 1916-1921* (London: Edward Arnold, 1929), p.290.
39 Smuts to Merriman, 4 March 1907 in Hancock and Van der Poel (eds.), *Selections*, vol.II, p.325.
40 Botha to Smuts, 1 February 1915 in Hancock and Van der Poel (eds.), *Selections*, Vol. III, p.235.
41 BL: Add MS 87052, Buxton Papers, 1914-1918, Buxton's notes on Botha, 6 March 1916.
42 BL: Add MS 87093, Buxton Papers, 1908-1929, Buxton's notes on Botha's life, no date.
43 BL: Add MS 87052, Buxton Papers, 1914-1918, Buxton's notes on Botha, 7 February 1918.
44 Meintjes, *Botha*, p.280; NARSSA: Preller Archive, 90, 'De Volksraad', *De Volksstem*, 2 February 1916.
45 NARSSA: Preller Archive, 90, 'De Volksraad', *De Volksstem*, 2 February 1916.
46 See N.G. Garson, 'South Africa and World War 1', *Journal of Imperial and Commonwealth History*, vol.8 (1979).

The forces in Europe were paid 1 shilling per day which was less than the amount paid to the soldiers in German South West Africa and German East Africa. The force was formed in accordance with the war establishments fixed for new armies and the British government assumed liability for pay.[47] Engelenburg agrees that Botha was in favour of increasing the payment to 3 shillings, however the National Party firmly opposed the idea of the Union 'losing money' on account of what they labelled a 'British war'. Botha attempted to justify the expenditure saying that the campaign in Europe would determine the war's outcome.[48] The point was put into context by the fact that many Afrikaners did not care about Britain's victory – they wanted practical outcomes like land, and opportunity – and for South Africa, any territorial aggrandisement would be a result of African campaigns.

During the break in December 1915, members of the Unionist Party put forward a strong public case for the equal pay for the forces in Europe and German East Africa, although limited to White soldiers. Botha and Buxton consulted with Smartt to hold back the motion during the parliamentary session in early 1916. The Unionists did not grasp the impact of the troubled relations between Boer and Briton and the legacy of the Anglo-Boer War, especially in the backveld. Smartt decided against introducing the motion to parliament in February 1916, but in a surprise move, the Unionist Party, in spite of their leader, decided to submit it.[49]

Botha regretted it. He said that the sensitive situation in South Africa had to be taken into account. He added, 'the motion will make no one happy and could only lead to problems'.[50] The result was a divided House. Botha claimed that the speaker who proposed the motion, Mr T. Boydell, lived in Durban and did not understand the desperate situation in the Free State. Botha went on that his personal feeling on the motion was for equal pay for all soldiers, but not at the cost of dividing his party.[51] The South African Party members of parliament, were in a difficult position, they agreed to support Botha on the motion out of loyalty but in the event of a vote, they would have to resign, because their constituents would not be in agreement.[52]

Botha agreed that the payment of the German East African contingent remained the responsibility of South Africa and the total cost of the East African campaign,

47 The infantrymen would each carry a rifle M.L.E. with oil bottle, pull through and sight protector, sword bayonet, pattern '88 with scabbard, and two hundred rounds of mark VI ammunition per rifle. See NARSSA: GG 667, file 9/93/7 War 1914-16: Imperial Army. South African Overseas Expeditionary Force, Botha to Buxton, 19 August 1915, and Bonar Law to Buxton, 17 July 1915.

48 Meintjes, *Botha*, p.280; NARSSA: Preller Archive, 90, 'De Volksraad', *De Volksstem*, 2 February 1916.

49 Mouton, 'The sacred tie', pp.17–19.

50 NARSSA: Preller Archive, 92, Botha quoted in 'De Volksraad', *De Volksstem*, 2 February 1916 and, *De Burger*, 16 February 1916.

51 NARSSA: Preller Archive, 92, 'De Volksraad', *De Volksstem*, 2 February 1916.

52 Buxton, *General Botha*, p.248.

estimated at £2.5 million would come from the Union's treasury.[53] Botha expressed his thoughts on the matter in a letter to Smuts:

> I enclose for you the full debate on the overseas payment. I was glad to get your telegram; no other way was open. Even our friend John X. came to me, after a three-day caucus in which he made three speeches and supported me strongly and said: I must now advise you to let this matter drop – So, only after I saw clearly that our party would break up did I make the statement. I am glad to say that it has done a great deal of good.[54]

The matter of the pay for soldiers on foreign service, in Europe and East Africa, was partially resolved in November 1916 when Britain agreed to the pay increase on condition that the Union made a financial contribution. Botha wanted the matter to be quietly resolved, but to no avail. Smartt put a motion to parliament in early 1917, and Botha responded by ensuring that that the motion was withdrawn.[55] A deeply frustrated Botha commented to Buxton that the Unionists were holding a loaded gun to the South African Party's head.[56] The matter of the sentencing of the rebels did not help things along at all.

Parliamentary Tussles and Public Opinion

Botha was in favour of leniency towards the rebels.[57] But he faced a complex situation – most Afrikaners wanted no penalty for the rebels; generally, Labour moderates supported clemency, however Sir Percy Fitzpatrick and Unionists criticised Botha demanding harsher sentences.[58] There was a mixed economy of opinion; C.P. Crewe supported Botha's 'forgive and forget' policy which he had promoted since the end of the Anglo-Boer War.[59] As Botha put it: 'Both the British and the Dutch have much to forgive and forget.'[60]

Drummond Chaplin voiced the hard-line view:

53 NARSSA: Preller Archive, 92, 'De Volksraad', *De Volksstem*, 2 February 1916.
54 Botha to Smuts, 23 February 1916 in Hancock and Van der Poel (eds.), *Selections*, Vol. III, p.336.
55 Mouton, 'The sacred tie', pp.19–20.
56 Buxton, *General Botha*, p.241.
57 NARSSA: PrellerArchive, 90, Botha quoted in 'Horses for Botha', *Pretoria News,* 18 December 1916.
58 L. Grundlingh, '"In the Crisis, who would Tamper with the Existing order?" The Political and Public Reaction of English-speaking South Africans to the 1914 Rebellion', *Historia*, vol.59, no.2 (2014), pp.164–165.
59 Grundlingh, 'In the Crisis who would Tamper?', p.165.
60 Buxton, *General Botha*, p.161.

> As regards the terms given to the Germans in S. West Africa, I think they were unduly lenient. I should have preferred to see the whole German population repatriated. I believe that would have been the cheapest policy in the end. These peoples, left in the country, with a fair supply of arms (they may have a good many hidden) will be sure to intrigue with the rebels in the Union and may give a good amount of trouble.[61]

However, these fears proved to be baseless. There were limited accounts of German and rebel sympathisers storing weapons, and these posed no legitimate threat. Afrikaner Nationalists had the political platform and did not need to resort to armed rebellion – this was proved in the 1915 elections where they won a significant number of seats. A large part of the Afrikaner Nationalist campaign involved justifying the actions of the rebels and advocating for leniency and blanket amnesty.

Steyn wrote to Buxton demanding that the governor general liberate De Wet and other convicted rebels, and that their fines be expunged. Buxton was not inclined to do this, nor could he reduce the sentences without the recommendation and advice of the responsible minister. Buxton responded that conciliation was important, but a complete amnesty was out of the question:

> The loyal Dutch who have kept their plighted faith, and who themselves have lost near relations and dear friends in the Civil War; and who, in so many places, have been plundered and retrenched (a persecution which is still going on with great virulence) are entitled, if not to reparation for the past, at least to absolute security for the future. The British are equally entitled to demand that no action shall be taken which would tend by condoning it to encourage the idea that a rebellion can be undertaken with impunity in this country … [we] need 'to draw a veil over all the ungracious past' – to heal wounds and bring about real and genuine atmosphere of conciliation and reconciliation between the Dutch, and between the Dutch and English.[62]

Hertzog did not help matters of conciliation and gave Buxton grave doubts which he shared with Botha and Smuts. Buxton put his views to Steyn, that Hertzog 'publicly justified the action of the "most noble and respected of their leaders", actions for which they have been found guilty of, or have pleaded guilty to High Treason'.[63]

Steyn replied that Buxton would 'not visit the sins of General Hertzog, the National Congress, and other sympathisers of the rebel prisoners who cannot be held responsible for them'.[64] Steyn's justification was one sided, but the reality for many was that they feared Nationalist reprisals, both socially and economically. Buxton explains:

61 WSHC: 947/468, Viscount Long Papers, Chaplin to Long, 14 September 1915.
62 BL: Add MS 86963, Buxton Papers, Buxton to M.T. Steyn, 18 July 1915.
63 BL: Add MS 86963, Buxton Papers, Buxton to M.T. Steyn, 18 July 1915.
64 BL: Add MS 86963, Buxton Papers, M.T. Steyn to Buxton, c. July 1915.

> Regarding rebels it is enough to say the position locally is critical. At least ninety per cent follow de Wet and no doubt the leniency shown by the Government backed mind you by Unionists is to blame. However, it's no use crying over the facts as the future has to be faced. A strong move against loyalists especially Englishmen is already noticeable ... they openly say they will make it too hot for every Englishman unless he comes to their way of thinking and behaves himself, otherwise out of the place he must go. ... Doctor de Villiers who was with the forces at the front and who refused to join Maritz after his life was threatened by the traitors has been told he must join the Nationalist Party ... Unfortunately through the fact that the rebels are so strong here the wretches are having their own way more or less.[65]

De Wet, who had been captured for his involvement in the rebellion, received an early release from prison in December 1915. This was on condition that he stayed out of politics and avoided making public addresses. Botha and Smuts were concerned about the old general again stoking the flames of rebellion.[66] In one case, the minister of justice pointed out that De Wet was allowed to visit Dewetsdorp but was not permitted to make any form of public address.[67] De Wet's release caused concern for the Unionists – many wondered whether a reconciliation between the South African Party and the Nationalists would divide the political landscape on racial lines.[68] Of course in practice this was not possible, at least not at this point in history. The schism between Botha and De Wet was profound – yet they had a long and deep, although not always easy, relationship. They came out of the Anglo-Boer War as two dashing supreme Boer generals; one commanding forces in the Transvaal and the other the Free State. Botha felt 'deep sadness at the miserable fall which my old comrade-in-arms has brought upon himself'.[69] It was in the hopes of placating his Boer countrymen, and his spirit of conciliation, that in 1916 Botha put out an amnesty law regarding offences committed during the rebellion.[70]

The Unionists had their reservations about the amnesty, but their most important policy was the continuation of the war effort, and for that they needed to keep Botha in power.[71] Inextricably tied to the war effort was the question of how to pay for it. In March 1916 Botha opposed a motion for a land tax, known as the Wyndham motion. Wyndham, of British descent and a member of Milner's kindergarten, stood unsuccessfully against

65 BL: Add MS 86963, Buxton Papers, Buxton's notes dated c. July 1915.
66 Meintjes, *Botha*, pp.281–282.
67 NARSSA: Preller Archive, 93, 'Botha over De Wet, *De Burger*, 21 January 1916.
68 I. van der Waag, 'Hugh Archibald Wyndham: His Life and Times in South Africa, 1901–1923', PhD thesis, University of Cape Town, 2005, p.265.
69 Buxton, *General Botha*, p.176.
70 NARSSA: Preller Archive, 90, 'De Volksraad Begrotindebat', *De Volksstem*, 23 April 1916.
71 See Van der Waag, 'Hugh Archibald Wyndham', pp.264–265.

Botha in 1906 for the Turffontein seat.[72] Fitzpatrick, to whom Botha had lost the Pretoria East constituency in 1910, put the Wyndham motion to the House.

Botha opposed it vehemently, referencing the difficulties facing farmers all over the country, the drought, and the politico-economic liability: the large amount of farmers who had become *bywoners*, and the overall strain it would place on the financial position of farmers.[73] *Bywoners* were of lower socio-economic status and often manipulated by an unfair power dynamic. A case in point, and demonstrating the economic dimension, was that during the Afrikaner Rebellion 90 percent of Beyers's commando were *bywoners*.[74] Buxton refers to the *bywoner* issue, offering a rather harsh description:

> … the poverty stricken hanger on, often unemployable, who number some 80,000 at least – the despair of South Africa … he is mainly a product of the old days of enormous farms, who squatted on the land and produced large families … the presence of a Black proletariat made him scorn unskilled work, and even for that he is unfit.[75]

Botha took on Fitzpatrick, saying that he had a good farm with all the resources he needed. However, many farmers in the rural areas were in a less fortunate position.[76] Like Botha, Wyndham was also a successful landowner, but the prime minister did not hammer this point home. The National Party press took Wyndham to task for his motion, publishing a cartoon of him as a jingoist squeezing the farmers to finance the war.[77]

72 Van der Waag, 'Hugh Archibald Wyndham'.

73 The Carnegie Commission produced five reports on the Poor White problem in South Africa. See Carnegie Commission, *The Poor White Problem in South Africa: Report of the Carnegie Commission: Joint Findings and Recommendations* (Stellenbosch: Ecclesia, 1932); E.G, Malherbe, *Educational Report: Education and the Poor White, Part III of The Poor White Problem in South Africa: Report of the Carnegie Commission* (Stellenbosch: Ecclesia, 1932); W.A, Murray, *Health Report: Health Factors in the Poor White Problem, Part IV of The Poor White Problem in South Africa: Report of the Carnegie Commission* (Stellenbosch: Ecclesia, 1932); R.W. Wilcocks, *Psychological Report: The Poor White, Part II of The Poor White Problem in South Africa: Report of the Carnegie Commission* (Stellenbosch: Ecclesia, 1932); J.R. Albertyn, A.D, Luckhoff, T.F, Cronje and M.E, Rothmann, Sociological Report: (a) The Poor White and Society, Part V (a) of The Poor White Problem in South Africa: Report of the Carnegie Commission (Stellenbosch: Ecclesia, 1932). Also see F.A. van Jaarsveld, *Die Afrikaners se Groot Trek na die Stede en ander Opselle* (Johannesburg: Perskor, 1982).

74 A. Grundlingh and S. Swart, *Radelose Rebellie, Dinamika van die 1914–1915 Afrikanerrebellie* (Pretoria: Protea, 2009), p.25.

75 Buxton, *General Botha*, p.200.

76 NARSSA: Preller Archive, 90, Botha quoted in 'Generaal Botha tegen Belasting op Landbougrond', *De Volksstem*, 20 March 1916.

77 Van der Waag, 'Hugh Archibald Wyndham', p.186.

The Nationalists saddled Botha with the Unionists. There was Nationalist criticism that the Botha government was not doing enough to support poor Whites, but Botha insisted that he was indeed in favour of improving the lot of the poor.[78] Botha put forward a high-level summary of support given, including approximately 8,400 jobs on the railways, 800 agricultural jobs, as well as further job creation initiatives on infrastructure and industrial projects.[79] The question of funding the war effort was inescapable and Hertzog criticised Botha. The prime minister countered that of all the Dominions, South Africa was spending the least on its war effort.[80]

Botha was able to promote his public image through the use of his mouthpiece, the *Volksstem*, In April 1916, he became aware of a film, *The Dop Doctor*, which was released in London, and which portrayed Afrikaners in a negative light. After writing to Engelenburg to find out more about the film, he declared that it made the Boer people seem characterless and simple country folk. The movie suggested that there was simmering tension and bitterness between South African Afrikaner and English speakers, something that Botha believed would have a negative effect on the complex political situation in the country.[81] It was bad enough that on the claim that the South African Party and the Unionists had an 'unholy covenant', Botha put forward the option of a vote of no confidence to the House.[82]

Botha gave Engelenburg permission to publish his response to the British high commissioner.[83] The movie was widely criticised in South Africa, and because of Botha's cable the film was withdrawn from the cinema circuit.[84] Perhaps the movie hit a nerve, showing parts of South Africa that Botha did not want exposed – it showed the animosity present in the Union.[85] Botha wanted to promote a modernising South Africa that had a growing role in the British Empire.

Although Engelenburg was a close ally and worked to the ends of Botha, the signs of frustration started to show. Convinced that the *Volksstem* was being taken over by Nationalists, he wrote to Engelenburg in May 1916 stating firmly that he had received a number of complaints about the *Volksstem* not being written in the 'desired tone'.[86]

78 NARSSA: Preller Archive, 90, Botha quoted in De Volksraad, Begrotindebat', *De Volksstem*, 3 April 1916.
79 NARSSA: Preller Archive, 90, Botha quoted in 'Armeblanken', May 1916.
80 NARSSA: Preller Archive, 90, Botha quoted in 'De Volksraad, Begrotingsdebat', *De Volksstem*, 3 April 1916.
81 NARSSA: Engelenburg Archive, 140, Botha to Engelenburg, 1 May 1916; Botha's private secretary to Engelenburg, 14 April 1916.
82 NARSSA: Preller Archive, 90, Botha quoted in 'Armeblanken', May 1916.
83 NARSSA: Engelenburg Archive, 140, Botha to Engelenburg, 1 May 1916; Botha's private secretary to Engelenburg, 14 April 1916.
84 See T. Gutsche, 'The History and Social Significance of Cinema in South Africa', PhD thesis, University of Cape Town, 1946, pp.394–395.
85 NARSSA: Preller Archive, 93, 'Crime against the People', *Rand Daily Mail*, 2 November 1916.
86 NARSSA: Engelenburg Archive, 140, Botha to Engelenburg, 10 May 1916.

He claimed there was a 'lack of neutrality' in the reportage. Botha had shares in the paper and made his influence felt.[87]

F.V. Engelenburg was an ally – he was a Dutch scholar, who originally came to support the Republic of Transvaal government under Paul Kruger in the late 1800s. He went on to become the editor of the *Volksstem*. His large and remarkable house, with Dutch architectural roots, still stands as a monument outside Pretoria. The house is today the headquarters of *Suid Afrikaanse Academie vir Wetenskap en Kuns* (The Afrikaans academy for science and art), and a museum. Engelenburg was an interesting man, a polyglot who could allegedly speak eight languages. Interestingly Buxton commented that Engelenburg was 'a strange creature', adding that he 'lived with a Portuguese lady for some years without marrying her.'[88] He went on to state that the 'hum-drum Damma Vittoria' could only speak a little Dutch and that he could not speak Portuguese. Perhaps the governor general was a little too quick to judge as it seems the good Dr Engelenburg could and did speak Portuguese.[89]

A group of influential businessmen reached out to Engelenburg and put forward the proposition that a South African Party Club, similar to the one in Johannesburg, be established in Pretoria.[90] Engelenburg asked Botha to speak to Sammy Marks, the industrialist, to secure funding for the establishment of the Pretoria South African Party Club. Botha trying to get some space, replied that Engelenburg should also ask Ewald Esselen to influence Sammy Marks.[91] The club became a hub for British upper-class socialites who were charmed by Botha. He used his personality for diplomacy, but his positive and contagious *joie de vivre* was just who he was – and he disarmed so many. A case in point was a comment by Edward Grey, the British foreign secretary, to Buxton, 'It must be very satisfactory to you and Mildred. Botha is a splendid fellow'.[92] Another by Lord Sandhurst, who sat next to Botha at a formal dinner in 1919 claimed he was, 'extremely interesting as well as pleasant'.[93]

Botha's magnetism was widely acknowledged and Olive Schreiner, who was critical of Botha's war policy, was also susceptible to his charm and on meeting him told Isie Smuts in a letter, 'It was the first time I had ever spoken to Botha though I shook hands with him once. I quite understand now why the Purcells and all my other

87 NARSSA: Engelenburg Archive, 140, Botha to Engelenburg, 7 December 1916.

88 WCARS: H.E.S Fremantle Collection, Vol. 3, A608, Diary, Tuesday, 12 March 1907.

89 See L. E. Brink, 'Die Lewe, Werk en Invloed van F.V. Engelenburg in Suid-Afrika (1889–1938)', PhD thesis, North-West University.

90 NARSSA: Engelenburg Archive, 140, Rooth & Wessels to Engelenburg, 12 January 1916; Engelenburg to Rooth & Wessels, 14 January 1916.

91 NARSSA: Engelenburg Archive, 140, Engelenburg to Botha, 4 May 1916; Botha to Engelenburg, 10 May 1916.

92 BL: Add MS 87094: Buxton Papers, 1891-1931, Grey to Buxton, 25 July 1914. Also see Add MS 87102, Mildred Buxton to Sydney Buxton,10 and 17 November 1916.

93 Sandhurst, *From Day to Day*, p.290.

friends are so fond of him. He has such a beautiful smile. I always believe there is something deep down very good in the people whose smile is good.'[94]

Armed with his smile, Botha continued with his political and administrative tasks throughout 1916. He visited various areas in the Cape, where he spoke about helping the farmers, especially during the drought.[95] He was a proponent of a good scientific agricultural education which would allow South Africa to compete internationally.[96] Botha felt comfortable in the agricultural world – it was slow, measured and without the vitriol of politics. The hard work and efforts of the farmer, if correctly applied, with skill and patience, the raising of crops and harvest season, the nurturing of cattle, played out slowly and with the fullness of time. It was diametrically opposed to the fast-moving, sharp, and toxic political issues that weighed heavy on him. This eventually had an impact on his health, and he asked Engelenburg to publish an update on his physical condition in the *Volksstem* in May 1916.[97]

There was no respite in June, and Botha faced a range of demands. He warned against the strong anti-German feeling in Durban, especially among the English-speaking population.[98] The Unionist jingoists placed Botha in a tight spot with their extreme anti-German propaganda that professed British superiority. Some National Party supporters, according to Buxton, were on the other end of the spectrum and had said that they were hoping for a German victory.[99]

Botha maintained that, 'Extremists on both sides are the difficulty and the danger. They keep alive the spirit of enmity and suspicion. That is what we have to battle against, else we never will secure harmony between the two races, and without harmony South Africa cannot progress.'[100]

Intelligence in the Face of Another Rebellion

Rumours of a second Afrikaner Rebellion circulated between July and August 1916. Approximately 8,000 commando members were said to be taking to the field in the Free State.[101] Gerrit van Niekerk Schonken and Christiaan Pieter van der Merwe, were two of the instigators whispering about a second rebellion. They approached De Wet with the idea but the old general, recently released from prison refused to be

94 NARSSA: Smuts A1, 191, Olive Schreiner to Isie Smuts, December 1908.
95 NARSSA: Preller Archive, 93, Botha quoted in 'Generaal Botha te Cradock', *De Burger*, 10 February 1916.
96 NARSSA: Preller Archive, 93, Botha quoted in Crime against the People', *Rand Daily Mail*, 2 November 1916.
97 NARSSA: Engelenburg Archive, 140, Botha to Engelenburg, 1 May 1916.
98 See T. Dedering, 'Avenge the Lusitania'.
99 BL: Add MS 87052, Buxton Papers, 1914–1918, Buxton's notes on Botha, 6 March 1916.
100 Buxton, *General Botha*, p.170.
101 Van der Waag, 'Hugh Archibald Wyndham', p.284.

drawn into the plan and promptly reported them to the authorities.[102] The National Party had just achieved a significant victory in October 1915, and had, in fact, little reason to take up arms.

Botha was at pains to deter this and warned against rebellious talks.[103] The prime minister was concerned enough to put loyal commandants on stand-by. However, in practice, the chances of a second rebellion remained slim.[104] Politically there would be little benefit and militarily it was a non-starter. As Olive Schreiner put it: 'Botha has all the money and guns ... he must win.'[105]

Following the declarations of loyalty, and later the recruitment of large numbers of Africans for the labour contingents through the offices of the chiefs, the primary internal-security and intelligence concern remained right-wing Afrikaners and the presence of 'enemy aliens'. From 1903, William Melville had monitored the movement of Germans and suspicious aliens in Britain. Dr W.J. Leyds, Kruger's former emissary, 'came in for much attention', as did the stream of 'South African suspects' that arrived in Britain in the years immediately after the Anglo-Boer War. To be fair, Leyds probably deserved some surveillance, as he was key in leading the Transvaal secret service, a role later adopted by Jan Smuts, when he became Transvaal State Prosecutor. Smuts went on to head up the rebadged 'intelligence service' during the Anglo-Boer War.[106]

Interestingly Smuts was intimately involved with the development of intelligence networks and organisations in South Africa, from the late 1890s, through the formation of the Union 1903–1910, the 1914 Afrikaner Rebellion and the First World War, and again, coming back as prime minister in the late 1930s and leading the Union during the Second World War. Smuts in his amazing career repeated the restructuring of the intelligence services – starting with his work in the Transvaal under Paul Kruger, he took responsibilities away from the police, provided greater funding and professionalised the intelligence service.[107] In 1939 he again modernised the intelligence apparatus, separating it from the police, and providing a suitable budget.[108] Botha's historical links with the intelligence service can be found in early reports of the Transvaal secret service. He went on to set up the secret service commission after the fall of Pretoria during the Anglo-Boer War. His objectives, always practical, were

102 Burton to Smuts, 12 September 1916 in Hancock and Van der Poel (eds.), *Selections*, Vol. III, p.402.
103 NARSSA: Preller Archive, 93, Botha quoted in 'General Botha's Big Bombshell, *Rand Daily Mail*, 24 August 1916.
104 Van der Waag, 'Hugh Archibald Wyndham', pp.271–276.
105 UCT: Olive Schreiner, BC16/Box8, Olive Schreiner to Frederick Pethick-Lawrence, October 1916.
106 See H.J.G. Kamffer, 'Om een scherpe oog in't zeil te houden: Die Geheime Diens in die Zuid-Afrikaansche Republiek', (PhD thesis, North West University, 1999).
107 Kamffer, 'Die Geheime Diens', p.203.
108 K. Fedorowich, German Espionage and British Counter-Intelligence in South Africa and Mozambique, 1938-1944, *The Historical Journal*, vol.48, no.1 (2005).

directed at receiving a consistent flow of intelligence for the conduct of guerrilla operations. The secret service commission even managed to plant an agent in the British field intelligence department.[109]

Smuts was an intellectual, but also a practical man – he needed the sources, the data, and the information to make the correct decisions, and he knew that it was through surveillance that he could control the situation. This was a tool of statecraft, and a means to maintain internal control. Alexander Scotland, a British spy who would go on to become a spymaster and interrogator extraordinaire reported to Smuts's agents before the First World War.[110] It was only on Smuts's recommendation that Scotland was taken into British military intelligence during the First World War. Scotland performed a similar service for Thomas Kendrick, who would have a tremendous impact on MI6, writing a letter of recommendation for his commission in the British intelligence service.[111] These early intelligence networks and spy rings, which touched on the mining sector, and covered much of Southern Africa, spanning the turn of the twentieth century, through the Anglo-Boer War, to the First and Second World Wars, require additional study.

During the Afrikaner Rebellion, Botha and Smuts drew on formal and informal networks of intelligence using the magistrates' offices (which consumed much of the older intelligence services), the police, and loyal personnel in the military districts.[112] This was intelligence on the tactical level, and was in response to the defection of Maritz, Beyers, and Kemp. The fomenting of the Afrikaner Rebellion was evidence of an intelligence failure, but luckily the ability to respond was on point; the tactical intelligence operations were a success. It could be argued that the lack of a formal secret service was partly to blame for the initial failure.

Reports from 1910 indicate that the British imperial defence council was aware of potential German attempts to foment rebellion in South Africa. However, prior to 1914, it was widely held that this option was not practicable or necessary.[113] With time and the Great War fast approaching, Germany reconsidered its strategic position. Cognisant that the force in German South West Africa was weak, the use of intelligence operations proved an attractive option. The German administration was well aware of the delicate political situation in South Africa, and one account claims that the Kaiser had conferred with Commandant General Beyers in 1913.[114] On 2 August 1914 the German Chief of the General Staff ordered that a rebellion be instigated in

109 Kamffer, 'Die Geheime Diens', p.386.
110 A. Scotland, *The London Cage*, (London: Evans, 1957), p.20
111 See H. Fry, *The London Cage: The Secret History of Britain's World War II Interrogation Centre* (London: Yale University Press, 2017); H. Fry, *Spymaster: The Man who saved MI6* (London: Yale University Press, 2021).
112 Meintjes, *Botha*, 239; Fedorowich, 'Sleeping with the Lion?', p.80. Ritchie, *With Botha*, p.4.
113 DODA: WW1 D, Box 8 instructions from Headquarters, 20 August 1910; Anon., *The Times History of the War*, p.9.
114 DODA: WW1 D, Box 8 instructions from Headquarters, 20 August 1910.

South Africa.[115] Maritz, Beyers, Kemp and other leaders defected.[116] Their motivations were complex and varied but, regardless, the offer of German support bolstered their position. The Germans hoped to achieve two objectives, firstly, to delay any potential Union invasion plans and secondly, to undermine the combat cohesion of the Union Defence Force.[117]

The British narrative of German spies infiltrating Britain had a limited evidence base, although the pre-war spy scares – of German agents visiting British territory under the cover of poultry farmers, teachers of foreign languages, commercial travellers, sellers of marine lamps in various shipping centres, and hotel waiters – led to the creation of the Special Intelligence Bureau in October 1909.[118] Soon after, the work was divided between Captain Mansfield Smith-Cumming (espionage abroad) and Colonel Vernon Kell, later Major General, (counterespionage inside Britain).[119] The formal organisational structures took a while to be implemented in South Africa.

Of the acute questions complicating the parliamentary crises in South Africa during the war years, Buxton thought the German presence to be 'the most important and worrying.'[120] Although South Africa's German population was small and presented no clear danger, 2,500 male 'enemy aliens' were interned at Fort Napier outside Pietermaritzburg – possibly 'as much for their own protection as for that of the State'.[121] Some had been detained immediately after the outbreak of the war; others after the anti-German riots following the sinking of the *Lusitania* in 1915.

As Botha told Buxton, in the matter of the internments, he was 'between the Devil and the Deep Blue Sea.' Sections of the British community pressed for the internment of every 'enemy alien', while many Afrikaners – particularly those with German links, and of nationalist politics – criticised the government's internment policy and exposed the fragility of definitions of nationality and the difficulties in establishing individual loyalties based simply on place of birth and whether they were ever naturalised.

In July 1915, officers of the Special Intelligence Bureau revisited the pre-war question of closer cooperation with the dominions and colonies in the monitoring of 'enemy agents, plots, and alien activities.' They approached Canada, Ceylon, Singapore, Hong Kong, Gibraltar, Malta, Egypt, and South Africa – essentially the five strategic naval gateways – for the identification of liaison personnel in the counter-espionage structures, appealing for the creation of such structures where none existed. Colonel Sir

115 S.B. Spies, 'The Outbreak of the First World War and the Botha Government', *South African Historical Journal*, vol.1, no.1 (1969), p.48.
116 Nasson, *Springboks*, pp.43–44; Warwick, 'The Battle of Sandfontein', p.74. See also, DODA: Diverse 1, Box 2, Evidence given in the Rebellion Commission of Enquiry.
117 Collyer, *Campaign in German South West Africa*, p.5; Farwell, *The Great War in Africa 1914–1918*, p.75; Garcia, *First Campaign Victory*, pp.31, 93.
118 TNA: KV 1/8: Memoir by William Melville, p.4.
119 TNA: KV 1/9, General Report by Capt. Kell, 7 November 1910.
120 Buxton, *General Botha*, p.265.
121 Buxton, *General Botha*, p.266.

Maurice Hankey, Secretary to the Committee of Imperial Defence, stressed the importance of a 'Colonial Special Intelligence work'. London received few reports bar causal references in despatches, and information was scant, beyond the occasional brief brought to the notice of MI5 through private sources, and others through intercepted letters forwarded by the censor. Better organisation and closer cooperation were needed. On 5 August 1915, the Colonial Secretary, Bonar Law, approached the governors general of the dominions and the governors administrating colonies. Their replies, all largely positive, arrived from September; in many cases, they submitted full reports on local conditions to Colonel Vernon Kell and by April 1916 MI5 was directly or indirectly in contact with every dominion and colony – except South Africa.

While Australia, East Africa and Malta created their own security bureaus, and communications with the naval authorities in Gibraltar and Egypt extended intelligence gathering across the Eastern Mediterranean, the South African officials ignored – or at best, delayed replying to – the missals sent from London. While Buxton, as high commissioner, assisted with minor queries, further approaches made throughout 1916 met the same lack of response. By February 1917, the Central Bureau felt the opening of direct communication with South Africa to be urgent. Walter Long, now Colonial Secretary, with Kell in tow, met with Smuts – who was then in London – in February 1917. They agreed that a suitable officer be sent to establish the liaison. Smuts cabled Botha pressing the need to satisfy London on the matter. But a wary Botha required convincing that the Bureau would do no more than monitor the movement and receive reports on the movements of foreign nationals. Lieutenant Colonel Hercules Pakenham, selected to confer with Buxton and Botha and their advisors, arrived in South Africa on 4 June 1917. An ever-astute Buxton explained that a 'Secret Service' would not be tolerated 'as the political condition of the country made the experiment too dangerous.'[122] Many members of the ruling party and the opposition Nationalists were bound to Germany by tradition and marriage and, as he noted, 'some even wished to see Germany victorious.' This made the treatment of Germans in South Africa a very thorny issue. Any bureau created with a view to uncover German plots, 'would disclose some very nasty places and involve many members of the legislature and even Cabinet Ministers – the result might be Civil War.'[123] Moreover, Hertzog's Nationalists hated the prime minister, whom they branded as a traitor, and any attempt to create a South African bureau would be seen as further evidence of his betrayal and they would seek to block its funding – it would require an increase in the Defence vote – in a hostile parliamentary sitting.

Cajoled from London, and perhaps mollified by Buxton and Smuts, Botha accepted a compromise arrangement whereby Lieutenant Colonel W.H. Hamilton-Fowle,

122 TNA KV 1/15: Appendix F to Report on the Establishment of a Counter Espionage Service in the Colonies and Overseas Dominions, 1921.
123 TNA KV 1/15: Appendix F to Report on the Establishment of a Counter Espionage Service in the Colonies and Overseas Dominions, 1921.

the Provost Marshal of the Union, became the special correspondent to the Central Special Intelligence Bureau. London was satisfied, for Fowle had a knowledge of the local conditions (he had served as an intelligence officer during the Anglo-Boer War) and was serving also as commissioner of enemy subjects, custodian of enemy trading and controller of the Pietermaritzburg Internment Camp, which gave him access to the ministers of justice and defence, the commissioner of the SAP, and the chief censor. However, Fowle would in this role report directly to the prime minister and so secure secrecy and full sanction. They adopted the term 'Special Intelligence' instead of 'Counter-Espionage', which they thought too narrow, misleading, and suggestive of a 'Secret Service'. The Bureau stated expressly that it aimed at harvesting information from official sources, not 'agents', and that its powers were prescribed by legislation.[124] Such arguments may have enticed Botha and Smuts to allow a seemingly limited and rather tenuous link between their Provost Marshal's Office and MI5 in London. In this way, Botha satisfied London while avoiding the conundrum of creating an organisation that would 'spy' on fellow South Africans – for which he had no taste – or for that matter the need to enact further enabling legislation. Notwithstanding, as Pakenham ominously reported, with Fowle and his two able Assistant Provost Marshals – Captains Trigger and Scott, both SAP – London 'practically' had their desired 'Special Intelligence Bureau in being.'[125] Pakenham's mission, Buxton argued to Walter Long, had the 'additional advantage that it [would] induce the people [in South Africa] to sit up, and to take a greater interest and care in these matters.'[126]

The Central Special Intelligence Bureau in London became the centre for information – and enquiries – from around the empire. Information was essentially of two kinds: on the activities of enemy agencies and societies and individual suspects in British territories; and details on individuals in foreign countries wanting to travel to Britain or within the empire. They maintained a 'Black List' of the names and profiles, which they shared also with South Africa. While the correspondence and personal files in the archives of the Provost Marshal documents the South African side, we do not know how many South Africans – whether British nationals or resident aliens – appeared on London's 'Black List'. Botha's dislike of secret organisations, a distaste shared by many Afrikaners, probably meant the sharing was largely one directional or at least limited. In any case, as he and Smuts realised, the greatest security threat to South Africa remained one from within – one best confronted openly through the moral force of their own personalities.[127]

124 TNA KV 1/16: Report on the Establishment of a Counter Espionage Service in the Colonies and Overseas Dominions, 1921, and Report on Lieutenant Colonel Pakenham's Mission to South Africa, 1 September 1917, with Annexures.
125 TNA KV 1/16: Pakenham's Mission to South Africa, 1 September 1917.
126 WSHC: 947/602, Viscount Long of Wraxall Papers, Buxton to Long, 26 June 1917.
127 TNA KV 1/15: Report on the Establishment of a Counter Espionage Service in the Colonies and Overseas Dominions, 1921.

It was a complicated matter – a mess, as family spats often are. Botha told Smuts at the start of June 1916 that all of the rebellion POWs had been released except for 22 – chiefly the Kemp group. The *Helpmekaar*, a majority women community led initiative, paid most of their legal costs and fines, mobilising from the pulpit, especially with younger ministers, who also managed to seize control of the Transvaal Synod of the Dutch Reformed Church.[128] '... one of the worst men locally is the Predikants and they are at the bottom of everything including this proposed move by the women.'[129]

Internal War

Lord Kitchener's death in June 1916, devastated Botha.[130] Buxton wrote that Botha was so affected by the passing of his old enemy that when he read the telegram to the House of Assembly his voice became so soft that he spoke in a whisper.[131] The loss of personal friends, relations and colleagues weighed heavily on the general, who had his work cut out for him – he tried to maintain his composure in the onslaught of Nationalist accusations.

The Nationalists attempted to create public dissent by claiming that military service was to be made compulsory. This already thorny issue was further complicated by some ambiguous and wrongly worded defence recruitment circulars. This added fuel to the already suspicious Nationalist fire, and a quote from a certain Paul Hubbel sums up the position, 'Don't enlist to fight the "Deutsch" if you can run away or get a chance to pull out on your "bike" when the recruiting sergeant comes to see you'.[132]

Botha spoke out against the so-called forced recruitment through the *Volksstem*, reiterating that overseas military service was voluntary, adding that he trusted that South Africans would rise to the challenge.[133] Botha realised that the recruiting committees, on some occasions, used questionable messaging, and he took additional steps to tackle the issue. He announced in parliament that he wholeheartedly supported volunteers looking to serve in German East Africa, but he was firmly opposed to forced recruitment. Hertzog asked whether any strongly worded recruitment circulars were still being distributed, Botha responded that the matter had been addressed and no bulletins demanding military service would be issued.[134] Botha had commanded

128 Botha to Smuts, 2 June 1916 in Hancock and Van der Poel (eds.), *Selections*, Vol. III, p.371.
129 BL: Add MS 86963 Buxton Papers, Extract from a letter from Vrede, c. July 1915.
130 Engelenburg, *Botha*, p.313; Meintjes, *Botha*, p.282.
131 Buxton, *General Botha*, p.157.
132 Wits: A1 J.H. Hofmeyer Papers, Aa.1-2,, Paul E. Hubbel, North Carolina, to Hofmeyer, 6 September 1915.
133 NARSSA: Preller Archive, 92, Botha quoted in 'Generaal Botha tegen Dwang', *De Volksstem*, 3 April 1916.
134 DODA: DC, Box 756, Botha quoted in Address at House of Assembly, 1916.

in German South West Africa, he had led the Union forces against the Afrikaner rebels, and he had never conscripted troops. He now took on the role of the minister of defence, a position previously held by his dear Smuts, and he balanced wartime practicalities and political sensitivities; without his trusted friend. It had been around six months since they last saw each other.

Botha was excited about seeing Smuts. His departure, in mid-July was supposed to have been kept quiet but he missed his old friend so much that he could not help telling everyone at the SAP club. Ironically, he added the caveat to everyone he told, that it was in confidence. The good general told so many people 'in confidence' that it became an open secret. According to Bourne, 'his departure was club gossip before he left'.[135]

Botha had been in close communication with Smuts during his time in East Africa. He had praised Smuts's successes against the German forces and offered him support both personally and officially. In characteristic Botha fashion he wrote, 'I was very glad to see your handwriting again especially in these times when I miss you so much'.[136] Botha offered his advice on the operations, from a removed position, not speaking to the tactics, but rather to the logistical support offered and matters of practicality and diplomacy. Botha suggested to Smuts that the captured Askaris be returned to their chiefs on condition that they would break ties with the Germans. Botha also suggested offering them bribes.[137]

On the home front he toured Pondoland and the Transkei to hold meetings with African populations.[138] Earlier in 1916 Botha opened the Black majority University of Fort Hare, an institution that would educate prominent figures such as, Nelson Mandela, Ntatho Motlana, Robert Mangaliso Sobukwe, Robert Gabriel Mugabe and many more. German East Africa had Botha's interest because Smuts was there. Botha was concerned with recruiting Africans for the South African Native Labour Corps, which would be hit-and-miss; but provided invaluable service in the European theatre.

The 1st South African Brigade, fought at the Battle of the Somme in July 1916 under Brigadier General Lukin. Botha and Smuts were not entirely convinced about Lukin's ability to command a mobile force in a war of manoeuvre and figured the European theatre would better suit his skill set.[139] The brigade had been deployed to participate in the Sanusi campaign in August 1915, and then to France in April 1916. Those same forces fought at the Battle of Delville Wood, a feat of which Botha was very proud.[140] Between 1 and 20 July 1916, the 1st South African Brigade experi-

135 NARSSA: GG 671, file 9/93/68 Recruiting, Bourne to P. Horsfall, 11 July 1916.
136 Botha to Smuts, 13 April 1916 in Hancock and Van der Poel (eds.), *Selections*, Vol. III, p.357.
137 Botha to Smuts, 13 April 1916 in Hancock and Van der Poel (eds.), *Selections*, Vol. III, p.357.
138 Engelenburg, *Botha*, p.313.
139 Van der Waag, *A Military History*, p.110; BL: Add MS 87052, Buxton Papers, 1914-1918, Buxton's notes, 6 March 1916.
140 Meintjes, *Botha*, p.287.

enced a horrific 3,155 casualties during the Somme offensive.[141] It was South Africa's contribution to the Allied Thermopylae. In 1926 Annie Botha would unveil the South African memorial at Delville Wood, an initiative sponsored by Percy Fitzpatrick, and many British politicians including Loyd George – it serves as a monument to all South Africans who served in the First World War.[142] See Chapter 8 for additional discussion on this important theme.

The year 1916 proved a demanding one for Botha. He struggled with the death of the former Free State president, M.T. Steyn, who passed away in November.[143] The two men had a complicated relationship but there was a mutual respect. Certainly not everyone felt that way about the Boer stalwart, and Mildred Buxton, wife of the governor-general, wrote in rather callous terms: 'I have been thrilled by Steyn's death – won't it be a great help to Botha? I wonder what he was saying to the Women's Congress when he fell down dead?'[144]

In December 1916 Botha reprimanded Engelenburg for publishing a pro-National Party article which eulogised President Steyn. Botha went on to say that the National Party's newspapers never published anything which put the South African Party in a positive light.[145] That aside the South African Party and the Nationalists were briefly united at Steyn's funeral. D.W. Krüger states that 'for a moment they forgot their differences … but with the death of Steyn an important link with the past had been broken and with him the hope of political reunification of Afrikanerdom.[146] The moment of closeness between Botha and the National Party caused some trepidation for the Unionists.[147]

It was Botha's isolation from friends and colleagues, by both death and departure that saddened him. Another matter which bothered Botha deeply, was closer to home. Annie became unwell in 1916, which understandably had a significant impact on the sensitive general. She remained unwell for a large part of 1916, something that no doubt weighed very heavily on Botha. He expressed his sadness in a letter to Smuts saying: 'She is very broken down and weak, her hair is cut short, but my heart is glad and filled with thankfulness that my poor dear little wife is again recovering.'[148] Botha and Annie were a true love match. Basil Williams, who worked in the service of Milner and later became a professor of history, comments that when Botha was away in Pretoria or Cape Town, he would ask his clerks to telephone Annie in Standerton

141 Van der Waag, *A Military History*, p.125.
142 For a discussion on the commemoration of the Battle of Delville Wood, see B. Nasson, 'Delville Wood and South African Great War Commemoration', *The English Historical Review*, vol. 119, no. 480 (2004).
143 Meintjes, *Botha*, pp.284–287.
144 BL: Add MS 87102, 1889-1918, Mildred Buxton to Sydney Buxton,7 December 1916.
145 NARSSA: Engelenburg Archive, 140, Botha to Engelenburg, 7 December 1916.
146 Krüger, *Age of the Generals*, p.105.
147 Van der Waag, *A Military History*, p.281.
148 Botha to Smuts, 13 April 1916 in Hancock and Van der Poel (eds.), *Selections*, Vol. III, p.358.

every night. After asking how she was, he would then ask about the farm and if the dam was full. Another story that shows their affection was in London, and although told through a third party, Williams recalls when Annie entered the room, dressed up for dinner, she asked Louis, 'How do I look?', to which he answered 'beautiful' and kissed her.[149] It was the personal life of the flawed general that buoyed him, but alas his world would 'get narrower'.

Conclusion

Buxton said that 1916 was a frustrating year for Botha. He described his anxieties in their meetings in Cape Town. Botha would often laugh when in good spirits, and at other times he would lament, 'the world is getting too narrow for me'.[150]

The death of Kitchener, and later Steyn weighed heavily on him. He had a layered, and complicated relationship with both men. Smuts and Bok took on roles a little away from the general. Botha was an emotional soul, he was moved and touched by contact with others. Hating to be alone, he internalised their suffering, and when Annie fell ill, it pushed him to the limit. His family was first in a very full life and their wellbeing was critical – after all they gave him support while he faced an almost impossible task. He was now fighting a war on two fronts: externally, a shooting war in German East Africa, and Europe; and internally a political war in the Union.

In August 1916 at the South African Party Congress, Botha gave an update on the war and on current affairs. He said that despite the critique of the German South West African campaign, many were now asking for farms in the new territory. Botha went on to speak of the German East African campaign, praising Smuts's efforts and saying that the enemy had been driven into the bushveld. He explained the difficulties of the campaign including disease.[151] After his return from East Africa in early August, Botha had a good understanding of the difficulties which Smuts faced and had unfortunately himself experienced a bout of dysentery.[152] Botha went on and perhaps unintentionally gave Smuts, and possibly himself, a backhanded compliment, saying that for the first time a man without military training was put in charge of a great army.[153]

149 Williams, *Botha, Smuts and South Africa*, p.118.
150 Buxton, *General Botha*, p.228.
151 NARSSA: Preller Archive, 93, Botha quoted in 'General Botha's Big Bombshell', *Rand Daily Mail*, 24 August 1916.
152 Botha to Smuts, 6 August 1916 in Hancock and Van der Poel (eds.), *Selections*, Vol. III, p.391.
153 NARSSA: Preller Archive, 93, Botha quoted in 'General Botha's Big Bombshell, *Rand Daily Mail*, 24 August 1916.

Chapter 7 examines Smuts's role, commanding a very different campaign to that what had been contested in German South West Africa. In German East Africa, Colonel von Lettow Vorbeck, a competent and determined commander, led the German force, maximising terrain in time and space; he was assisted by the Askaris, environmental disease which affected Smuts's troops, and climatological factors. Smuts on the other hand was in command of a polyglot force and managed to make some significant territorial gains in pursuit of the elusive German commander.

7

Campaigning in Africa and Europe, 1916

> *Good-bye, good luck. I wish you a safe delivery from Germans, Portuguese, Belgians and all miasmatic microbes, and that Cicero may soon return from Cilicia in triumph.*
>
> Merriman to Smuts, 20 November 1916[1]

> *No time will be lost in pressing this campaign to a conclusion. But it bristles with extraordinary difficulties.*
>
> Smuts, May 1916[2]

> *Once more I wish to thank ... all ... members of staff for efficient and unselfish service and many kindnesses. In spite of all difficulties of our work this campaign and my association with GHQ will ever remain a treasured memory.*
>
> Smuts, January 1917[3]

With the general election over and their political position steady rather than stable, Botha and Smuts, urged on by the Unionists and loyalist Afrikaners who were concerned that South Africa was not doing enough, turned to the wider war. South Africa was exporting steel, war-related materials, and foods to Britain, Russia, France, Italy, and Japan, but, recognising that the Union's economic wellbeing was tied to the fortunes of the British Empire, they felt obliged to do more than simply support the wider war effort through South African trade and industry.[4] A new realism was now dawning too. For the British sector, the early war enthusiasm, experienced by many Afrikaners as ultra-jingoistic, had gone, while many nationalist Afrikaners came to accept that the war would not provide the much-wanted opportunity to fix old

1 Merriman to Smuts, 20 November 1916 in Hancock and Van der Poel (eds.), *Selections*, vol. III, p.414.
2 Smuts to Gillett, 2 May 1916 in Hancock and Van der Poel (eds.), *Selections*, vol. III, p.362.
3 NARSSA: Smuts Papers, vol.202, Smuts to GHQ, c. January 1917.
4 See the files in NARSSA: GG 586, file 9/51/52 War 1914-16: Trade. Exportation of certain forms of steel, and GG 586, file 9/51/54 War 1914-16, Trade.

grudges with Britain. Moreover, many South Africans, men like Lieutenant Cyril Newton-Thompson, having left to join the British armed forces, were already serving on the Western Front, and there had been some talk of recruiting men in South Africa for a 'New Army'.[5] The Afrikaner Rebellion, while coming at great political cost to Botha and Smuts, had proved indispensable in making the Union Defence Force into the modern force the defence minister had always desired. With the voices of the Beyers cohort silenced, Smuts could work with alacrity and a 'new look' armed force, which began to emerge in the short months between September 1914 and March 1915, was battle-hardened in German South West Africa. A chance illness at the end of 1915 would give an at first reluctant Smuts the opportunity to command his own 'show', test the instrument of his design somewhere else in Africa, and – in the process – extend South Africa's influence and possibly her borders.

Two South African expeditionary forces left South African shores from the end of 1915. Lukin's 1st South African Infantry Brigade mobilised first, served briefly in Egypt against the forces of Ahmed as-Sharif as-Sanusi, and, leaving for the trenches of the Western Front, famously stood at Delville Wood – 'the bloodiest battle-hell of 1916', according to Liddell-Hart in the face of overwhelming odds.[6] John Buchan, who would write their history, was already in France. He had visited the fleet in 'the far Northern Seas' and had observed the naval activity in the Channel. Writing to John Edgar in Cairo, he explained that, as much as he would like, he would be unable to visit Egypt for some time: 'like a stormy petrel, I follow the chief war zone, and the centre of gravity seems to be shifting rapidly from the Near East.'[7] For the moment, congruently and somewhat reluctantly, Smuts seemed to follow on to the next 'sideshow'. In addition, batteries of South African artillery deployed to Palestine during the summer of 1916, and the Cape Corps battalion arrived there in 1918, its 1st Battalion having earned its stripes in Tanganyika. The Cape Corps fought bravely in September 1918 at the battle of Square Hill and Smuts lauded them later: 'You fought as bravely and as well as any other unit of the British Army and established a brilliant record for your Corps.'[8] This was a remarkable tribute from a man who in 1914, had made cutting comments on the value of 'Coloured' troops.[9]

Of the war's 'sideshows', the East African campaign has drawn substantial attention. Ross Anderson and Anne Samson stand at the forefront of this scholarship; the first presented a magisterial examination of the campaign at a military-operational and tactical level set against the strategic background of the war; the second in two books,

5 NARSSA: GG 667, file 9/93/1 War 1914: Imperial Army. Suggested recruiting of men in South Africa for enlistment in the 'New Army'. See also UCT: BC915 James Metcalfe Papers, A1 to A5.
6 Basil Liddell Hart, *History of the First World War* (London: Macmillan, 1997), p.247.
7 QUA: Buchan fonds 2110, box 2, John Buchan to John Edgar, 28 March 1916.
8 I.D. Difford, *The Story of the 1st Cape Corps* (Cape Town: Hortors, 1920), p.253.
9 Ian Gleeson, *The Unknown Force; Black, Indian and Coloured Soldiers Through Two World Wars* (Rivonia: Ashanti, 1994), p.92.

narrated the political dimension, uncovering the personalities and the intrigue.[10] Our focus here is to add to this scholarship by examining the roles Botha and Smuts played during this crucial year: of Smuts's campaigning in East Africa where, as Merriman suggested, he faced the combined perils of friend and foe and disease, whilst – as shown in chapters 5 and 6 – Botha attempted to steady an unstable home front in South Africa. Meintjes writes that '1916 was a weary and dreary year for Botha'.[11] He faced a divided House from late 1915 and in the new year he would have to do so without Smuts. When Parliament convened, Smartt put forward a motion to thank Botha for the roles he had played during the German South West African campaign. This inadvertently opened the doors for a full National Party assault in parliament on the prime minister. Notwithstanding a tumultuous debate, Botha's services and that of his troops were recognised, and the motion passed by a comfortable 86 votes to 26 votes.[12] However, this was a harbinger for a difficult year.

Things Take New Turns

The war had come to Africa immediately with the activation by the belligerents of their pre-war plans. Each of Germany's colonies – surrounded by enemy territory, at first British, French, and Belgian, and later Portuguese too – sought to exploit the military advantages of a central position and interior lines. This led to a first phase in the African campaigning, lasting to late 1915, during which the four German colonies were invaded and two – Togoland and German South West Africa – were conquered. By late 1914, the British had been forced onto the defensive along the Nigerian and Kenyan frontiers. Assumptions regarding a limited war in Africa remained largely valid well into 1915 when the campaigning entered a second phase; one marked by the widening of the warfighting in Africa as the realities of total warfare began to overwhelm the belligerents in Europe.[13]

The early optimism that a quick victory in Europe would limit direct colonial involvement evaporated and local German commanders, most notably, Paul Emil von Lettow-Vorbeck in East Africa, sought to protract the campaigning in Africa and tie down as many Entente troops as possible – something he did with great success. As Lord Buxton noted:

10 R. Anderson, *The Forgotten Front: The East African Campaign, 1914–1918* (Stroud: Tempus, 2004); A. Samson, *Britain South Africa and the East African Campaign, 1914-1918: The Union Comes of Age* (London: I.B. Tauris, 2006); and Anne Samson, *World War I in Africa: The Forgotten Conflict Among the European Powers* (London and New York: I.B. Taurus, 2013).

11 Meintjes, *Botha*, p.283.

12 BL: Add MS 87052, Buxton Papers, 1914-1918, Buxton to Law, 27 November 1916.

13 I. van der Waag, 'The First World War in Africa: Impact and Consequences' in António José Telo (ed.), *A Grande Guerra e a Construção do Mundo Moderno* (Lisbon: Academia Militar, 2016), pp146–148.

> The first Campaign against German East Africa in 1914-15 in which the Union had no share, was unsuccessful and somewhat disastrous. Subsequently, for many months the British, mainly Indian troops, remained on the defensive; and it was not until the autumn of 1915 that the Imperial Government came to the conclusion that a serious effort must be made to occupy the country – the only remaining Colony still in the hands of the Germans.[14]

This tied with the end of the German South West African campaign and Botha's signal to London that in addition to providing an infantry brigade for France, his government would form a second brigade for service somewhere in Africa. They argued the South African soldier was better suited for warfare in Africa than were their British counterparts. The idea was attractive and not without merit: the South Africans were attuned to an African way of warfighting, and they had recently concluded a successful campaign, while their mounted brigades – based on the tradition of the Boer commandos – could not be deployed with effect on the Western Front. The British and Indian troops had made no headway since their bloody repulse at Tanga in November 1914.[15] British prestige, a crucial ingredient for imperial control, had been in decline since the sinking of HMS *Pegasus* near Zanzibar by the German cruiser *Königsberg* on 20 September. Dogged by poor leadership, low morale, and poorly prepared troops, the British would remain on the defensive throughout 1915.

Greater intensity now marked this second phase – which lasted until late 1916 – as the British, French, Portuguese, and Belgians went onto the offensive in East Africa and West Africa. While conducted with greater determination, campaigning in Africa contrasted sharply with the mass mobilisation, the enormous firepower, the trenches, and the extensive battle-related casualty lists of the Western Front. As South Africa's shadow defence minister noted of the fighting in Europe: 'Modern war for most people seems to entail a painfully stationary existence'.[16] Instead in Africa, the war remained mobile, was fought over large tracts of land by relatively small forces that were invariably able to manoeuvre, exploit open flanks, and sometimes adopt indirect approaches – at which both Smuts and Lettow-Vorbeck, his German quarry, would excel. Due to the absence of infrastructure and the presence of debilitating diseases, East Africa would be predominantly an infantry affair, dependent on vulnerable lines of communication that remained constantly on the verge of breakdown.[17]

14 Buxton, *General Botha*, p.290.

15 Ross Anderson produced a model examination of this battle with his *The Battle of Tanga 1914* (Stroud: Tempus, 2002).

16 WSRO: Petworth House Archives, Hugh Wyndham to Lady Leconfield, 2 May 1915.

17 Hew Strachan, *The First World War in Africa* (Oxford: Oxford University Press, 2004), pp.32–33; and Van der Waag, 'The First World War in Africa', pp.146–148.

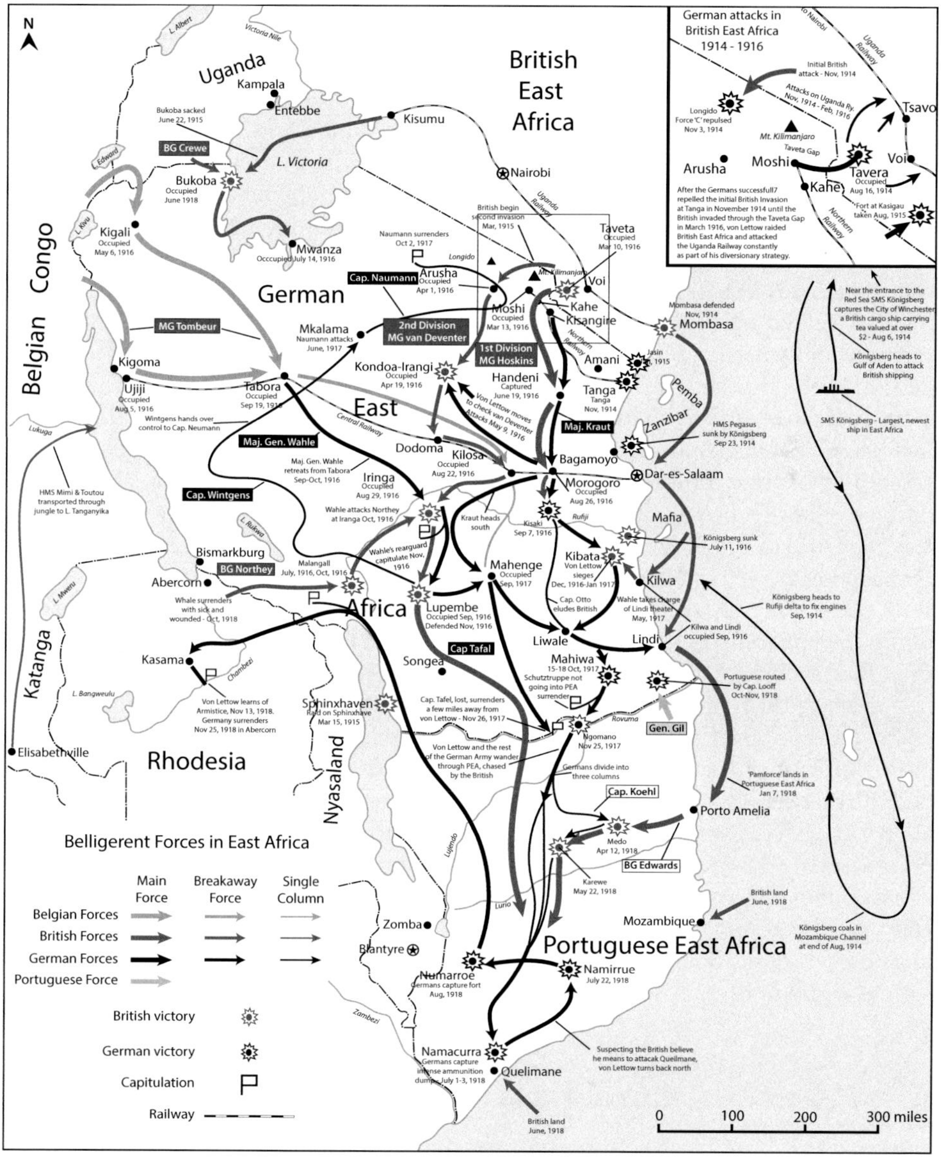

Map 7.1 German East Africa, 1914-18.

Smuts in East Africa – 'The Modern Napoleon'?

A turning point in the campaign, aimed now at the conquest of German East Africa and followed by steady if costly progress, certainly came in early 1916 with the arrival of Smuts and large numbers of South African troops. By October 1915, a hard-pressed London determined that something be done to push the German troops, then still threatening the Kenyan railway into the hinterland from Mombasa, from the frontier and so earn further campaign spurs in Africa – something that seemed impossible in Europe at the time. The War Office had offered Smuts the command of the East Africa contingents when they were formed in November 1915. But, with Smuts unable to accept at the time, Lieutenant General Sir Horace Smith-Dorrien was appointed. When the offer was made again – due to Smith-Dorrien's illness – Smuts accepted immediately and on 8 February 1916 was appointed with the temporary rank of lieutenant general in the British Army.[18] He was also 'the second youngest general in the British army.'[19] Buxton felt the need to remove any jealousy that might exist on the part of British officers, and especially if there was any feeling that Smuts had 'ousted S.D.'. A special public statement was issued.[20] The governor general later assured Smuts that Smith-Dorrien had suggested him for the command, although he did not want this made public knowledge.[21] Smuts sailed on the *Professor Woermann*, leaving Durban on 12 February and, stopping in Delagoa Bay to confer with the Portuguese, arrived in Mombasa a week later. Crewe, who arrived with Smuts and his staff, noted ominously at the time: 'On the whole most of the Indian people and some of the Imperial officers look upon us as intruders and fear that they may be superseded or pushed into more violent action than they are accustomed to.'[22]

For many, the South Africans were intruders into British East Africa, and the new commander-in-chief of the 'British Expeditionary Force' was unwelcome. Their criticism, and that of succeeding generations of British historians of the campaign, was based largely, and not without some merit, on Smuts's military background and his ability to exercise command over a large, regular army. Ross Anderson cements these points – with the matter of his appointment to the command – in his *The Forgotten Front*: Smuts, he argues, had not only, 'helped manoeuvre himself into the position [but had] been instrumental in instigating an aggressive policy in East Africa and arranging a large South African contingent. If politically favourable, Smuts had serious limitations as a soldier.'[23] As we shall see, there is another side to Smuts,

18 NARSSA: Smuts Papers, vol.198, Bonar Law to Buxton, c. February 1916.
19 Lentin *Jan Smuts*, p.32.
20 NARSSA: Smuts Papers, vol.198, Buxton to Bonar Law, 8 February 1916.
21 NARSSA: Smuts Papers, vol.198, Buxton to Smuts, 18 February 1916.
22 DODA: 2, Diverse Group 1, Box 13, Diary of the Mission of Brig. Gen. Hon. Sir C.P. Crewe, KCMG, CB, to the Belgians.
23 See Anderson, *The Forgotten Front*, pp.110-111. Smuts had neither formal military training nor experience of higher command, and his position was made more complicated

which is largely ignored and, to be fair, at the time, the British Army lacked men with exactly those competencies they demanded of Smuts, which is why London had turned to Smuts in the first place.[24]

But Smuts was a novel appointment in many respects. Before leaving Durban, he had enquired through Buxton how he should communicate with the War Office. He suggested that he send his official reports to both the War Office and Pretoria, and that any reports that were published be published in both countries simultaneously.[25] London agreed and would also take steps to minimise any friction between the civil and military authorities in East Africa, which had been considerable during the first 18 months of the war. The critical question was whether Smuts, as the GOC in East Africa, had full authority in the last resort? Bonar Law thought it unnecessary to make formal arrangements between civil and military authorities in East Africa but undertook to back Smuts: 'I shall take care that Smuts is not hampered by civil Authorities.'[26] Buxton had discussed these matters with Botha and Smuts before the latter's departure for Mombasa and forwarded copies of correspondence from London. He asked that they be kept well locked up. But Smuts's appointment proved as difficult as it was complicated. When writing in November 1916, Merriman might jokingly have wished Smuts delivery too from the British in East Africa.

Botha assured Smuts that as prime minister he would 'do everything to help' him: 'Just tell me what can be done.'[27] Smuts's South African troops comprised two infantry brigades, a mounted brigade, an unbrigaded mounted regiment, a Cape Corps battalion, and artillery and supporting services.[28] Representing an initial strength of 18,700, they served mostly in Imperial Service units raised on a volunteer basis.[29] Thousands of South Africans enlisted. Many of them for the first time. One young South African, a university student who went with a friend to the recruitment office in Cape Town in early 1916, noted later that 'young men not in uniform were receiving white feathers through the post and even having them presented to them by girls in the streets.'[30] Some units, such as the

by the multiple roles he played – including politician and government minister. Anne Samson makes a similar argument that 'Smuts's appointment was a political one.' Samson, *World War I in Africa*, p.132.

24 Mark Frost, 'Staff training in the British Army during the two world wars', unpublished research paper.

25 NARSSA: Smuts Papers, vol.198, Governor General to Secretary of State, 9 February 1916.

26 NARSSA: Smuts Papers, vol.198, Bonar Law to Buxton, 8 February 1916. See also Buxton to Bonar Law, 7 February 1916 in the same file.

27 Botha to Smuts, 23 February 1916 in Hancock and Van der Poel (eds.), *Selections*, vol. III, p.336.

28 Anderson, *The Forgotten Front*, p.297.

29 Collyer, *The South Africans with General Smuts in German East Africa* (Pretoria: Government Printer, 1939), p.50. The 5th Battery, SAMR, was the only Permanent Force unit to serve in East Africa, though with volunteer personnel.

30 J.E.P. Levyns, *The Disciplines of War; Memories of the War of 1914-18* (New York: Vantage, 1984), p.23.

South African Field Artillery Brigade, formed in 1915 for service on the Western Front, were diverted shortly before departure to East Africa. As one gunnery officer recounts, it was a blow to the men of the brigade: 'everyone wanted to go to Europe, the focal point of the War. There was glamour about England and Europe, but nothing of that sort in East Africa, as we found to our cost.'[31] This statement might reflect the individual prejudices of 1916 but some of the argument also made sense. Deneys Reitz, a close confident of Smuts, articulated his reasons for volunteering as follows: 'I had no animus against the German people … my chief [Smuts] was going and, further, I could not hang back while so many of my countrymen were moving forward to an adventure in the wilds of Africa.'[32]

The men of the brigade knew of the rigours of East Africa and of the equine diseases. Some mounted infantry and artillerymen feared more for the welfare of their animals than for themselves: 'We argued that the guns were of no use, if it hadn't the means to bring them into action.'[33] Some men, who had volunteered for European service, refused to go to East Africa and some 300 fresh recruits had to be found and trained for the artillery brigade. As Lettow-Vorbeck noted later, Smuts's appointment proved to be a recruitment elixir. But, based on their first encounter at Salaita, he was probably also correct in thinking that 'the training of these newly raised formations was slight, and the conduct of the Europeans, many of whom were very young, proved that many had never yet taken part in a serious action.'[34] For many, it *had* been their first action. Writing in grandiloquent style in 1937, Smuts described them as follows:

> … to me the real hero of the East African campaign is the South African citizen soldier … They were mostly young men, civilian volunteers from the veld and the towns, from the open country and the unrivalled climate of their native land, with scant military training, with no knowledge or thought in any quarter of what awaited them in East Africa, either in the manner of fighting or in the climatic or biotic conditions of nature. [Yet] From the Lumi to the Rufiji, from the Indian Ocean to the Great Lakes they fought their way through, and in eleven months had mastered a huge stretch of primeval Africa.[35]

This achievement, largely under his own command, was, he argued, the equal of 'the effort of the Great Trek and of the Boer War.' Yet, his troops in East Africa would never be recognised, and – with East Africa relegated as a 'little side-show' – they would have to endure seeing the accolades go to their compatriots who had gone to the Western Front.[36]

31 Frank H. Acutt, *Sailing Through the Rainbow* (Durban: Knox, n.d.), p.70.
32 Reitz, *Trekking On*, p.54.
33 Acutt, *Sailing Through the Rainbow*, p.73.
34 Paul von Lettow-Vorbeck, *East African Campaigns* (New York: Robert Speller & Sons, 1957), p.92.
35 Smuts's Foreword to Collyer, *The South Africans*, p. viii.
36 Smuts's Foreword to Collyer, *The South Africans*, p. ix.

Their first-battle experience had not been a good one. On the day Smuts left Durban, Major General Wilfred Malleson, an Indian Army officer, launched a precipitous attack on the German positions at Salaita. The result was a tactical disaster. The British artillery targeted the German secondary trenches and alerted the defenders of the impending attack. Colonel P.S. Beves's 7th South African Infantry broke into the German line but were repulsed with significant casualties after heavy fighting. Crewe was correct in his summation that the attack had failed 'owing to lack of coordination and preparation, the artillery was not properly employed, the operation orders were ridiculous, and the Commanding Officers had neither been properly consulted nor directed. The blame was with Gen. Malleson.'[37] Malleson, who had been a staff officer, became the bungling fool to South African troops. Frank Acutt, a South African gunner, recounts:

> [Malleson] thought he would try out his skill as a "general" by attacking a comparatively small hill occupied by the enemy, known as "Salaita", which stood between our position and the German frontier. The attack was a complete failure, and we lost a lot of men.[38]

The notion that British general officers were careless when it came to colonial lives was taking root. The change in mood following Smuts's arrival is reflected in the memoirs these men wrote. For example, Acutt refers to the news they received of Smuts's appointment shortly after 'the disastrous Salaita affair. ... Things [then] began to move.'[39] Smuts and his staff, Crewe tells us, had at first not realised 'the strength of the position on the German right flank where the North Paré Mountains offer mountain positions the like of which I had not seen outside of Basutoland.'[40] However, Piet van der Byl – then on Smuts's staff, and in the next war in Smuts's cabinet – notes that, when examining the German front at Salaita, Smuts had commented sardonically on the British approach to warfighting in Africa: 'British generals seem to take a fortified position as a personal affront and attack it head on. We believe in going round it.'[41] Here was a man they knew. Somebody seemingly with answers, and one they trusted. For Brett Young, Smuts was a romantic and inspiring figure, a man of 'unquestionable wisdom and military genius.'[42]

Smuts's campaign in East Africa contrasted quite dramatically to the campaign he and Botha fought in German South West Africa. All South African soldier-narrators

37 Crewe's Mission Diary, p.1.
38 Acutt, *Sailing Through the Rainbow*, p.74.
39 Acutt, *Sailing Through the Rainbow*, p.75.
40 Crewe Mission Diary, p.1.
41 Piet van der Byl, *From Playgrounds to Battlefields* (Cape Town: Howard Timmins, 1971), p.205.
42 This comes through too in his fictional work. Francis Brett Young, *Jim Redlake* (London: William Heinemann, 1930), p.570.

– Smuts himself and members of his personal staff included – contrast their experiences in East Africa with those they had faced in South West Africa. Reitz and Van der Byl outline the differences between the two campaigns most clearly. As soon as the troops moved forward, they realised that this campaign would be very different and much more arduous. German South West Africa, as Reitz noted, had 'open plains and, above all, there were no fever, no horse sickness, and no tsetse fly.' There the operations were widespread and their troops had to cover enormous distances through vast country. Instead in East Africa, they faced 'a thousand miles of dense forest and bush, and a deadly climate, and with the lowered spirits that come on most South Africans when there is no sunshine.'[43] The Germans had a strong garrison of 3,000 men supported by perhaps 10,000 well-trained Askaris or African troops. Their commander, Lettow-Vorbeck, a professional soldier, was able, innovative, and charismatic. Prepared to lead from the front he spared neither himself nor his troops. Smuts once described him as 'a very gallant gentleman', and he contrasted sharply with Lieutenant Colonel Viktor Franke. Recognising that the fate of Tanganyika would be decided in Europe, he used his army to prevent far larger numbers of Entente troops from participating in the main theatres of war and in the meantime, cause them as many losses as possible. The British, hard-pressed in France and the Middle East, were unable to substantially reinforce their Anglo-Indian forces in Kenya which remained cowered by the Germans who had crossed the frontier and threatened the railway. Smuts had his work cut out for him. The nature of the terrain the frequent movement of troops over impassable roads, and the scourge of fever, which steadily sapped troop strengths, meant a hard and hazardous campaign.

Tanganyika was ill-suited to the type of campaigning at which Botha and Smuts excelled. The physical environment – the terrain, thick vegetation, and disease ecology – foiled the wide, sweeping movements of mounted troops. Losses of manpower from malaria, tick-bite fever, dysentery, and bites and stings from a long list of arachnids, insects, and worms, were unexpectedly high. While the African campaigns of the Great War were but a continuation of earlier colonial campaigning, the nature of the opposing armies differed too. All belligerent armies in Africa, were comprised of small numbers of White officers and troops, substantial numbers of African troops, and enormous numbers of porters. The British forces Smuts commanded in East Africa were substantially larger than those under Lettow's command and the Royal Navy controlled the seas, but this was a polyglot army, possibly approaching 100,000 in strength and drawn from South Africa, East and West Africa, the Belgian Congo, Lusophone Africa, and of course Britain and India. Enjoying the advantages of a central position, and the use of interior lines of communication, Lettow fought first in the foothills of Kilimanjaro, from where he threatened British rail communication between Kenya and Uganda, and later drew the campaign deep into the jungles of central and southern Tanganyika, exposing Smuts's troops to lengthening lines

43 Reitz, *Trekking On*, p.55.

of communication – which were harried by guerrilla activity – erratic supply, and growing medical complications.[44]

Typical of all multinational forces, Smuts also had difficulty in commanding his army. He started with a confidence deficit. The regular British Army and Indian Army officers – all White, and graduates of the military schools and staff colleges of the empire – considered their new commander an amateur. Most of these men, according to Van der Byl, who has his own axe to grind for Smuts, felt that this had been especially so in camp – the province of 'some of the senior British 'dug-outs', who had not been very successful elsewhere'.[45] Smuts was unconventional at the best of times. In East Africa his approach – as we shall see – was foreign and unorthodox. And, to crown it all, Smuts only a decade before had faced some of them in the field during the Anglo-Boer War. Like Lettow-Vorbeck, Smuts was wont to leave his base, move well forward to reconnoitre personally, and commune with his troops. Smuts – intellectual in approach, unflappable in battle, and the darling of the British Press – did not go down well. They fed an anti-Smuts narrative into their networks within the British Army, which resounds loudly in the historiography. At the time, Smuts had to manage the personalities with diplomacy and already in April Botha expressed his admiration for the 'attitude' Smuts had taken 'towards the officers and the manner in which [he] conducted the battles' – which the reader might interpret as both against Lettow and within Smuts's own camp. 'The prevailing jealousy', Botha opined, 'would have quite prevented you from making a success of the campaign.'[46] The first battlefield successes in East Africa, won so quickly and dramatically, won Smuts local spurs and an enhanced reputation in the press.

Of course, the jealousies and competition for promotion extended further. This had been seen in German South West Africa when the staff appointments were made and command positions filled. And it happened again. Botha selected the men for the senior commands. His nephew, Manie Botha, went out with the first of the reinforcements to command the 1st South African Mounted Brigade under Brits whom he knew personally. L.A.S. Lemmer was selected too; as Botha noted, he had long held a grievance for not becoming a brigadier-general in the march to Windhoek and beyond. Now Lemmer was given the opportunity but declined due to his wife's illness. But, politically, Botha had made the offer and then sent Myburgh instead.[47] And then there was the question of Sir Charles Crewe, the Unionist member of the legislature and, at the start of the war, Director of War Recruiting. Crewe was to have been on Smith-Dorrien's staff and remained on when Smuts assumed the command.

44 Strachan, *The First World War in Africa*, p.131 *passim*.
45 Van der Byl, *From Playgrounds to Battlefields*, p.200.
46 Botha to Smuts, 13 April 1916 in Hancock and Van der Poel (eds.), *Selections*, vol. III, pp.345–349.
47 Botha to Smuts, 21 March 1916 in Hancock and Van der Poel (eds.), *Selections*, vol. III, pp.345–349.

As noted in chapter two, Botha viewed him as the fifth wheel on Smuts's coach.[48] Unsurprisingly, on his arrival in Kenya, Smuts despatched him first on a mission to the commander of the Belgian Congolese forces and then to command the Lake Force in the far west.

Friends, acquaintances, and colleagues wrote Smuts letters of congratulation and sent him newspaper cuttings proclaiming his success following his dramatic Kilimanjaro operations. In March, Buxton congratulated him on 'the promptitude of [his] operations [which] were remarkable, and … obviously founded on sound strategy.'[49] A fortnight later, he professed the wonders of Smuts's achievement.[50] George Fiddes, an old acquaintance, wrote from the Colonial Office of the rapidity of Smuts's advance which 'almost took people's breath away here.'[51] Aston praised him and his campaign, which 'seems to be going splendidly'[52], while Michael Furse, the Bishop of Johannesburg, who had recently visited the chaplains in East Africa, told everyone on his return to the Witwatersrand:

> Smuts is doing wonderfully well and impresses all the Generals and soldiers with his ability. He rushes on and on and has an unnerving eye for tactics – and leaves all details to those under him – which of course they like and is just how it ought to be – but not so easy as it sounds they say. He neither bothers about details in politics either and when he was Treasurer a million more or less meant nothing to him.[53]

Smuts had tremendous energy. It did not flag in East Africa. By July, he seemed 'to be reaping the result of all the hard work'.[54] An enthusiastic Aston felt the whole war was going well now that the Allies were working to a combined plan. Henry Burton wrote on 12 September 1916, that

> … a fellow called Rowden has written in the English papers to support that, when you are done in E. Africa, they should get you to the French Western Front as he is certain you will prove to be 'the Modern Napoleon'! This, perhaps, is what an old acquaintance of mine would call 'laying it on with a trowel'.[55]

48 Botha to Smuts, 13 April 1916 in Hancock and Van der Poel (eds.), *Selections*, vol. III, p.359.
49 NARSSA: Smuts Papers, vol. 198, Buxton to Smuts, 22 March 1916.
50 NARSSA: Smuts Papers, vol. 198, Buxton to Smuts, 7 April 1916.
51 George Fiddes to Smuts, 9 June 1916 in Hancock and Van der Poel (eds.), *Selections*, vol. III, p.376.
52 NARSSA: Smuts Papers, vol. 198, Maj. Gen. Sir George Aston to Smuts, 2 July 1916.
53 WSRO: Petworth House Archives, Maud Wyndham to Lady Leconfield, 9 July 1916.
54 NARSSA: Smuts Papers, vol. 198, Major General Sir George Aston to Smuts, 2 July 1916.
55 NARSSA: Smuts Papers, vol. 198, Henry Burton to Smuts, 12 September 1916.

Despite the flurry, Smuts seemed to have time for everything – even the maintenance of his extensive correspondence.

Smuts conducted a voluminous correspondence throughout the campaign. His letters to Isie and to Botha, in particular, describe the campaign, its phases, and its difficult circumstances. Those to his wife are delightful and written with enthusiasm. To Botha, they were personal but, as one would expect, also business-like. On 14 March, for example, he told Isie of the encircling movements that unlocked the Kilimanjaro complex and the Meru district – describing with delight 'the spirit among our young burghers', the similarities with the battle fought in the previous war against the British at Spioenkop, and the taking of the Reata and Latema ridges.[56] These attacks, Botha wrote, had been 'carried out beautifully.' Botha shared his correspondence with Smuts with opinion leaders in the Union and explained to them how Smuts, 'in so short a time,' had made himself 'master of the situation.' His victories led to an improvement in the general spirit in South Africa. Reported in the English-medium press reports on Smuts headlined above the battle at Verdun then raging in France.[57]

Yet, while recounting the hardships of such an arduous campaign, Smuts took time to take in the country around him. He delighted in its beauty. Writing in March, he described the countryside: 'This is a lovely country. Yesterday I was in Moschi and you can have no idea how beautiful the slopes of Kilimanjaro are.'[58] He wrote about the fauna and flora, the majesty of the mountains and the thickness of the bush. He found fruits and vegetables – mandarins and oranges, wild pea, and wild guava – and he kept seeds of the varietals, hoping to plant them after his return to South Africa.[59] As one British soldier noted of campaigning in Africa; this was a 'natural history lecture.'[60] But, perhaps most of all, Smuts had space and relative solitude to think about large issues. The Great Rift Valley proved a wonderful stage to further develop his ideas of Holism.

In March 1916, with all eyes fixed on him, Smuts was the man of the moment in East Africa. Until his arrival it seemed as if there had been 'no definite plan of campaign.' The Allied forces had adopted defensive postures after their initial offensives had been repulsed at the end of 1914. As Crewe opined, clearly the British forces in Kenya and Uganda, and the Belgian forces, had to 'undertake a reasonable but active offensive instead of guarding extinct volcanos, and a boundary line which is of no consequence

56 Smuts to his wife, 14 March 1916 in Hancock and Van der Poel (eds.), *Selections*, vol. III, pp.340–341.
57 Botha to Smuts, 21 March 1916 in Hancock and Van der Poel (eds.), *Selection*, vol. III, p.356.
58 Smuts to his wife, 14 March 1916 in Hancock and Van der Poel (eds.), *Selections*, vol. III, pp.340–341.
59 Smuts to his wife, 16 August 1916 in Hancock and Van der Poel (eds.), *Selections*, vol. III, pp.395–396.
60 Essex Record Office (ERO), Chelmsford, UK:TS 634/1, Bernard Harris to Zillah Harris, 28 June 1915.

whatever.'[61] As Buxton, with whom both men were intimate, noted, 'General Botha had much to do with the initial stages, and with the preliminary plan of the German East campaign: and he had, as Prime Minister, full responsibility for raising the necessary troops, and especially the Burgher Brigades.'[62] Botha and Smuts discussed via telegram the strategy for the campaign following the advance into Tanganyika, the details of which Botha shared with the governor general. Three possible routes of advance had presented themselves.[63] First was an inland advance from the coast, using the German railroads, from Tanga or Dar-es-Salaam. Botha and Buxton favoured this option: for Botha, it offered greater security although it would be slower; for Buxton, the occupation of Tanga would have an important 'moral effect' in East Africa and more widely.[64] But Smuts rejected this option, as he had already effectively turned Tanga with his seizure of the Usambara railway, while Dar-es-Salaam would hold all of the difficulties of a seaborne invasion and his troops, who would arrive there at a bad time of year, would be stricken with disease. An advance on Tabora via Lake Victoria was a second option. Smuts reasoned, this would entail the transfer of large numbers of troops to the north-west and so weaken the position in Kenya immediately to the north of Lettow's troops and endanger the Ugandan railway. Moreover, he felt the British troops already in the north-west should have been able to hold their own and take their part in the larger concentric advance he planned.

For these reasons Smuts adopted a third option, which the War Office approved.[65] This involved an advance into the heartland of Tanganyika – along the Pangani River and Usambara railway with possibly a second column moving from Aruscha to Kondoa Irangi. He gave command of the second column to Major General Jacobus van Deventer, another former Boer general. Acutt, who served under him, described Van Deventer as 'a man with a gruff voice, an astute but cautious general, and probably the only soldier of note who had fought for and against three nations': Britain Germany, and the Dutch-speaking South Africans.[66] This line of advance was more direct than option two – they had also 'lost' five to six weeks which greatly limited the sphere of operations – and it would avoid a contested seaborne invasion. Smuts later explained:

> I decided to push the whole of the 2nd Division into the interior under van Deventer, and for the present to keep the other two divisions with me in rain

61 Crewe's Mission Diary, pp.2–3, 5.
62 Buxton, *General Botha*, p.290.
63 Collyer, *The South Africans*, pp.99–100.
64 NARSSA: Smuts Papers, vol. 198, Buxton to Smuts, 18 May 1916.
65 NARSSA: Smuts Papers, vol. 198, See for example. Buxton to Smuts, 1 March 1916, Buxton to Smuts, 22 March 1916.
66 Acutt, *Sailing Through the Rainbow*, p.82. For an insightful examination of the command exercised by Smuts and Van Deventer, see Ross Anderson, 'J.C. Smuts and J.L. van Deventer: South African Commanders-in-Chief of a British Expeditionary Force', *Scientia Militaria*, vol. 31, no. 2 (2003), pp.117–141.

> quarters. In this way it would be possible to occupy a valuable portion of the country with the next two months; and if, as I expected, this move would and must have the effect of compelling the enemy to withdraw large forces from the Pares and Usambaras to stem the tide of invasion into the interior, I could, if necessary strengthen van Deventer still further and yet have sufficient troops left to make a comparatively easy conquest of these mountains against the enemy's weakened defence. These anticipations were fully realised.[67]

By the close of August, his troops and those of Van Deventer reached the Central Railway, and by the end of the year, they had corralled Lettow's forces into the malaria-ridden, south-western quadrant of the territory. However, Lettow would remain undefeated in the field and the campaign would only end after the cessation of hostilities in the European theatre. Buxton, who had echoed Smuts's belief that the campaign in German East Africa would prove more suited to South African methods and experience, would be proved wrong.[68] And, no doubt, a statement Smuts made during one of the recruitment drives would later haunt him, that his 'men should not be under the impression that they were being sent to a country where fever, fly, and sleeping sickness prevailed. Nothing of the kind. They were being sent to a perfectly healthy country and perfectly suited to South African modes of warfare.'[69]

In his history of the campaign, Jack Collyer, chief of the general staff to Smuts in East Africa, explained the enormous tactical advantages Lettow-Vorbeck had held. Kilimanjaro stood sentinel on the frontier, barring movement completely except around the lower reaches of its foothills. The only open routes to the south led to the interlocking mountains of the Paré and related ranges, while the rivers – described by Collyer as considerable, unfordable, and infested by crocodile – 'combined with the mountain range and fever-laden swamps and dense bush to produce as formidable an obstacle to movement on the south of the theatre of operations as did Kilimanjaro on its north.'[70] This natural fortress presented advantages on which Lettow capitalised. His troops were almost entirely concealed and, when the campaign got under way, they held all the high ground overlooking the approaches the South Africans would have to take, which they had reconnoitred thoroughly. According to Collyer, the South Africans were 'almost as ignorant of the terrain as the former were well posted in its features.'[71]

Thick bush, uncut forests, and mountainous country created difficulties and Smuts's style of operations – widely dispersed forces, operated simultaneously on several fronts – would demand 'eyes in the air'. There had been no air arm in East Africa up to this point other than a small flight of the RNAS and a few gentleman amateurs.

67 As quoted in Collyer, *The South African*, pp.102–103.
68 BL: Add MS 87052, Buxton Papers 1914-1918, Buxton's notes, 6 March 1916.
69 BL: Add MS 87052, Buxton Papers 1914-1918, *Cape Times,* 29 November 1915.
70 Collyer, *The South Africans*, pp.62–63.
71 Collyer, *The South Africans*, pp.62–63.

The size and nature of the battlespace demanded more and better types of aircraft to assist Smuts in his inexorable advance. The SAAC had been disbanded after the German South West African campaign, but the majority of the pilots had volunteered for further service in Britain where they were to form the nucleus of No. 26 (South African) Squadron of the RFC. However, after being brought up to strength by further recruits from the Union, No. 26 Squadron was dispatched to East Africa in December 1915 with B.E.2e and Henri Farman aircraft to carry out reconnaissance, bombing and communication missions in support of Smuts's operations.[72] Pilots flew a few daily reconnaissance flights, with some opportunistic bombing, but it was as Kenneth van der Spuy tells us 'more in the nature of a pleasant holiday.' It was 'quick and light and easy' and very different to aviation on the Western front, and even more so in comparison with the ground troops in Tanganyika that 'toiled and sweated their way through bush and swamp'.[73] Pilots played probably little more than a reconnaissance role. When at the hospital at Morogoro, British doctor Norman Jewell met a wounded German Askari, who informed him that his injuries had been caused by 'a bird [that] laid an egg on him.'[74] Jewell records that this was the only man he encountered for the whole campaign wounded by aerial bombardment. The remoteness of the war theatre, and impossible lines of communication introduced near insurmountable difficulties in obtaining spares and replacements, ordnance and ammunition, and petrol for trucks and aircraft, unknown on other fronts. As a result, East Africa would become even more of a war of improvisation that German South West Africa had been.

Some of the men who fought in East Africa were colourful to say the least. Some, like Lieutenant Colonel Jerry Driscoll had raised a battalion that served in the Anglo-Boer War, and he did the same again. He, Frank Selous, and others, who had conducted nefarious operations in the former Boer republics, now came under South African higher command.[75] The warfighting in East Africa allowed such men to define their own roles – something again that contrasted sharply with circumstances on the Western Front.

At about the time Smuts was at Moshi, two interesting men joined his staff: Denys Reitz and Piet Pretorius. Aboard the same ship that conveyed No. 26 South Africa Squadron to East Africa, Reitz provided congenial conversation and told of dramatic accounts of warfighting in Africa to the young pilots.[76] Son of a former Boer president and something of a South African hero, his Second Anglo-Boer-War journal was the finest book King George V later claimed to have ever read. He had served under Smuts during the Anglo-Boer War, under Botha in South Africa and then in

72 TNA AIR 1/690/21/20/26: History of 26 (South Africa) Squadron, RAF.
73 K.R. van der Spuy, *Chasing the wind* (Cape Town: Books of Africa, 1966), p.94.
74 Norman Parson Jewell, *On Call in Africa in War and Peace, 1910–1932* (Hove: Gillyflower Publishing, 2016), p.69.
75 Jewell, *On Call in Africa in War and Peace*, pp.48–49.
76 Van der Spuy, *Chasing the Wind*, p.89.

German South West Africa, and joined Smuts in East Africa, and would end his war in command of a British infantry regiment on the Western Front.[77] A family friend, Reitz was close enough to Smuts to tell yarns about him. During one of their dinners in the veld, he shared the story about Sammy Marks's order of a replica of the Venus de Milo. When the statue arrived in Pretoria, Marks was distressed to find the arms missing and sought compensation from the South African Railways. Smuts, his mind on some larger matter interjected: 'My dear fellow, do stop talking all this nonsense and let me think'. But Reitz continued – Smuts, then Acting Minister of Railways, allowed the claim! Marks's financial sinew had no doubt weighed in.[78]

Smuts camped with his troops and ate his meals with his personal staff. He enjoyed communing with his troops and was surprised to find that many of them were farmers – perhaps as many as half of his South African infantry – 'and all fight splendidly.'[79] Most had enormous admiration for him and drew him on topics, often fun, but sometimes equally serious. Spellbound they listened to him soliloquising. 'It was always a joy', Piet van der Byl records, 'to listen to this brilliant brain thinking out loud.'[80] One evening Smuts spoke of evolution, of the development of reason in man, and of instinct in the animal kingdom. Developing his thoughts on leadership, he said that every hundred years or more a leader emerged able to combine a logical and trained mind with instinct. If the conditions were favourable, such a 'superman' – combining military skill with political leadership – became 'a world shaker.' As noted in chapter 9, he would have a similar discussion in London with Baron Sonnino and Sir George Riddell the following year.

The other man, Piet Pretorius, who Smuts chose for his chief scout, was another colourful figure. Descendant of Andries Pretorius, the Voortrekker general who had founded Pretoria, and son of a Boer commandant who had fought the British on two separate occasions, Pretorius was a well-known hunter and poacher – by his own admission – and knew Tanganyika intimately. When the war broke out in 1914, he adjusted to its demands. As he admitted, 'in a way it was the same job, tracking though the veld and mountain and jungle, with the exception that my quarries were no longer elephant or lion, but men who had become greater enemies to peace and freedom.'[81] This was a somewhat ironic statement; Pretorius was known to poach game and impress labour under conditions that may have approached slavery. Yet, for his contemporaries, he was a feature of the landscape and something of a hero rather than a villain. Brett Young's semi-fictitious Jim Redlake was thrilled to meet him: '... for Pretorius, with his crew of savages, was

77 Deneys Reitz, *Commando: A Boer Journal of the Anglo-Boer War* (London: Faber and Faber, 1929).
78 Van der Byl, *From Playgrounds to Battlefields*, p.207.
79 Smuts to his wife, 14 March 1916 in Hancock and Van der Poel (eds.), *Selections*, vol. III, pp.340–341.
80 Van der Byl, *From Playgrounds to Battlefields*, p.189.
81 Piet Pretorius, *Jungle Man: The Autobiography of Major P.J. Pretorius* (London: George G. Harrap and Company, 1947), pp.15, 152.

perhaps the most striking figure of that romantic campaign: a great hunter, the hero of a hundred hair-breadth escapes and feats of incredible daring.'[82] At Morogoro, Pretorius formed a new battalion, 1,000 strong, from captured German Askaris. They were first-class troops – the Germans had trained them well – and re-equipped as British auxiliaries they served on the Allied side to the end of the war. Legendarily, Pretorius had used his tracking and fieldcraft skills to locate the position of the *Königsberg* in one of the more dramatic, and certainly strategically significant, operations of the campaign. Recognising this utility, Smuts appointed him as his chief scout. Major Richard Meinertzhagen, head of intelligence for the British forces, was cut from similar cloth, while the 25th (Frontiersmen) Battalion of the Royal Fusiliers and Cole's Scouts, raised specifically for the campaign included such notable hunters as Frederick Selous, Denys Finch-Hatton, and Berkeley Cole.[83] Many of these men were no doubt heroes. Some were villains. And some were perhaps both.[84] Harry Trew, who later became Deputy Commissioner of the South African Police, noted that 'several ex-criminals' mentioned by him in *African Man Hunts* – the prequel to *Botha Treks* – 'rendered gallant service during the Great War, and quite a number died for their country.'[85] This was probably true of all armed forces.

Smuts and Van Deventer fought the campaign in 'Boer War' fashion. Tents were unknown outside the base camps. The men camped and slept sometimes in torrential rain. 'We barged ahead', Acutt tells us, 'irrespective of whether the transport carrying supplies and medical necessities kept up with us. ... If there were no rations, the soldiers were expected to live on the country (what a country!), and the animals too.'[86] Roland Bourne, the Secretary for Defence, noted in one of his ministerial missals that this was the South African way of campaigning.[87] For the troops on the ground this would be cold comfort. Food became increasingly scare the further south they moved as the logistic lines were stretched to breaking point. A firm foraging sequence was established: the mounted forces had the first opportunity to loot, then came the horse artillery, and finally the footslogging infantry. A farmhouse not yet looted was rare and a greater find than 'a river bed with nuggets of gold', while at Kondoa Irangi, the commissariat scraped up rice from the floors of the German barracks, which the men refused as it had too much grit, and 'secured' instead quantities of sweet potatoes from the fields of a nearby African village.[88] The P.B.I. (Poor Bloody Infantry) would arrive after everyone else and collapse from exhaustion, disease, and want of sustenance. At Kilossa, Acutt encountered a heart-rending sight:

82 Brett Young, *Jim Redlake*, p.559.
83 Timothy J. Stapleton, *Warfare and Tracking in Africa, 1952-1990* (London and New York: Routledge, 2015), pp.39–40.
84 Peter Stanley, *Bad Characters; Sex, Crime, Mutiny, Murder and the Australian Imperial Force* (Millers Point, NSW: Murdoch, 2010).
85 H.F. Trew, *African Man Hunts* (London and Glasgow: Blackie and Son, 1938), p.vii.
86 Acutt, *Sailing Through the Rainbow*, p.82.
87 NARSSA: GG 597, file 9/57/40, Secretary for Defence to Ministers, 13 November 1916.
88 Acutt, *Sailing Through the Rainbow*, pp.83, 86.

> On both sides of the street were the South African Infantry … lying on the pavements in their hundreds, just dying from neglect. Some were dying of disease, some of thirst, some of want of something in their bellies – not one made a complaint as we walked by – they were too weak and exhausted even to make a sign or utter a word.[89]

By mid-August, Smuts realised the campaign would take a different turn. Instead of 'fighting it out', it was now apparent that Lettow would 'retire southwards and prolong the war.'[90] Tanganyika is blessed with many rivers and Lettow and his troops burned or blew up the bridges. As a result, Smuts had to concentrate on bridge-building and railway-construction programmes and the establishment of a more regular intelligence system. As Crewe noted, 'Smuts also desires that some form of Intelligence Base should be established, for hitherto our information seems to have been very indifferent and probably all of it obtained through Belgian sources, and they are naturally from their position scarcely likely to be able to secure the full knowledge which is so desirable.'[91]

However, living off the land meant different things. According to Crewe, Smuts immediately stressed the importance of paying the local Africans 'full reasonable value … for all cattle, grain and other supplies taken or bought for the use of the troops.' This had not always been the case during the colonial conquest of the region in the previous decades. However, by 1916, with the war gearing up, he and his staff recognised the need to 'avoid setting all the natives [*sic.*] against us.' The straight requisitioning of cattle and grain from Africans, even if friendly to Britain could easily turn people all over East Africa against Britain whereas paying a reasonable price for what was taken 'would dispose natives in German East to be friendly.'[92] Crewe's argument is couched in turn-of-the-century colonial terms, and he does not address the matter of a willing seller. Moreover, news that the troops were suffering from a shortage of supplies was worrying and Smuts and his staff kept Vere Stent, the Reuters correspondent who had accompanied the troops in the field, 'in reserve' in case he was needed to 'contradict exaggerated stories about sufferings due to shortage of supplies.' Smuts and Botha were careful not to ventilate the complaints.[93]

Some characteristics of the campaign including the scorched-earth methods the Germans used as they withdrew to the south, ruined local economies. All combatants pressed men to serve as porters to carry the vast quantities of supplies needed, while large tracts of rural land were devastated – crops destroyed, villages burned – to deprive opponents of supply and support. A doctor with Lettow's forces noted, 'Behind us we

89 Acutt, *Sailing Through the Rainbow*, p.100.
90 Smuts to his wife, 16 May 1916 in Hancock and Van der Poel (eds.), *Selections*, vol. III, p.396.
91 Crewe Mission Diary, pp.3–4.
92 Crewe Mission Diary, pp.3–4.
93 Krige to Bourne, 18 November 1916, DC.

leave destroyed fields, ransacked magazines and, for the immediate future, starvation. We are no longer the agents of culture; our track is marked by death, plundering and evacuated villages.'[94] All too often combatants on all sides seized food and other supplies – if not in policy, certainly in practice. This differed vastly from the intent earlier in the year to pay a reasonable price for goods acquired locally.

The casualty lists of the armed forces were also frighteningly long. In April, the Buxtons visited the first two contingents of sick and wounded at Wynberg. They had come on the *Armadale* and *Ebani* and numbered about 300 British and South African troops. Most were from the Salaita battle, although some had seen action at Taveta.[95] For the duration of the campaign, the numbers of battlefield wounded and the missing as registered in the casualty books of the South African Medical Corps are given in Figure 7.1. These show that the advances conducted by Smuts, while constant, often rapid and very different to the immobility of his predecessors in this campaign, came at a price. Van Deventer, who succeeded him in early 1917, fought a different kind of campaign. Most of the heaviest fighting, as Smuts himself noted, happened in 1916, when almost all of Tanganyika was occupied. In the subsequent campaign involving its own arduous marches and disease-related casualties, 'the military performance and its significance were on a comparatively minor scale.'[96] Van Deventer could focus more on consolidating Smuts's achievement by containing the German forces and holding the territory already occupied. His battle-related casualty rate would necessarily be much lower.

As shown in Figure 7.2, the South African battlefield casualties in East Africa, at 7.24 per cent, while higher than in German South West Africa (0.56 per cent) and Egypt (6.92 per cent) did not approach the 25.09 percent of force strength on the Western Front. However, adding the numbers for illness from disease presents a vastly different picture. Taken holistically, the Allied battlefield casualties in East Africa were 71.46 per thousand troops; the non-battle causalities were a staggering 2,244.36 per thousand troops.[97] In May 1916 in a letter to Merriman, Smuts acknowledged that the South African casualties were much heavier than they had been in South West Africa: 'fever has for the time filled our hospitals.'[98] But, as he promised his correspondents he would press on: to Gillett – 'No time will be lost in pressing this campaign to a conclusion.'[99] And to Merriman – 'But I shall press on resolutely'.[100] As

94 Ludwig Deppe quoted in Martin Meredith, *Diamonds, Gold and War: The British, the Boers and the Making of South Africa* (New York: Public Affairs, 2008), p.495.
95 NARSSA: Smuts Papers, vol. 198, Buxton to Smuts, 7 April 1916.
96 Smuts's Foreword to Collyer, *The South Africans*, p.vi.
97 Anon., 'Casualties in War', *The Indian Medical Gazette*, vol. 67, no. 2 (Feb 1932), p.100.
98 Smuts to Merriman, 12 May 1916 in Hancock and Van der Poel (eds.), *Selections*, vol. III, p.366.
99 Smuts to Gillett, 2 May 1916 in *Selections*, vol. III, p.362.
100 Smuts to Merriman, 12 May 1916 in Hancock and Van der Poel (eds.), *Selections*, vol. III, p.366.

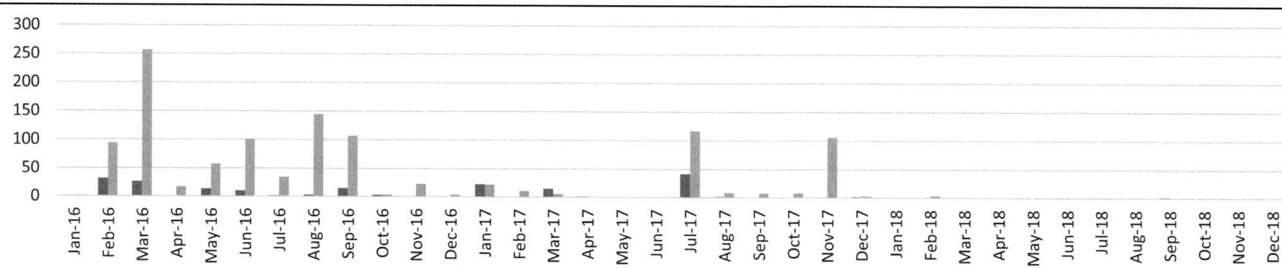

	Jan-16	Feb-16	Mar-16	Apr-16	May-16	Jun-16	Jul-16	Aug-16	Sep-16	Oct-16	Nov-16	Dec-16
Missing	0	32	26	0	14	10	2	3	15	3	0	0
Wounded	2	94	257	17	58	101	35	145	107	4	23	4

	Jan-17	Feb-17	Mar-17	Apr-17	May-17	Jun-17	Jul-17	Aug-17	Sep-17	Oct-17	Nov-17	Dec-17
Missing	23	1	15	2	0	0	42	2	0	0	1	2
Wounded	22	11	6	0	0	1	117	9	8	8	106	3

	Jan-18	Feb-18	Mar-18	Apr-18	May-18	Jun-18	Jul-18	Aug-18	Sep-18	Oct-18	Nov-18	Dec-18
Missing	0	1	1	0	0	0	0	0	2	1	1	1
Wounded	1	4	1	0	1	0	0	0	0	0	0	0

Figure 7.1: Wounded and Missing, SAMC, German East Africa, 1916–1918. (Source: SAMC, box 22, Casualty Books.)

discussed in the next chapter, the porters suffered the most from disease. Theirs was a story of 'sorrow, suffering and glory.'[101]

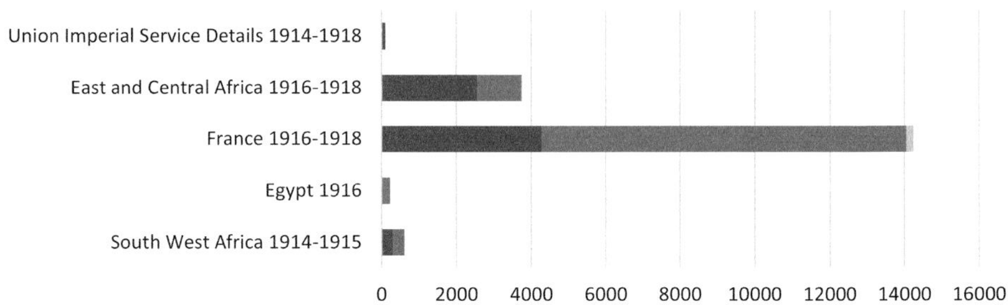

	South West Africa 1914-1915	Egypt 1916	France 1916-1918	East and Central Africa 1916-1918	Union Imperial Service Details 1914-1918
■ Dead from all sources	295	24	4275	2548	99
■ Wounded	318	201	9752	1173	
■ Missing			23	10	
■ POWs			194	1	

Figure 7.2: South African casualties in the First World War.

Twenty-five years later, when South African troops again deployed to East Africa, Lieutenant Colonel H.W. Vaughan-Williams, who had been Assistant Director Medical Services (ADMS) with the 3rd East African Division, published an article on the medical services rendered during the campaign and of 'the chief causes of the troubles, mistakes, and even partial chaos that occurred' – at least as far as his division was concerned.[102] He distilled the problems into seven categories: in sum, poor training of medical staff, shortages of transport and medical supplies, poor cooperation between the medical officers and the medical staff in the field and the supplies and logistics personnel of the quartermaster sections, shortages of books for training, and the absence of the Director Medical Services and high-ranking officers of his staff at times of military emergency. Vaughan-Williams was arguably correct: East Africa, with a sickness death rate higher than any other campaign, had been 'almost entirely a medical war' in 1916 and 1917.[103] The colonial forces were variegated, comprising small numbers of White officers and troops, larger number of Black troops, and vast

101 Geoffrey Hodges, *Kariakor – The Carrier Corps; The Story of the Military Labour Forces in the Conquest of German East Africa, 1914 to 1918* (Nairobi: Nairobi University Press, 1999), p.1.
102 H.W. Vaughan-Williams, 'Medical Services in the East African Campaign, 1916-1917', *South African Medical Journal*, vol. 15, no. 1 (11 January 1941), p.9.
103 Vaughan-Williams, 'Medical Services in the East African Campaign', p.9.

numbers of porters, who, suffering terribly, carried tons of ammunitions and rations through vast, often inhospitable areas. The political consequences of the failing medical system are discussed in chapter 8.

France

At the beginning of August, Smuts was recovering from malaria. Buxton wrote him hoping his own health and the health of the troops was improving. Botha had just been to East Africa and Smuts had recently captured the central railway, which the governor general hoped 'ought to knock the enemy out a bit.'[104] The news from Europe also appeared to improve. The naval action off Jutland seemed to proclaim continued superior British seamanship, while the Russian advance – 'real and substantial' Buxton told Smuts – encouraged Romania to join the Entente. Without tangible progress at Verdun, and suffering tremendous casualties and food deprivation, Germany appeared to be weakening. Yet Buxton did not think the end was yet in sight: 'The Germans are not going to accept any terms to which the Allies could (I hope), agree until they are beaten in the field and driven at least out of Belgium.'[105] Smuts could certainly agree. In Britain the financial, economic, and commercial position appeared to be sound. Exports were increasing despite the blockade of the Central Powers and increased activity on the London Exchange encouraged optimism.[106] This made Buxton confident of a satisfactory peace.

And, of course, news of the 1st Brigade in France, and the heavy casualties sustained in mid-July, reached Smuts in East Africa too. While frustrated by the meagreness of the news from the Western Front, he conveyed the thanks of Botha and the cabinet to Lukin 'on their gallantry and dash whilst participating in [the] capture of Longueval and storming [of] Delville Wood.' He was joined by others. Colonel Dalrymple of Johannesburg, while expressing his elation, mourned 'the passing of our heroes who can ill be spared'. Lord Selborne, who had been high commissioner in South Africa, professed that his 'heart is full of pride though my eyes are full of tears.' Merriman, almost ticking off the Springbok virtues, was more cryptic: 'Well done South Africans. Discipline. Pluck. No swagger. God bless you all.'[107] The casualty lists were heavy. Buxton wrote of the '332 killed and 1,696 wounded in four days.' The lists, and the price paid, would more than anything, he felt, 'bring home to the people here the gigantic nature of the struggle, and the sacrifices which it involves.'[108] But, most of all, the Brigade had made a reputation for itself and had earned South Africa

104 NARSSA: Smuts Papers, vol. 198, Buxton to Smuts, 2 August 1916.
105 NARSSA: Smuts Papers, vol. 198, Buxton to Smuts, 10 July 1916 and 2 August 1916.
106 NARSSA: Smuts Papers, vol. 198, Buxton to Smuts, 10 July 1916.
107 UCT: BC676 Major General Sir H.T. Lukin Papers, A1.10, Messages and Telegrams of Appreciation.
108 NARSSA: Smuts Papers, vol. 198, Buxton to Smuts, 2 August 1916, Buxton's emphasis.

spurs. Lukin noted in his first brief account: 'I am sad and proud – sad to lose so many gallant comrades – proud that South Africa's representatives upheld her honour under a very severe trial. The fighting at Delville Wood was as bitter and stubborn as any that took place along the line. Our men did grand work, their bulldog courage was worthy of all praise.'[109]

If the two African campaigns compared so dramatically, their contrast with the war on the Western Front was greater still. Here the leadership and command was more remote and much less personal – in East Africa they knew each other. East Africa, many record, was fought on more gentlemanly terms. Corporal Hausmann, a despatch rider, notes: '… very often we would receive mail intended for the enemy, as they would for us. At pre-arranged signals, mail, prisoners and an occasional bottle of whisky would be exchanged between the two sides, under a white flag.'[110] The Western Front was more anonymous, the men nameless, replaceable, expendable. And, most of all, it seemed far from the South African approach to warfighting. As Corporal Doitsh notes:

> We found it difficult to adapt ourselves to trench fighting, as this was not the South African method of warfare. Give our men the open, where we can face the enemy and fight, and we are at home; but trench fighting was, as it were, a new toy to us. But at the same time we made the best of it. We kept strafing the Hun, and of course got back as much as we gave. It is, however, curious how the Huns knew when they were put up against new troops, and also it was strange to know that they knew that we were the South Africans, as they posted a notice up saying that they would skin and burn alive the first South African they captured.[111]

Doitsh later thought that this may have been a response to their loss of German South West Africa, but – captured soon after on 19 July 1916, with at least seven others – he was relieved to find the threat empty. But there is an interesting point here. This is the South African distinctiveness on the battlefield. Differences between the Springbok and counterparts in other 'British' forces – sometimes noted by their British counterparts – permeate the literature. They introduced cultural practices, such as lighting fires and barbecuing meat, to the Western Front, made noises, and were viewed by some at least as 'less disciplined than Imperial troops.' These practices drew German

109 UCT: BC293 Sir Walter Stanford Papers, B112.2, Lukin to Stanford, 25 July 1916.
110 Colin Martin (ed.), *Corporal Haussmann Goes to War; Armed with Motor-cycle and Camera* (Kenilworth: private, 2000), p.53. On the more personal nature of the campaign in east Africa, see Samson, *World War I in Africa*, pp.142–143.
111 Corporal E. Doitsh, *The First Springbok Prisoner in Germany; Being the Thrilling Experiences of the First South African to return* (London: McBride, Nast & Co., 1917), p.59.

fire onto their positions, reflecting an apparent mix of inexperience and innocence – a kind of colonial naivety when it came to European warfare.[112]

The Wider War

At home, Botha and Smuts had the larger goal of nation building; of welding together the English and Dutch-speaking sectors of South African society. By 1916, men in uniform were reaching out to each other. In German South West Africa they had fought in self-contained units and the campaign was quickly over. But in East Africa and France, where the volunteers served in more mixed units and formations, and suffered together to a greater degree, friendships based on need and companionship developed across language lines.[113] But a large issue clouded South Africa's participation in the war and, with it, the dreams Botha and Smuts shared of increased national status and possibly territorial acquisition. This was the question of military manpower and the ability to expand the pool of military personnel to meet the demands of the war.

From the start, the mobilisation had been plagued by difficulties emanating largely from the limitations imposed by the *South Africa Defence Act*. Only White males could be attested and then deployed only in direct defence of South Africa. As a result, the pool from which soldiers could be drawn – White male volunteers, and largely supporters of the government's war policy – was small and inadequate for South Africa's military tasks.[114] Buxton articulated the problem as follows:

> Recruiting is not good. The fact is that the source from which recruits can be obtained unfortunately has been seriously tapped and has nearly run dry. After all, the whole of the various contingents have been obtained from only about a half of the white population. The war, moreover, has never been actively brought home to the people here as in Europe. At the request of the Mayor of Cape Town I am issuing an Appeal endorsing your recruiting message.[115]

From April 1916, following the first of the battles fought in Egypt and East Africa, Roland Bourne strained to fill the manpower requirements for Smuts in East Africa and Lukin in France. Botha applied increasing pressure on the secretary for defence; he told Smuts, 'I am putting the screw on Bourne a little to economise as much as

112 MacDonald to his wife, Mary, 4 January 1917. Transcript of letters written by Colin MacDonald, chaplain 8th Black Watch, BEF, January to August 1917, private collection.
113 Acutt, *Sailing Through the Rainbow*, p.77.
114 I. van der Waag, 'South African Manpower and the Second World War' in Douglas E. Delaney, Mark Frost, and Andrew L. Brown (eds.), *Military Manpower and the Armies of the British Empire in the Two World Wars* (Ithaca and London: Cornell University Press, 2021), p.186.
115 NARSSA: Smuts Papers, vol. 198, Buxton to Smuts, 7 April 1916.

possible.'[116] But, as Bourne told Smuts, it was 'no use pretending that the supply of useful infantry men is not getting rapidly exhausted.' The Botha Cabinet went so far as to consider the diversion of the 1st Brigade from France to East Africa – to 'force the pace' against Lettow and allow Smuts to complete the operations using primarily South African troops – but the War Office, before Pretoria could ask for them, sent Lukin's contingent to France.[117] With the Brigade en route to the primary war theatre, Bourne reverted to doing 'everything possible ... to cajole, bully and shame men into coming forward.'[118] As discussed in the next chapter, the new measures included a personal appeal by Botha and Smuts for recruits, the staging of the recruitment drive, and the harnessing of government employees and civil servants. By mid-May, Buxton told Smuts that recruiting was improving, but that 'the material that is now obtained is very raw – A footman and a chauffeur of mine have at last been passed and have just gone to Potchefstroom!'[119]

The territorial growth of the Union of South Africa had been an imperative of the Botha Government. The war provided a means to achieve this. However, tensions between their colonial policies divided Britain, France, Belgium, and Portugal. There were vocal critics of each other in each country and South Africa's sub-imperialist goals complicated matters further. The Belgians railed against the idea of British administration over the districts Smuts captured and, by May, Buxton told Smuts they might have wanted 'to peg out a claim' and, writing as the governor general of the Union, added: 'perhaps we do too!'[120] He was certainly not wrong. Smuts used South Africans where he could for the civil administration of the territory he conquered.[121] H.S. Cooke, who had been acting director of Native Labour on the Witwatersrand and then director of the Information Bureau, was brought in as chief political officer and a temporary major. Several experienced officials of South Africa's Native Affairs Department, sent out specially for purpose or recruited from their regiments in East Africa, served under him, while from August 1916 a specially selected detachment of SAMR, all well trained in policing duties, policed the northeast quadrant of Tanganyika. Adam Payne, an official in the Department of Native Affairs, numbered among the civil servants from Pretoria sent to serve as assistant political officers in occupied Tanganyika. Sent to Mwanza, on the shore of Lake Victoria, and

116 Botha to Smuts, 13 April 1916 in Hancock and Van der Poel (eds.), *Selections*, vol. III, p.358.
117 NARSSA: Smuts Papers, vol. 198, Buxton to Smuts, c. April 1916, and Buxton to Smuts, 3 May 1916.
118 Bourne to Smuts, 14 April 1916 in Hancock and Van der Poel (eds.), *Selections*, vol. III, p.360.
119 NARSSA: Smuts Papers, vol. 198, Buxton to Smuts, 18 May 1916.
120 NARSSA: Smuts Papers, vol. 198, Buxton to Smuts, 18 May 1916.
121 There were of course notable exceptions. Sir Theodore Morrison, then on his way to East Africa to assist in the civil administration of the territory Smuts was then occupying, was a distinguished Indian civil servant. NARSSA: Smuts Papers, vol. 198, Buxton to Smuts, 25 July 1916.

then to Musoma, he had to convince and cajole the local sultans to send recruits to serve as porters in the British transport service. Those that refused, Payne punished personally.[122]

Botha, after his return from East Africa, raised the matter of the difference in the methods of government especially in terms of the treatment of Africans. Most disquieting for Botha was the future impact of the millions of Africans in Central and East Africa and their impact on South African policy. The gruelling campaign and shared hardships fostered comradery across national and ethnic lines and potentially formed a fertile seedbed for the export of ideas highlighted by the Chilembwe revolt in Nyasaland in early 1915.[123] This was suppressed by the British. In turn, the Botha government responded rapidly when Mandume ya Ndemufayo challenged the imposition of South African rule in Ovamboland (South West Africa) following the armistice in July 1915. There were few South African officials: a Major Fairlie of the SAMR and a clerk at Namakunde in the neutral zone, and a resident commissioner for Ovamboland at Ondonga. They were, Bourne reminded the Cabinet, 'the sole exponents in that territory of the might and majesty of the Union.' Described as a 'savage chief' – and 'this turbulent fellow' – Mandume refused Pretoria's demand that he and his headmen 'place themselves unreservedly in our hands.'[124] He died in battle in February 1917.

South Africa's relations with her Portuguese neighbour were equally difficult. While never resorting to armed conflict, distrust was high, and the diplomatic contest was at times intense. In Southern Africa, this manifested in two practical instances. First was the role of the Portuguese forces in the prosecution of the campaign in East Africa. Buxton told Smuts that he very much doubted whether the Portuguese – 'our "ancient ally"'[125] – would 'be much help' although they had perhaps 12–15,000 troops on the Tanganyikan frontier: 'They seem so far instead of getting to Lindi and to Kilwa as they boasted, to have got only a few miles beyond their own border.' Buxton shared with Smuts intelligence he had received from the British Consul General at Lourenco Marques, a Mr Macdonnell, who thought 'some of the men were pretty good, but the forces as a whole and the officers were a wretched lot, and they had no proper organisation and no intelligence or transport department.' This does not seem too different from the difficulties Smuts had faced himself. However, as Buxton and Smuts recognised, while a substantial Portuguese advance might have corralled Lettow in late 1916, their failure for having done so would undermine any claim they would make at the end of the war – 'if and when the question of the partition of the territory arises.'[126]

122 Adam Payne, *Blow Blow The Winds Of Change* (Johannesburg: Pens Editorial and Publishing Enterprises, 1989), pp.96–139. See also Samson, *World War I in Africa*, p.149.
123 NARSSA: GG 597, file 9/57/40, Secretary for Defence to Ministers, 18 September 1916.
124 NARSSA: GG 597, file 9/57/40, Secretary for Defence to Ministers, 6 November 1916.
125 NARSSA: Smuts Papers, vol. 198, Buxton to Smuts, 4 November 1916.
126 NARSSA: Smuts Papers, vol. 198, Buxton to Smuts, 30 September 1916.

The second instance related to the territory of Mozambique itself and official Portuguese views of South Africa's 'north' policy. For some time, Portuguese officials were very wise in keeping a tight hold on information pertaining to Mozambique. The South African Department of Defence was forced to use the Reuters news service to fill information voids and, under Major Johan Leipoldt, then South Africa's chief intelligence officer, run agents in Lourenco Marques to monitor the movement of prominent Portuguese nationals. As one of the South African agents reported: 'the Portuguese were by a long way not as anti-German as he liked to see them.'[127] But, of course, by this stage, the expansionist desires of her South African neighbour represented a far greater threat to the Portuguese in East Africa than Germany ever did. As Leipoldt noted: 'The Official and Military element have no sympathy with us and view the Imperial and especially Union Governments with grave suspicion.' One official told him that 'whenever they come into contact with the Union Octopus, it gets its tentacles closer around them and they were fully convinced that the ultimate aim was the loss to them of Portugal's most valuable colonial asset.'[128]

Smuts Leaves East Africa

In December 1916, London approached Botha to attend an Imperial War Conference in Britain scheduled for February 1917, but Botha declined on account of his health, his wife's frailty, and the threat of an apparent second rebellion. Most of all, he did not feel up for the trip and questioned the role he might play. Lloyd George suggested that Smuts be brought back from Tanganyika and sent to London in his stead. Botha and Buxton readily approved and urged Smuts to go to London to represent South Africa. He was according to Buxton: 'the most suitable alternative.'[129] Smuts was ready to go. This meant that Botha would become the only Dominion premier not to visit London during the war. As he told Buxton: 'I could at present do more good here by seeing things through than by going to England.' He would also miss the 1918 Imperial War Conference, claiming that he was not a great talker and Smuts would take care of things just as well as he could.[130]

The War Office instructed Smuts to hand over his command in East Africa to Major General Reginald Hoskens as soon as military operations allowed and to return

127 DODA: DC, box 356, file DC 40057 Intelligence Section, quoted in Major J.G.W. Leipoldt to Adjutant General, 22 December 1917. See also, NARSSA: GG 597, file 9/57/40, Secretary for Defence to Ministers, 4 September 1916.
128 DODA: DC, box 356, file DC 40057 Intelligence Section, Major J.G.W. Leipoldt to Adjutant General, 22 December 1917.
129 WSHC: 947/540, Viscount Long of Wraxall Papers, Long to Drummond Chaplin 16 January 1917.
130 Buxton, *General Botha*, p.160.

to South Africa before leaving for Britain. Lord Derby, the Secretary of State for War, wrote a personal letter to Smuts in January 1917:

> I cannot but regret that you should have to leave East Africa before the conclusion of the campaign in which you are now engaged, but I fully realise the larger issues at stake and the very great value of your presence at the Conference.
>
> I take this opportunity to congratulate you sincerely on the ability and uniform success with which you have conducted the campaign in the face of great natural difficulties and of thanking you in the name of the Army Council for the whole-hearted support which they have throughout received from you.[131]

Derby hoped that the campaign in East Africa was in its final phase. It was not. Hoskens carefully prepared the British forces for a fresh offensive in East Africa in early 1917, but, having lost the confidence of the Chief of the Imperial General Staff, General Sir William Robertson, he was replaced in April by Major General Jacobus van Deventer, another South African. As Walter Long realised, there was 'some feeling about Van de Venter's [*sic.*] appointment' and discussed it at great length with Robertson, 'who felt satisfied that he was the best man for this particular campaign.'[132]

Smuts returned to South Africa in January 1917. He proposed to leave Dar-es-Salaam on 20 January and to proceed to Lourenço Marques to discuss the war situation with the Portuguese Governor General in Mozambique.[133] But he was clearly unwell. While in Tanganyika, he had been exposed to Merriman's miasmatic microbes and the biotic conditions of the campaign. He had been bitten at least once – by a venomous spider – and suffered from dysentery and recurring bouts of malaria. He was ill while in South Africa; for nine days he lay in bed in Irene with malaria, which again struck him in Cape Town shortly before his departure. This prevented him from visiting Windhoek, conferring with Howard Gorges, the administrator of the conquered territory of South West Africa, and discussing questions of soldier settlement.[134]

Smuts was also forced to postpone his departure by a week and eventually sailed on the evening of 15 February aboard the *Dunvegan Castle*, which had been delayed for two days to enable Smuts to finalise discussions with his colleagues in the South African cabinet. It had been universally known in South Africa that he would be leaving by the *Walmer Castle*, but Smuts, not a man for taking chances, thought it

131 WSHC: 947/636, Viscount Long of Wraxall Papers, Lord Derby to Smuts, 8 January 1917.
132 WSHC: 947/602, Viscount Long of Wraxall Papers, Long to Buxton, 31 May 1917.
133 NARSSA: Smuts Papers, vol. 202, Smuts to Theron, 11 January 1917.
134 E.H.L. Gorges to Smuts, 25 February 1917in Hancock and Van der Poel (eds.), *Selections*, vol. III, p.453.

wiser to leave by an earlier ship. But, the news slipped, out; as Buxton wrote to Long, 'secrecy is not a South African virtue.'[135]

Collyer, who Smuts described as 'the very able and experienced officer who was my chief of the General Staff', produced a lessons-driven textbook for the instruction of officers at the South African Military College.[136] In his foreword, Smuts noted that the first phase:

> ...was carried on – in British territory – with many ups and downs until my arrival in February, 1916, and after I left in January, 1917, it continued till the Armistice. But during the eleven months of my command the greatest effort on the Allied side was made, most of the fighting on the various fronts took place and almost the entire enemy territory was occupied.[137]

As many recognised, this was a tremendous achievement. But it had also come at a huge human cost. Smuts readily pays tribute to Lettow and his 'brilliant performance':

> Outnumbered most of the time, during my command greatly outnumbered and continuously outfought, this black army under highly trained white officers put up a fight so skilful, so prolonged under the most discouraging conditions of continuous retreat, that it stands out in my memory of seven years' war experience as one of the most striking military feats I have known.[138]

Collyer highlighted the mistakes made and opportunities missed by the opposing commanders – as well as the 'defects and faults' in the administration, logistic, and medical organisation. In the end, Smuts praised Lettow: 'all his record as a whole remains a fine one in which his old opponents also take great pleasure.'[139] The German armed forces were much better led in East Africa than they had been in South West Africa. Lettow not only organized a very large Askari army but he trained them to 'fight with great skill and bravery.'[140] And here, Smuts believed, were the 'lessons' of the war – taught in the main by his German adversary. Africa campaigning demanded mobile infantry, troops fleet of foot; the resourceful use of the African bush, adroit night fighting, the skilful handling of reserves, and the seizure of opportunities for counterattack.[141]

135 WSHC: 947/636, Viscount Long of Wraxall Papers, Buxton to Long, 16 February 1917.
136 Smuts's foreword to Collyer, *The South Africans*, p. v.
137 Smuts's foreword to Collyer, *The South Africans*, p. v–vi.
138 Smuts's foreword to Collyer, *The South Africans*, p. vii.
139 Smuts's foreword to Collyer, *The South Africans*, p. vii.
140 Smuts to Merriman, 12 May 1916 in Hancock and Van der Poel (eds.), *Selections*, vol. III, p.366.
141 Smuts's foreword to Collyer, *The South Africans*, p. vii.

Conclusion

Matters in South Africa prevented Botha from attending the Imperial War Conference, convened in London by Lloyd George, who had just lifted Asquith from the seat of power. Smuts would go in his stead. As Crafford suggests, this was for Smuts a heaven-sent opportunity. The campaign in East Africa seemed to be drawing towards its end and its final phase – of mopping up and cornering Lettow-Vorbeck – might be left to others and so free him to tackle larger issues. Once back in South Africa, Smuts spoke in laudatory terms of conquest, and of having 'secured a voice in the ultimate disposal of this subcontinent.'[142] Even if some of his fellow Dutch-speaking compatriots fulminated against him, and his body was wracked with malaria, this Cicero had indeed returned from his Cilicia in triumph.

Smuts's departure from East Africa coincides with the start of a third phase in the campaigning in Africa during the Great War. This period is marked with crisis and revolution in Europe and the intensification of the campaigns against Turkey in Egypt and the Middle East, and against the Germans in East Africa. Time and again Lettow-Vorbeck seized the initiative invaded Northern Rhodesia, Uganda and the Belgian Congo, and increased the size of his forces by adding larger numbers of African soldiers, until they numbered more than 20,000 men. This phase is marked by increasing 'Africanisation' and guerrilla warfare. Lettow's troops lived off the land, harried their opponents – numbering some 160,000 troops – and ranged the countryside, crossing borders at will, until the armistice in Europe was declared.[143]

East Africa proved to be a much larger, more difficult campaign and presented problems – of a political and military nature – greater even than South Africa's deployments to Egypt and the Western Front. In his own brief account, Smuts described the performance of his troops in Tanganyika as 'a great human performance [and] an unusual and arduous task.' Writing in 1937, he expressed the hope that the East African campaign would 'long remain the outstanding example of tropical African warfare.'[144] Two years later South Africa once again poised to send troops to East Africa to counter the armies of Mussolini.

In October 1915, Crewe, then Director of War Recruiting, had expressed his gratitude to Colonel M.C. Rowland, the Quartermaster General, for the work his section had done in preparing the departing contingents: 'They were collected hurriedly, equipped and sent forward in I should say record time and all the arrangements made for them in camp and on their journey both by land and sea were most satisfactory.'[145] There may have been no complaints in October 1915, but – as discussed in the next chapter – these would certainly come.

142 Crafford, *Jan Smuts*, p.133.
143 Van der Waag, 'The First World War in Africa: Impact and Consequences', pp.146–148.
144 Smuts's foreword to Collyer, *The South Africans*, p. v.
145 DODA: DC Group2, box 690, file DC 128/958/9199, Applications for Overseas Contingent, Colonel Charles Crewe to Colonel M.C. Rowland, 12 October 1915.

8

'Not a Serial Fairy Tale', 1916–1918

All this rot about 'equality of sacrifice' bores me stiff. You can't get equality of sacrifice ... Catelwords and catchphrases are the source of many mistakes and many wrong actions. We had 'business as usual' at the beginning of the war and then you have that foolish one 'when in doubt do nothing' which may lead you astray unless you remember 'he who hesitates is lost'.

South African serviceman to his fiancé, 2 June 1916.[1]

The fact that ... after we returned from France, having sacrificed our lives, no recognition whatsoever has been shown us, assures us and confirms the fact that the natives of this country, in spite of their loyalty, are a nonentity, and are only called upon when the Government are in dire straits, and then not recognised when their services are finished with.

S.T. Zondani and E. Ntusi to Magistrate of East London, 24 January 1920.[2]

Botha and Smuts needed a reliable senior civil servant in Pretoria to run the Department of Defence. They found him in Roland Bourne: a former military officer who had served during the Second Anglo-Boer War with the 1st Royal Scots before taking up service in Milner's administration in the Repatriation Department.[3] He was capable of enormous quantities of work, forceful in approach, and ardent in upholding, and at times protecting, his position as secretary for defence. This last quality, which placed him at times at odds with high commanders, led Botha to believe that Bourne

1 UCT: Joyce Newton-Thompson Collection, B1.17, BC643, Cyril Newton-Thompson to Joyce Nettlefold, 2 June 1916.
2 As quoted in Albert Grundlingh, *War and Society, Participation and Remembrance, South African black and coloured troops in the First World War, 1914-1918* (Stellenbosch: SUN Press, 2014), p.102.
3 I. van der Waag, 'Smuts's Generals: Towards a first portrait of the South African high command, 1912-48', *War in History*, vol.18, no.1 (2011), pp.33–61.

would sometimes overegg matters but trusted his judgement.[4] Smuts, another not to suffer fools gladly, recognised his value too – something seen in their long and detailed correspondence; between them they held together the logistic and organisation framework during the early war. The bond was strong and formed on a common understanding of service and of the peculiar role of defence policy in the exertion of dominion autonomy. This was something these men understood.[5] Bourne was later knighted in recognition of his service.

As Secretary for Defence, Bourne wrote a weekly memorandum for the Cabinet on the operations of the South African contingents on the war fronts. These started in mid-July 1916, after the South African deployments had become more complicated, and covered the campaigns in East Africa and 'Overseas', that is the Western Front. Matter of fact, they tell mostly of 'progress' made on the war fronts but also of the steps taken in South Africa to prepare new recruits and remounts to replace 'wastage' in the war zones. As he noted in September, 'these memoranda are not a serial fairy tale, there are to be reported, in addition to good news, some set backs [*sic.*] and disappointments.'[6] These setbacks included a growing manpower crisis, escalating casualties and recruitment problems despite Botha's personal recruitment appeal, and Smuts's travails in East Africa and – implicitly at least – their likely political impact. They are examined in this chapter.

Casualties and War News

The South African casualties, first sustained in East Africa at Salaita, were immediately controversial. As Botha admitted, the first list of killed, wounded, and missing in East Africa created 'a rather painful situation'.[7] He had to rely on Smartt – the leader of the official opposition – to help him avoid a debate in the House of Assembly. The first casualty reports from France were heavier still and seemingly prompted the writing of Bourne's weekly memoranda. Clerks at the Defence Secretariat adjusted the casualty numbers each week as finer details of those killed in action or had died later from wounds became available. Casualties were difficult to ascertain, even in static operations, unless the wounded could be counted, and the dead registered. Through August 1916, the numbers of Springbok casualties confirmed from the fighting on

4 See for example, Botha's impression of Bourne's handling of the report on the War Stores Commission in Botha to Smuts, 21 March 1916, Hancock and Van der Poel (eds.), *Selections*, vol. III, p.347.

5 Similar understandings were held in the other Dominion capitals. See, for example, Desmond Morton, *A Peculiar Kind of Politics; Canada's Overseas Ministry in the First World War* (Toronto: University of Toronto Press, 1982).

6 NARSSA: GG 597, file 9/57/40, Secretary for Defence to Ministers, 11 September 1916.

7 Botha to Smuts, 23 February 1916 in Hancock and Van der Poel (eds.), *Selections*, vol. III, p.337.

the Somme rose steadily from 2,054 to 2,924 – the overwhelming majority sustained in the fighting at Delville Wood. In August, men were dying from wounds sustained in the fighting in mid-July, but the most dramatic increase – rising from 0.73 per cent to 16.75 per cent – related to men reported as missing in action. Increasingly, from the end of August, much to the comfort of their families, who were demanding news, men first identified as missing were now confirmed to be prisoners of war.[8] By 11 September, a further 110 other ranks – of the seven officers and 372 other ranks still missing in France, the week before – were reported to be POWs.[9] More and more men were found over the following weeks by the official POW bureaux in Britain and Germany and 'the great Bureau in Geneva.'[10] However, by October, officials feared that the vast majority of those still missing from the fighting in Delville Wood – six officers, and 242 other ranks – had to have been killed although their bodies had not been recovered. Botha and Smuts had to carefully manage the release of accurate news and satisfy the families of the killed and missing men, while dealing with widely circulating rumours that the Dominion troops were utilised as cannon fodder, or that Lukin's Brigade – within a month of their heroic stand at Delville Wood – was again in action when it was not.[11]

8 There was considerable concern about the fate of South African prisoners of war and civilian internees. These had been present in German South West Africa. On 12 June, after some eight months in captivity, the South African prisoners of war at Tsumeb were allowed to write home. They bought or borrowed postcards or writing paper and for two days they could only discuss the passage of their mail. They did not know then that their letters – burned on the day of their release – never reached the Union. Their lot improved in other ways as the campaign drew to an end. On 24 June, they received for the first time as POWs, soldiers' rations and, on 4 July, a South African airman spotted their enclosure; the long-lost prisoners had been found. Percy L. Close, *A Prisoner of the Germans in South-West Africa* (Cape Town and London: T. Maskew Miller, 1916), pp.289–290, 292, 301. But concerns about POWs reached new heights in East Africa. Belgian Ministry of Colonies, *The Fate of the Prisoners during the East African Campaign* (London: Gabriel Devreese, 1919). The Boer farmers in Tanganyika were also a concern. Some had joined Smuts: the whereabouts of others were unknown. Botha wanted to know whether there had been any instances of abuse by the Germans. Botha to Smuts, 21 March 1916 in Hancock and Van der Poel (eds.), *Selections*, vol. III, p.348.

9 NARSSA: GG 597, file 9/57/40, Secretary for Defence to Ministers, 11 September 1916.

10 NARSSA: GG 597, file 9/57/40, Secretary for Defence to Ministers, 3 October 1916. For a personal, war-time description of the search for the missing on the battlefields of the Western Front, see Lord Northcliffe, *At The War* (London: Hodder and Stoughton, 1916), pp.133–149. Comité International de la Croix-Rouge (CICR): C G1 A 10-02A, Stanley, British Red Cross Society, London, to Le Comité International de la Croix-Rouge, Geneva, 23 September 1914.

11 NARSSA: GG 597, file 9/57/40, Secretary for Defence to Ministers, 21 August 1916.

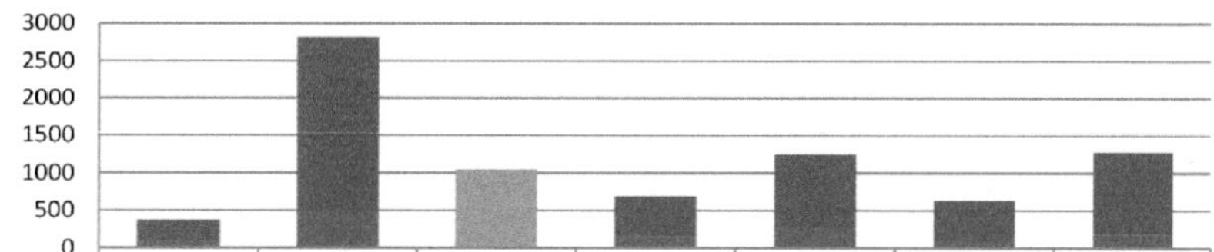

	German South West Africa	Somme: Delville Wood July 1916	Somme: Butte de Warlencourt Oct 1916	Arras 1917	3rd Ypres Sep 1917	Battle of the Lys: Messines Apr 1918	Le Cateau operations Oct 1918
Killed and wounded			1050				
Wounded and missing	288	2313		549	995	550	1086
KIA	88	502		145	263	89	190

Figure 8.1: South African casualties in Western Front battles compared to the whole of the German South West Africa Campaign.

The escalating casualties on the warfronts created a demand for accurate news on the part of the public but also the government. Botha and Smuts needed detailed updates, especially from France, where they had no press representative or military office, so that they might respond as required.[12] However, by early September there were still no official reports or commendations regarding the action at Delville Wood to counterpoise the heavy casualties sustained there. The War Office, after a query by William Schreiner, the South African high commissioner in London, first suggested that Pretoria 'take Reuters cables to be accurate' as far as news was concerned, but then detailed an officer to write an article on the South African stand at Delville Wood.[13] The first official reports 'of our gallant fellows' doings Overseas' arrived in September. These included an account written by Lukin, and appreciations of the work done by the bearer division of the South African Field Ambulance and the South African Signal Company. Aspects of these, with Rawlinson's Special Order, were prepared for the Press.[14] Lukin's account is vivid, telling of hardship, endurance, valour, and suffering. Ordered to capture and hold Deville Wood at all costs, the brigade had suffered 75 per cent casualties but had persevered. The message was clear: the South

12 Schreiner, the high commissioner, explained the position in a letter in August 1916, NARSSA: GG 597, file 9/57/40, Schreiner to Creedy, 15 August 1916.

13 NARSSA: GG 597, file 9/57/40, Secretary for Defence to Ministers, 4 September 1916. As noted in chapter 7, the Reuters news service was already used by the South African Department of Defence to fill information gaps when the Portuguese officials in Mozambique issued no official reports. In September 1916, the first news that the 1st SA Infantry Brigade was again in the fighting line – on Vimy Ridge – came from Reuter's.

14 NARSSA: GG 597, file 9/57/40, Secretary for Defence to Ministers, 11 September 1916.

Africans had done their duty.[15] Yet, the Department of Defence battled to get official news. As Bourne noted that November, they had no official news of the Brigade 'beyond a very formidable casualty list.'[16]

Botha and Smuts recognised the importance in proclaiming South Africa's battlefield achievements if South Africa was to secure a voice at the peace conference. Yet nothing had been done about the writing of the history of the South African operations. As Schreiner noted, unlike the other Dominions, South Africa had 'none of the machinery for recording and publishing the exploits of our men, which Canada, Australia and New Zealand have, in one form or another.'[17] Collyer, who had served as Botha's chief of staff in German South West Africa, and then as chief of staff to Smuts in East Africa, had expressed an interest in writing the campaign histories, but growing public demand and the government's media interest meant this could not wait for the end of the war.[18] Bourne approached Smuts in November 1916 to appoint Wyndham and Buchan – two old acquaintances from 'Kindergarten' days – to write the histories of the South African campaigns in German South West Africa and on the Western Front.[19] The histories they wrote, which formed part of the government's larger information programme, would stress the valour and success of the Springbok soldier, and the importance of Allied solidarity, and advanced Botha's goals in nation-building.[20] However, as Bourne argued: 'events in South Africa move with such astounding rapidity that there is only time to deal with them,

15 NARSSA: GG 597, file 9/57/40, Lukin to Secretary for Defence, 4 August 1916. Read this with the messages Lukin received from various personages; an assortment may be found in the Lukin Papers, UCT: Major General Sir H.T. Lukin Papers, BC676, A1.10, Messages and Telegrams of Appreciation.

16 NARSSA: GG 597, file 9/57/40, Secretary for Defence to Ministers, 6 November 1916.

17 NARSSA: GG 597, file 9/57/40, Schreiner to Creedy, 15 August 1916.

18 DODA: DC, Box 189, file 11122, Correspondence with various people re History of the German South West African Campaign, Acting Adjutant General to Brigadier General J.J. Collyer, 19 July 1916.

19 Buchan was then restructuring Whitehall's propaganda machinery into a new Department of Information. TNA: CAB 21/37, Buchan to Lloyd George, 2 February 1917, and Minutes of a Meeting of the War Cabinet, 24 January 1917. Buchan's 'History of the War', serialised for popular consumption, was avidly read by Dominion soldiers. See UCT: Purland Family Collection, BC 477, N.W. Nichol to Captain Purland, 12 November 1916.

20 The four campaign historians were military officers (Wyndham, Buchan, Leipoldt, Collyer): one Afrikaans, three English-speakers. Wyndham produced the first draft on the German South West Africa campaign (1916–1917), which was revised by Leipoldt (1918–1919), and then subsumed into *The Union of South Africa and the Great War: Official History* (1924), of which Leipoldt was the primary author. The remaining campaign histories were produced by Buchan in 1920 (the Springboks on the Western Front) and Collyer in 1937 (German South West Africa) and 1939 (German East Africa). See I. van der Waag, 'Recording the Great War: military archives and the South African official history programme', *Scientia Militaria: South African Journal of Military Studies*, vol.44, no.1 (2016), pp.81–110. Republished with permission in *Nuova Antologia Militare, Rivista Interdisciplinare della Società Italiana di Storia Militare* (Rome), n.1 (2020), pp.3–53.

and little left to "make a song" about them.'[21] Much of the writing would inevitably await the end of the war.

But there had been complaints from the start. The war correspondents had been laudatory in their despatches from German South West Africa creating the impression in the UK, some editors felt, 'that practically the whole affair was carried through by Dutch-speaking South Africans and that the English South Africans performed but a very minor part.'[22] While this generated some resentment, things did not improve. In fact, the first despatch from East Africa – published in South Africa on 1 April 1916 after a long wait – seemed to continue the narrative taking a figurative turn as B.H. Dodd, the editor of *The Daily Dispatch* (East London) complained. It was little more than a 'summary of operations' and as Dodd argued contained laudatory references to Smuts and his exploits in the Anglo-Boer War with 'the figurative statement about his burghers "having their horses' feet in the Atlantic Ocean" [which were] more likely to be appreciated in the Old Country than here.'[23] Nation-building had certainly been a government imperative, but some editors of English-medium newspapers demanded more war news that was plausibly balanced.

The government and civic organisations took greater steps to proclaim the sacrifice of the predominantly English-speaking infantry brigade in France. The first Delville Wood anniversary presented an opportunity. The Cape Musicians' Association organised a musical memorial service on 18 July 1917 under the patronage of Buxton, as Governor General, Brigadier General Cavendish the commander of the Imperial garrison, Rear Admiral O.F. Gillett of the Royal Navy at Simon's Town, Sir Frederic de Waal, Botha's son-in-law and the Administrator of the Cape Province, and Chief Justice Sir James Rose-Innes. The proceeds went to the Governor General's Fund for the relief of returned soldiers and their families. Reported as 'a most impressive tribute to the memory of the noble band of South Africans who a year ago made the supreme sacrifice at Delville Wood under circumstances which have won imperishable glory for their country', it was 'in every respect worthy of the great anniversary that it marked.' South Africa's elder stateman, John X. Merriman, gave the tribute:

> You know the story of the combat, the courage of the attack and the indomitable tenacity which marked its every stage and served to show that our South Africans were worthy to take their place with the bravest from every part of the British Commonwealth, and to stand by the side of our heroic allies, the French, who have given the world such an example of enduring sacrifice for their country and the cause. It was an episode. Yes, but it was far more for us! It was the first stiff fight in which the forces of our new-born Union have met under the most

21 NARSSA: GG 597, file 9/57/40, Secretary for Defence to Ministers, 6 November 1916.
22 DODA: CSO, Box 2, file 2/6/20, Press Correspondents reports re B.E.A., 'The East Africa Despatch', *The Daily Dispatch* (East London), Saturday, 1 April 1916.
23 DODA: CSO, Box 2, file 2/6/20, Press Correspondents reports re B.E.A., 'The East Africa Despatch', *The Daily Dispatch* (East London), Saturday, 1 April 1916.

> extreme conditions of modern warfare and have shown themselves not unequal to the dreadful task.

From such episodes, Merriman argued, nations derive strength. Delville Wood would become South Africa's Thermopylae or Morgarten, a critical story in South Africa's foundational narrative and a future touchstone on the international stage. South Africans, as citizens of a young nation, could hold their heads high among the peoples of the world.[24]

Supply and Disease

Difficulties in East Africa particularly had highlighted the need to control the flow of information and construct an official narrative to counter growing criticism, much of which centred on the dual, inter-related questions of supply and disease. As Smuts intimated in a telegram on 24 September, this was exacerbated by bad weather:

> During the last three days general continuous rains of unusually severe character have fallen, roads and rivers are impassable, bridges washed away and all transport from Korogwe to Kissaki and from Kondoa–Irangi to Kidodo is at a standstill. As we are at present living from hand to mouth supply situation is very critical. I also fear heavy increase of sick rate.[25]

The government was forced to concede an inquiry following serious allegations made of corruption and improper or negligent conduct. Smuts had first noticed improprieties in 1915, before leaving for East Africa, when he started a preliminary investigation. A can of worms was opened. The evidence presented before the War Stores Commission of Inquiry was damning. The regimental medical officer of 12th South African Infantry testified:

> Rations have been consistently inadequate throughout. Not on one occasion were full rations received. Not only were rations insufficient in quantity but they were frequently unsuitable in quality – as witness the sandy rice at Kondoa; rancid mealie meal; and meat so appallingly tough that it was imperfectly digested, and consequently lost much of its value as a food. This type of food resulted in diarrhoea. Fat was almost unobtainable. (I have seen men frying meat in dubbin.) The issue of jam was negligible. Sugar was deplorably scarce. Vegetables were

24 NARSSA: PM 1/1/48, file 4/84/1917, European War SA Brigade Successes, 'Union's Roll of Honour; Deathless Deeds at Delville Wood; Musical Memorial Service in the City Hall; Mr Merriman on South Africa's Heritage', *The Cape Times*, 19 July 1917.

25 NARSSA: GG 597, file 9/57/40, Secretary for Defence to Ministers, 3 October 1916.

> issued on rare occasions, but only as a substitute for some other portion of the ration. It is my deliberate opinion that on the average throughout the above period [6 April 1916–26 September 1916] men were subjected to a process of semi-starvation. At times this state of affairs was mitigated to some extent by the men's own efforts in obtaining food from natives [*sic*.]. At other times – notably at Kidodi – the men suffered from acute starvation.[26]

The Commission's final report – extending to 77 printed pages, with 5,328 typeset pages of evidence – found that several officers in the Transport and Remounts and the Veterinary Services branches, including the Director of Transport and Remounts, Lieutenant Colonel Victor Hosken, and his son Captain C.C. Hosken, were under suspicion of corruption, negligence, and behaviour unbecoming officers in their posts. While the government acknowledged that Hosken's post had been one of 'very great difficulty', the matter entered the press where Hosken faced severe criticism. Hosken was relieved of his appointment from 15 September 1916 and reduced in rank to captain. Several remount and veterinary officers were dismissed, others were reprimanded. Some of the officers felt they had been treated highhandedly, had no opportunity to confront their accusers, and had no definite charges facing them. Hosken was, he complained to Bourne, 'a discredited man [with] little hope of any success in procuring further employment'.[27] Ingeniously, Hosken reverted to the politics of the 1912 integration; he had integrated into the UDF having served as a major and as Director of Transport in the Natal Militia. He not only reminded the reader of his previous career but hinted at the neglect of Natal men in the UDF. The report and associated correspondence was tabled in Parliament during the 1917 Session.

The fitness of the Springbok soldier in East Africa depended on an efficient supply system and a satisfactory medical service. Where these failed, the government paid the price at home. The allegations of starvation dogged Botha and Smuts. On 12 November, 'an unctuous leading article' appeared in the *Sunday Times* (Johannesburg). An exasperated Bourne opined in his weekly memorandum to the cabinet:

> Those who have read this series of memoranda will understand fully how impossible it has been to carry out the immensely successful operations and keep the troops well fed, how this failure has been the chief source of General Smuts' anxiety and worry, and now though conditions may improve, it will probably be impracticable always to keep advanced troops on regular full rations during the final phase of the campaign. It is, of course, easily understood that the troops themselves do not realise all the difficulties. They very seldom do. Men

26 Wits: AB1219, Rev. Edward Francis Paget Papers, Report by Captain Grantley Barrett, RMO, 12th SAI, to OC 9th SAI, undated.

27 UG 12–1917 Correspondence and Other Documents relating to the Report of the War Stores Commission, 30. Hosken to Bourne, 11 September 1916. We are grateful to Anri Delport for securing an electronic copy of this document.

> returning ill and debilitated owing to bad and insufficient food even though they do not intend to 'grouse', will naturally lay emphasis on the want of food and exaggerate it.[28]

His statement that South African troops traditionally forage and feed themselves was cold comfort, as was Smuts's response to the complaints: 'Beyond general hardships these complaints are unfounded.'[29] In November, the leading South African newspapers took up the story once again. The *Rand Daily Mail* and the *Sunday Times*, Buxton wrote Smuts, 'have been running-a-mock over the question of the discomforts endured by the troops during the campaign.' The *Rand Daily Mail* carried a cartoon that Buxton described as 'really disgraceful' and one that would 'have harrowed the hearts of a very large number of parents and others.' These were things 'they probably did not think of this when they thought they would make a scoop.' Smuts responded with a personal message and Botha addressed the matter on his public campaign trail.[30]

East Africa had a sickness death rate higher than any other campaign. The wastage of manpower from environmental conditions and disease was appalling. The troops and porters contracted malaria, tick-bite fever, and dysentery in large numbers and suffered from the lesser ills of heat rashes and veld sores, and the bites and stings of various tropical insects, worms, and arachnids. Collyer records that, in December 1916, an astonishing 10,700 British troops were hospitalised during a single week, while the battle-related deaths for the entire four-year campaign numbered 3,443.[31] Various equine sicknesses decimated animal transport. Trooper L.R. Simes records that the South African Medical Corps staff issued mounted troops with injectable arsenic for general equine strengthening and quinine for themselves.[32] East Africa demanded thousands of replacements in horses, mules, and donkeys and on a monthly basis: 7,793 were shipped in July 1916, and a further 6,120 in August.[33] The campaign had become, as Merriman noted, more a campaign against climatological conditions and a tropical disease environment; severe tests of nature and of sheer physical endurance. Figure 8.2 demonstrates that the African porters suffered measurably worse than the combatant troops; at the peak of the 1917 campaigning season, their death rate from disease per thousand men reached a staggering 27.6, whereas the high number for troops – reached in the previous month – was six.[34]

28 NARSSA: GG 597, file 9/57/40, Secretary for Defence to Ministers, 13 November 1916.
29 NARSSA: GG 597, file 9/57/40, quoted in Secretary for Defence to Ministers, 13 November 1916.
30 NARSSA: Smuts Papers, vol. 198, Buxton to Smuts, 21 November 1916.
31 Collyer, *The South Africans*, p.277.
32 Natal Carbineers Archives, Pietermaritzburg (NCA): Trooper Lyle Richmond Simes Collection, L.R. Simes, 'The Three Campaigns First World War: West and East Africa and Overseas'.
33 NARSSA: GG 597, file 9/57/40, Secretary for Defence to Ministers, 4 September 1916.
34 The story of the Carriers – 'the feet and hands of the army' according to Rudyard Kipling – is told by Hodges, *Kariakor – The Carrier Corps*.

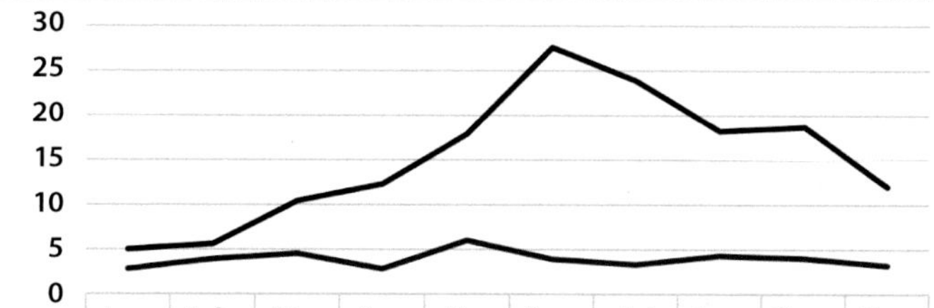

	Jan	Feb	Mar	Apr	May	Jun	Jul	Aug	Sep	Oct
Troops death rate per 1,000 of strength per month	2.8	3.9	4.5	2.8	6	3.9	3.3	4.3	4	3.2
Followers death rate per 1,000 of strength per month	5	5.6	10.4	12.3	17.9	27.6	23.9	18.2	18.7	12

Figure 8.2: Death rates per 1000 of strength per month: troops and 'followers' (porters, carriers) in East Africa, January to October 1917.

Smuts, who also contracted malaria and suffered with dysentery, acknowledged in May 1916 that: 'Our casualties have been much heavier than in the German South West Africa campaign, and fever has for the time filled our hospitals.'[35] He wrote that he might see to the early evacuation of the most serious cases and take steps to alleviate some of the concerns, but, as he and Botha knew, the arrival of casualties in Durban would 'make a very bad and unpleasant impression.'[36] Botha, who had acknowledged that 'In war, there can hardly be a more important branch of military organisation than the care of the wounded, the sick and the dying',[37] made a point to visit the South African sick and wounded invalided from East Africa. They were, he believed, receiving the best treatment available.[38]

Mothers approached Smuts for information on their sons. When in London, a Mrs Hodgson approached him. Her son had contracted malaria in East Africa and was hospitalised in Pretoria, where Mrs Smuts and other members of the Smuts family visited him and other invalids from East Africa. Smuts had said: 'He is a good boy and has served me very well, and I shall always be glad to do for him what I can.'[39] Determined to avoid the physical exertion of the campaign fought against Lettow-Vorbeck and its political fallout, Smuts would fight a different campaign in East Africa in 1940–1941.

35 Smuts to Merriman, 12 May 1916 in Hancock and Van der Poel (eds.), *Selections*, vol. III, p.366.
36 Smuts to his wife, 26 September 1916 in Hancock and Van der Poel (eds.), *Selections*, vol. III, p.407.
37 DODA: UWH, box 25, Botha quoted by J. Halsted, 'The South African Red Cross in War, 1939-45', p.13.
38 Botha to Smuts, 13 April 1916, and 6 August 1916 in Hancock and Van der Poel (eds.), *Selections*, vol. III, pp.358, 391.
39 NARSSA: Smuts Papers, vol. 202, Smuts to Mrs Hodgson, 29 March 1917.

The losses in manpower had been high. Following complaints – including a report written in October 1916 by Colonel H.J. Kirkpatrick, of the 9th South African Infantry Regiment – the War Office instituted an official enquiry into the medical services rendered in East Africa since the start of the campaign. The enquiry, led by Major General W.W. Pike, the Surgeon General of the British Army Medical Service, was disquieting. It found that 'from the beginning' medical services rendered in East Africa had been 'obviously unsatisfactory.' The conditions in East Africa, as the report acknowledged, were entirely different to those prevailing in other war theatres and required specific 'scientific and sanitary organisation ... to investigate and fight against preventable disease.' The campaign needed an army of bacteriologists, protozoologists, and other specialists, and adequate supplies of microscopes, malarial prophylaxis, and other equipment, and the chlorination of water, and other interventions, but the omission of even basic safeguards had had serious consequences to force strength. They found that this had been partly due to the want of funds and partly to the neglect of the senior and general officers in charge, including the DA & QMG in East Africa, Major General Ewart, and his staff officers. As the Quartermaster General in the UK noted: 'The extent of the theatre of operations, and of the lines of communication called for specially strong staffing, and great vigilance and activity in inspection, especially having regard to the climatic conditions.'[40] Significantly for Smuts, who is often blamed, and solely so, for the neglect of the health of his men, most of those censured in the report were imperial officers: especially doctors in the RAMC or the Indian Medical Service.

Of all maladies, venereal disease carried a social stigma and, where questions of race and sex intersected, it raised a potential political issue for the government to manage. For this reason, venereal diseases possibly vexed Botha and Smuts in ways other diseases did not. A small number of venereal cases had occurred in German South West Africa, but with the later deployments to Egypt, France and East Africa these intersecting questions – particularly complicated in the South Africa of the time – re-emerged and a raft of measures were instituted; men inflicted with the disease were hospitalised and treated until the active symptoms disappeared – and their pay stopped until their mandatory discharge from service.[41] The question took a new, interesting turn, when the Springboks left for Egypt. Corporal E. Doitsh, of the 1st South African Infantry, who published his narrative in 1917, proclaimed that Alexandria was a 'most immoral town', putting 'the well-known quarters of some of the Continental cities ... out into the shade'.[42] Such disclosures horrified the members of Johannesburg's Ladies Reform Club and the government responded with additional measures like those taken by Britain and the other Dominions: an

40 TNA WO 141/31: Report on Medical Arrangements East Africa, QMG to AG, 29 April 1918.
41 Union of South Africa. *Debates of the Senate*, 12 April 1915, col 210.
42 Doitsh, *The First Springbok Prisoner*, p.24.

education programme with lectures in English and Dutch, preventative measures, and strict medical treatment. In September 1916, the Department of Defence produced a pamphlet for distribution to the troops before their return to South Africa. Botha and Smuts had signed the original foreword, which included 'selected and striking passages' from the report of the Royal Commission on Venereal Disease, and 'giving facts and figures which, were they better known and realised, would act as a most powerful deterrent to all except the most depraved.'[43] Stereotypically, the pamphlet petitioned soldiers returning from the front 'not to have anything to do with women of loose character', while Bourne expressed the hope 'that the distribution will be carried out in the full spirit of General Botha's and Lt-General Smuts' appeal to South African soldiers.'[44] Smuts appointed a medical board to investigate the prevalence, control and treatment of venereal disease. They reported in September 1918, shortly before the wider repatriation of troops. He supported their recommendations with two exceptions: the free issue of prophylactic outfits would not be supplied to the men on demand, and the Early Treatment Depots – to be known as 'Blue Light Depots' – would be established but not in the towns.[45] Smuts further instructed medical staffs to avoid as far as possible 'giving publicity outside the Forces to these establishments.'[46] Venereal disease in the military had become a South African political issue.

Manpower and the Racial Politics of Recruitment

These vexatious issues made recruitment for the fresh drafts more difficult. As discussed in chapter 6, recruitment for two expeditionary forces – one for East Africa, the other for overseas, that is France – opened in August 1915. Volunteers came forward in ready numbers, but there was soon concern in Pretoria and London regarding reinforcements. In March 1916, after the ending of the Sanusi campaign, the Army Council suggested that South Africa reopen recruiting for Lukin's Brigade and the auxiliary troops in France up to a monthly intake of 10 percent of establishment. Four months later, just as the Entente offensive astride the Somme started, they repeated their suggestion. However, Botha would not commit himself and, leaving for

43 NARSSA: GG 597, file 9/57/40, Secretary for Defence to Ministers, 3 October 1916.

44 DODA: CSO, box 20, file CSO 22/38 Syphilis and Severe Gonorrhoea, Circular from Assistant Secretary for Defence to Camp Commandants, 6 November 1916.

45 The UDF pamphlet, *Sexual Hygiene*, was adapted from a British Army pamphlet drafted by 'An Experienced Physician'. DODA: DC, box 1193, file 191 Treatment of Venereal Cases, Report of Medical Board on Prevention of Venereal Disease, Defence Headquarters, Pretoria, 11 September 1918, and Acting DMS to ADMS Durban, ADMS Cape Town, SMO Potchefstroom, SMO Kimberley, SMO Roberts Heights, 11 November 1918.

46 DODA: DC, box 1193, file 191 Treatment of Venereal Cases, Bourne to DMS, 18 October 1918.

East Africa, postponed his answer until he had consulted Smuts.[47] Neither man would commit themselves until they conferenced on the campaign in Tanganyika. Botha would be away for three weeks, and at the beginning of August when the 'wastage' from Delville Wood had already nearly exhausted the Brigade's trained reserve, Bonar Law enquired again.[48] Following Botha's return, two recruiting campaigns started: one for France, the other for East Africa. However, Botha and Smuts had decided that, should the simultaneous recruiting drives reduce the numbers Smuts required for Tanganyika, they would close recruiting for France.

Recruiting reopened at the start of August. As Botha and Smuts had feared, for the moment, it was impossible to recruit more than Smuts's requirement for East Africa. Following his return, Botha made a special appeal for volunteers and hoped to meet the demand for Smuts's divisions as well as Lukin's brigade.[49] Absurdly optimistic, Botha even suggested that South Africa complete a division with reserves for France. He was grounded by Buxton's realism. A six-month estimate – and the war was unlikely to be over that soon – required 28,500 men in addition to the Brigade already in France. Botha had hoped for a larger, more visibly South African presence. Buxton suggested that instead they ask the War Office to brigade the South African units on the Western Front with the 1st Brigade 'so that all South Africans [would] be in the same Division.'[50] However, by mid-August 1916, recruiting for the two expeditionary forces reached crisis proportions. Only about 10 volunteers came forward on an average day and the casualties at Delville Wood had consumed the strong reserve maintained in Great Britain. By the end of September, despite Botha's 17 August appeal, only 2,084 recruits came forward of which just 146 were for the Brigade in France.

In some ways, the result, though disappointing, was unsurprising. Political divisions meant possibly 50 percent of possible recruits would never volunteer and large numbers of the remaining 50 percent were already serving abroad. Moreover, a considerable proportion of the men serving in East Africa and those who had volunteered since Botha's appeal, would have volunteered for France but 'felt that the first call on them was for the arduous campaign close to their gates.'[51] The better rate of pay for East Africa had no doubt played a role too.

Another recruiting campaign was conducted 'with greatest vigour' and, combined with a personal appeal by Botha, brought some results: 741 Europeans and 849 for the Cape Corps within two weeks. Civil servants were 'combed out' of government

47 NARSSA: GG 671, file 9/93/68 Recruiting, Bonar Law to Buxton, 4 July 1916.
48 NARSSA: GG 671, file 9/93/68, Recruiting, Bonar Law to Buxton, 4 August 1916.
49 NARSSA: GG 671, file 9/93/68, Recruiting, Bourne to Horsfall, 5 August 1916.
50 NARSSA: GG 671, file 9/93/68, Recruiting, Buxton to Botha, 8 August 1916. Absurdly, Smuts would make the offer of a further South African division during the Second World War and at a time when a manpower crisis had made the offer impossible. See, Van der Waag, 'South African Manpower and the Second World War'.
51 NARSSA: GG 671, file 9/93/68 Recruiting, Ministers' Minute 1426, 30 September 1916.

departments. As Bourne argued, the 'public service can well be reduced and curtailed even if the public are inconvenienced.'[52] The main difficulty was sustaining the reinforcements for the two warfronts – East and Central Africa, and the Western Front. Recruiting for the infantry brigade in France reopened on 1 September as for five months, all recruits had been destined for Smuts in East Africa. However, in the face of heavy casualties, Smuts had insisted that South Africa was 'honour bound to make every effort to prevent our infantry brigade in France becoming depleted and therefore useless for want of adequate reserves to replace casualties and wastage.'[53] Notwithstanding, while recruiting remained steady, most of the men coming forward volunteered for East Africa; of the 1,832 men who enlisted between 17 August and 10 September, only 12 volunteered to serve with the brigade in France. This, as Bourne noted, was 'terribly disappointing' and related to the pay question: 'human nature being what it is, it would be surprising perhaps if South Africans did not choose the one of two equal paths of duty which was the most lucrative.'[54] Botha and Burton met with the Johannesburg Recruiting Committee in October but many recruiting committees, possibly hoping to secure the excess pay for the overseas contingents, fostered the idea that the men could not be expected to serve in France unless they received equal pay.[55] The question of manpower remained a headache for Botha and Smuts.

By the start of September 1916, 43,223 South Africans were serving in uniform in one of the expeditionary force contingents; approximately a quarter were in France, the remainder in East and Central Africa. In addition, while the *South Africa Defence Act* proscribed the recruitment of Black and Coloured men into the UDF – except in times of emergency when People of Colour through special proclamation by the governor general could be enlisted for mostly non-combatant tasks – there were 9,250 Black men and 1,030 Coloured men with the labour battalions. The Act provided for military service by citizens of European descent, entrenched a racially differentiated military service, and seriously constrained the pool of people on whom the government might otherwise have had a call. Soon the realities of the war highlighted the folly of this discrimination. Pressure to recruit People of Colour would come from two sources: the Imperial War Cabinet to alleviate the manpower shortages and supply problems on the Western Front, and the military necessity for increased numbers of combatant troops. This would lead to the formation of the South African Native Labour Contingent (SANLC) and two Cape Corps battalions.

The SANLC was formed in September 1916 to satisfy London's demand for labour, but its creation was immediately controversial and highly politicised. Botha agreed to its formation but only under specific conditions; they would serve in non-combatant

52 NARSSA: GG 597, file 9/57/40, Secretary for Defence to Ministers, 14 August 1916.
53 NARSSA: GG 597, file 9/57/40, Secretary for Defence to Ministers, 4 September 1916.
54 NARSSA: GG 597, file 9/57/40, Secretary for Defence to Ministers, 11 September 1916.
55 NARSSA: GG 597, file 9/57/40, Secretary for Defence to Ministers, 16 October 1916.

roles under the supervision of South African officers, many of them officials of the Department of Native Affairs, and they would be housed in separate compounds. Moreover, the SANLC was formed under the Department of Native Affairs, and not Defence, placing the men administratively outside of the Union Defence Force. However, the SANLC formed part of the Imperial forces and this had several implications. Firstly, Botha did not need parliamentary approval in South Africa – the men of the SANLC would be a cost to the British government – and so he dodged the immediate political debate.[56] Second, as part of the Imperial forces, the SANLC wore military-style uniforms, received military-style rations, and received the standard medical care; all drafts were vaccinated and inoculated against enteric fever and pneumonia before sailing. This, with an Army Council decision to re-designate the units of the South African Native Labour Corps as South African Native Labour Companies, gave the men their identity as soldiers denied them in their own country.[57]

Notwithstanding, by the war's end, 82,769 Black South African men joined the contingent and served in a variety of supporting and auxiliary roles in East Africa and France and made a significant contribution to the war effort.[58] The Department of Native Affairs used its network of officials for recruiting. The men were engaged for one year, which could be extended by mutual agreement, and were paid £3 per month, two thirds of which was deferred until discharge, although allotments were made to dependents. The chaplains, NCOs, interpreters, and hospital orderlies received more. But most of the men were assigned to menial roles in the supporting and auxiliary services; drivers and labourers, dock workers and storemen, stretcher bearers and cooks' assistants. In all, 292 officers, 1,204 White warrant and non-commissioned officers, and 25,090 Black men served in the SANLC in France, of whom 27 were killed in action or died as the result of active service and more than 600 tragically drowned in the English Channel when the Royal Mail Steam Packet *Darro* collided with the transport *Mendi* on 21 February 1917.[59] The death rate while in France from diseases alone was 5.3 per 1,000 in February and 8.7 in March.[60] Colonel P.G. Stock, the South African DMS on the Lines of Communication in France, submitted a report on the health of the men of the SANLC up to 31 January 1917. Complete returns were not available, but the figures, though approximate, allow the drawing of deductions. In addition to cases requiring hospital admission, the men suffered from trench foot, which Stock believed to be the primary cause of 'inefficiency'.

56 Gleeson, *The Unknown Force*, p.25.
57 TNA DO 119/924: Overseas Native Labour Contingent Medical Report, Long to Buxton, 3 March 1917.
58 TNA WO 106/5827: South African war effort 1939-1946. Peacetime organisation of the Union Defence Force.
59 Anon., *Official History*, pp.218, 230; TNA: DO 119/924: Overseas Native Labour Contingent Medical Report, DAAG France to Secretary, War Office, 31 March 1917.
60 TNA DO 119/924: Overseas Native Labour Contingent Medical Report, Lieutenant Colonel P.G. Stock to the DMS LoC, 17 February 1917 and 23 March 1917.

Prophylactic measures were taken to keep feet clean and dry, but ill-fitting boots – the ordinary ammunition boot was issued – were arguably an aggravating cause.[61] Trench foot accounted for the highest incidence of hospital admissions, followed by cases of frostbite, bronchitis, pneumonia, silicosis, and other respiratory conditions.[62] Pneumonia, bronchitis, and tuberculosis were the main causes of death during that first winter. One of the chaplains, W.H. Hallowes, mentioned in *The Church Chronicle* that on Sundays 'The extreme cold rather limited his efforts [to hold services], as the men were reluctant to leave their blankets and warm fires.' The winter of 1916–17 was particularly severe. As a group the SANLC stood up to it well. The general health was better than expected. Although chilblains, trench foot and frostbite were common. There were, according to Hallowes, 11 cases requiring amputation of 'portion of their lower limbs … I don't think that anyone could visit our hospitals and see those terribly mutilated feet and frostbitten hands without being deeply moved.'[63]

There were growing problems. Many stemming from the inequalities in South African society. African men – housed in compounds reminiscent of the South African mines and treated as non-combatants in a foreign warzone – felt unwanted and far from home. France was considerably colder, but the confiscation of home comforts, including dagga (cannabis) smuggled in their kits, increased the alienation.[64] Limits on promotion to nothing more than lance corporal also influenced recruitment. The men of the first contingent had received appointments as sergeants and corporals, especially those who enjoyed traditional status as chiefs or headmen. For many African men, committing themselves to a foreign venture, the will of their traditional leaders weighed as heavily as 'pure patriotism and mercenary impulse.'[65] The *Mendi* disaster and the loss of more than 600 men of the Seventh Contingent, had a profound effect. Botha acknowledged their tragic loss in Parliament. By the second quarter of 1917, the supply of new recruits for the SANLC was falling off dramatically. There were concerns too not to attest men showing signs of tubercular infection – something which had affected the casualty rate in France.[66]

In response, the Botha government undertook to take 'more vigorous measures of recruiting' through the assistance of officials, missionaries, traders, and of course the

61 TNA DO 119/924: Overseas Native Labour Contingent Medical Report, Lieutenant Colonel P.G. Stock to the DMS LoC, 17 February 1917.
62 TNA DO 119/924: Overseas Native Labour Contingent Medical Report, Lieutenant Colonel P.G. Stock to the DMS LoC, 23 March 1917.
63 Hallowes cited in Norman Clothier, *Black Valour: The South African Native Labour Contingent, 1916-1918, and the sinking of the Mendi* (Pietermaritzburg: University of Natal Press, 1987), p.113.
64 TNA DO 119/924: Overseas Native Labour Contingent Medical Report, D Company, Walter Long to Buxton, 17 April 1917.
65 TNA DO 119/924: Overseas Native Labour Contingent Medical Report, Buxton to Long, 25 May 1917.
66 TNA DO 119/924: Overseas Native Labour Contingent Medical Report, Long to Buxton, 17 May 1917.

traditional leaders.[67] However, holistically, most recruits came from one district – the Zoutpansberg – and for much of the Transvaal, the Cape and Transkei there were very few volunteers, 'and Zululand has been an absolute frost.' Buxton acknowledged that there may have been reason to believe that in parts of these provinces, 'disloyal Nationalists and German agents have got at the natives [*sic.*] in order to persuade them against recruiting, telling them that if they do they will be either put into the firing line or drowned as in the case of the "Mendi". It is difficult to get proof of this, and I doubt if there is any great foundation for it.'[68] Yet, for Buxton, the greatest disappointment lay with the average 'Natal Britisher':

> … a great man to talk of Natal as British to the backbone, abuse Botha and the loyal Dutch in a blackguardedly way in his newspapers as slackers and what not but flaunts the Flag on every occasion and sings 'Rule, Britannia!' But when it comes to helping the Empire in the concrete he pauses if his own interests are involved or affected.[69]

Not only had Natal – of all the provinces, bar the Orange Free State – contributed the fewest volunteers for the expeditionary forces, but, when the recruiters for the SANLC came round, Natal employers shielded their labour force from enlistment. Botha asked Buxton to speak to some of the leading Natal men, but this seemed to have only short effect.

The question of non-racial units in the Union Defence Force – politically tortuous and under the constant gaze of the Nationalists – came to a head in late 1917 as the manpower problem pressed. Reports from France, unofficial but strong, indicated that Coloured men had been sent with the reinforcements for the 1st S.A. Infantry brigade. For the ever-practical Smuts, while he appreciated the 'services rendered by this loyal section of the community [it] would be a pity to give cause for resentment amongst European troops which could be obviated by Non-Europeans being drafted into other units which are open to them.'[70] The Chief of the General Staff took the matter up. The Director of War Recruiting, then Colonel R.H. Price, felt that the procedure laid down in 1913 ought not be abandoned and any decisions regarding what was termed 'doubtful decent' remain with the medical officers. The officials hoped to prevent legal liability for the state relating to the classification of volunteers in terms of the racial legislation of the time. As Price argued: 'The medical officer has an opportunity of seeing the recruit stripped which should facilitate a decision in this matter and should any disputes arise the professional opinion of a medical officer would naturally carry

67 TNA DO 119/924: Overseas Native Labour Contingent Medical Report, Buxton to Long, 25 May 1917.
68 WSHC: 947/602, Viscount Long of Wraxall Papers, Buxton to Long, 5 June 1917.
69 WSHC: 947/602, Viscount Long of Wraxall Papers, Buxton to Long, 5 June 1917.
70 DODA: AG 1914-1921, box 189, file 489, Coloured Men in Overseas Brigade, Smuts London to Defence Pretoria, 6 September 1917.

more weight in a matter of this sort than that of a layman.'[71] Collyer, then the Chief of the General Staff, instructed that the necessary steps be taken to ensure that no more Coloured recruits were enrolled for the European units for overseas, or sent forward to Britain and the High Commissioner was requested to post these men either to the Cape Auxiliary Horse Transport Companies if they were willing, or return them to South Africa for discharge. Collyer also asked for a complete roll of these men, so that he might ascertain where they were recruited and by whom they were passed fit for service in the 1st Infantry Brigade.[72]

Racial profiling and the identification of men of 'doubtful colour' was as difficult as it was disagreeable. Recognising its distastefulness, Smuts had expressed himself on the matter in February 1916, but he was seemingly careful not to commit himself on paper and in the meantime the Director for Medical Services reported that, due to the shortage of medical officers, his staff was unable – and to their credit, perhaps unwilling – to comply with the procedure Price had requested.[73] But their situation remained unchanged. In October, a further 17 Coloured men arrived at Woking and reported to the second reserve battalion.[74] Moreover, Colonel R.C. Grant – of Sandfontein fame, and now part of the recruiting organisation – asked whether the rules regarding the enlistment of men should also be applied to South African units not destined for Europe. A 'special case' had occurred. A man called Hulley had joined the King's African Rifles as a platoon sergeant. He was 'undoubtedly Coloured' and Grant, declaring that he would reject him for the overseas contingent, noted that Hulley had already rendered good service in several units: in Hartigan's Horse from January 1915 to May 1915; in the SAMR from May 1915 to May 1916; and as corporal in the 9th SA Horse from May 1916 to February 1917. As Grant argued, he could 'hardly see

71 DODA: AG 1914-1921, box 189, file 489, Coloured Men in Overseas Brigade, Director of War Recruiting to Chief of General Staff, 25 September 1917.

72 DODA: AG 1914-1921, box 189, file 489, Coloured Men in Overseas Brigade, Chief of General Staff to Director of War Recruiting, Director of Medical Services, and the Officer in Charge of Records, 27 October 1917.

73 The Director for Medical Services refers to Smuts's guideline; however, no document is on file, DODA: AG 1914-1921, box 189, file 489 Coloured Men in Overseas Brigade, DMS to CGS, 28 September 1917. Collyer confirmed that the practice laid down for the ACF in the matter of Coloured persons was as stated in Confidential Circular 21/2616 of 18/2/1913. The ruling from the Minister, conveyed in the Assistant Secretary's letter CSO 1346 of 25/2/1916, confirmed that the final responsibility for the rejection of a recruit on account of colour rested with the Attesting Officer. Under the circumstances, Collyer did not think any good purpose would be served by the expression of further opinion on his part and requested the Directors of Medical Services and War Recruiting to arrange closer cooperation between the Medical Officers and Attesting Officers 'should any doubt as to colour arise in the cases of candidates for enlistment.' See, AG 1914-1921, box 189, file 489 Coloured Men in Overseas Brigade, Chief of General Staff to Directors War Recruiting and Medical Services, 3 October 1917.

74 Oppositely London to Defence, 24 October 1917.

how he can now be rejected'.[75] Sadly, Collyer decided that Hulley – once identified as 'undoubtedly Coloured' – had to be discharged.[76] Botha and Smuts knew all too well that this was an insult to the Coloured community. And, when Colonel H.W.M. Bamford, commander of the Second Reserve Battalion, interviewed the 20-plus men in France all but two stated that they would rather return to South Africa than be transferred to Cape Auxiliary Horse Transport companies. As the authorities recognised, it would be a grave mistake to send the aggrieved men back to South Africa as they would adversely affect recruiting. Smuts, then in London, intervened as, in his view, the feeling of the Coloured community in South Africa would be wounded after their exemplary behaviour throughout war, and advised that the men be allowed to complete their training and then take their place in France on the understanding that they be utilised as far as possible in the South African Brigade.[77] Botha agreed, and the defence officials concurred. This was contrary to policy, although the 1912 Defence Act provided for special enlistment during emergencies. A brave political decision, it was absolutely the correct one although not unmixed with self-interest. The Nationalists and government backbenchers, and some Unionists, would attack Botha and Smuts on the matter of raising and deploying Black and Coloured South African troops, particularly in Europe.[78] But, that this news did not break in the press, is yet further evidence of the remarkable hold Botha and Smuts had on the flow of information.

Conclusion

Botha and Smuts had traded roles at the start of 1916 when Smuts left for East Africa. Botha took on the position of minister of defence, while Smuts became the field commander. The two men, despite the 5,000 kilometres that now separated them, maintained their close working relationship and, in terms of their planning, their focus was on South Africa's constitutional status and position on the world stage. The older man remained loyal to a fault, always considering Smuts's requirements in East Africa and giving them primacy. But, by September 1916, the offensive on the Somme had clearly petered out and the realisation had dawned too that the campaign in Tanganyika, where the progress was slow and the complaints many, would not be

75 DODA: AG 1914-1921, box 189, file 489, Coloured Men in Overseas Brigade, Colonel R.C. Grant to Director of War Recruiting, 27 October 1917.
76 DODA: AG 1914-1921, box 189, file 489, Coloured Men in Overseas Brigade, Chief of General Staff to Director of War Recruiting, 2 November 1917.
77 DODA: AG 1914-1921, box 189, file 489, Coloured Men in Overseas Brigade, High Commissioner London to Botha Pretoria, 26 November 1917.
78 J.X. Merriman to Lord Buxton, 5 December 1916 in P. Lewsen (ed.), *Selections from the Correspondence of J.X. Merriman 1905-1924* (Cape Town: Van Riebeeck Society, 1969), pp.285–86.

soon over. This stalling on the military fronts, and the inquiries into some of their vexatious issues – coinciding as they did with a parliamentary debate on the Rebellion Commission and the allegedly poor way in which the enquiry had been handled – did much to undermine Botha's position in South Africa.[79] The disappointing recruitment drives were symptomatic of this.

New realities set in for the public and especially for the troops on the battle fronts. Assumptions regarding a limited war in Africa, which remained largely valid well into 1915, now evaporated and a new phase, marked by the widening of the war in Africa as the realities of a total war were impressed upon the belligerents in Europe, opened. The men sent abroad seemed to be paying a tremendous price, exposed either to the malarial jungles and rigours of East Africa or the trenches and brutalisation of industrial warfare in France. With each passing war year, soldiers increasingly questioned the price exacted by their service. They did so in all countries, on both sides, and South Africa was no different. Cyril Newton-Thompson, a young, South African subaltern with a British regiment, was not alone in interrogating the popular catchword in 1916 of 'equality of sacrifice'. There could never be equality and certainly not in a country like South Africa where large portions of the population either refused or were denied the opportunity of military service. Moreover, while life in South Africa seemed to go on 'as smug and comfortable almost as if there was no war',[80] things were changing here too although many questioned the direction of that change. After the first week of fighting at the start of what became the Battle of the Somme, Newton-Thompson noted on 7 July 1916, 'The soldiers will have gone to their last long rest reckoning little of why it all was, except that they thought our cause the better, and it will be left to the historian and especially the student of military history to determine whether in the great offensive of June – July – August 1916 the game was worth the candle.'[81]

79 BL: Add MS 87052, Buxton Papers, 1914-1918, Buxton to Law, 27 November 1916.
80 WSRO: Petworth House Archives, Maud Wyndham to Lady Leconfield, 2 and 7 October 1916.
81 UCT: Joyce Newton-Thompson Collection, B1.43, BC643, Cyril Newton-Thompson to Joyce Nettlefold, 7 July 1916.

9

High Politics, 1917–1918

The only unwounded statesman [Smuts] of outstanding ability in the Empire.

Winston Churchill[1]

The General [Botha] is a cross between a very self-willed naughty child and a fowl of the air.

Buxton[2]

The year 1916 had been a dark and bleak. Amidst sweeping changes in the political and military leadership of Britain, Asquith had finally fallen from power and Kitchener was dead. Lloyd George, the interim War Secretary, was now prime minister. Walter Long was his Secretary of State for the Colonies and Lord Derby was at the War Office. Churchill still harboured the damage of the Dardanelles debacle; he would return to the cabinet as the Minister of Munitions in July 1917. Few military men were untainted with defeat, or perhaps rather the failure to find success. Blamed for the costly failures of the war, military commanders on all sides were criticised for the callous waste of human life in a succession of futile offensives while popular notions of 'chateaux generals' gained steady currency. Maud Wyndham, wife of South Africa's shadow defence minister, vocalised these notions in a letter to her mother-in-law in early December 1916. She blamed the Allied generals for these military 'muddles' and accused many of them of incompetence and poor mental agility. But, writing at the time of Asquith's fall, she was even more critical of the politicians whom she accused of not supporting the military commanders with a workable and realistic grand strategy to win the war. 'Providence', she lamented, 'has not given us a Chatham and a Marlborough to guide us through this period.' Yet, while it was 'no use girding against the poor minnows we have got,' Mrs Wyndham was convinced, as many may have

1 Churchill quoted in Lord Riddell, *Lord Riddell's War Diary, 1914-1918* (London: Ivor Nicholson & Watson, 1933), p.251.

2 BL: Add MS 87093, Buxton Papers, 1908-1929, Buxton's notes on Botha, not dated.

felt, that there were 'things even a minnow might avoid.'[3] An honourable death in the war was in days past enough – or perhaps the only way – to safeguard reputation.

In South Africa, the political and military leadership was wrapped up firmly in the personae of Botha and Smuts, and both were still very much alive. True to their word, they had entered the war on Britain's side. They had suppressed a rebellion by their own people. And between them, they had given the Allies the first of their campaign victories with the conquest of German South West Africa and then the corralling of Lettow-Vorbeck in disease-ridden southern Tanganyika, while adding to the Entente strength on two other fronts – in France and Palestine. Praised in Britain for their stance, both men were at times – for the British sector in South Africa as well as the Afrikaner right – objects respectively for amusement or scorn. Walter Long, while acknowledging that there were 'no great difficulties' confronting them in South Africa in January 1917, recognised several 'causes for anxiety'. Botha, he feared, would have a difficult time for Hertzog's Nationalists had gained substantially in numbers. As Long noted, they became a 'serious thorn in Botha's side'.[4] This chapter examines their work at this difficult juncture in time, covering Smuts's arrival, work in London at the Imperial Conference, and then in the War Cabinet, as well as Botha's growing troubles at home.

Smuts Arrives in London

Richard Hannay, the literary figure in Buchan's *Greenmantle*, reached London at about the same time Smuts did. 'One felt the war', Hannay narrates, 'more in its streets than in the field, or rather one felt the confusion of war without feeling the purpose.'[5] Public criticism was still muted, but politicians, including Lloyd George, Walter Long, and Edward Carson, had been perturbed for some time about the war's direction and the laissez-faire approach of Asquith's large, unwieldy, cabinet. With powerful press support, Lloyd George, backed by Long and other cabinet colleagues, approached Asquith and demanded 'the appointment of a Committee of three without portfolios to "run the war" and do nothing else.' Real constitutional reconstruction was urgent and it was vital, they argued, that 'the men who are to wield great powers should be vigorous both in mind and body, ready and able to press their policy regardless of any consequences other than those which will contribute to final and complete victory.'[6]

3 WSRO: Petworth House Archives, Maud Wyndham to Lady Leconfield, 8 December 1915. Mrs Wyndham, an amateur family historian, was descended from the very core of those families that had governed Britain during the eighteenth and nineteenth centuries; her ancestors, as she well knew included both Chatham and Marlborough.

4 WSHC: 947/636, Viscount Long of Wraxall Papers, Long to Lloyd George, 3 January 1917.

5 John Buchan, *Greenmantle* (London: Hodder & Stoughton, 1937), p.2.

6 WSHC: 947/636, Viscount Long of Wraxall Papers, Long to Bonar Law, 2 December 1916.

At the war's start, a War Council had developed from the pre-war Committee of Imperial Defence, but this and its successors – the Dardanelles Committee, and the War Committee created in November 1915 – were advisory only; the executive power remained firmly in the Cabinet chaired by Asquith, a man noted for his intellect but also his slowness in decision-making. The Easter Rising and 'an ill-conceived spell of repression' in Ireland, and the perceived 'military muddles' on the war fronts, added to Asquith's political woes. On 7 December 1916, amidst the demand for more centralised control of the war by a smaller, empowered and directed war cabinet that would meet daily, Lloyd George replaced the long-embattled Asquith as prime minister.[7]

Shortly after, Smuts arrived in London to the adulation of the British public. As Crafford notes, he had a 'propaganda value.'[8] His successes in East Africa had been spectacular and they came at a time when Entente successes were few. Lionised as a former enemy now friend, who had brought the Entente its only campaign successes, he received a hero's welcome. According to Walter Long: 'He has done extremely well. All men speak well of him, and I hope that now it is only the question of sweeping up [in East Africa].'[9] Writing years later, Admiral Edward Ratcliffe Garth Evans, noted, 'What a lot of distinguished men we carried on board the Broke and my other destroyers! Kings, potentates and princes, prime ministers of Britain and the Dominions, several times the whole War Cabinet; and it was during my "taxi-cab" time with Admiral Bacon that I first met General Smuts.'[10]

Lloyd George had called a conference of Dominion leaders in London to discuss the growing role for the Dominions in the expanding war effort. In the South African representative, he finally found a man with energy and drive equal to his own. Two conferences would meet simultaneously: an Imperial War Conference convened on the pre-war pattern of imperial conferences, and the newly created Imperial War Cabinet established to coordinate war policy.[11] Smuts was soon associated with both.

Smuts arrived in London on 12 March. As he told Wolstenholme, he had left his 'family quite well though far from happy at [his] constant absences.'[12] But this was important work, and his first few days were exceptionally busy. Amidst the War Office work, there were requests for personal interviews, the offer of an honorary doctorate from Trinity College, Dublin, and endless invitations to lunch or to dinner or for a visit in the country. These came from the Selbornes, the Harcourts, Lady Gladstone, the Maitlands, the Royal Colonial Institute, with senior imperial officers who had served in South Africa against Smuts, or in East Africa with him. A Miss

7 Arthur Marwick, *The Deluge; British Society and the First World War* (Boston and Toronto: Little, Brown and Company, 1965), pp.40, 179–183.
8 Crafford, *Jan Smuts*, p.134.
9 WSHC: 947/636, Viscount Long of Wraxall Papers, Long to Drummond Chaplin 16 January 1917.
10 Admiral Lord Mountevans, *Adventurous Life* (London: Hutchinson, 1946), p.124.
11 Lentin *Jan Smuts*, p.34.
12 NARSSA: Smuts Papers, vol. 202, Smuts to Wolstenholme, 13 March 1917.

Dorothy Craik asked for a photograph of him. Lady Phillips asked Smuts to sit for 'a portrait sketch made at the expense of a few friends.'[13] Botha pressed him to make time for 'old friends of better days.'[14] Smuts longed to spend time in Cambridge as well, but each day it seemed as if 'something else of an urgent character turned up.' As he told Wolstenholme: 'I find this world much distracted and even mystifying and am now groping about to get my bearings.'[15] Most of these invitations Smuts turned away. He was then immersed in work and did not anticipate being in Britain for long. There was little time and he longed to return to South Africa – where his family, Botha, and domestic politics called for him.[16]

New work returned Smuts to the company of old friends and a few old enemies. At Cambridge, where he received an honorary LLD, he was hailed as 'like the younger Scipio, our Second Africanus.'[17] Emily Hobhouse, staunch reformer and monitor of the British concentration camps in South Africa, had told Smuts years before that his name would be read in large print in the British newspapers. This had now come to pass, but Hobhouse was much less sanguine about Smuts sitting in the same councils as Alfred Milner, a man much despised in South Africa and in some quarters in Britain, for his polices in South Africa when he had been high commissioner.[18] But, significantly, Milner was one of the first to write to Smuts after his arrival in London, praising the former Boer general for his 'great achievements, political and military ... and especially ... the fine work lately accomplished in East Africa' and with it invited Smuts informally to the inner counsels of cabinet business.[19]

The Imperial War Conference met from 23 March and at intervals over the succeeding weeks. The Imperial War Cabinet had first to decide upon and approve resolutions moved at the Imperial War Conference.[20] From it, the British people – in the United Kingdom and the Dominions – expected definite progress regarding closer union and imperial preference. The topics they would discuss ranged from demobilisation and the standardisation of military stores and equipment, and of training for ordnance personnel, to naval defence, trade commissions, and patents. On 4 April, the Canadian prime minister, Sir Robert Borden, tabled far-reaching resolutions on food supply, the control of natural resources within the Empire, and their economic utilisation. Staunch support came from the other Dominion representatives, but Smuts faced peculiar difficulties. As Long noted,

13 NARSSA: Smuts Papers, vol. 202, Smuts to Lady Phillips, 26 March 1917.
14 NARSSA: Smuts Papers, vol. 202, Smuts to Lord Harcourt, 17 March 1917.
15 NARSSA: Smuts Papers, vol. 202, Smuts to Wolstenholme, 15 March 1917.
16 NARSSA: Smuts Papers, vol. 202, Smuts to Lady Maitland, 22 March 1917.
17 As quoted by Crafford, *Jan Smuts*, p.136.
18 Emily Hobhouse to Smuts, 7 March 1917 in Hancock and Van der Poel, *Selections*, vol. III, p.414.
19 Milner to Smuts, 12 March 1917 in Hancock and Van der Poel, *Selections*, vol. III, p.414.
20 WSHC: 947/645, Viscount Long of Wraxall Papers, Long to Lloyd George, 4 April 1917.

> Smuts is of course in a difficult position, he would face the music I feel confident if he had only himself to consider, but Botha and his Government are very much afraid of both questions and Buxton does not help so Smuts is all for putting off 'till after the war.' To meet his views and carry him along Borden toned down his Resolution – Borden talked this all over with me very fully and confidentially.[21]

Long sent his press release on the proceedings of the conference to Smuts for his endorsement prior to their publication. Long included all resolutions considered suitable for publication but omitted three: those on the control of wool production in the Empire to safeguard Imperial resources and meet the industrial needs of the Empire and the Allies, on the control of the ownership and production of metals and ores, and on making the Empire self-sufficient in meat production and supply. He did not think Smuts would object as Long wrote it in general terms, but – in view of Smuts's remarks about 'dumping' – thought it right to mention this to him first.[22] Notwithstanding such stratagems, the Nationalists in South Africa alleged in Parliament and the press 'that Smuts in England was "selling them".'[23] Moreover, as discussed later in this chapter, the so-called 'Wool Crisis', caused by the sale of the wool clip to Britain, troubled South African domestic politics for the remainder of the war. Botha bore the brunt in South Africa and as Sir Drummond Chaplin, the Administrator of Southern Rhodesia, noted to Long: Botha was 'getting weaker rather than stronger.'[24]

But Smuts, his able lieutenant, would have to remain in London, for the moment at least, for there were meetings of the Imperial War Cabinet as well as a range of large questions then drawing attention. One was the future of the German territories in Africa. Botha and certainly Smuts had dreamed of an expanding Union of South Africa that would grow organically, much as the United States had done, and embracing perhaps the territories stretching north to the equator. South Africa's war had been fought, in part, with territorial aggrandisement in mind. German South West Africa was under South African occupation and German East Africa had almost entirely fallen to troops commanded by Smuts and Lieutenant General Sir Jaap van Deventer, his successor in Tanganyika. These military successes had to be converted into political outcomes, and Smuts – while South African agents conducted rather indelicate operations in Mozambique – had to be in London to press South Africa's interests.[25] Smuts had the qualified support of some politicians in Britain and Southern Africa who saw the importance of establishing British supremacy in subcon-

21 WSHC: 947/645, Viscount Long of Wraxall Papers, Long to Lloyd George, 10 April 1917.
22 WSHC: 947/645, Viscount Long of Wraxall Papers, Long to Smuts, 30 April 1917.
23 WSHC: 947/602, Viscount Long of Wraxall Papers, Note by Buxton, 26 June 1917.
24 WSHC: 947/540, Viscount Long of Wraxall Papers, Drummond Chaplin to Long, 13 March 1917.
25 DODA: DC, Box 356, DC40057 Intelligence Section, Secret report from Major Leipoldt to the Adjutant General, dd 22 December 1917.

tinental Africa in terms of prestige and the maintenance of power. This involved three broad principles articulated in 1916 and 1917: the exclusion from Southern Africa of any possible future enemy power; the building of a British society north of the Limpopo River as a possible counterpoise to the Dutch-speaking population of South Africa; and the creation of a contiguous strip of 'British' territory stretching from Cape Town to Cairo. The first implied the removal of Germany from Africa. The second, an enlarged Rhodesia – something that appealed to Chaplin. And the third, acquisition by Britain of territory around the Great Lakes joining Northern Rhodesia to Kenya and possibly affecting an exchange of territory with Portugal. London, however, guarding her relationship with Lisbon, and wary of South Africa and Rhodesia's sub-imperial aims, would license no precipitate moves. Chaplin envisioned a grandiose scheme:

> It would be a splendid thing if a deal could be arranged with the Portuguese by which they would retire north of the Zambezi and east of the Shire. Then Lourenço Marques and the area south of the Sabi would go to the Union (as well as S. West Africa) and Beira and the rest of the Portuguese territory south of the Zambezi and east of the Shire would go to Rhodesia. The Portuguese might receive in return the greater part of 'German East Africa', including the German railways. In some ways I think this would be facilitated by the fact that all or practically all the Portuguese territory in question is controlled by the Mozambique, Nyasa and Zambesia Chartered Companies, which might be amenable to some cash consideration. The control of Beira would enormously help the development of Rhodesia. No doubt, however, a scheme of this kind would not be too easy to arrange.[26]

Everything depended on an Entente victory, and the completeness of that victory, and at the same time reassuring Lisbon – a longstanding friend, already articulating her refusal to 'give up any territory' – of her place in Africa.[27] Lisbon, in official communication with Whitehall, made it clear that she resented 'any suggestion that she is not able to make the best use of the territory she now possesses.'[28]

The role played by the Dominions and their status within the British Empire was a second matter of concern. On 2 May 1917, Lloyd George spoke about 'the great experiment of setting up a real Imperial War Cabinet', including as it did Dominion representatives, and of the importance of repeating this experiment and incorporating it into 'the machinery of the British Empire.' Such a body would, after the war, discuss

26 WSHC: 947/540, Viscount Long of Wraxall Papers, Drummond Chaplin to Long, 13 February 1917.

27 WSHC: 947/540, Viscount Long of Wraxall Papers, Long to Drummond Chaplin 14 April 1917.

28 WSHC: 947/540, Viscount Long of Wraxall Papers, Long to Drummond Chaplin 14 April 1917.

matters of common concern, including foreign policy and imperial defence. Lloyd George thought it 'inconceivable that in the future the Dominions should be neither fully informed nor consulted on questions which might lead to war.'[29] Sir Robert Borden, W.F. Massey, and Sir E.P. Morris, the prime ministers of Canada, New Zealand, and Newfoundland, respectively, embraced the idea, although Smuts and the representatives from India – the Maharaja of Bikaner and Sir S. Sinha – were much less sanguine. The Indian representatives called for 'a larger voice' for the people of India as opposed to the Government of India, while Smuts, taking the road of caution, suggested that they all first return to their '*own* countries, where they were dealing with their *own* problems and developing on their *own* lines.'[30] Smuts needed time to confer with Botha and consider more fully the effect the proposal – edging as it did towards imperial federation – might have on the domestic politics of South Africa. Members of Milner's Kindergarten and the later Round Table Movement propagated the notion of imperial federation, which was unpopular in South Africa and rejected by Dutch-speaking Nationalists. Later that month, in a speech to the joint houses of parliament at Westminster, Smuts introduced the idea of 'the British Commonwealth of Nations', a concept – pushed along by Hertzog when he came to power in 1924 – that led steadily to full independence though the Statute of Westminster in 1931.[31]

Sent by Lloyd George to meet the French president, fortify the Belgian king, and examine the military situation, Smuts visited the Western Front in early April 1917.[32] He took Captain F. Guest, who had been his staff captain in East Africa, with him. Lukin had initially asked him to come. The brigade's commander was concerned that recruiting was slowing down, and Smuts sought to reassure him of the government's support: 'we know what our responsibility to the Brigade is and hope that we shall not fail them.'[33] What Smuts saw of the larger picture unsettled him. Britain had entered the war in August 1914 'in a very small way' – sending an expeditionary force to France but relying on the sea power exerted by the Royal Navy. Over the following three years, the British Army in France had grown and had steadily taken over more and more of the frontline. Yet even though the British Empire had become the principal partner in the Entente – in financial, naval, and possibly military terms – British war policy remained subordinate to France. For Smuts, 'three curious respects' reflected this anomalous situation. Firstly, while the armies of the British Empire were defending French soil, Paris had taken the military and diplomatic initiative in

29 TNA CAB 23/40/14: Minutes of a Meeting of the Imperial War Cabinet, 2 May 1917.
30 TNA CAB 23/40/14: Minutes of a Meeting of the Imperial War Cabinet, 2 May 1917. The emphasises are ours.
31 The Union's proposal for full independence which chimed with the Wilsonian principle of self-determination was contrasted by its policy towards South West Africa, that remained a colony in everything but name. Namibia would be a province of South Africa until the late twentieth century, when it finally achieved independence.
32 Crafford, *Jan Smuts*, p.138.
33 NARSSA: Smuts Papers, vol. 202, Smuts to Lukin 20 March 1917.

the Balkans and – if they made no serious miscalculations, something Smuts seemingly doubted – they would enjoy the prestige rightfully due to Britain as 'the most powerful and disinterested member of the Entente.' Secondly, British strategy on the Western Front had to conform to French direction. A direction based on French considerations and suborned by the dangers of political instability in Paris and rivalries among the senior French commanders. But, for Smuts, the third aspect was the most serious of all. By April 1917, the whole of the British Army, excepting small forces conducting campaigns elsewhere, had been 'locked up on the Western Front.' This left no large reserves to meet contingencies, possibly including a German invasion of the Netherlands. The problem was how to create such a reserve. For Smuts, the only answer lay in extricating British forces 'partially from the Western Front' and leaving France to 'their legitimate task of defending French soil as far as their power permits.' This would mean a concentration of the British Army towards the north, and towards the Belgian border, and as far south as the Lille-Roubaix-Turcoing sector; enabling operations to secure the Belgian coast and the elimination of the German submarine bases at Ostend and Zeebrugge. This would place London in a position to consider the creation of a reserve army; and weaken the hold on British war policy by a government in Paris that was 'neither stable nor far-sighted.'[34] It all seemed fanciful – most soldiers believed the Western Front, the only place for a conclusive victory, ought not be weakened in favour of 'sideshows' – but Smuts's *Memorandum on the Military Situation*, delivered to the War Cabinet in April, strengthened Lloyd George's resolve to keep Smuts close at hand.

The Imperial War Cabinet dissolved in June. In the meantime, Smuts was offered two jobs, each of which had its own allure but also drawbacks. Smuts had already become the British prime minister's fix-it man. Lloyd George asked him to take the Palestine Command and Smuts had refused. He sought Botha's advice when the War Cabinet pressed him further. Botha had advised him to take the command if it was to be a position that would influence the war: 'this will depend upon the scale on which the operations there are to be carried on. If on a large scale it would be very difficult to refuse the offer.'[35] In typical Botha fashion he reached out to Isie and kept her abreast of the War Office's offer, while attaching confidential telegrams to his correspondence:

> … enclose herewith for your strictly confidential information a first telegram A, from Jannie, a telegram B from me, and C, from Jannie. These telegrams speak for themselves. I have no time to write and thought it best to keep you informed in this way. Please treat them as entirely private, but I should like to hear your views about them, for I should also want to transmit that to Jannie.[36]

34 TNA CAB 24/11/49: Smuts to Robertson, 13 April 1917.
35 Botha to Smuts, 26 April 1917, Hancock and Van der Poel (eds.), *Selections*, vol. III, p.494.
36 Botha to Isie, 4 May 1917, Hancock and Van der Poel (eds.), *Selections*, vol. III, p.493.

Botha considered all sides of the equation and confirmed that some of Smuts's friends had thought he should turn down the command and return to South Africa – their urging had no doubt influenced Smuts in his refusal. However, when Botha consulted the Cabinet, they had unanimously thought Smuts should accept if the War Cabinet pressed him once more.[37] They did not, but instead asked whether Smuts might assist in dissolving the standoff in Ireland. This too did not happen.[38] Long was no doubt correct in his thinking that Smuts could bring little; the Irish, he told Buxton, 'are very sensitive about what they call outside interference.'[39] Again Smuts read the room. He also awaited something much bigger. Moreover, Smuts was 'in his element in London, the hub of the universe, giving advice to important men, solving problems, and settling difficulties.'[40]

Impressed by Smuts's abilities and energy, Lloyd George convinced him to remain in Britain and join the War Cabinet proper – 'the Prime Minister's inner Cabinet and supreme executive body in the waging of the War.'[41] Churchill, who described Smuts as the 'only unwounded statesman of outstanding ability in the Empire', thought that the South African defence minister should be elected as member of the War Council. By 'unwounded' Churchill had meant 'the only one who is fresh and bright, unwounded mentally and physically.'[42] These traits appealed to Lloyd George too. The Asquiths, wanting to undermine Lloyd George, had tried to dissuade Smuts from joining the War Cabinet but Smuts owed them little. Historically Lloyd George had supported the Boers. This was a debt not easily forgotten. Grigg puts it well: 'even in the world of politics where absolute loyalty is in short supply he [Smuts] is one of the sharpest operators.'[43] But not all thought the same and some political manoeuvring was required.[44] But Lloyd George had found his Hannay in Smuts. If modern armies – large machines with standardised parts – demanded the average, here was an 'exception in human nature', a man not short of a job, unafraid of danger and fighting for ideals higher than narrow nationalism.[45] In Smuts, Lloyd George had found somebody – independent, able, and popular without constituting a political threat to Downing Street – to tackle a range of difficulties. Lloyd George described Smuts at length in his war memoirs; he did so in the following terms:

37 WHSC: 947/602, Viscount Long of Wraxall Papers, Buxton to Long, 11 May 1917.
38 Smuts to Isie, 9 June 1917, Hancock and Van der Poel (eds.), *Selections*, vol. III, p.532.
39 WHSC: 947/602, Viscount Long of Wraxall Papers, Long to Buxton, 31 May 1917.
40 Crafford, *Jan Smuts*, p.138.
41 Lentin *Jan Smuts*, p.36.
42 Churchill quoted in Riddell, *Lord Riddell's War Diary*, p.251.
43 J. Grigg, *Lloyd George: War Leader* (London: Allen Lane, 2002), p.175. As quoted in Lentin *Jan Smuts*, p.35. Asquith, Riddell thought, 'held a very moderate opinion of Smuts at the time of the South African War' and 'did not appreciate what a remarkable man he was.' Riddell, *Lord Riddell's War Diary*, p.166.
44 Keith Wilson (ed.), *The Rasp of War; The Letters of H.A. Gwynne to The Countess Bathurst, 1914-1918* (London: Sidgwick & Jackson, 1988), p.327.
45 Buchan, *Greenmantle*, pp.6–7.

> South Africa was represented by General Smuts, the gifted and versatile Dutchman. He had made a study of war and had no mean experience of it. He had just conducted a successful campaign in the vast jungles of tropical Africa, where he fought the most resourceful of all the German Generals – von Lettow-Vorbeck.
>
> Smuts is one of the most remarkable personalities of his time. He is that fine blend of intellect and human sympathy which constitutes the understanding man. Although he had proved his courage in many enterprises which demanded personal valour, and although he had shown his powers in many a fight which had called for combative qualities, his sympathies were too broad to make him a mere fighting man. His rare gifts of mind and heart strengthened those finer elements which are apt to be overwhelmed in an hour of savage temper and pitiless carnage. Of his practical contribution to our counsels during these trying years, it is difficult to speak too highly.[46]

Richard Steyn recently argued that 'at a time of national emergency, no one in London seemed too concerned about political or constitutional niceties.'[47] However, some men – even at the heart of the British establishment – clearly were.

The Only Unwounded Statesman of Outstanding Ability in the Empire

On 8 June, at Lloyd George's invitation, Smuts joined a meeting of the War Cabinet shortly before its closure. The prime minister explained, much to the surprise of those around the table, that the former-Boer general would join them as a cabinet member. Walter Long was opposed to Smuts's appointment and on the same day commiserated with Maurice Hankey, the secretary, regarding the intricacy of the War Cabinet's workings and the nature of some of its decisions – most of all the unforeseen decision reached that morning on Smuts. As Long explained, this was 'a very big question' and yet, without full discussion, Smuts's entrance into the full War Cabinet was already considered settled.[48] The idea of Dominion representation on the War Council was hatched in early 1916 in a discussion between Milner, Lloyd George, and William Hughes, the Australian prime minister who had approached Lloyd George regarding the 'unsatisfactory condition of affairs' in British politics. All three men sought change in the political leadership and strategic direction of the war and Hughes had expressed a desire to join the Council. However, as they recognised, if Hughes stayed in London

46 David Lloyd George, *War Memoirs of David Lloyd George* (London: Ivor Nicholson & Watson, 1934), vol. IV, pp.1743–1744.

47 Steyn, *Jan Smuts*, p.84.

48 WSHC: 947/636, Viscount Long of Wraxall Papers, Long to Hankey, 8 June 1917. Hankey 'only got wind' of Smuts's appointment on the afternoon of 8 June, Hankey to Long, 9 June 1917.

for anything shorter than six months, he would be little more than a visitor at the Council. George Riddell, a press baron and ardent Lloyd George supporter, explained, 'It is invidious to criticise a visitor's proposals. Suggestions made by members are discussed and criticised. Sometimes they are adopted; sometimes they are rejected; and sometimes a compromise is reached. No one is hurt or offended because his views are not accepted.'[49]

Any Dominion representative had to have impeccable credentials, the ability to study themselves into the meeting, the capacity to read up all past minutes and documents, and, if necessary, the preparedness to butt heads and take no offence. The person would also have to stay for six months and preferably longer. Lloyd George had wanted to see Borden, Botha, and Smuts on the Council, but 'particularly Smuts, of whom [he] spoke very highly.'[50] Even Long later conceded that Smuts was 'certainly a very able man' and able to take 'a broad view of things.'[51]

However, Smuts's appointment raised all kinds of constitutional and procedural impediments. Wanting his independence, he had turned down Lloyd George's suggestion that he stand for Parliament in the United Kingdom, which brought the unprecedented position that somebody sitting in the Cabinet might be member of neither the Commons nor the Lords. The work of sorting out the details, was left to an astonished Long, who met with Smuts on 8 June to finalise the negotiations. Smuts, the lawyer, aware of the constitutional delicacies, consented on condition that he attend for military matters only. On 10 June, Long wrote to Hankey again. 'There must be no mistake. Smuts can, and *will*, only join for *Military* questions. He selected this term himself. We may easily get into serious trouble.'[52] Long felt that Smuts was correct – 'both for his own sake and ours.' Should Smuts, as a South African, speak on 'overseas interests' such as Canadian and Australian affairs, 'there must be a big row' and on this Long would not have agreed.[53] For this reason, as he wrote to Lloyd George, Smuts 'could not become an ordinary member.'[54]

Telegrams passed between Britain and South Africa over the following days. Smuts cabled Botha for consent, which the older man readily gave. This meant that he would not return to South Africa, which, while hard on his family, gave him unsurpassed opportunity, 'never in our life or in history will there again come a time so critical for mankind, and it would be cowardly and selfish if I were to refuse all requests for help and co-operation.' Membership of the War Cabinet, he told his wife, was 'much better' than either the chairmanship of the Irish Convention and the command in Palestine, both of which he had turned down, and gave him 'the right position to do good work in

49 Riddell, *Lord Riddell's War Diary*, p.166.
50 Riddell, *Lord Riddell's War Diary*, p.166.
51 WSHC: 947/602, Viscount Long of Wraxall Papers, Long to Buxton, 4 July 1917.
52 WSHC: 947/636, Viscount Long of Wraxall Papers, Long to Hankey, 10 June 1917. Long's emphasis.
53 WSHC: 947/636, Viscount Long of Wraxall Papers, Long to Hankey, 8 June 1917.
54 WSHC: 947/636, Viscount Long of Wraxall Papers, Long to Lloyd George, 8 June 1917.

connection with our war policy.'[55] In the meantime, Long contacted Buxton and Hankey. He warned Hankey to proceed cautiously, at first only 'summoning' Smuts for military items on the agenda.[56] Hankey, in turn, would keep Smuts at arm's length – going 'slow about sending papers to Smuts' – until the whole matter was settled. In the meantime, Smuts had been placed on 'a new and important Cabinet Committee on War Policy' and Hankey promised vainly to 'keep [Smuts] quiet with paper on this subject.'[57] Long made his final move on 10 June. He pressed Lloyd George to make Smuts a member of the Imperial General War Staff instead; Smuts could then be called to attend whenever Lloyd George wished and without constitutional difficulty.[58] But Lloyd George had found his man and on 15 June he issued his statement in the House of Commons, the text of which had been approved by the War Cabinet and read beforehand to Smuts, 'The War Cabinet, in order to avail themselves of the special military knowledge and experience of General Smuts, have invited him to attend their meetings during his stay in this Country.'[59] And so, 'urged by Lloyd George, encouraged by Botha, moved by his own inclination', Smuts joined the War Cabinet as a minister without portfolio but remained a South African minister and he refused the additional salary.[60] True to his roots, while he lived at the Savoy Hotel, he eschewed its luxury and fine living, preferring *biltong* and *beskuit* sent him from South Africa. Neither did he dress the part. C.P. Scott, the editor of the *Manchester Guardian*, records that Smuts dressed invariably in 'ordinary officer's khaki, without a scrap of decoration – gold or red tab [and that] he might have passed for the least distinguished of the soldiers present ... Obviously a very big man.'[61] He made an impression wherever he went, and his speeches were published in London and New York in June 1917; Smuts dated his foreword 31 May – a significant date in South Africa history.[62] He teasingly told his wife that he hoped 'all this applause will not turn my little head'.[63] Buxton, watching from South Africa, wrote to Long: 'It is pleasant to hear your warm appreciation of Smuts – though it is what I expected. But I hope the B[ritish] P[ress] won't overdo it as they did in the case of Hughes. But Smuts's head is harder and less swellable than Hughes'!'[64]

55 Smuts to Isie, 9 June 1917 in Hancock and Van der Poel (eds.), *Selections*, vol. III, pp.531–533.
56 WSHC: 947/636, Viscount Long of Wraxall Papers, Long to Hankey, 8 June 1917. See also Hankey to Long, 9 June 1917.
57 WSHC: 947/636, Viscount Long of Wraxall Papers, Hankey to Long, 9 June 1917.
58 WSHC: 947/636, Viscount Long of Wraxall Papers, Long to Lloyd George, 10 June 1917.
59 WSHC: 947/636, Viscount Long of Wraxall Papers, J.T. Davies to H.F. Batterbee, 15 June 1917.
60 Hancock and Van der Poel (eds.), *Selections*, vol. III, p.529.
61 As quoted in Lentin *Jan Smuts*, p.37.
62 J.C. Smuts, *War -Time Speeches; A Compilation of Public Utterances in Great Britain* (London: Hodder and Stoughton, 1917).
63 Smuts to Isie, 9 June 1917 in Hancock and Van der Poel (eds.), *Selections*, vol. III, pp.521–533.
64 WSHC: 947/602, Viscount Long of Wraxall Papers, Buxton to Long, 7 July 1917.

While people from all walks of life queued to meet him, Smuts's reception by military men sometimes contrasted remarkably from the popular sentiment. Kitchener, when tested on the idea of giving Smuts command of Imperial troops, had predicted that: 'My generals', who had fought against the Boers in South Africa, 'will not accept Mr Smuts.'[65] Kitchener's disregard of Smuts's military rank – shown in this statement – was echoed by some of his subordinates during the later war years. Smuts no doubt was aware of this when turning down the command in Palestine. For some at least, Smuts became an object of some distrust and much jealousy. In November 1917, when addressing a meeting of the St John's Ambulance in London, Brigadier General Alfred Cavendish, then the general officer commanding the South African Military Command in Cape Town, described Smuts as 'that modern miracle' who 'for the beaten enemy … had a very nasty knack of asserting himself at times.'[66] Cavendish was recalled in March 1918 and his military career effectively terminated.[67] William Carter, the Archbishop of Cape Town, who knew the parties and issues in the fracas, noted guardedly that Cavendish had 'somehow … not been a great success [and had] not got on with the Authorities here.'[68]

Smuts became a convenient handyman. He not only had significant and relevant military experience, but was one who could be trusted with difficult, often unpleasant tasks, the successful completion of which would bolster Lloyd George without constituting a political threat to the prime minister. There were the special missions – to the United States, to North Africa, the Middle East, and with Lloyd George and Sir Henry Wilson to Italy to bolster morale after Caporetto.[69] As well as the settlement of strikes in South Wales – by the police and coalminers, and the possibility of his chairing an Irish convention. Woodrow Wilson's special envoy in the UK, Colonel House, remarked of Smuts in November 1917, 'He has grown to be the lion of the hour … He is one of the few men I have met in the Government who do not feel tired, He's alert, energetic, and forceful.'[70]

Smuts was kept busy over the following months as Lloyd George came to rely increasingly on his sagacity, meticulousness, and capacity for plain hard work. Lloyd George's biographer, John Grigg, commenting on Smuts's position on the Imperial and British War Cabinets, said 'he was talented enough to count for two.'[71] On 8

65 As quoted in Lentin *Jan Smuts*, p.34.
66 DODA: DC, Box 1142, file DCDB23/94/7, suggested recall of Brigadier General Cavendish GOC South African Military Command and appointment of General Martyn, Speech made by Cavendish at a meeting of the St John's Ambulance on 2 November 1917.
67 In January 1918, Cavendish had instructed Surgeon General William Pike, of the Army Medical Service, who was then visiting South Africa, not to confer with South African officials. NARSSA: GG 675, 9/93/196, Colonel Stock to Defence, 29 January 1918.
68 Wits: AB186 Archbishop William Carter Papers, Carter to Lawley, 10 March 1918.
69 Keith Jeffrey, *Field Marshal Sir Henry Wilson; A Political Soldier* (Oxford: Oxford University Press, 2006), p.206.
70 Crafford, *Jan Smuts*, p.142.
71 Grigg, *Lloyd George*, p.63.

June 1917, the day after the assault at Messines, Lloyd George appointed a cabinet committee to consider War Policy in its broadest terms; it comprised Curzon, Milner, and Smuts, with himself as chair. Bonar Law and Balfour were added shortly after.[72] Smuts advised on military questions and helped shape military policy. On 11 July 1917, the War Cabinet decided that he and Lloyd George, in consultation with representatives from the armed forces, examine 'the defence arrangements for Home defence against air-raids' and 'the air organisation generally and the direction of aerial operations.'[73] The frighteningly new strategic threat presented by aerial warfare led to two separate reports, written largely by Smuts.

The first report related to the air defence of Great Britain. London was the nerve centre for the Empire and the hub of its financial sinew. Pre-war air enthusiasts and writers of fiction had predicted the disappearance of the customary separation between the battlespace and home front, and between soldier and civilian, and the loss of Britain's traditional immunity to invasion. Britain had been at first slow to respond but, by 1917, as Richard Overy argues, 'small though the human cost was compared with the campaigns of the next war, the sheer novelty of attacks on British soil against British civilians explains the exaggerated reaction of press and public.'[74] Press baron, Lord Northcliffe wrote at the time:

> Let it be realized that the practical aeroplane is not yet ten years old, that already our shores are within less than twenty minutes by air from the Continent of Europe. Let it be realized that aeroplanes are very cheap to make and will become cheaper. The vast change that this invention has produced in the position of England does not even now seem to be understood by one person in a hundred.[75]

Air raids were predicted to escalate over the ensuing months and London was expected to become part of the battlefront. The need to adapt defences, from simply meeting Zeppelins at night with ack-ack and slow aircraft, to meeting daytime 'invasions by squadrons of aeroplanes in formation' was now apparent and Smuts urged the implementation of additional precautions without prejudicing aerial operations on the high seas and in the field. Air defence meant the ability to reply to an aerial attack by means of a heavy barrage of gunfire and interdiction by concentrated air units under unified command, which required a reserve squadron of fighters and the ability to destroy a second strike should it follow close on a first

72 John Terraine, *Douglas Haig; The educated soldier* (London: Hutchinson, 1963), p.319.
73 TNA CAB/24/20: First Report, Committee on Air Organisation and Home Defence Against Air-Raids.
74 Richard Overy, *The Birth of the RAF, 1918: The World's First Air Force* (London: Allen Lane, 2018), p.13.
75 Lord Northcliffe, *At the War* (London: Hodder and Stoughton, 1916), p.46.

attack.[76] If this seemed revolutionary, their examination of the issues in the second report – on the air organisation and aerial operations, which led to the formation of the Royal Air Force (RAF) – was more so.

At its centennial, Richard Overy argued that 'the birth of the RAF was surrounded by argument and controversy.' The creation of a new service for the air defence of the UK was a political decision to address the apparent failure in home defence and the gruelling rivalry between the two existing air services – the Royal Naval Air Service and the army's Royal Flying Corps – for human and material resources including the appropriation of land for aerodromes and the workings of industry.[77] The War Cabinet discussed Smuts's aerial operations report on 21 September 1917. He highlighted what he described as 'the real question', namely the presence of two air programmes: one provided for 80 squadrons operational on the Western Front, the other, under the Air Board, provided for a Royal Flying Corps of 200 squadrons. Both programmes, Smuts argued, had to be properly resourced if Haig was to receive the forces he needed. Churchill, then Minister of Munitions, differed. The acceleration of supply was no easy matter when changes of design necessarily affected output. Moreover, the allocation of skilled labour remained a problem. Sir David Henderson and Sir Eric Geddes chimed in. As there was a considerable difference of opinion regarding the facts, a committee was formed under Smuts to investigate the conditions of air production – the other members were Lord Derby (War), Sir Eric Geddes (First Lord), Churchill, and Lord Cowdray.[78] Smuts loved working with large questions. Here he was, at the head of yet another committee and one examining a marvellous new technology. Speaking that August in dramatic terms he spoke of passenger air services that would dramatically change international travel. A trip to South Africa would take just four days: 'the travellers to sleep at an hotel *en route* each night, and described in a dramatic way the change which this would work in the world.'[79] Later that week, Germany made a combined airship and aeroplane attack. Between 15 and 20 aeroplanes attacked the south-east coast between Dover and Harwich, while nine airships half-heartedly attacked the east coast between the Wash and the Tees. Four or five aeroplanes had attempted to reach London but seemingly only one plane succeeded in dropping no more than six bombs, which led to 12 deaths and 35 other casualties. It was impossible to 'conceal London'; the air defences had seemingly done their work.[80]

76 TNA CAB/24/20: First Report, Committee on Air Organisation and Home Defence Against Air-Raids.
77 Overy, *The Birth of the RAF*, p.16; TNA: CAB 23/4/11, Minutes of a Meeting of the War Cabinet, 21 September 1917.
78 TNA CAB 23/4/11: Minutes of a Meeting of the War Cabinet, 21 September 1917.
79 Smuts quoted by Riddell, *Lord Riddell's War Diary*, pp.260–261.
80 TNA CAB 23/13/18: Major General Sir F.C. Shaw, the Chief of the General Staff, Home Forces. Minutes of a Meeting of the War Cabinet, 25 September 1917.

Lloyd George hosted an inter-ally conference in London during the first week of August 1917. A small group gathered at Great Walstead for a weekend-in-the-country before its start. Lloyd George, Riddle, Robert Cecil, Milner, and Smuts were there, as well as Baron Sonnino, the Italian foreign minister. In an aside, Smuts, Sonnino and Riddell considered the magnitude of the events taking place. This was a moment of historical crisis, too big then to appreciate and only seen by those who would succeed them. Smuts agreed, although he felt that perspectives were already being revised – too much he thought had certainly been made of small things at the war's start. Now, Smuts noted, in 1917 they stood at one of history's crisis points; at one of the great milestones – Hannibal, Alexander, Caesar, Napoleon, the war of 1917. But unlike other great milestones, the three men agreed, the crisis of 1917 centred on no one individual.[81] There was – in answer to Maud Wyndham's rhetorical question posed at the start of this chapter – no Marlborough and no Chatham, but rather a concert of great men working for victory. Afterwards Riddell and Smuts talked alone. Smuts confided that:

> … the War Cabinet is snowed under by papers and details, and that some drastic revision of the organisation was necessary. There is no sufficient delegation and Ministers have no time to think out the really great problems of the war. At the end of the week the mind is in a haze owing to the number and complexity of the problems which have arisen.[82]

Smuts left for London at 11:00 p.m.; the others stayed the night and resumed their conference over breakfast.

The next day, Smuts attended a meeting of the War Cabinet. There was reason for optimism. Recent intelligence confirmed that Germany was thinly stretched. Austrian troops had mostly faced the Russian offensive in Galicia, but these were now reinforced from Germany – which was drawing strength from the Western Front and from the Balkans to do so. Moreover, there was hope that Korniloff's army, more disciplined than the other Russian armies, would be the start of a regeneration in the armed forces of their eastern ally. Then on the Western Front, 'the proportion of killed to wounded in the recent offensive was very small.'[83] While others reported on the major fronts, Smuts again reported on rather technical matters. He came in on the tonnage for the conveyance of horse, on this occasion serving as the link between the War Office, the India Office, and the Ministry of Shipping.[84]

81 Sonnino and Smuts agreed that of these great leaders Hannibal was the greatest. Riddell, *Lord Riddell's War Diary*, pp.260-261.
82 Riddell, *Lord Riddell's War Diary*, p.261.
83 TNA CAB 23/3/52: Minutes of a Meeting of the War Cabinet, 3 August 1917.
84 TNA CAB 23/3/52: Minutes of a Meeting of the War Cabinet, 3 August 1917.

He dined with Riddell, Donald, and Garvin in his private rooms at the Savoy on 26 September. They first questioned him as to what he had meant in saying that the allies had won the war. He explained:

> The Germans know they have lost the war. Psychologically we have won. They know that the whole world is against them, and that although from a military point of view they may not yet be defeated, yet the longer the war continues, the worse their condition will be. Their trade, which they have built up with such assiduity, has been destroyed. They know how difficult they will find it to recover any part of their lost ground and that as the war proceeds their difficulties will increase. The Boers knew months before they were actually defeated from a military point of view that they were beaten. The Germans are in the same position.[85]

For Smuts, the position was clear; 1917 was about settling the post-war world – the empires of continental Europe, Belgium, France, and Alsace-Lorraine, the Middle East, and of course Africa. In this context, South Africa's role in the African campaigns and the presence of South African troops in France, the pivot of the battlefronts, was critical. At the end of the year, the War Office asked South Africa for a despatch on the German South West Africa campaign with recommendations for medals and decorations. Piet van der Byl, who had served under Botha during the campaign and Smuts in East Africa, arrived in London in early 1918. He went to the Savoy each day to work with Smuts on the finalisation of the despatch and the nominations for the honour roll.[86] Several awards were made. Amongst others, Howard Gorges was knighted, and the wife of the Archbishop of Cape Town received a CBE for charitable work at the Wynberg Hospital, the Gifts and Comforts Depot, and the Rest House for Soldiers. The Lloyd George government and the Royal Household, aware of the limited civilian honours available for war service, created new honours including the Order of the Companions of Honour. The first on Lloyd George's list was ironically a military man, although perhaps not to some – Lieutenant General Smuts.

Smuts understood the significance of the complex webs behind government, public opinion, and the press. In November 1917, he put forward Roderick Jones, the general manager of Reuter's, for an award. Knighted in the 1918 New Year's Honours list, Jones was an enigmatic figure. He had arrived in Pretoria in 1895, headed the Reuters South Africa office from 1905, and had worked with Smuts in managing the press at the time of the Afrikaner Rebellion in 1914. He was now in London and since October 1915 had been in charge of Reuter's, instituting a special cable service to the Dominions.[87] Until 1915, British propaganda had been directed almost solely at

85 Summation of Smuts's views in Riddell, *Lord Riddell's War Diary*, p.277.
86 Van der Byl, *From Playgrounds to Battlefields*, pp.247, 263.
87 Had Jones not left South Africa, Botha would have recommended him for an award in recognition for his services in the Union. WSHC: 947/563, Viscount Long of Wraxall Papers, Smuts to Long, 14 and 20 November 1917.

opinion makers. This changed when the government realised it had to reach the broad public and approached Reuter's, the largest of the news agencies based in London.[88] Jones felt the needs of the war justified his sending government propaganda through his news service. The desperate financial position in which Reuters found itself had no doubt been an added incentive.[89] The value of the news service, tracked by the value of Reuters shares, increased with each war year.[90] News, which would not reach the Dominions, or arrive very much later, could now be placed in the Dominions' Press while still newsworthy, for example news of soldier settlement plans, and schemes for imports and food controls. As the Reuters dominions' editor noted, due to the rapid passage of news, the South African Minister of Agriculture even announced a soldier-settlement scheme for South Africa; something thought revolutionary due to 'the deep-rooted natural hostility of S. Africa's ruling powers to any policy of land settlement.'[91] But there were other advantages. The new service enabled Reuters to tell Britain's side of the war – giving 'adequate prominence to the deeds of Imperial troops in recent operations' and stressing that their roles in the actual fighting, and the casualties they sustained, were proportionately higher than among Dominion troops. This they did to counter German propaganda that Dominion and Colonial troops 'were bearing the brunt of the fighting' on the Western Front. Importantly, for Smuts, his speeches could be sent verbatim throughout the Empire; for example, until the institution of the news service, the Associated Press of America had only sent redacted reports of similar speeches to Canada.[92] The work of this largely privatised

88 Buchan headed the new Department of Information: created to address the unsatisfactory state of Whitehall's propaganda machine and provide detailed news that was disseminated rapidly. His advisory committee included a mix of British editors and newspaper proprietors, and the manager of Reuter's. TNA CAB 21/37: Buchan to Lloyd George, 2 February 1917, and Minutes of a Meeting of the War Cabinet, 24 January 1917.

89 Taylor Downing, *Secret Warriors: Key Scientists, Code-breakers and Propagandists of the Great War* (London: Little Brown, 2014), p.284.

90 The South African Department of Defence recognised the value of the Reuters news service by August 1916. Reuters filled an important gap when the Portuguese officials in Mozambique issued no official reports. And, as the South African high commissioner in London confirmed, 'we could take Reuters cables to be accurate.' NARSSA: GG 597, 9/57/40, Secretary for Defence to Ministers, 21 August 1916 and 4 September 1916.

91 South African governments discouraged immigration and land settlement. As Kent Fedorowich explains, 'Throughout 1917 and 1918 the South African government remained resolute in its determination not to introduce special soldier settlement projects, state-aided migration programmes or participate in an imperial free passage scheme.' Kent Fedorowich, *Unfit for Heroes: Reconstruction and Soldier Settlement in the Empire between the Wars* (Manchester and New York: Manchester University Press, 1995), p.124.

92 WSHC: 947/563, Viscount Long of Wraxall Papers, Dominions Editor to Managing Editor Reuter's, 23 October 1917. 'I do not know how this would be attainable without the Imperial Service, because the newspapers of each Dominion, I will not say only want, *but certainly will not complain if they only get*, chiefly news of their own soldiers' doings when big operations are taking place.'

propaganda machine played no small part in creating Smuts's image as an Empire-statesman – and this Empire-statesman could shape the narrative.

During the first quarter of 1918, Smuts visited several of the warfronts. At Lloyd George's behest he and Hankey visited Haig on the Western Front, where they were received with smiles at Haig's headquarters. However, their real mission was 'to find a replacement for Haig.' Their report would disappoint the prime minister but, as Lloyd George questioned in his *War Memoirs*, who could credibly have replaced him? Military men, skilled, qualified, and possessed of average intelligence, were many 'but Haig was all that and probably better within those limits than any others within sight.'[93] Haig was no doubt aware too that there was no replacement for him, and he could manipulate the situation to his advantage.

Then, on 5 February 1918, Smuts left London with a small retinue for the Middle East.[94] Travelling quickly they reached Cairo on 11 February having stopped in Paris, Rome, Taranto, and Alexandria en route. Senior British operational commanders met them at different points on their journey; sometimes they accompanied Smuts part of the way. At Versailles, they discussed various questions relating to their mission with Sir Henry Wilson and collected information relating to the campaigns in Palestine and Mesopotamia. The group reached Rome on 8 February, where they discussed questions of transportation with the First Lord of the Admiralty and Sir Guy Granet, the Director General of Military Transport, and General Nash. General Grey, who had overseen Inland Water Transport in Mesopotamia, explained the transportation situation on the Tigris. Granet went with them to Egypt. The group reached Taranto on 9 February, where they inspected the camp through which British troops to and from Salonica and Egypt transited and reached Alexandria on 11 February. Here they discussed the possibility of landing stores on the Palestine and Syrian coasts to support Allenby's advance – especially after Haifa was taken and opened for traffic. In Alexandria, they met with Admiral Jackson and General Hopwood – Maude's chief of the general staff, who accompanied him part of the way to Cairo to discuss the situation in Mesopotamia. Hopwood strengthened Smuts's 'impression that the Mesopotamian campaign would have to be reduced to a strictly defensive basis in future.'[95] In Cairo he met Sir Reginald Wingate, Major General Bols (Allenby's chief of the general staff), and Brigadier General Macauley, who oversaw the Egyptian and Palestine railways. They analysed the strategic and transportation aspects of the campaign and discussed the political relations between the Arabs and Jews with Wingate, Allenby, and Clayton. In Cairo, Smuts met Major General John Salmond, who oversaw aviation in the Middle East and inspected the aerodromes, as well as the repair and training facilities at Heliopolis and Alexandria. Smuts's report on his

93 John Terraine, *Douglas Haig; The educated soldier* (London: Hutchinson, 1963), p.389.
94 Brigadier General Stewart, of Haig's Headquarters, Colonel Kirke, of the Imperial General Staff, Lieutenant Colonel Amery, of the Staff of the Supreme War Council, and Captain Lane of the War Cabinet Staff, went with him.
95 TNA CAB 24/4/50: Report by General Smuts on his Mission to Egypt, 1 March 1918.

mission to Egypt reads like the passage of a military mogul, something not unseen – mostly by the envious and less kind – in the United Kingdom and South Africa.

Lieutenant General Sir Philip Chetwode, then commander of XX Corps in Palestine, wrote to the editor of London's *Morning Post*, Howell Gwynne, telling 'a pretty tale' of the visit of Smuts and Amery, then on the personnel of the Cabinet Office, who had been sent to Palestine to study and report on the situation. They advised on an expedition to the Hedjaz railway, which, undertaken against Allenby and Chetwode's advice, failed.[96] Gwynne, by no means a neutral player, was less than charitable in his transmission of the story:

> Smuts and Amery, a civilian – both civilians really – were sent out to Palestine, without consultation with the General Staff, to persuade Allenby to undertake operations which the Prime Minister wanted to carry out against the wish of the General Staff. These proposals were condemned by Allenby, by Chetwode, and by Bulfin as being dangerous. But Allenby's rigid idea of a soldier's duty to obey, even when he thinks obedience is dangerous, was the reason why he undertook the offensive against his own better judgement and the better judgement of his Generals.[97]

Smuts had spent three days (14–16 February) at Allenby's headquarters. These discussions led to Smuts's telegram to the War Office of 15 February, which had indeed set out his recommendations for the coming campaign, and a sequence of further missals on the future of railways, matters of transport, and other requirements.[98] Returning through Cairo, Smuts met with Major General Webb Gillman, Mesopotamian Expeditionary Force commander General Sir William Marshall's chief of general staff, who shared his views that the railway and transportation problems prevented a simultaneous advance by the Tigris or Euphrates routes.

The Military Representatives of the Supreme War Council had decided at the start of 1918 that the coming campaign against the Ottomans embody a coordinated scheme rather than a series of disconnected operations. There were two options: conduct simultaneous, convergent operations from Palestine and Mesopotamia; or a concentrated attack from either Palestine or Mesopotamia while reducing the other front momentarily to a purely defensive role. Convinced that an offensive from Mesopotamia would achieve little beyond tactical success, Smuts advocated an advance on Aleppo. There was much to recommend the western approach. It did not require right flank

96 H.A. Gwynne to Lady Bathurst, 29 April 1918 in Keith Wilson (ed.), *The Rasp of War; The Letters of H.A. Gwynne to The Countess Bathurst, 1914-1918* (London: Sidgwick & Jackson, 1988), p.271.
97 Attached to Gwynne to Lady Bathurst, 28 May 1918 in Wilson (ed.), *The Rasp of War*, p.285.
98 TNA: CAB 24/4/50, Smuts to Chief Imperial General Staff, London, 15 February 1918, Annex 1 to Report by General Smuts on his Mission to Egypt, 1 March 1918.

protection, while it offered possibly 500 miles of additional railroads, extending the lines of communication, and fewer climatic difficulties. Furthermore, he argued, that an attack from Mesopotamia would in any case probably require a supporting advance from Palestine towards Aleppo. And then, should Allenby reach Aleppo, the Turks would be unable to maintain a large force in Mesopotamia and 'the task of clearing Mesopotamia will, to a large extent, have been accomplished automatically.'[99] All in all, the conditions for an advance from Palestine and into Syria were much more favourable than from Mesopotamia.

Smuts loved the Middle East. The healthy appearance of the troops, and high spirits, despite their recent hardships, impressed him. They were, he reported, universally confident in Allenby, their commander-in-chief. The region also appealed to his sense of the great and the old. It was a place for contemplation and rigorous living. Often open space and a dry climate. He thought Egypt imminently suitable for air training, not only for the Air Service in the Middle East, but for large numbers of pilots destined for the Western Front. The weather conditions were ideal, and the establishment of air schools in Crete and on the Egyptian coast, for example at Sollum, would alleviate the congested conditions at British aerodromes. Moreover, Constantinople, the railway infrastructure, and the supply depots in Thrace and Asia Minor presented suitable, viable targets. While the aerodromes at Mudros and Imbros might become the centre for continuous bombing missions, flying day and night, against these objectives. He certainly thought big, and there was a willing Salmond to carry with him the suggestions to the Air Council and the Air Policy Committee.[100]

The whole policy in the Middle East had to be directed in operations against Turkey. This raised several points. In the first instance, 'nothing should be done which might upset our Arab Allies, whose military usefulness is being increasingly felt, and may assume yet greater importance as we get in touch with the Hauran and the powerful tribes east of Damascus.' The Turks had made the most of the declaration on Zionism and the publication of the Sykes-Picot Agreement of May 1916. He stressed the importance of practicing good faith towards the Arabs through recognition of their position in Damascus and Syria more generally. The Arabs understood from the agreement that much of Syria and the whole coast would become a French colony after the war. This had increased their distrust. At the same time, while taking the war to the Turks, the Turks had to know that Britain did not wish to deprive them of Constantinople or their remaining European districts where the Turks formed a majority. The promise of a Turkish national state after the war might present the chance for a separate peace.[101] Smuts may not have passed through the military training establishments of the UK, but he certainly had an eye for the large, and the dramatic, something that continued to appeal to those in search of solutions.

99 TNA CAB 24/4/50: Report by General Smuts on his Mission to Egypt, 1 March 1918.
100 TNA CAB 24/4/50: Report by General Smuts on his Mission to Egypt, 1 March 1918.
101 TNA CAB 24/4/50: Report by General Smuts on his Mission to Egypt, 1 March 1918.

Smuts returned to a heavily depressed London. At the start of 1918, the balance of the war had seemingly shifted against the Entente powers with revolution in Russia, defeat for Italy on the Isonzo front, the munities in the French Army, declining manpower reserves, and the exhaustion of British forces after Passchendaele. After the German offensive starting on 21 March, the British armies in France were in retreat. At this gloomy time, a cable arrived from Botha stating that the Germans 'had shot their bolt'. Smuts read it to a disheartened war cabinet. A year later, when Botha was in Paris for the peace conference, Smuts asked what he had meant. Botha's reply was emphatic: 'In the first breakthrough, they drove the Allies back 36 miles and then paused, refitted and attacked again – advancing only some 16 miles. Again they halted and poised themselves for a third time and only advanced some 6 to 7 miles. Surely it was obvious they had shot their bolt.'[102] To Botha, out in South Africa, the strategic picture was clear. Van der Byl tells us: 'He had that vision denied much cleverer men, which could see over the mountains and into the future.'[103] Van der Byl undoubtedly lionised Botha and his instinctive sense of strategy and tactics – something that no doubt nettled Smuts.

At this point, Smuts delivered his note on the controversial question of a diplomatic mission to Russia to discuss the war situation with Trotsky and the Soviet regime. This was thought important enough to have a cabinet minister lead it. However, Lloyd George hesitated and asked Smuts to investigate it. Smuts reported – as many already thought – that such a member of the British government might be pressed when there to recognise the new republic and so 'give the Bolsheviks an enormous advantage over the other parties.'[104] This would raise a double quandary. On the one hand, if the minister declined Trotsky's invitation to recognise the new regime, the mission would be shown to have been 'foolish and futile.' If on the other hand, Trotsky was willing to accept the British proposals in exchange for recognition, London might be pushed prematurely in making such a far-reaching decision without proper consideration and consultation with their Allies and at a time when 'everything, even our own ideas, are still hazy and unformed.'[105]

While a minister was not sent, Smuts did have another mission to Europe before the war's end. On 13-14 July 1918, he was at Danny, the house in Sussex rented by Lloyd George. Borden and Henry Wilson were also there. Smuts arrived having travelled from Oxford. He, Lloyd George, and Borden climbed the hill behind the house: the first two, having returned covered in perspiration, had to bathe before a War Council deliberation in the hall. They spoke about the war and the disposition of the American troops.[106] Riddell was back at Danny a week later. He found Lloyd George in the dining room. The prime minister told him that Smuts had been to Switzerland

102 As quoted in Van der Byl, *From Playgrounds to Battlefields*, p.189.
103 Van der Byl, *From Playgrounds to Battlefields*, p.189.
104 TNA CAB 24/49/23: Note by Smuts on 'Russian Mission', 24 April 1918.
105 TNA CAB 24/49/23: Note by Smuts on 'Russian Mission', 24 April 1918.
106 Riddell, *Lord Riddell's War Diary*, p.339.

some time before to meet a leading Austrian statesman, Count Mensdorff, to discuss possible peace terms. Mensdorff was not an official representative of his government, but, as Lloyd George put it, a useful contact. His government could not countenance such a move, but not discourage it either.[107] Nothing came of Smuts's meeting in Switzerland. Official news of the visit came from Britain but had been cabled to the South African press weeks before. 'Because it was in the press', Maud Wyndham told her mother, 'no one believed it.'[108]

Botha's Battles on the Home Front

While his loyal lieutenant was away, Botha remained under constant siege in South Africa. Smuts's successes in London did little to assist the older man's policy of conciliation and at home both men remained under constant attack by the Nationalists. While pleased to note Britain's gratitude to South Africa for her role in the war, he knew the Nationalists were responsible for much public bitterness. Botha used the press to counter the onslaught and he travelled the country shaking hands and making speeches.[109] In Malmesbury, he made a special mention of Smuts as a son of whom Malmesbury should be proud. Smuts, he argued, was in that moment one of the most sought-after intellectual men in the world, and that anyone who was not proud of Smuts was most likely jealous.[110] Botha praised Smuts also for his work during the rebellion, 'No one can ever appreciate sufficiently the great work that General Smuts has done – greater than that of any other man during this unhappy period. At his post day and night, his brilliant intellect, his calm judgement, his amazing energy and his undaunted courage have been assets of inestimable value to the Union in her hour of trial.'[111]

Botha met with key Unionists that May – including Smartt, Duncan, Walton, Crewe and Jagger – to ensure their continued support. Some friction had developed between the parties. The Unionists rightly felt that Botha came to expect their support; an expectation that verged on a demand or South Africa risked leaving the war. Botha, Buxton recounted, had told them: 'We are all sinners, and I daresay I am the biggest sinner of all.' There was the promise of improved relations. Buxton had always warned Botha of 'the necessity and the expediency, in the circumstances in which he is placed (i.e. that he is in the minority and depends in the final resort on the Unionist vote) of consulting Smartt more than he does. It is only fair to the Unionists that he should do so.' However, while Botha agreed in principle, and sometimes spoke to Smartt in detail, some of his party were 'opposed to any truck with the Unionists,

107 Riddell, *Lord Riddell's War Diary*, p.341.
108 WSRO: Petworth House Archives, Maud Wyndham to Lady Leconfield, 26 April 1918.
109 NARSSA: Preller Archive, 90, 'Botha', *De Volksstem*, 26 June 1916.
110 NARSSA: Preller Archive, 93, Botha quoted in 'General Botha to Malmesbury', *De Burger*, 6 June 1917.
111 Buxton, *General Botha*, p.195.

and consultation does not take place sufficiently often.'[112] During the 1917 Session of Parliament, Botha did not consult Smart on new legislation and the budget. Botha felt that Smartt had been too demanding – wanting to be consulted regarding all legislation and financial matters. But Botha remained opposed to a coalition government, although relying on the Unionists' pledge of support as long as the South African Party continued its support of the war effort.[113] Gradually, as the Unionists were well aware, their party lost its identity and would disappear after the war.

That January, Botha had addressed the Coloured community in Carnarvon. He thanked them for their service in East Africa and Europe.[114] The Cape Corps, raised in August 1915, comprised of Coloured soldiers, was deployed to German East Africa and later Palestine. It was thought that they would be hardier in the face of environmental disease – but this did not prove to be the case. Furthermore, in September 1916, the South African Native Labour Contingent had been formed to mitigate the labour shortages on the Western Front and by 1918 approximately 22,500 Black men had seen service.[115] Any discussion of the franchise, as a reward for war-time service, was political dynamite. While Botha told his Carnarvon audience of the possibility of extending the political franchise for the Coloured community throughout the Union, he would remain vague on this matter and – watched by hawk-like Nationalists – could never be a strong advocate for the rights of People of Colour.

The politicking between the South African Party and Hertzog's Nationalists remained vociferous. Firmly opposed to Botha and Smuts, D.F. Malan agitated against their policies and in absolute frustration Botha blurted out in a meeting in Vosberg that he had sacrificed far more for South Africa than Malan ever would.[116] Whilst claiming a history of struggle against the British Empire during the Second Anglo-Boer War, Botha continued to stress the importance of seeing the war effort through and that South Africa, if it wanted to be a respected member of the international community, could not turn its back on Britain. Any challenge to the constitutional dispensation would have to wait for the end of hostilities in Europe.

But Hertzog quickened the pace in two lectures he gave at Stellenbosch University. They were a media sensation; many commentators saw them as 'constituting a definition of the Nationalist position.'[117] His principal point was that South Africa was entitled to neutrality in times of war and ought not become involved in disputes that did not affect her interests – even if they affected the interests of Britain or the other

112 WSHC: 947/602, Viscount Long of Wraxall Papers, Buxton to Long, 11 May 1917.
113 NARSSA: Engelenburg Archive, 140, Botha to Engelenburg, 13 June 1917; NARSSA: Preller Archive, 93, Botha quoted in 'Premier and his Critics', *Rand Daily Mail*, 21 January 1917.
114 NARSSA: Preller Archive, 93, Botha quoted in 'De Victoria Wes Zetel', *De Volksstem*, 21 January 1917.
115 Van der Waag, *A Military History*, pp.114, 129.
116 NARSSA: Preller Archive, 93, Botha quoted in 'Victoria West Election', *Unknown*, January 1917.
117 WSHC: 947/602, Viscount Long of Wraxall Papers, Buxton to Long, 25 May 1917.

Dominions. He spoke on 4 May on the position of South Africa with respect to the British Empire, and of the 'goggas' (bogeys) with regard to 'the Empire'; on the 'the Flag' question, and possible 'Independence'. His second lecture followed on 11 May. Walter Long summed it up as follows: 'He is evidently dissatisfied with everything and everybody, and occasionally some of the sentences quoted by you [Buxton] look as if he was a real rebel. But I cannot help thinking it is more appearance than reality … of course it adds unnecessarily to Botha's difficulties.'[118]

Clearly, while gaining social capital in some circles, Botha was losing political ground. The provincial elections that June shattered any illusions that remained. The Nationalists swept the Orange Free State, which was expected, but now gained substantially in the Cape Province reflecting large gains since the General Election of October 1915.[119] Again Botha vainly attempted to justify the results saying that 55,000 Union soldiers and hence his supporters were on the fronts.[120] Wyndham had predicted correctly that Botha had been too confident in his thinking that the soldiers' votes would not be needed, but he was clearly wrong.[121] The slide had been gradual at first, starting soon after 1910. Even Olive Schreiner, who could be sharply critical, noted to her brother, the South African high commissioner in London: 'I am sick of Botha.'[122] But she disliked Smuts too. She did not trust him, thought him something of a Trojan horse in the South African Party ('He's in the wrong place') and a bad influence on Botha, 'The Cape is mainly rising against the Dictatorship of Smuts; and secondarily of Botha as his instrument. Jan Smuts is hated by our up-country people as even Rhodes & Milner were never hated.'[123] Schreiner no doubt overestimated Smuts' power over Botha. But, by the war's end, the influence of both men in South Africa was vastly diminished.[124]

Botha remained active. He addressed sometimes contentious issues and throughout maintained a high degree of logic and compassion in his thinking. A case in point, which also demonstrated that Botha did not hate People of Colour, was correspondence between the prime minister and Van Deventer, who replaced Smuts as commander of the British forces in East Africa. Van Deventer had made a request for 500 Africans (Basotho or Zulu) to assist with the campaign in dangerous areas as well as 200 Coloureds for service in less dangerous areas. Van Deventer referred to danger in terms of tropical disease. Botha said that he would try and raise the required Coloured servicemen, but he refused to allow Africans to be sent to dangerous locations in East

118 WSHC: 947/602, Viscount Long of Wraxall Papers, Long to Buxton, 4 July 1917.
119 WSHC: 947/602, Viscount Long of Wraxall Papers, Note by Buxton, 15 June 1917.
120 NARSSA: Preller Archive, 93, Botha quoted in 'Fatherland First', *Sunday Times*, 24 June 1917.
121 Van der Waag, *A Military History*, p.322.
122 NARSSA: Smuts Papers, A1, 191, Schreiner to Isie Smuts, 18 October 1913.
123 UCT: Olive Schreiner BC16, Box5, Olive Schreiner to William Schreiner, 6 December 1914.
124 BL: Add MS 87005, Buxton Papers, Buxton to Dulane, 1 November 1918.

Africa, saying that they had suffered enough on campaign.[125] On the sinking of the SS *Mendi*, Botha acknowledged the service of the labour corps members who died with a minute's silence in parliament in 1917.

Botha was now a tired man. From London, Smuts reassured him and encouraged him to stand fast until the end of the war because South Africa was depending on him.[126] After a troublesome parliamentary session, Botha in poor health took much-earned rest on his farm Rusthof.[127] In June 1917, Botha and Annie – herself recovering from a spell of illness – attended the grand opening of the South African Party club.[128] Botha's condition worried Engelenburg, the party's vice-chairperson, and others present. Botha afterwards went to Warmbaths to take the waters and F.S. Malan deputised for Botha during this time.[129] Leyds asked Engelenburg, who remained in contact with Botha throughout his recuperation, to keep a close eye on events and where possible to keep him informed without bothering the general.[130] During this time Smuts, with Botha's encouragement, had taken up his position in the War Office.[131]

Botha remained relatively cheerful. In June 1917, he had told a provincial council election meeting at Robertson, and through them the country, how the Nationalists had misled and deceived the electorate on four particular scores: the Rebellion, the commandeering for the overseas contingents, the 'One Million' question, and the allegation that Smuts in England was 'selling them'.[132] In referring to the rebellion and the wider war, Botha affirmed his understanding of the Afrikaner people:

> How could the older section of the people be expected to have the same enthusiasm for war or the British Empire as the English Afrikander. But I desire to emphasise that they cannot be accused of disloyalty if perhaps they did not display that great enthusiasm. And no one would blame them because of that. While as regards to honesty and loyalty they stood back for no one.[133]

The 'One Million' colloquially was the 'Overseas Pay' issue that gave regular trouble. Buxton, who felt that Botha's government had mishandled it and was as a result 'in a

125 DODA: Secretary for Defence Group 2, 765, Correspondence between Botha and Van Deventer, June 1917.
126 Smuts to Isie, 31 March 1917, Hancock and Van der Poel (eds.), *Selections*, vol. III, p.471.
127 Engelenburg, *Botha*, p.286.
128 NARSSA: Engelenburg Archive, 140, Botha to Engelenburg, 13 June 1917.
129 Meintjes, *Botha*, p.288. See also F.A. Mouton, *Prophet without Honour, F.S. Malan: Afrikaner, South African and Cape Liberal* (Pretoria, Protea Boekhuis, 2012).
130 NARSSA: Leyds Archive, 262, Part II, Leyds to Engelenburg, 6 August 1917; Engelenburg Archive, 140, Botha to Engelenburg, 20 August 1917.
131 Hancock and Van der Poel (eds.), *Selections*, vol. III, p.529.
132 WSHC: 947/602, Viscount Long of Wraxall Papers, Botha quoted in a note by Buxton, 26 June 1917.
133 Botha quoted in Buxton, *General Botha*, p.174.

tangle', approached London for a concession. But this was complicated by the government's negotiations to sell the maize crop, other foodstuffs, and the wool clip to a hungry, needy Britain. Buxton had urged the South African government to send all they could to the UK, but, Botha's government, wanting to respond, feared criticism from farmers and the electorate in a country where – in Buxton's view – there was 'no apparent need for economy of consumption'.[134] Botha could only do what he could, not what he might have wished to do.

In September 1917, after his spell in Warmbaths, Botha visited Buxton. He unburdened himself to the governor-general, who, in many ways, assumed the role of Smuts as Botha's friend and confidante. After his death, Annie would write to Buxton to tell him how much Botha had appreciated his trust and enjoyed being called upon by Buxton to discuss matters of state. In turn, Buxton was taken with Botha's manner and the interesting way he phrased things in English, with an Afrikaans twang. Allowing graphic expression, Botha would say 'we are not yet out of the bush', or in moments of crisis, speaking about his opponents, he would say, 'knock 'em in the veld'.[135] One can almost imagine a dashing Botha leading the first raid into Natal during the Anglo-Boer War saying 'knocking 'em in the veld' or perhaps before the final envelopment of the *schuztruppen* in German South West Africa. Buxton's fondness for Botha was personified in a statement he made in January 1918: 'it is always a pleasure to do anything for Botha, as he always makes such nice acknowledgements of our efforts'.[136]

On this visit, Botha revealed the truth about his health to Buxton. His first meeting with his doctor, a Dr Smith, had revealed that he was not ill but was overworked. On consultation with a Dr Knight and after undergoing a second examination, Botha was diagnosed as having a heart condition, which required immediate treatment. Botha promised that he would adhere to the prescription and treatment suggested by Dr Knight. Buxton then recommended that Botha go for another consultation, because Dr Knight had said that if Botha did not 'take care of himself' he would die in four to five years. But Botha did not lessen his workload. He was desperately concerned about the wool clip and the Wolmarans libel lawsuit. Meanwhile, Buxton was worried about Botha's health condition, saying that it, 'gave cause for serious anxiety.'[137] Buxton began to make contingency plans in the event that Botha passed away, in which case Smuts would be forced to return.[138]

In September 1917, Botha was in court. Senator A.W.D. Wolmarans had attacked Botha's character, accusing Botha of boasting about killing rebels and – colluding with Smuts – of changing the borderline of German South West Africa on a map,

134 WSHC: 947/602, Viscount Long of Wraxall Papers, Buxton to Long, 7 June 1917.
135 Botha quoted in Buxton, *General Botha*, pp.223–225.
136 BL: Add MS 87052, Buxton Papers, 1914-1918, Notes taken by Buxton, 4 January 1918.
137 BL: Add MS 87005, Buxton Papers, Buxton to Dulane, 1 November 1918.
138 Memorandum by Lord Buxton, 14 September 1917 in Hancock and Van der Poel (eds.), *Selections*, vol. III, p.561.

which then gave an inaccurate position of the German troops to justify the German South West African campaign. Wolmarans also alleged that Botha had said that 'he was going to have a whole lot of our people shot'.[139] Botha had opened a case of libel in October 1916, and Wolmarans counter-sued for a remark that Botha had made about his courage. Botha in his reply explained that the area in question on the map was in and around Nakob and that the map had not been altered in any way. He also explained that the alleged comment about shooting his people took place when he fought Beyers during the rebellion in 1914. Botha explained that, when he went out to Commisiedrift, he gave the order for the rebels to be captured and specifically not shot.[140] And this, as he noted, at a time when the rebels were using white arm bands – then used as identifiers for government commandos – to ambush government forces.[141] If Botha had used words along the lines of killing rebels, then he most likely had done so at this time.[142] Botha, clearly pained by the accusations and the ensuing court case, recalled an occasion, following the accidental death of De la Rey, when Wolmarans had said that Botha had blood on his hands. Botha also explained his own impugning of Wolmarans's courage. This related to events during the Anglo-Boer War when Wolmarans had accompanied Kruger to the Netherlands. Wolmarans had not returned but stayed in Europe until after the end of the war, instead of returning and taking up arms. In the end, the two men settled their dispute out of court. Wolmarans covered Botha's costs.[143] This was a moral victory if not a complete one, but it came at an important time for the prime minister.

Botha never got the rest he needed, although he assured Smuts that his health was improving and that Smuts should remain in London while he took care of local politics.[144] In October 1917, he was at the South African Party Congress, where in a speech he seamlessly addressed political, strategic, domestic, and agricultural matters and appeared to do so with aplomb. In his characteristic manner, he welcomed and charmed conference delegates and party members and spoke of the difficulties while thanking them individually for their sacrifices and hard work 'in these dark days.' The South African Party had 'shown what it means to be a South African'.[145] Botha's tone and enthusiasm impressed the governor general, who wrote to Smuts: 'I am glad to say

139 Meintjes, *Botha*, p.288.

140 NARSSA: Preller Archive, 106, Botha quoted in 'De Botha-Wolmaranszaak', *Ons Vaderland*, 21 September 1917.

141 DODA: Diverse 1, Box 57, General Botha's Operations against the Rebels, Botha to Smuts, 13 November 1914.

142 A case in point of this tactic was when J.J. Alberts was deployed to engage Kemp. His advance force was captured after being lured in under a rebel white flag of surrender. DODA: AG 1914–1921, Box 8, Armoured Trains Colonel, Alberts report to General Smuts after the action at Treurfontein 19 October 1914.

143 Meintjes, *Botha*, p.289.

144 Smuts to Isie, 5 October 1917, Hancock and Van der Poel (eds.), *Selections*, vol. III, p.556.

145 UNISA: South African Party Central Congress 1911-1923, 2, Address by General Botha, September 1917.

that Botha has, in spite of heavy physical and mental strain involved in attending the South African Party conference, continued to improve.'[146]

Botha solidified his reputation as a war leader at this conference. His main address was imposing and appropriate, and, ranging matters political and strategic, he had defined his understanding and his government's objectives in terms of a better peace for the war-weary world. As he explained himself:

> In guns of heavy calibre, we are safe, and we can meet the enemy on any battlefield. In aeroplanes we are the masters. Our whole organization shows it is growing and therefore no one need be a pessimist over the result of the war in Europe. Our position today is better notwithstanding a serious revolution has broken out in Russia. Our case is good, and the war will result in our favour.[147]

He received loud applause. He had spoken as a son of the Empire, an imperial general, and South Africa's prime minister. His reference to 'our whole organisation' meant the armed forces of the Empire and, while a military man himself, he never presumed to know the intimate details of campaigns in which he was not directly involved. And he referred to Smuts, showing his own pragmatism and faith in his good friend, 'I am talking from afar, where one does not have anxiety and care and hunger, and where one never hears a cannon-shot or sees an aeroplane, and I am not in the best position to judge. I know your judgments and know they are good, and I abide by them.'[148]

At the conference, Botha also referred to the Nationalist attacks on his war policy and his reputation as well as the missed opportunity – due to internal political differences – to sell the maize crop at a higher price and control the monopoly. He likened this to the politics of the wool clip and the sacrifice of real economic opportunities on petty political altars.[149]

Some months before, the Imperial Wool Scheme had been the cause of earlier political heckling that was now characteristic of South African domestic politics. In May 1917, the British government offered to buy the entire wool clip for 55 percent above the pre-war rate. Following this announcement, Japan and the United States put forward a greater demand for wool at higher prices. The increased demand made the farmers, who had already committed to the wool scheme, feel that they were hard

146 Buxton to Smuts, 5 October 1917, Hancock and Van der Poel (eds.), *Selections*, vol. III, p.558.

147 UNISA: South African Party Central Congress 1911-1923, 2, Address by General Botha, September 1917.

148 Botha to Smuts, 26 February 1918 in Hancock and Van der Poel (eds.), *Selections*, vol. III, p.610.

149 NARSSA: Preller Archive, 93, 'ZAP Kongress', *De Volksstem*, 2 October 1917. See also Garson, 'South Africa and World War 1'; Nasson, *Springboks*; Krüger, *Age of the Generals*, 108; Van der Waag, 'Hugh Archibald Wyndham', p.282.

done for their loyalty to the Botha government.[150] The matter was immediately political. Many farmers, a considerable number of whom were National Party supporters, believed that the government was attempting to coerce farmers to sell their stock to the state, and Nationalist politicians – seizing the moment – advised them not to sell their wool to the Botha government. The situation was eventually resolved. Botha and Buxton had to convince Whitehall to allow farmers who had entered the scheme to withdraw voluntarily if they so wished and sell their clip to Japan or the United States. However, Botha succeeded in persuading a significant number of wool producers to adopt the deal. While producers that sold to the United States and Japan made better returns, those who opted for the imperial scheme received good returns too.[151]

For Botha, the matter had been very serious, and the wool crisis – as it came to be called – continued into 1918. Yet, Engelenburg, who perhaps had reason to do so, brushes over the whole matter in his Botha biography. As editor of the *Volksstem*, a government-inclined newspaper, Engelenburg published another article on the 'wool question' in early 1918. This frustrated Botha, who wrote to Engelenburg and dressed down his old colleague for publishing articles that created further divisions and possibly even unrest and referred specifically to the wool clip.[152] In contrast, Buxton dedicates a section of a chapter in his Botha biography to the wool question, which he identifies as one of several alarums or crises affecting the government during the war, and suggests that it gave him, as governor general, 'almost more trouble and anxiety than any other that arose'.[153] As a newspaperman, Engelenburg was impelled to report on the matter, despite Botha's frustration and ire. Engelenburg's article appeared to have had an internal source, which Botha addressed. But the *Volksstem*'s editor denied any government source; the information had come from one external source.[154] But Botha, who would have nothing of it, produced documentary evidence of a leak and told Engelenburg plainly that the *Volksstem* as a 'so-called' government newspaper had the responsibility of due diligence and responsible reporting.[155] The prime minister was convinced that a significant number of *Volksstem* employees were National Party sympathizers.[156] Botha reached out to Buxton, his confidant, on many occasions regarding the wool clip. In December 1917, he told Buxton: 'I am worried to death … I might have to resign'.[157] The wool crisis was a heady mix of politics and economics, and the Nationalists exploited the situation to Botha's detriment.[158]

150 Buxton, *General Botha*, pp.259–260.
151 Buxton, *General Botha*, pp.259–260; Engelenburg, *Botha*, pp.285–286; NARSSA: Preller Archive, 93, 'ZAP Kongress', *De Volksstem*, 2 October 1917.
152 NARSSA: Engelenburg Archive, 140, Botha's private secretary to Engelenburg, 16 January 1918.
153 Buxton, *General Botha*, p.256.
154 NARSSA: Engelenburg Archive, 140, Botha's private secretary to Engelenburg, 16 January 1918, and Engelenburg to Botha, 21 January 1918.
155 NARSSA: Engelenburg Archive, 140, Botha to Engelenburg, 20 February 1918.
156 Botha to Smuts, 13 April 1916 in Hancock and Van der Poel (eds.), *Selections*, vol. III, p.358.
157 BL: Add MS 87052, Buxton Papers, 1914-1918, Botha to Buxton, 21 December 1917.
158 Krüger, *Age of the Generals*, p.106.

For the prime minister, the wool question remained serious. As Buxton noted, this, with several other crises, 'raised unforeseen storms and jeopardised the life of the Government.'[159] But the mealie question was equally significant. Botha was critical of the South African farmer – they had sold their maize for less than the minimum amount agreed by the government – and in a speech he questioned: 'why don't they become more business-like? Let them remove politics from their business then we can carry on a business that can pay us in this country.'[160] Botha remained the conscientious farmer and businessman at heart and was never satisfied when he proposed a system, strategy, or course of action aimed at better results, which was then turned down by others without real justification. In September 1917, he told his party's Congress: 'what hurts me is people saying we cannot get trucks and sell their mealies at any price. I say do not be in too great a hurry, see that your mealies are properly dried, and you will get your money.'[161] This may have reminded Botha of the time when his siblings opted to sell their parents' estate instead of allowing him to continue farming there. South Africa was developing at a rapid rate, but the opposition refused to acknowledge this. Now national politics, based on emotion and ties of loyalty, scuppered sensible business at a time when South African industry was modernising and agriculture and trade, so critical to war-time Britain, were also important on Botha's agenda.[162] As he noted to Smuts, agricultural issues had foiled political majorities at the recent provincial elections in rural districts including Standerton.[163]

Attempts to create a new political platform – in Hertzog's view, 'a closer union between a certain section of the English people and the Dutch represented by my party'[164] – came to nought. While many White South Africans were anxious to reach a better understanding between the two language groups and create a foundation of common national feeling, a majority recognised that the Constitution – the Act of Union, freely adopted in 1910 – had provided a foundation on which South Africans might build their national life. As Patrick Duncan told Hertzog, the Act had 'laid down a fair settlement as between the two White races and providing a guarantee for our external protection and free internal development.'[165] While neither perfect nor 'the last word in our history', the very peace of South Africa depended on '*our* abiding by it' especially with 'this war raging and the feelings aroused by recent wounds in S.

159 Buxton, *General Botha*, p.262.
160 UNISA: South African Party Central Congress 1911-1923, 2, Address by General Botha, September 1917.
161 UNISA: South African Party Central Congress 1911-1923, 2, Address by General Botha, September 1917.
162 NARSSA: Preller Archive, 93, 'Generaal Botha te Elandsfontein' *De Volksstem*, 5 November 1917.
163 Botha to Smuts, 26 February 1918 in Hancock and Van der Poel (eds.), *Selections*, vol. III, pp.607–608.
164 UCT: D1.19.1, BC294, Sir Patrick Duncan Papers, Hertzog to Duncan, 4 August 1917.
165 UCT: D1.19.2, BC294, Sir Patrick Duncan Papers, Duncan to Hertzog, 10 August 1917.

Africa still so fresh.' Rather, the best they might do, Duncan chided, 'to bring about a better state of things will be a service to our country.'[166]

Botha spread his message and earned the respect of some Nationalists. A discussion between Botha and a National Party member was a case in point. He told Botha, 'General, I was present at the meeting and I am glad that I attended. You clarified certain matters.' Botha responded, 'I am glad to hear that from you Bul [colloquial address].' The conversation proceeded on a friendly note and ended with the Nationalist saying to Botha:

> It is my honour to greet you in front of all these people. I was in the rebellion and your forces shot me, but here I am, there was no other way. Things cannot go on the way they are going now ... we should be closer ... thank you for the advice today ... I am here today ... I will remain a nationalist but here is my hand. Good day general.[167]

Political feeling, however, remained tense. The message to Haig and news of the German advance on the Western Front encouraged nationalist agitation in April 1918 and riots broke out in Johannesburg between National Party supporters and the more extreme Unionists. Hugh Wyndham called the latter 'loyalists' – in the sense that they stood for a rigid upholding of the Act of Union. The riots were worrying. Wyndham, who had served as chief intelligence officer for South Africa, believed that another rising had threatened. Groups of armed men (commandos), buoyed perhaps by the war news from France, formed in the surrounding farming districts and some eight thousand 'Boers' were alleged to have sworn an oath – reminiscent perhaps of the oath taken at Paardekraal in December 1880. Engelenberg suspects that Botha attempted to re-appropriate the Paardekraal celebration, recasting it as a Boer and British event, epitomising the new united White South Africa. But the Nationalists were not biting.[168] It was a clumsy attempt by Botha. There are some parallels with Botha's earlier attempt at drawing attention away from the Boer War's Women monument, an initiative promoted by Steyn and Hertzog. On that occasion Botha put forward the idea of a Voortrekker monument and tried to use it to commemorate Boer and British histories. Botha tried to re-write history using cultural symbols. Steyn was quick to point out the historical disharmony, and the sheer lack of logic in such a proposition. One can only imagine the outrage given that trekboers and voortrekkers were in large part motivated by disdain of British rules, taxes, and laws. The monument was a non-starter. However, the theme was to re-emerge during the twentieth century, when Afrikaner Nationalism peaked, and the so called 'Great Trek' became their founding story, an origin myth – again

166 UCT: D1.19.2, BC294, Sir Patrick Duncan Papers, Duncan to Hertzog, 10 August 1917.
167 NARSSA: Preller Archive, 93, 'Ik is nie Bang vir Jou nie', *De Volksstem*, 1 November 1917.
168 Engelenburg, *Botha*, p.314.

a historical revision. It was the expression of Afrikaner Nationalist independence, a theme closely tied with anti-British sentiment.

Speeches and leading articles appeared in the press and a Cape Nationalist – 'one of the most bitter' Maud Wyndham tells us – spoke at a meeting in the Johannesburg Town Hall where they took down the Union Flag. A rumour spread that the flag had been dishonoured ('torn into shreds and spat on') and the British crowd outside, then at fever pitch, marched to and raided the Nationalist Club. Nobody was hurt but the event had a sequel when Hertzog was assaulted on the steps of Parliament in Cape Town by an excited Johannesburg railway fitter.[169] Colin Steyn appeared to assist Hertzog and 'a very truculent little wife of a Unionist member (a niece of Dr Jameson's) went and belaboured Colin Steyn.' Three policemen, unwilling to intervene in a fight between members of parliament, watched until, in a bizarre twist of events, Wyndham and Colonel T.E. Fowle, the Provost Marshal, went to Hertzog's assistance. Mrs Wyndham noted: 'Someone said it was such a sign of the times that after it was all over the only thing left on the scene of the fray was a woman's broken umbrella.'[170] Nationalists from all parts of the country were outraged. They held public meetings, made resolutions, and demanded that Botha take steps to charge 'the rabble' that had burned the Club and assaulted Hertzog, their general, in such cowardly fashion.[171] The *Volksstem*, Botha's mouthpiece, happily proclaimed that two 'Englishmen' had saved the old general.[172]

The political situation seemed to improve through May. The South African Party had their provincial congresses during the month and Botha, generally pleased with their outcome, retried to Pietermaritzburg, where his daughter lived, for some rest. But the country was in poor shape. Services strikes took their toll. No trains were running in Johannesburg, where the men at the power station demanded higher wages. The Nationalists, some Unionists argued, 'have a great opinion of strength and success.'[173] They would be subdued as long as the Entente and Associated Powers appeared to be winning the war but should the balance shift in Germany's favour, they would become more energised and forceful. That March, Hester Carter, wife of the archbishop of Cape Town, sat next to Botha at a luncheon at Government House. Botha, very pessimistic, told her that 'he thought if the war went on much longer there would be a revolution in every country.'[174] South Africa, like so many other countries, faced further industrial action and rampant Afrikaner separatism. Troops were

169 WSRO: Petworth House Archives, Maud Wyndham to Lady Leconfield, 26 April 1918.
170 WSRO: Petworth House Archives, Hugh Wyndham to Lady Leconfield, 26 April 1918, and Maud Wyndham to Lady Leconfield, 26 April 1918.
171 NARSSA: PM 1/1/48, file 4/75/1917 European War Resolutions re War, P.C. van Niekerk to Botha, 24 April 1918, and Bestuur Publike Vergadering, Brakpan, to Botha, 23 April 1918.
172 NARSSA: Preller Archive, 93, 'Generaal Botha', *De Volksstem*, 17 May 1918.
173 WSRO: Petworth House Archives, Maud Wyndham to Lady Leconfield, 9 August 1916.
174 Wits: AB186 Archbishop William Carter Papers, Carter to Lawley, 3 March 1918.

mobilised in July 1918 to protect the mines and a general strike was averted. Many wanted dramatic security intervention; Wyndham sardonically remarked that nobody but 'a comparatively harmless international socialist called Bunting' was arrested for 'Bolshevism'.[175] More seriously the 'Great Flu' arrived in South Africa in October, taking six per cent of the population in just six weeks.[176] The world was changing.

During mid-1918, Botha's physical condition deteriorated and during a tour he caught a cold. He increasingly complained of feeling faint and took some time off for rest and recovery in August 1918. At the end of the month, D.F. Malan, the ardent Cape nationalist, made his famous declaration on South African independence.[177] F.S. Malan, then acting prime minister, 'took the battle to the NP.'[178] Botha had cancelled his tour of the Orange Free State which had been scheduled for August.[179] His state of health caused considerable concern to those close to him and to the centrist people of South Africa. A.G. Robertson, the Administrator of the Transvaal, who then chaired a provincial council dominated by Nationalists and Labourites, wrote to Smuts saying that Botha was despondent and believed that he would not live beyond 56 years because his brother and father had died at that age. Robertson reported also that when it came to his diet, Botha was 'like a child.'[180] Meintjes makes a similar point; when on the ship on the way to London to attend the peace negotiations, Botha would squabble with Annie when she refused to give him preserved ginger, which he found delicious. He would then threaten that unless he was given his treats, he would not do his morning exercises.[181] Buxton despairingly wrote of Botha: 'the general is a cross between a very self-willed naughty child and a fowl of the air.'[182]

Conclusion

The war ended on 11 November 1918. The world had changed in all spheres. South Africa, despite the turmoil and unjust political dispensation, had settled down to a

175 WSRO: Petworth House Archives, Hugh Wyndham to Lady Leconfield, 12 July 1918. Bunting would become a key figure in the Communist Party of South Africa. The events of 1918 are discussed in Allison Drew, *Between Empire and Revolution; A Life of Sidney Bunting, 1873-1936* (Pretoria: Unisa Press, 2009), pp.108–110.

176 Howard Phillips, *Plague, Pox and Pandemics* (Auckland Park: Jacana, 2012), p.68.

177 D.F. Malan, 'Die Onafhanklikheid van Suid-Africa', 31 August 1918 in S.W. Pienaar and J.J. Scholtz (eds.), *Glo In U Volk; Dr D.F. Malan as Redenaar, 1908-1954* (Cape Town: Tafelberg, 1964), pp.19–36.

178 Mouton, *Prophet Without Honour*, p.127.

179 NARSSA: Preller Archive, 106, 'Generaal Botha's Gezondheid', *De Volksstem*, 9 August 1918.

180 Robertson to Smuts, 11 August 1918 in Hancock and Van der Poel (eds.), *Selections*, vol. III, pp.669–670.

181 Meintjes, *Botha*, p.293.

182 BL: Add MS 87093, Buxton Papers, Buxton's notes on Botha, not dated.

normality, a normality disrupted by the outbreak of a world war. But, as Lady Cobham assuaged her family in Johannesburg, life had 'a weird way of "settling down" again. In 1916, they had had to "settle down" to the war.'[183] After 1918, they would have to 'settle down' to the peace and what it brought.

Botha and Smuts, while sharing many experiences, including command in their first campaign, had two very different wars. After returning victorious from Windhoek in July 1915, Botha remained largely at home. He was constantly perturbed by events that seemed beyond his control, or soon became so. There were numerous issues: the maize, wool, espionage, Natal and Native contingent issues, German charges regarding Ovamboland, the question of the war estimates, and the changing political face of South Africa. His rejection by his people – first during the rebellion and then at the ballot box – came as a particularly heavy blow. He felt let down. Nationalist agitation in and out of Parliament spread from the Orange Free State to the Transvaal. The Unionists, Botha's war-time political allies, shifted uneasily with the Nationalists emboldened by Woodrow Wilson's 14 principles including that on self-determination. Neither Botha nor Smartt thought another rebellion likely.[184] But both were certainly worried men.

On the other hand, Smuts, who spent the first months of the war in its administrative machine in Pretoria, left South Africa in early 1916. For him, the war presented opportunities to prove his mettle on a larger stage; first in East Africa in command of British troops, and then in London in his extraordinary role with the War Cabinet. This he seized, taking considerable care to shape a public narrative of South African loyalty and military success at a time when Botha experienced increasing difficulty in showing political accomplishment at home. Once in London, then still the hub of the largest empire in history, he commented publicly and shaped thinking on several matters that lay close to his post-war vision: the recasting of the British Empire as a Commonwealth of Nations; the Allied war aims and the nature of the peace; and the first formulation of the idea of a League of Nations. Others argue that Smuts's 'wisdom came to be exaggerated', and that he took a 'lordly philosophical view of world affairs', but his 'versatility and industry are beyond question'.[185] Regardless of the many interpretations, Smuts was uniquely placed to achieve these aims. He was in London, at the centre of imperial power, and in a cabinet where, constituting no political threat to his colleagues in the War Cabinet, he provided their counterpoise in the eyes of a distrusting British public.[186] This independence and the 'unpleasant tasks' that Lloyd George asked him to undertake, gave Smuts the unique opportunity to reach for objectives – political and constitutional – otherwise beyond the purview of such a young country.

183 HHA: 2/30/12, Lady Cobham to Maud Wyndham, 26 January 1917.
184 WSHC: 947/602, Viscount Long of Wraxall Papers, Note by Buxton, 7 and 14 June 1917.
185 Grigg, *Lloyd George*, pp.64, 540.
186 Crafford, *Jan Smuts*, p.141.

10

A Better Ending?

There is much to make us profoundly sad and almost to despair of the future of the race when we see our greatest intellectual and scientific discoveries turned like so many daggers at the heart of civilization.

Smuts to Wolstenholme, 29 November 1915[1]

Through our own efforts and our own sacrifices, we have secured a voice in the ultimate disposal of this subcontinent ... South Africa, instead of being a small, cramped, puny country, gnawing at its own entrails, will have a larger freedom and a better life, and will become the great country which is its destiny.

Smuts[2]

Botha's policy of conciliation was a symptom of his philanthropy; Smuts's League of Nations Covenant was the creation of a virtuoso in the sphere of constitutional law. Botha's intellectual biography might be compressed into a single monumental chapter; General Smuts's runs into periods, embracing whole phases of mental endeavour.

Engelenburg[3]

The Union of South Africa was unique among the Dominions of the British Empire. Her geo-strategic position at the southern tip of Africa, where sea routes converged and her soil gave of its bounty in food and resources, was of vital importance to Britain and her allies. South Africa was also the only Dominion to border the German Empire, which had incited an internal rebellion and offered the opportunity for Botha and Smuts to fight their own campaign and secure an early victory for Britain and her hard-pressed allies in Europe. However, the constraints of the Defence Act

1 Smuts to Wolstenholme, 29 November 1915 in Hancock and Van der Poel (eds.), *Selections*, vol. III, pp.324–325.
2 As quoted in Crafford, *Jan Smuts*, p.133.
3 Engelenburg, *Botha*, p.333.

– which allowed only the attestation of soldiers from the small White, male population – and the political and racial divisions in the country, dramatically and needlessly restricted the available manpower pool for South Africa to contribute to the war effort. Notwithstanding this, several expeditionary forces crossed South African borders or left its shores. An infantry brigade, heavy artillery batteries, and several ancillary units sent to France earned a reputation around which Botha and Smuts – using novelist and war writer John Buchan in no small measure – constructed an interwoven narrative of Dominion valour and South African nationalism.[4] In so doing, as Smuts noted, South Africa had 'secured a voice' in her future and 'the ultimate disposal of this subcontinent.' While a significant building block in the construction of a White South Africanism, the war did not come cheaply. Heavy casualties and the extended campaign in East Africa opened a debate – argued throughout this volume – on South African participation in foreign wars, the development, design and preparation of appropriate, modern, armed forces and their use as foreign policy instruments in far-off theatres, on military planning and, as the armed Rebellion illustrated, on the interface between foreign campaigning and domestic politics.

Botha and Smuts were lionised abroad; they were former Boers, successfully reformed, and firmly part of a British Empire for which they had recently fought – on the field of battle and in the halls of diplomacy. In South Africa, where the political and military leadership was combined in the duo, the two men together bore responsibility for the design, pursuit, and execution of South Africa's war policy. Following the fall of the Tsar, this placed them in a unique position in terms of the Allied wartime leadership. On them alone rested the heavy burden of explaining to the South African public the necessity of Union participation in the war, of their conduct of the war, and their achievement of war goals. Globally the public were tired of the war, and of its human and material costs. South Africa was no different. Ideas that the German East African campaign had been 'badly bungled' and that Lettow 'ought to have been caught' received wide currency. Others saw it as 'a shocking waste of money.'[5]

Eric King, a sapper from the South African Signal Company, tried to gain entry to a university in Britain after the war. But his health broke and he had to be invalided back to South Africa. This was, as he explained, 'a severe disappointment but quite unavoidable. My plans for the future are still to be extracted from chaos.'[6] Others seemingly managed to pick up the pieces more easily. Harry Marshall, an officer with the 1st Cape Corps Labour Regiment, wrote to James Metcalf from Rouen of a friend of theirs, a certain George, who had been gassed at Delville Wood but was

4 Nasson, *Springboks*, pp.205–218. See also I. van der Waag, 'Contested histories: official history and the South African military in the 20th century' in J. Grey (ed.), *The Last Word? Essays on Official History in the United States and British Commonwealth* (Westport, Connecticut and London: Praeger, 2003), pp.27–52.

5 UCT: BC 477 Purland Family Collection, J.B. Moffat to Captain Purland, 5 January 1919.

6 UCT: BC 477 Purland Family Collection, Eric B. King to Captain Purland, 30 July 1919.

then convalescing, married in the meantime, and with the Reserve Battalion of the 4th South African Infantry.[7] However, there were many that sympathised with N.W. Nichol's argument regarding politicians of all nationality: 'There is no doubt the politicians ought to get it in the neck, it's an awful shame that the soldiers should be the only ones to suffer.'[8] The politicians, Newton-Thompson complained, were 'prepared to fight to the last drop of blood of the soldiers at the front.'[9] Many politicians in belligerent states would suffer dramatic losses in electoral support and the loss of office at the next elections. This chapter addresses these issues in three ways: Botha and Smuts's attendance of the Paris Peace Conference, Botha's death and legacy, and the poisoned chalice Smuts inherited.

Coming to Terms with the Carnage: Armistice, Vereeniging and Versailles

Prime Minister Louis Botha was in Cape Town when the news of the Armistice came. November 11 was the birthday of the Italian king, and his consul general hosted a lunch at the Civil Service Club. Their repast was interrupted by a telephone call for Vice Admiral Edward Fitzherbert, the commander-in-chief at Simon's Town. The admiral – with 'sailor-like brevity' according to Rose-Innes – announced that an Armistice had been signed and hostilities on all fronts had ceased. For a moment, there was absolute silence. Then all present 'sprang to their feet, cheered, drank the Sovereign's health and sang God Save The King.'[10] The lunch ended quickly and those there sallied out onto the streets and down to the Grand Parade, where a hymn was sung, and Botha and Smartt addressed the gathering crowds.

Smuts was in London ruminating on the meaning of the war for the post-war world. He had penned the lines in the first epigraph to this chapter in November 1915. War saddened him immensely and offended his deep sense of the generosity of the human spirit. Yet, at the same time, the war offered him unparalleled opportunities: not only to command his own 'show' and test the UDF as an instrument of policy but increase South Africa's influence and perhaps extend her borders to the north. These lay at the heart of South Africa's war policy. Three years later, with the war at an end, Smuts had time on his hands. Moving between London and Paris over the next months, he wrote assiduously to his family, to friends in Britain, and to political and other acquaintances in South Africa. As a result, this period – from the Armistice to

7 UCT: BC 915 James Metcalf Papers, Harry Marshall to James Metcalf, undated.
8 UCT: BC 477 Purland Family Collection, N.W. Nichol to Captain Purland, 1 August 1917.
9 UCT: BC643, Joyce Newton-Thompson Collection, B1.53, Cyril Newton-Thompson to Joyce Nettelfold, 21 July 1916.
10 B.A. Tindall (ed.), *James Rose Innes, Chief Justice of South Africa, 1914–27 Autobiography* (Cape Town: Oxford University Press, 1949), p.265.

the death of Botha and his own accession as prime minister – is the most closely documented phase of his life. Significantly, these 10 months also form their own volume in the seven-part series, *Selections from the Smuts Papers*. In their introduction to this volume, Keith Hancock and Jean van der Poel defined four clear phases in Smuts's writing at this time: a period when he was full of hope for a 'good peace', followed (late March to late April) by growing apprehension, then (first three weeks of May) a period a despair, and finally a time (20 May to 28 June) when Smuts agonised over his personal decision whether to sign the Treaty or not.[11]

But we do not have a similar layer of documentation for Botha, and we need to rest more heavily on the writings of those close to him or who engaged with him in an official capacity. The governor general knew Botha in both roles. Buxton, while never occupying a position in Britain for which his ability and charm entitled him, certainly – as Walter Long noted – had 'come into his own in South Africa.'[12] Local politicians of all hues trusted and confided in him, and all spoke highly of him. In particular, he got on with Botha and Smuts, and in the latter's absences provided one of the supports – alongside Merriman – that buttressed the ailing prime minister. The warmth and closeness of their relationship, and Buxton's deep concern for Botha's health and well-being, permeates the biography he wrote of his prime minister – one of only a few instances where a proconsul did so.

Botha was particularly unwell in November 1918. He and Smuts had caught the 'Great Flu' and were experiencing symptoms at the time of the Armistice.[13] Dr Hugh Smith, Botha's physician, confided to the governor general:

> His illness is to a certain extent as much mental as physical; by which I mean that he is very despondent about himself much more than I have ever seen him before. One bad feature of his illness is this: for some time past he has been obsessed with the idea that he has only about a year to live.[14]

Botha's father had died at the age he would reach at his next birthday, and his older brother had died two years before he reached their father's age. They all shared the same symptoms. Botha was recuperating as a guest of David Graaff at De Grendel and was considering a sea voyage for relaxation when the news of the Armistice arrived together with an urgent call from London to attend a prime ministers' conference. He arrived at Southampton in high spirits and feeling physically restored, although Buxton tells us the strain of official duty in Britain and of the Peace Conference in Paris taxed his health severely.[15] Even at this stage, English-speakers demanding that

11 Hancock and Van der Poel (eds.), *Selections*, vol.IV, p.3.
12 WSHC: 947/540, Viscount Long of Wraxall Papers, Long to Drummond Chaplin16 January 1917.
13 Tindall (ed.), *James Rose Innes*, p.266.
14 Buxton, *General Botha*, p.326.
15 Buxton, *General Botha*, p.327.

he had not done enough, criticised him. Sir Lewis Michell of Cape Town noted in his diary of Botha's reception in London:

> I hope that in making so much of Botha the British public are not worshipping an idol for with perpetual friendliness in speech, he has always, *in S. Africa*, been anti-English in his actions i.e. against giving promotion or fair play to British, as compared with Dutch, citizens of the Union. Coalition is often on his lips, but his words have never been translated into actions. Mrs Botha ... is a clever helpmeet – but also devoted to Boer interests, still they are a fine couple.[16]

Botha and Smuts attended the conference at Versailles as representatives of the Union of South Africa. Men who had signed an instrument of surrender in 1902 sat now around a conference table in Europe – Botha ironically in the chair alongside Milner – and had an opportunity to raise their voices against the intentions of some victors to exert vengeance on the Germans as a people. In this respect they would achieve nothing.[17] The irony, of two former Boer generals supporting Milner in an appeal for moderation in the treatment of defeated Germany was not missed.[18]

While in Paris, Botha and Smuts unexpectedly encountered a situation that forced them to take a stand regarding the constitutional position of South Africa. France, wanting to ensure a weakened Germany, requested the assistance of the other associated powers to achieve this goal. France hoped to bind her war-time allies by treaty to assist her should Germany attack her again in future. On 6 May 1919, in a letter Smuts drafted, Botha raised his objections with David Lloyd George, the British Prime Minister. Any commitment, without the support of the United States, to support France in case of unprovoked German aggression 'would be a most dangerous thing for the British Empire.'[19] Should Lloyd George intend to bind the Dominions in common treaty, he and Smuts wanted the opportunity to discuss the matter with him. Lloyd George placated them for the moment, but Botha followed this up with a second letter – also written by Smuts – that pointed to a future changed constitutional dispensation:

> One result of the perfectly correct exclusion of the Dominions from the obligation which it is proposed to lay on the British people may well be that, in some future Continental war, Great Britain may be at war and one or more of the Dominions may stand out and maintain their neutrality. But that result is inevitable and flows from the status of independent nationhood of the Dominions.[20]

16 WCARS: A540 Sir Lewis Michell Collection, Diary, Monday, 28 July 1919.
17 G.D. Scholtz, *Hertzog en Smuts en die Britse Ryk* (Cape Town: Tafelberg, 1975), p.70.
18 Meintjes, *Botha*, p.296.
19 Botha to Lloyd George, 6 May 1919 in Hancock and Van der Poel (eds.), *Selections*, vol.IV, p.150.
20 Botha to Lloyd George, 15 May 1919 in Hancock and Van der Poel (eds.), *Selections*, vol. IV, pp.158–159.

As the nationalist historian G.D. Scholtz notes, this was eight years after Botha and Frans Malan had declared that South Africa could not remain neutral should Britain be at war; and only two years after Malan repeated this on behalf of the government. And here, while in Paris settling the terms of one war, Botha and Smuts, albeit in private communication, had affirmed the possibility of Dominion neutrality in the next war.[21] Scholtz correctly detects the beginnings of a duality in Smuts's attitude on the constitutional question and South Africa's position in international law, which he would maintain for many years; namely, to maintain different positions in private conversation and in public speech. In large part, Smuts's political position in South Africa depended on the 'English' voter for whom talk of right of neutrality or of secession from the Empire was anathema. As far as his public remarks were concerned, Smuts had to reckon with the feelings of this sector of the South African public. In 1939, when Smuts was prime minister once again, these came to a head when his government was caught between support for the wider war effort and political survival.[22]

Botha and Smuts signed the Treaty of Versailles on 28 June 1919 – on the fifth anniversary of the assassinations in Sarajevo. Botha shared his thoughts on the Treaty with James Rose-Innes, the South African chief justice, on their return voyage to South Africa:

> Of all the brilliant assemblage in the Hall of Mirrors, he and Smuts alone had known, from personal experience, the bitterness of total defeat, and were able to realize the wisdom of clemency. Some of the terms imposed were harsh and unwise. He had been unable to modify them. 'But if we South Africans had refused to sign, we would have been met with the remark that it was good enough for the Germans, but not good enough for us.' That was not a convincing argument, because the Germans had signed under duress; but the difficulty of standing out was obvious. I did not ask why, with his views, he had not associated himself with Smuts's published protest, which subsequent events have so fully justified. But it would seem from Dr Engelenburg's apparently authorised statement that it was Lloyd George who persuaded Smuts to sign, subject to a public protest. Botha had already agreed to become a signatory. His feelings may be gathered from the facsimile of his endorsement upon the agenda papers of 28th June 1919, which ended with the significant words – *Vandag gedenk ek 31st*

21 Scholtz, *Hertzog en Smuts en die Britse Ryk*, p.71.

22 Smuts wrested control of the RNVR and coastal defences from the Royal Navy and established the foundations, much to the chagrin of men in the Admiralty, of a separate, dominion navy. See Ian van der Waag, '"The thin edge of the wedge": Anglo-South African relations, dominion nationalism and the formation of the Seaward Defence Force in 1939-40', *Contemporary British History*, vol. 24, no.4 (2010), pp.427–449.

> *Mei 1902* [To-day I remember 31st May 1902]. Vereeniging was a background to Versailles.[23]

For both men, this was a tangible acknowledgment of South Africa's international status. When Botha returned to South Africa on 24 July, he declared in newsprint, 'They had been successful in obtaining for South Africa a higher independent position. South Africa had been placed on the same footing and treated in the same way like Belgium, Greece and similar small nations … I place this recognition of our status next to the establishment of the Union as one of the milestones in our history.'[24]

Botha and Smuts heralded this enhanced constitutional status as an outcome of their government's war policy. However, the Nationalists viewed matters differently. Hertzog, deputised at a National Party Congress held on 16 January 1919, had been in London and Paris too – at the head of a delegation of eight, two from each province – to demand the right to self-determination and a restitution of the independence of the Boer republics. English-speakers in South Africa were outraged. One veteran wrote: 'The Nationalists are growing strong & are allowed to talk openly of establishing a Republic. They are asking to be allowed to send delegates to the Peace Conference. Did you ever hear of such cheek?'[25] The Hertzog delegation met with Lloyd George on 5 June. The British prime minster replied in writing that neither the British government nor the British parliament could 'reopen a great settlement', which would 'constitute an interference with those rights which were once and for all conceded to South Africa.' He continued, 'At the most solemn moment in its history, the people of South Africa exercised a free, deliberate final choice in a free Constitution of its own creation … The proclaimed principle of self-determination to which you refer has been given effect to by the people of South Africa in the fullest, freest, most solemn and deliberate manner.'[26]

No doubt, Hertzog and his delegation did not expect Lloyd George to fulfil their request; they certainly did not expect him to reply in such definite terms and, using the opportunity they had afforded him, proclaim the success and standing of their political opponents. South Africa had been represented, at 'the greatest conference in history', 'by two statesmen of indubitable Dutch origin who have won for South Africa an extraordinary influence in the affairs of the world.'[27]

Such a public demonstration in Paris of South Africa's control over her own national destiny was enormous. But Smuts in his correspondence with the Gilletts and Wolstenholme had addressed several larger war-related issues and questions

23 Tindall (ed.), *James Rose Innes*, pp.271–272.
24 *Rand Daily Mail*, 25 July 1919, as quoted in Scholtz, *Hertzog en Smuts en die Britse Ryk*, p.71.
25 UCT: BC 477 Purland Family Collection, J.B. Moffat to Captain Purland, 5 January 1919.
26 As quoted in Scholtz, *Hertzog en Smuts en die Britse Ryk*, p.73.
27 As quoted in Scholtz, *Hertzog en Smuts en die Britse Ryk*, p.74.

affecting the post-war world. They had shared ideas on the dangers of a stalemate, of a war of attrition, and of an inconclusive peace. The war had shattered the world order. Dynasties, which had ruled for centuries, fell. Empires, once powerful, dissolved. And Britain, as Margaret Gillett thought, had been thrust into European affairs: 'I suppose England in the rank and file has never been so conscious of "Europe" before, even in the days of Napoleon – that in itself seems to suggest a hope.'[28] Smuts agreed and found solace in deeper, spiritual things. The regeneration, he told Margaret Gillett, 'must come from within, from the soul; mankind must feel the pulsation of a new spiritual life before the wounds will heal and the new order will arise.' He was not particularly troubled in 1916, when he penned these lines, about talk of vengeance on the part of the victors. The war certainly needed a decisive result – as he told Wolstenholme, 'an inconclusive peace might be merely the prelude to a new era of preparedness and costly preparations'.[29] But the war's cost in the destruction of life and material he hoped would be enough to turn people away from bitterness and hatred.[30] Writing in December 1918 in a similar vein, John Buchan noted of the post-war world: 'I am every day more convinced that if we do not secure a workable scheme, we shall not have won the war, and we shall have missed the greatest opportunity in all history. There is a great deal to fight against, hasty idealism as well as perverse stupidity'.[31]

Significantly, at much the same time that Botha departed for Europe, the Inter-Denominational Conference of Native Ministers and Christians of South Africa assembled in South Africa to discuss world affairs. Reverend J. Manille, the conference's secretary, sent a resolution adopted at the conference to the prime minister. The conference protested, on legal grounds and Christian principles, against the legislative frameworks various governments, including Botha's own, had adopted since the end of the Anglo-Boer War. The settlement founded at Vereeniging, and enshrined in the Act of Union, had disenfranchised Black South Africans, while the Native Land Act of 1913 introduced residential and agricultural segregation, and reserved only small parts of the country for African use. Botha, also the minister of native affairs, answered through Edward Dower and maintained that the Land Act was but temporary legislation. His attempts at appeasement were hollow and the largest political question in South Africa's history remained unanswered.[32]

28 M.C. Gillett to Smuts, 14 March 1916 in Hancock and Van der Poel (eds.), *Selections*, vol. III, pp.337–338.
29 Smuts to Wolstenholme, 21 May 1916 in Hancock and Van der Poel (eds.), *Selections*, vol. III, pp.367–368.
30 Smuts to M.C. Gillett, 2 May 1916 in Hancock and Van der Poel (eds.), *Selections*, vol. III, p.362.
31 QUA: John Buchan fonds 2110, box 3, John Buchan to Gilbert Murray, 17 December 1918.
32 NARSSA: Preller Archive, 106, 'Fair Play and Justice', *Rand Daily Mail*, 29 July 1919.

Botha's Death

Botha, then a very tired man, sailed from Britain on the *Llanstephan*. The Peace was proclaimed on the day the ship sailed, and large crowds gathered at Waterloo and Southampton to see him off. A quiet, recuperative voyage of three weeks was required, but no sooner had they left British shores than Botha's health broke and he was confined to his cabin – unable to exercise and troubled 'by profuse haemorrhage from an abscess on the thigh, probably symptomatic of some graver condition.' Rose-Innes, returning to South Africa aboard the same ship, found him 'strangely depressed.' Botha shared his family history with the chief justice: telling him that 'he was nearing the age limit of his kin.'[33] This did not make for pleasant conversation.

On arrival in South Africa, they received a mixed reception. He and Smuts had secured a League Mandate to administer the territory of South West Africa but this fell short of their hoped outright territorial aggrandisement. The National Party and the nationalist press scorned them, painting Botha and Smuts as the lackeys of the British Empire.[34] During August, Botha toured the country, and received ovations and praise from his constituents and party members, but he was clearly a shadow of his former self. He retired briefly to Rusthof, his farm, where he contracted an influenza-like illness, and returned to Pretoria to consult his doctor. He was ordered to bed and strict instructions were issued that he not to be bothered.[35] The incidence of so-called 'Spanish' influenza had been increasing in South Africa since 1918.[36] Buxton believed that the Department of Health had taken insufficient measures to quarantine the disease.[37] On the night of 26 August 1919, Botha passed away in his sleep.[38] Rose-Innes, who spoke to Botha at the funeral of Lord de Villiers, the first chief justice of the Union, recalled that the prime minister had said: 'this is the road we must all travel.'[39]

A state funeral was held for Botha four days later. The South African Party's mouthpiece *De Volksstem* and other newspapers, such as the *Sunday Times*, eulogised him and broadcast news of the funeral.[40] Coen Brits, his close friend and political ally, led a commando of over 100 men who mourned the loss of their general, while soldiers lined the streets of Pretoria West with their weapons behind them. Smuts

33 Tindall (ed.), *James Rose Innes*, p.271.
34 Meintjes, *Botha*, p.301.
35 NARSSA: Preller Archive, 105, 'Generaal Botha's Gezondheid', *De Volksstem*, 25 August 1919.
36 Smuts to Isie, 22 October 1918 in Hancock and Van der Poel (eds.), *Selections*, vol. III, p.681.
37 BL: Add MS 87005, Buxton Papers, Buxton to Long, 5 November 1918.
38 Meintjes, *Botha*, p.302.
39 Innes, *James Rose Innes*, p.273.
40 NARSSA: Preller Archive, 105, 'Generaal Botha's Uitvaart', *De Volksstem*, 30 August 1919; 'Wijlen Generaal Louis Botha', *De Volksstem*, 29 August 1919; 'Patriot and Statesman', *The Sunday Times*, 31 August 1919.

extolled Botha's virtues: 'Botha had a vision ... a South Africa formed of both sections of the White population ... his great work was the Union of South Africa.'[41] Olive Schreiner wrote at the time: 'I've just seen General Botha's death in the papers. There's something sad when the old landmarks disappear one by one.'[42] At the time of the Dominions conference, Maud Wyndham had speculated whether Botha would go; 'it would be unthinkable to be left without him', she thought at the time, 'sheep [the people of South Africa] without a shepherd indeed.'[43] And now he was gone.

With the old landmark gone, and the people of South Africa without their shepherd, the country appeared to be at a turning point. Archbishop Carter, expanding on Botha's significance, compared him to Smuts and the possible road ahead. He told Algernon Lawley, his friend in Britain: 'He was a great man, really great in my opinion, certainly the greatest that this country has produced. And his death coming at this moment is a calamity.' Smuts was clever – 'one of the cleverest' – but he had no influence compared with Botha – not on the platteland. Carter's introspection would be proved correct. Smuts was unable to carry the electorate alone. Many did not trust him. And they in turn were 'too slow for him, and he does not suffer fools gladly.' The Unionists, then still the official opposition, were weak, having lost substantial support at recent provincial and municipal elections. While Botha's death might 'soften the bitter feelings of the Nationalists', Carter predicted that Smuts would become prime minister, unite with the Unionists to form 'a Constitutional party' and in so doing he would 'probably alienate some of the Dutch.'[44]

Yet, surprisingly perhaps, Botha remained a figure of contempt in Natal, the most 'British' of the four provinces, too. Some months after his death, a group of Natalians brought the old man's name into disrepute. For some time, the Defence Council, a statutory body established in terms of the *South Africa Defence Act* and representing language and provincial interests, had become a site of contention. Largely impotent, it met on only 13 occasions between 1912 and July 1918 – a period that witnessed the military integration, the rebellion, and the Great War. Several councillors felt superfluous and objected to being 'merely ... a registering machine for actions by the Department.'[45] Crewe resigned, possibly in protest.[46] After the war, Botha's government had considered a change in colour of the Citizen Force uniform. The members of the Defence Council agreed to the change. Brigadier General Sir Duncan McKenzie, who then represented Natal on the Council, had expressed his preference for retaining the existing colour but did not oppose the government's argument that a change was

41 Meinjes, *Botha*, p.294.
42 HRC: Olive Schreiner Letters, Olive Schreiner to Joan Hodgson, 29 August 1919.
43 WSRO: Petworth House Archives, Maud Wyndham to Lady Leconfield, 14 April 1918.
44 Wits: AB186 Archbishop William Carter Papers, Carter to Lawley, 31 August 1919.
45 DODA: DC, Box 348, file 35930, 14th Meeting of Defence Council, Minutes of 13th Meeting, 20 June 1918.
46 URU: 383, f.2863, De Wet to Buxton, 19 December 1918; NARSSA: GG 29, 1/1149, Ministers' Minute No 2863 of 20 December 1918.

desirable. Colonel Edward Greene, who had commanded the Natal Carbineers, later alleged that McKenzie had not approved of the new cloth and publicly 'charged the Prime Minister with having deliberately made false statements showing them to be false.'[47] Greene came from one of the Old Natal Families with military and naval men on all sides. Well-connected, his kin included the magistrate James Stuart, the last prime minister of Natal, Sir Frederick Moor, and the future chief justice Sir William Solomon. He was no man to trifle with, but Sir Thomas Watt – a draftee of the National Convention, and then a member of the cabinet – wanted to 'expose the hound and turn the tables on him.'[48] In death, Botha remained a divisive figure even in English-speaking circles.

Smuts's Poisoned Chalice

The world breathed a collective sigh of relief following the armistice of November 1918 and braced itself for the inevitable post-war changes. Some forecast a wave of revolutions. Bolshevism, following the October Revolution in Russia, and the export of ideas to countries ready for change, was 'very catching.'[49] In South Africa, the catalogue of immediate concerns included: the inability to reach agreement on questions that were political, economic and social, including the constitutional relationship of the Union to the British Empire; the real prospect of a Nationalist government; and internal dissent and social turmoil, including a range of labour troubles and whispers of revolt. As Maud Wyndham noted in May 1921, the strikes and revolts in Britain were 'just like reading of the war over again.'[50] She was convinced that the one solution to all this revolution and tumult was 'for the last trumpet to sound.' And she wished it would before things got worse.[51] She was referring to Britain, but social turmoil was about to engulf South Africa.

The euphoria of the new South Africa had been short-lived and the fault lines, partly racial, partly ecclesiastical, partly political, but, as Selborne expected, mainly economic, had been exacerbated by the war.[52] The internal threats to the South African state remained three-fold. The first was the perception of a general rising of Black Africans, which, although holding the greatest danger to the colonial state,

47 DODA: DC, box 418, file 51107, 16th Meeting of Defence Council, Bourne to J.W. Moor, 16 February 1920, and Sir Thomas Watt to Secretary for Defence, 18 February 1920.
48 DODA: DC, box 418, file 51107, 16th Meeting of Defence Council, Bourne to J.W. Moor, 16 February 1920, and Sir Thomas Watt to Secretary for Defence, 18 February 1920.
49 HHA: 2/31/68, Lady Cobham to Maud Wyndham, 13 November 1918.
50 HHA: 2/4/35, Maud Wyndham to Lady Cobham, 10 May 1921.
51 HHA: 2/4/34, Maud Wyndham to Lady Cobham, 4 May 1921.
52 Wits: A881 Pim Papers, BL.1, Lord Selborne to Howard Pim, 30 November 1915.

was thought unlikely to occur soon. The second was a workers' revolution inspired by events in Russia, and the third an Afrikaner uprising and seizure of the state, both of which seemed possible, perhaps probable, during the period immediately after the Armistice. In April 1919, Wyndham noted that Johannesburg had a 'taste of Soviet government', when the tramway men and power station men assumed control and turned out the town council.[53]

Yet, perhaps even more disturbingly, Hertzog seemed to draw the support of young Afrikaner men, both in the 'backveld' but increasingly also in the towns, many of whom were intoxicated by the vision of a restoration of the old republics. The defeat of Germany had not assuaged these views as Smuts had hoped. The recent bye elections showed the contrary.[54] The Allied victory had had no effect in stemming the tide of republicanism.[55] Having split with Botha and Smuts and, according to their critics, having violated the spirit of the Union constitution and the 'solemn agreement between the British & Dutch', the Nationalists pushed for secession from the empire and the resurrection of a Boer republic.[56] Their ultra-fringes, according to the 'British' section in South Africa, were again close to outright rebellion in 1919.[57] Keeping the Smuts government in, the Nationalists out, and labour down was becoming increasingly difficult. The continued progress of Afrikaner nationalism was for Smuts, the governing party, and the official opposition – still the Unionists – most disconcerting. It challenged not only the position of English-speakers in South Africa but the very link with the Empire and its institutions.

The Unionists had expected a snap election in 1919. Alfred Hennessey, their chief party organiser, thought Botha would return from Paris with Rhodesia, German South West Africa and possibly a lease of Delagoa Bay 'in his pocket' and go to the country immediately without even whispering coalition.[58] Botha certainly hoped to reunify the Afrikaner people politically – of this the majority of Unionists had never had any illusions. They knew that Botha would take every advantage of their erstwhile, war-time cooperation. Yet, they were confident that they had 'done the right

53 WSRO: Petworth House Archives, Hugh Wyndham to Lady Leconfield, 4 April 1919.
54 BLO: Ms Curtis 802, f. 155, Hugh Wyndham to Reginald Coupland, 4 January 1919.
55 Kent Fedorowich, '"The Weak Link in the Imperial Chain": South Africa, the Round Table and World War One' in A. Bosco and A. May (eds.), *The Round Table, the Empire/Commonwealth and British Foreign Policy* (London 1997), pp.149–150.
56 Wits: AB186 Archbishop Carter Letters, William Carter to Algernon Lawley, 17 January 1919 and 7 June 1919. This view is carried in 'The Men who wanted to break up the Union; UNISA: United Party Archives, Central Head Office, Pamphlets, The Republican Deputation to Europe', anonymous pamphlet published by Wallach's Ltd, Pretoria, 1919. See also 'The Nationalists and the Peace Conference', *The Round Table*, vol.9 (no.34) March 1919, p.620.
57 Wits: A881 Howard Pim Papers. BL.1, see, for example, Selborne to Pim, 10 October 1919.
58 UCT: BC294 Duncan Papers, D1.18.15, Alfred Hennessey to Patrick Duncan, 21 November 1918.

thing' in placing the interests of the Empire before any personal or party advantage.[59] Botha hoped for a majority over all parties, but, if he did not get this, at least for increased strength and that the Unionists would be weakened by Labour, so that if Unionist support had to be obtained, on the numerical basis, it would not mean more than a couple of seats in the cabinet.[60] As Jan Hofmeyr noted, the SAP were unwilling to amalgamate with the Unionists, while the latter remained home to what he described as jingo extremists.[61]

The 1919 parliamentary session opened with a fierce debate on the question of the independence of South Africa from the British Empire. Fired with Wilsonianism, the Nationalists declared themselves in favour of complete independence even if this meant the dismemberment of the Union to attain it. The only hope for the Unionists and the maintenance of the imperial link lay with Botha's supporters – Afrikaners loyal to the Union constitution. The formation of a new party, with Botha as leader, appeared as the only alternative to a possible civil war in which the loyalists could not hope to prevail without imperial military intervention.[62] But this died with Botha. Smuts, for so long heir apparent, did not have Botha's extensive network of patronage, kinship, and broad-based appeal. While Smuts attempted to follow Botha's policy, a great many Afrikaners, who may have followed Botha, refused to follow him.[63]

At the next general election, held on 10 March 1920, Smuts was unwilling to risk coalition with the Unionists before the poll and opposed them in all constituencies.[64] The outcome came as a thunderbolt. The key electoral questions related to soldiers' pensions, profiteering, the cost of living, and increased taxation. All related to the war, and Smuts's South Africa Party and the Unionists, their war-time allies, were held to answer. Voter apathy had also increased among erstwhile supporters of these parties. As a result, support for the SAP and the Unionists declined sharply across South Africa. As shown in Figure 10.1, they were returned with 13 and 14 fewer seats respectively. 'The mistake' always made in South Africa, a newspaper columnist noted after the poll, was 'to imagine that elections are won by a spasmodic blast of wind and thunder for some six or eight weeks before an election contest.' Smuts had simply not done enough on the electoral trail – he had neither the personality nor the inclination to traverse the country as Botha did and at one time enjoyed. The Nationalists, on the other hand, had developed a party machinery capable of forming opinions

59 UCT: BC294 Duncan Papers, D1.34.13, Thomas Smartt to Patrick Duncan, 23 November 1918.
60 UCT: BC294 Duncan Papers, D1.18.16, Alfred Hennessey to Patrick Duncan, 29 November 1918.
61 UCT: BC294 Duncan Papers, A1.28, J.H. Hofmeyr to Patrick Duncan, 22 March 1919.
62 UCT: BC294 Duncan Papers, E41.6.2, Patrick Duncan to Thomas Smartt, 26 July 1919.
63 I. van der Waag, 'Boer generalship and the politics of command', *War in History*, vol.12, no.1 (2005), pp.15–43.
64 RHO: Feetham Papers, Box 5, file 1, ff.1–3, Richard Feetham to his mother, 7 January 1920.

in the press, in the clubs, on the street corners, and in farmers' fields. 'No man', the columnist warned, 'however eminent, must expect that, with our shifting population and the constantly changing borders of constituencies, his personality is known to the electors of his division.'[65] Smuts certainly paid the price.

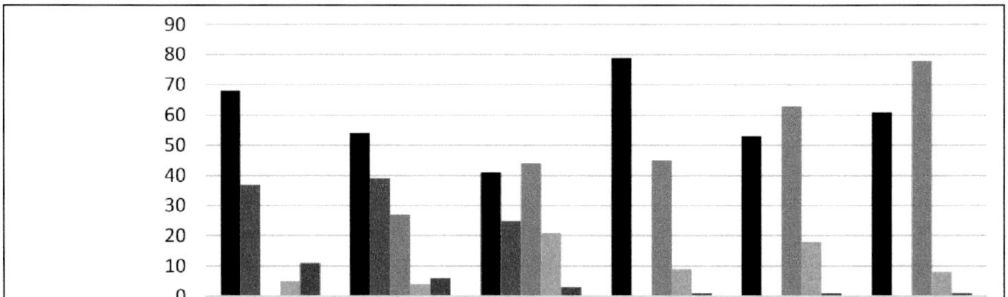

	1910	1915	1920	1921	1924	1929
■ South Africa Party	68	54	41	79	53	61
■ Unionists	37	39	25			
■ National Party		27	44	45	63	78
■ Labour	5	4	21	9	18	8
■ Independents	11	6	3	1	1	1

Figure 10.1: Results of South African general elections held between 1910 and 1929.

The electoral results were catastrophic at the national level. The Nationalists were now the strongest party in the house and Smuts, with the support of the Unionists and independents, could obtain only a bare majority. 'The worst prognostications', Wyndham noted in a post-election letter to his mother, had 'been fulfilled.'[66] Smuts now had to come to terms with the Nationalists and Labour, both of whom had made great gains. Smuts had not garnered a substantial number of Afrikaner votes but, instead, drew substantial 'British' support without which he would have been beaten by the Nationalists. This as some Unionists noted was a good lesson as in the build-up to the election he had 'behaved with his usual slimness in several of the constituencies.' And now with the Unionists considerably weakened, he would have to contend with Hertzog and Cresswell, and without the help of the Unionists 'to pull his chestnuts

65 UNISA: United Party Archives, Transvaal Head Office, Scrapbook No. 1, Chairman of the SA Party Club to Louis Esselen, undated (c.1921). Similar arguments are made in 'S.A.P. Organisation. Questions of Failure and Success', *The Star*, 17 July 1924.
66 WSRO: Petworth House Archives, Hugh Wyndham to Lady Leconfield, 15 March 1920.

out of the fire.'[67] Yet, with no party having an outright majority, and Labour and the Nationalists uncertain as to what to do, another election seemed certain.

Smuts spent the Easter recess trying to form a coalition government, but Labour refused to lose their independence and the Nationalists were prepared to agree but on impossible terms. As a coalition with the Unionists alone would not give Smuts a working majority, the country braced itself for another election. That September, Smuts suffered severe reversals in the provincial council elections held in the Cape and Transvaal and attended the Hereenigings conference at great disadvantage, increasing the bitterness between his own party and the Nationalists. Smuts, however, reluctantly, was forced to a rapprochement with the Unionists, which led to the disbandment of the Unionists Party rather than a merger. Appealing to the South African voter to consider the consequences of his vote, the new South Africa Party claimed a vote for them was the only way to prevent South Africa from becoming another Ireland.[68] But this was not enough. Wyndham had hoped that the formation of a 'constitutional party', embracing loyalists of both languages, would 'tide us over the next few years.'[69] It bought just three years.

While the election, held on 8 February 1921, ended with Smuts remaining in power with 79 seats in the House of Assembly and a majority of 24, it was clear the levee would not hold.[70] Over the next two years, several magisterial districts were convulsed by social turmoil – not in the least on the part of Black South Africans eager to push their legitimate political and socio-economic aspirations. Armed conflict occurred regularly in South Africa and the feelings of fresh bitterness and increasing unemployment pointed to further unrest. At this time, as an expression of South Africa's new status, the last elements of the imperial garrison were withdrawn in December 1921. The rural unrest of 1918 was followed by the Israelite protest at Bulhoek in May 1921, and the Rand Revolt and Bondelswarts uprising in 1922.[71] A sequence of events commencing with the general election in March 1920 had seemingly cumulatively pointed to the end of an era. The rise and then confluence of Labour and

67 WSRO: Petworth House Archives, Maud Wyndham to Lady Leconfield, 9 March 1920. Written over several days.

68 UNISA: United Party Archives, Central Head Office, Pamphlets, 'Gaan Suidafrika 'n tweede Ierland word?' Anonymous pamphlet published by Wallach's Ltd, Pretoria, 1921. The SAP appealed to the voters to 'Vote S.A.P. and Kill Secession' – 'The Voter's Duty', *Rand Daily Mail*, 26 January 1921. For an interesting comparison between the Afrikaner Rebellion (1914) and the Easter Rising (1916) in Ireland see B.M. Nicholls, 'Rebellions in retrospect: "Die rebellie" of 1914 and the Easter rising of 1916 revisited', *Southern African-Irish Studies*, vol.3 (1996), pp.67–88.

69 WSRO: Petworth House Archives, Hugh Wyndham to Lady Leconfield, 13 October 1920.

70 UNISA: United Party Archives, Transvaal Provincial Head Office, Scrapbook No. 1, 'General Elections 1921: Transvaal'.

71 H.A. Wyndham, 'Some aspects of South African defence', *The State: A South African National Magazine*, vol. 2, no.6 (June 1909) and vol.2, no.7 (July 1909). See DODA: DC, Box 451, file 52002 Recalcitrant 'Israelite' Natives.

a resurgent Afrikaner nationalism, representing in the combination of mostly rural Dutch-speakers and the working-class English, the two archenemies of everything Smuts represented, brought his downfall in 1924. This alliance, 'unholy' – in the view of Smuts's South Africa Party – and in the context of the recent past almost unnatural, seemed to usher in a dark age.[72] Politically, South Africa could no longer be saved for the empire and, as an erstwhile Unionist colleague noted, with 'no great national British question at stake' South African politics had become 'dull and degrading.'[73] Their dreams of creating a new White South Africanism as a Dominion within a British Commonwealth had seemingly failed.

Conclusion

The varied, complex roles played by Generals Louis Botha and Jan Smuts during the First World War repay close examination. Unique in this war, they formed the apex of the country's political and military leadership. Fascinating and enigmatic figures, they loom large on the South African, British Imperial and Commonwealth historical landscapes. Exploring their similarities and differences, we find the emotional intelligence of Botha – a man lionised in his own day, and the Union's first Prime Minister – and the intellectual prowess of Smuts, his deputy and the Minister of Defence. They are flawed yet significant figures. Botha appealed to different audiences in a fractured South Africa, demonstrated his understanding and pragmatic approach to business, agriculture and war; but Smuts applied his intellect and energy to South Africa's problems, using the pen and the sword in equal measure, but seemingly with little long-term resolution for the national problems they and succeeding generations of South Africans would face – most of all in creating a free society and equitable political dispensation for all South Africans.

Once prominent, they are today divisive figures that represent different things to different people. This volume attempts to place them in the context of the ongoing historical dialogue. These brilliantly imperfect figures were in some ways like Greco-Roman heroes. They fought seemingly insurmountable odds, and at times achieved great victories, but they were also warriors who made startling errors, and ultimately – in classical fashion – they were crushed by the weight of the world they tried to create.

72 UNISA: United Party Archives, Central Head Office, Pamphlets, 'The Unholy Alliance: What the labour-allies of the National Party think of Religion', anonymous pamphlet published by Wallach's Ltd, Pretoria, 1921.

73 WCARS: A.540 Sir Lewis Michell Collection, vol.1, Charles Crewe to Lewis Michell, 11 December 1925.

Sources

Archival Sources

Private Papers

Bodleian Library, Oxford (BLO)
Curtis – Papers of Lionel Curtis and the Round Table – Mss Curtis
Dawson – Geoffrey Dawson Papers – Mss Dawson
Milner – 1st Viscount Milner Papers – Mss Milner dep., Milner Adds

British Library, London (BL)
Buxton – Sydney Charles, 1st Earl Buxton, personal and family papers – Add MS 86849–77

Essex Record Office, Chelmsford (ERO)
Harris – Letters from Bernard Harris, surgeon, to his wife and daughter, 1915 – TS 634/1

Free State Archives Repository, Bloemfontein (FSAR)
De Villiers – C.C. de Villiers papers – A64/93

Hagley Hall Archives, Worcestershire (HHA)
Cobham – Papers of the 8th Viscount Cobham
Wyndham – Papers of Hon. Mrs Hugh Wyndham

Harry Ransom Center, University of Texas (HRC)
Schreiner – Olive Schreiner Letters

Natal Carbineers Archives, Pietermaritzburg (NCA)
Simes – Trooper Lyle Richmond Simes Collection

National Archives and Records Service of South Africa (NARSSA)
Beyers – General C.F. Beyers Collection – A.414
Engelenburg – Dr F.V. Engelenburg Collection – A.140
Lleyds – Dr Leyds Collection
Preller – Dr G.S. Preller Collection – A.747
Smuts – Field Marshal J.C. Smuts Collection – A.1

National Library of South Africa, Special Collections, Pretoria (NLSA)
Motlke – Dorothy von Moltke papers – MSC 26/2.7/12

Queen's University Archives, Kingston, Ontario (QUA)
Buchan – John Buchan fonds 2110

Rhodes House Library, Oxford (RHO)
Farrar – Sir George Farrar Papers – Mss.Afr.S. 2175
Feetham – Richard Feetham Papers – Mss.Afr.S. 1793
Stanley – Sir Herbert James Stanley papers – Mss Af S.1250

Royal Marines Archives (RMA), Eastney Barracks, Portsmouth
Aston – Major General Sir George Aston Papers – 11/12/38

University of Cape Town Libraries, Cape Town (UCT)
Chaplin – Drummond Chaplin Collection – BC 831
Duncan – Patrick Duncan Papers – BC 294
Lukin – Major General Sir H.T. Lukin Papers – BC 676
Metcalfe – James Metcalfe papers – BC915
Newton-Thompson – Joyce Newton-Thompson Collection – BC 643
Purland – The Purland Family Collection – BC 477
Schreiner – Olive Schreiner Papers – BC16
Stanford – Colonel Sir Walter Stanford Papers – BC293

University of South Africa Library, Archives and Special Collections, Pretoria (UNISA)
Conradie – Senator J.M. Conradie Collection

Western Cape Archives and Records Service, Cape Town (WCARS)
Fremantle – H.E.S. Fremantle Collection – A.608
Malan – F.S. Malan Collection – A.583
Michell – Sir Lewis Michell Collection – A.540
Te Water – Dr T.N.G. te Water Papers – A.467

West Sussex Record Office (WSRO)
Leconfield – Papers of Constance, Lady Leconfield, Petworth House Archives
Wyndham – Papers of Hon. Hugh Wyndham, Petworth House Archives

William Cullen Library, University of the Witwatersrand, Johannesburg (Wits)
Carter – Archbishop William Carter Papers – AB186
Hofmeyr – Jan H. Hofmeyr Papers – A.1
Nourse – The Nourse Family Records – A.743
Paget – Rev. Francis Edward Paget Papers – AB1219
Pim – Howard Pim Papers – A.881

Wiltshire and Swindon History Centre, Chippenham (WSHC)
Long – Viscount Long of Wraxall Papers
Methuen – Field Marshal Lord Methuen Papers

Private Collections
MacDonald – Transcript letters of Padre Colin MacDonald, January to August 1917

Organisation Papers

Archives du Comité International du Croix Rouge/International Committee of the Red Cross, Genève (ACICR)
C G1 A 10-02, Listes de prsionniers allemands et turcs capturés par les Britanniques et listes de prisonniers britanniques capuréres par les Allemands 12.09.1914 – 08.11.1918
C G1 A 24-09, Statistiques mensuelles de la correspondance émise par les prsionniers en mains allemandes et passée par l'Agence, ordonnées par camp, 20.05.1915 – 09.12.1920

William Cullen Library, University of the Witwatersrand, Johannesburg
Church of the Province of South Africa

Archives and Special Collections, University of South Africa Library, Pretoria
United Party Archives – Papers of the Central Head Office, Papers of the Transvaal Head Office, Papers of the South African Party Central Congress

Official Papers

Department of Defence Archives (SANDF Documentation Centre), Pretoria (DODA)

Adjutant General 14
Box 13, Report on the Battle of Sandfontein, 26 September 1914

Adjutant General 1914-1921
Box 8, file Rebellion
Box 8, file Armoured Trains

Box 8, file G5/305/9199 Commander-in-Chief, Government Notice for the next issue of the Government Gazette.
Box 27, file G.23/9199, vol.1, Grant of Commissioned Rank in UDF during Hostilities
Box 150, file Strengths, General Summary, Southern Force
Box 182, file Mounted Strengths, Field state
Box 189, file 489 Coloured Men in Overseas Brigade

Chief Staff Officer (CSO)
Box 2, file 2/6/20 Press Correspondents reports re British East Africa
Box 20, file 22/38 Syphilis and Severe Gonorrhoea

Diverse
Box 1, file 2493 Intelligence Reports.
Box 1, file 2493 Intelligence Reports South West Africa
Box 1, Treason Trials, Rebels Captured and Surrendered
Box 2, Rebellion Commission of Enquiry
Box 2, Evidence given in the Rebellion Commission of Enquiry
Box 13, Diary of the Mission of Brig. Gen. Hon. Sir C.P. Crewe, KCMG, CB, to the Belgians
Box 15, file 199 Colonial Defence Committee Memoranda on General Defence Matters
Box 57, file General Botha's Operations against the Rebels

SA Citizen Force
Box 4, file 61 SA Mounted Rifles
Box 67, file 2508/1 Purchases of Horses

Secretary for Defence (DC)
Box 1, file 12 Members who took part in the debate in Parliament
Box 20, file 51/274
Box 47, file 1063 South Africa Defence Bill
Box 57, file General Botha's Operations against the Rebels
Box 109, files 2270 and 2271 Meetings of the Defence Council
Box 189, file 11122 Correspondence with various people re History of the German South West African Campaign
Box 252, file 17138 Reports of Force Commanders in GSWA, Operations in and around Sandfontein
Box 252, file 17138 IO Historical Record of the campaign in German South West Africa
Box 252, Casualty Lists
Box 252, file Correspondence between General Botha and Lieutenant Colonel Franke on the subject of a breach of armistice by Union troops at Tsumeb
Box 348, file 35930 Meetings of the Defence Council

Box 365, file DC 40057 Intelligence Section
Box 418, file 51107 Meetings of the Defence Council
Box 451, file 52002 Recalcitrant 'Israelite' Natives
Box 573, file D.9199 European Crisis General, vol.7
Box 632, file General Botha
Box 689, file 958/9199 Overseas Contingent
Box 690, file DC 128/958/9199 Applications for Overseas Contingent
Box 756, file Address at House of Assembly by General Louis Botha
Box 765, file Correspondence between Botha and Van Deventer
Box 1142, file DCDB23/94/7 Suggested recall of Brigadier General Cavendish GOC South Africa Military Command and appointment of General Martyn
Box 1193, file 191 Treatment of Venereal Cases

South African Mounted Riflemen (SAMR)
Box 1044, file 516/69 Colonel Brits
Box 1046, file 516/33 Nervous unrest amongst the Public of the North West

World War I German South West Africa (WWI GSWA)
Box 23a, Citations GSWA

World War I War Diaries (WWI WD)
Box 1, file AIR/1/1247/204/1 Report by major Wallace on the campaign in GSWA
Box 2, file AIR/1/1247/204/7/4 Historical record of No. 26 (SA) Squadron South African Aviation Corps and Historical record of the South African unit of the Royal Flying Corps

World War I Diverse (WW1 D)
Box 8

The National Archives of the United Kingdom, Kew (TNA)
Air Ministry
AIR 76/474/129
AIR 1/690/21/20/26 History of 26 (South Africa) Squadron, RAF

Cabinet Office (CAB)
CAB 21/37 War Cabinet and Cabinet Minutes
CAB 23/3/52 War Cabinet and Cabinet Minutes
CAB 23/4/11 War Cabinet and Cabinet Minutes
CAB 23/4/48 War Cabinet and Cabinet Minutes
CAB 23/4/49 War Cabinet and Cabinet Minutes
CAB 23/4/52 War Cabinet and Cabinet Minutes
CAB 23/5/58 War Cabinet and Cabinet Minutes
CAB 23/5/69 War Cabinet and Cabinet Minutes

CAB 23/6/26 War Cabinet and Cabinet Minutes
CAB 23/6/27 War Cabinet and Cabinet Minutes
CAB 23/6/34 War Cabinet and Cabinet Minutes
CAB 23/6/45 War Cabinet and Cabinet Minutes
CAB 23/7/27 War Cabinet and Cabinet Minutes
CAB 23/8/15 War Cabinet and Cabinet Minutes
CAB 23/13/18 War Cabinet and Cabinet Minutes
CAB 23/40/14 War Cabinet and Cabinet Minutes
CAB 24/4/50 Report by General Smuts on his Mission to Egypt, 1 March 1918
CAB 24/11/49 War Cabinet and Cabinet Memoranda
CAB 24/20 First Report, Committee on Air Organisation and Home Defence Against Air-Raids
CAB 24/37/80 Smuts on War Aims January 1918
CAB 24/49/23 War Cabinet and Cabinet Minutes
CAB 38/14/16 South Africa: Defence Scheme (internal), revised to April 1907, 1908
CAB 40 War Cabinet: War Priorities Committee: Minutes and Memoranda, 1917-1919
CAB 45/112 The Campaign in GSWA, Narrative of Events

Colonial Office (CO)
CO 537/521 Defence of South Africa 1909

Dominions Office (DO)
DO 119/890 War Prisoners of War
DO 119/910 War Intelligence German South West Africa
DO 119/924 Oversea Native Labour Contingent Medical Report

Security Service (KV)
KV 1/8 Memoir by William Melville.
KV 1/9 General Report by Captain Vernon Kell, 7 November 1910
KV 1/15 Report on the Establishment of a Counter Espionage Service in the Colonies and Overseas Dominions, 1921
KV 1/16 Report on Lt Col Pakenham's Mission to South Africa, 1 Sep 1917, with Annexures

War Office (WO)
WO 95/4632 1st Battalion Cape Corps, 1918-1919
WO 106/5827 South African war effort 1939-1946, Peacetime organisation of the Union Defence Force
WO 141/31 Report on Medical Arrangements East Africa

National Archives and Records Service of South Africa, Pretoria (NARSSA)

Governor General (GG)
GG 29, file 1/1149Ministers' Minute No. 2863
GG 568, file 9/51/52 War 1914-16: Trade, Exportation of certain forms of steel
GG 568, file 9/51/54 War 1914-16: Trade
GG 597, file 9/57/40 German East Africa to close of campaign
GG 597, file 9/57/41 War 1914-1918: German East Africa
GG 597, file 9/57/42 Personnel: Transport of unfit men from East Africa
GG 597, file 9/57/44 War 1914-1918: German East Africa
GG 597, file 9/57/45 War 1914-1918: German East Africa
GG 597, file 9/57/48 War 1914-1918: General van Deventer's appreciation of the Co-operation of the Belgian Troops in the East African Campaign
GG 667, file 9/93/1 War 1914: Imperial Army
GG 667, file 9/93/7 War 1914-16: Imperial Army, South African Overseas Expeditionary Force
GG 668, file 9/93/19 War 1914-15: Army, Imperial
GG 668, file 9/93/24 War 1914-15: Army, Imperial
GG 668, file 9/93/26 War 1914-15: Army, Imperial
GG 671, file 9/93/68 Recruiting
GG 675, file 9/93/196 War 1914-1918. Army Imperial. Visit of Surgeon-General Pike to Union

Prime Minister (PM)
PM 1/1/30, file 4/93-4/95 European War
PM 1/1/31, file 4/95 European War
PM 1/1/32, file 4/95 European War
PM 1/1/32, file 4/97/1914 War: German South West Expedition & Supply of Ammunition & Guns
PM 1/1/48, file 4/75/1917 European War Resolutions re War
PM 1/1/48, file 4/84/1917 European War SA Brigade Successes
PM 1/1/271, file 147/1 Military

Executive Council of the Union of South Africa (URU)
URU 383, f.2863

Published Sources

Newspapers, Journals and Periodicals

Allen, H.M., 'Louis Botha: Boer and Briton', *The Sewanee Review*, April 1918
Anon., Review of L. Botha's article, 'The Boers and the British Empire', *The Spectator: A Weekly Review of Politics, Literature, Theology and Art*, vol.89 (1902)

Anon., 'Lord Gladstone leaves for home', *The African Review* (July 1914)
Anon., 'Die Appel wat onder die Botha – boom geval het', *Die Beeld*, 17 August 2013
Anon., 'The East Africa Despatch', *The Daily Dispatch* (East London, South Africa), 1 April 1916
Anon., 'Botha', *De Volksstem* (Pretoria), 26 June 1916
Anon., 'Premier and his Critics', *Rand Daily Mail* (Johannesburg), 21 January 1917
Anon., 'De Victoria Wes Zetel', *De Volksstem* (Pretoria), 21 January 1917
Anon., 'Generaal Botha te Malmesbury', *De Burger* (Cape Town), 6 June 1917
Anon., 'Union's Roll of Honour : Deathless Deeds at Delville Wood : Musical Memorial Service in the City Hall : Mr Merriman on South Africa's Heritage', *The Cape Times*, 19 July 1917
Anon., 'Fatherland First', *The Sunday Times* (Johannesburg), 24 June 1917
Anon., 'De Botha-Wolmaranszaak', *Ons Vaderland* (Pretoria), 21 September 1917
Anon., 'ZAP Kongress', *De Volksstem* (Pretoria), 2 October 1917
Anon., 'Lord Gladsone, the Union's first Governor-General', *The Times*, 30 March 1930
Anon., 'Casualties in War', *The Indian Medical Gazette*, vol. 67, no. 2 (February 1932)
Anon., 'Ik is nie Bang vir Jou nie', *De Volksstem* (Pretoria), 1 November 1917
Anon., 'Generaal Botha te Elandsfontein', *De Volksstem* (Pretoria), 5 November 1917
Anon., 'Generaal Botha', *De Volksstem* (Pretoria), 17 May 1918
Anon., 'Fair Play and Justice', *Rand Daily Mail* (Johannesburg), 29 July 1919
Anon., Generaal Botha's Gezondheid', *De Volksstem* (Pretoria), 9 August 1918
Anon., Generaal Botha's Gezondheid', *De Volksstem* (Pretoria), 25 August 1918
Anon., 'Generaal Botha's Uitvaart', *De Volksstem* (Pretoria), 30 August 1919
Anon., 'Patriot and Statesman', *The Sunday Times* (Johannesburg), 31 August 1919
Anon., 'The Nationalists and the Peace Conference', *The Round Table*, vol.9, no.34 (March 1919)
Anon., 'Vote S.A.P. and Kill Secession, The Voter's Duty', *Rand Daily Mail* (Johannesburg), 26 January 1921
Anon., 'S.A.P. Organisation, Questions of Failure and Success', *The Star* (Johannesburg), 17 July 1924
Beaton, A.J., 'Notes on Railway Construction during the campaign in German South West Africa', *Civil Engineering*, vol.14, no.1 (1916)
Vaughan-Williams, Lt Col H.W., 'Medical Services in the East African Campaign, 1916-1917', *South African Medical Journal*, vol. 15, no. 1 (11 Jan 1941)

Published Diaries, Memoirs, Speeches and Letters and Autobiographies

Acutt, F.H., *Sailing Through The Rainbow* (Durban: Knox, n.d.)
Baden-Powell, B.F.S., *War in Practice, some Tactical and Other Lessons of the Campaign in South Africa, 1899 – 1902* (London: Isbister & Co, 1903)
Boyce, George D. (ed.), *The Crisis of British Power: The Imperial and Naval Papers of the Second Earl of Selborne, 1895-1910* (London: The Historians Press, 1990)

Churchill, W.S., *London to Ladysmith via Pretoria* (London: Longmans & Green, 1900)
Churchill, W.S., *My Early Life* (London: Thornton Butterworth, 1930)
Close, Percy L., *A Prisoner of the Germans in South-West Africa* (Cape Town and London: T. Maskew Miller, 1916)
De Wet, C. R., *Three Years War* (New York: C. Scribner & Sons, 1902)
Doitsh, Corporal E., *The First Springbok Prisoner in Germany : Being the Thrilling Experiences of the First South African to return* (London: McBride, Nast & Co., 1917)
Gandhi, M.K., tr. Desai, M., *An Autobiography: The Story of My Experiments with Truth* (Nerul: Prakash Book Depot, 2009)
Gandhi, M.K., *My Experiments with Truth* (Auckland: The Floating Press, 2009)
Hancock, W.K. and Van der Poel, J. (eds.), *Selections from the Smuts Papers* (London: Cambridge University Press, 1966)
Headlam, C. (ed.), *The Milner Papers: South Africa 1899-1905 Volume II* (London: Cassell & Company, 1933)
Jewell, N.P., *On Call in Africa in War and Peace, 1910-1932* (Hove: Gillyflower Publishing, 2016)
Kemp, J.C.G., *Die Pad van die Veroweraar* (Cape Town: Nasionale Pers, 1946)
Lettow-Vorbeck, P.E. von, *My Reminisces of East Africa* (London: Hurst and Blackett, 1920)
Lettow-Vorbeck, P.E. von, *East African Campaigns* (New York: Robert Speller, 1957)
Levyns, J.E.P., *The Disciplines of War : Memories of the War of 1914-18* (New York: Vantage, 1984)
Lloyd George, David, *The War Memoirs of David Lloyd George* (London: Ivor Nicholson & Watson, 1934)
Marais, A.H. (ed.), *Politieke Briewe, 1911-1912: Deel 2* (Cape Town: Tafelberg, 1973)
Maritz, M., *My Lewe en Strewe* (Johannesburg: privately published, 1939)
Maurice, F. (ed.), *The Life of General Lord Rawlinson of Trent: From his Journals and Letters* (London: Cassell, 1928)
Martin, C. (ed.), *Corporal Haussmann Goes to War: Armed with motor-cycle and camera* (Kenilworth: privately published, 2000)
Masterman, L. (ed.), *Mary Gladstone (Drew) Her Diaries and Letters* (London: Methuen & Co., 1930)
Mountevans, Admiral Lord, *Adventurous Life* (London: Hutchinson, 1946)
Natrass, G. and Spies, S.B. (ed.), *Jan Smuts: Memoirs of the Boer War* (Johannesburg: Jonathan Ball, 1994)
Northcliffe, Lord, *At The War* (London: Hodder and Stoughton, 1916)
O'Shaughnessy, W.W. and Rayner, W.S., *How Botha and Smuts Conquered German South West* (London: Simpkin, 1916)
Payne, Adam, *Blow Blow the Winds of Change* (Johannesburg: Pens Editorial and Publishing Enterprises, 1989)

Pienaar, S.W. and J.J.J. Scholtz, eds., *Glo In U Volk: Dr D.F. Malan as Redenaar, 1908-1954* (Cape Town: Tafelberg, 1964)
Reitz, Deneys, *Commando* (Johannesburg: Jonathan Ball, 2012)
Reitz, Deneys, *Trekking On* (London: Travel Book Club, 1947)
Riddell, Lord, *Lord Riddell's War Diary, 1914-1918* (London: Ivor Nicholson & Watson, 1933)
Ritchie, M.E., *With Botha in the Field* (London: Longmans, 1915)
Robinson, P.K.J., *With Botha's Army* (London: Allen & Unwin, 1916)
Rose-Innes, James, *James Rose Innes: Chief Justice of South Africa, 1914-1927* (London: Oxford University Press, 1949)
Sandhurst, Viscount, *From Day to Day, 1916-1921* (London: Edward Arnold, 1929)
Scotland, A., *The London Cage* (London: Evans, 1957)
Seely, J.E.B., *Adventure* (London: William Heinemann, 1930)
Sibley, J.R., *Tanganyikan Guerrilla: East African Campaign 1914 –1918* (London: Pan Books, 1973)
Smuts, J.C., *War-Time Speeches : A Compilation of Public Utterances in Great Britain* (London: Hodder & Stoughton : New York: George H. Doran Company, 1917)
Solomon, V. (ed.), *Selections from the Correspondence of Percy Alport Molteno, 1892-1914* (Cape Town: Van Riebeek Society, 1981)
Tindall, B.A. (ed.), *James Rose Innes, Chief Justice of South Africa, 1914-27, Autobiography* (Cape Town: Oxford University Press, 1949)
Trew, H.F., *Botha Treks* (London: Blackie & Son, 1936)
Trew, H.F., *African Manhunts* (London and Glasgow: Blackie & Son, 1938)
Van der Byl, P., *From Playgrounds to Battlefields* (Cape Town: Howard Timmins, 1971)
Van der Spuy, K.R., *Chasing the Wind* (Cape Town: Books of Africa, 1966)
Viljoen, B.J., *My Reminisces of the Anglo-Boer War* (London: Hood, Douglas and Howard, 1902)
Walker, H.F.B., *A Doctor's Diary in Damaraland* (London: Edward Arnold, 1917)
Warwick, G.W., *We Band of Brothers: Reminiscences from the 1st S.A. Infantry Brigade in the 1914 – 1918 War* (Cape Town: Howard Timms, 1962)
Whittal, W., *With Botha and Smuts in Africa* (London: Cassell, 1917)
Wilson, Keith (ed.), *The Rasp of War : The Letters of H.A. Gwynne to The Countess Bathurst, 1914-1918* (London: Sidgwick & Jackson, 1988)
Young, F.B., *Marching on Tanga: With General Smuts in Africa* (London: W. Collins, 1917)
Young, F.B., *Jim Redlake* (London: William Heinemann, 1930)

Contemporary Literature

Albertyn, J.R., Luckhoff, A.D., Cronje, T.F. and Rothmann, M.E., *Sociological Report: (a) The Poor White and Society, Part V (a) of The Poor White Problem in South Africa: Report of the Carnegie Commission (*Stellenbosch: Ecclesia, 1932)
Anon., *The Times History of the War* (London: The Times, 1915)

Anon., *Union of South Africa and the Great War, 1914-1918: Official History* (Pretoria: Government Printer, 1924)

Bellairs, B., *The Transvaal War 1880-1881* (Cape Town: Struik, 1972)

Bodenstein, H.D.J., *Was Generaal Botha in 1900 'n verrader?* (Amsterdam: J.H. De Bussy, Holl, 1916)

Brunker, H.M.E., *Boer War, 1899 – 1902: Chart showing Organisation and Distribution of the British Forces with a List of Military and Naval Officers and an Account of the Organization and Administration of the Boer Forces* (London: W. Clowes & Sons, 1900)

Buchan, J., *The History of the South African forces in France* (London: Nelson & Sons, 1920)

Buxton, J., *Greenmantle* (London: Hodder & Stoughton, 1937)

Buxton, Lord, *General Botha* (London: Hazel, Watson & Viney, 1924)

Churchill, W.S., *Great Contemporaries* (London: Macmillan, 1937)

Churchill, W.S., *Ian Hamilton's March* (London: Longmans & Green, 1900)

Carnegie Commission, *The Poor White Problem in South Africa: Report of the Carnegie Commission: Joint Findings and Recommendations* (Stellenbosch: Ecclesia, 1932)

Collyer, J.J., *The Campaign in German South West Africa, 1914–1915* (Pretoria: Government Printer, 1937)

Collyer, J.J., *The South Africans with General Smuts in East Africa, 1916* (Pretoria: Government Printer, 1939)

Courtney, W.L. and Courtney, J.E., *Pillars of Empire: Studies and Impressions* (London: Jarrolds, 1918)

Cunliffe, F.H.E., *The History of the Boer War: Volumes 1 and 2* (London: Methuen & Co, 1904)

Dane, E., *British Campaigns in Africa and the Pacific 1914-1918* (London: Hodder & Stoughton, 1919)

Difford, I.D., *The Story of the 1st Cape Corps* (Cape Town: Hortors, 1920)

Doyle, A.C., *The Great Boer War* (London: Smith, Elder & Co, 1900)

Engelenburg, F.V., *General Louis Botha* (Pretoria: J.L. Van Schaik BPK, 1928)

Kestell, J.D., tr., Van Velden, D.E., *The Peace Negotiations: Between the Governments of the South African Republic and the Orange Free State and the Representatives of the British Government, which terminated in the Peace concluded at Vereeniging on the 31st May 1902* (London: Richard Clay & Sons, 1912)

Levi, N., *Jan Smuts: Being a Character Sketch of Gen. the Hon. J.C. Smuts, K.C., M.L.A., Minister of Defence, Union of South Africa* (London: Longmans, 1917)

Methuen, Lord and Brig.-Gen. Aston, *Empire Strategy : With special reference to South Africa* (Johannesburg: The Transvaal Leader, 1908)

Phillips, L., *Transvaal Problems Some Notes on Current Politics* (London: John Murray, 1907)

Preller, G.S. and Engelenburg, F.V., *Onze Krijgs Officieren: Album van Portretten met Lewens-schetsen der Transvaalse Generaals en Kommandanten* (Pretoria: Volksstem, 1904)

Rodgers, T., *The Story of Holland* (New York: G.T. Putnam's Sons, 1889)
Sampson, P.J., *The Capture of De Wet: The South African Rebellion 1914* (London: Edward Arnold, 1915)
Wyndham, H.A., 'Some aspects of South African defence, Part 1', *The State : A South African National Magazine*, vol.2, no.6 (June 1909)
Wyndham, H.A., 'Some aspects of South African defence, Part 2', *The State : A South African National Magazine*, vol.2, no.7 (July 1909)

Government Publications

Hansard

Debates of the House of Assembly of the Union of South Africa, 1914-1918
Debates of the Senate of the Union of South Africa, 1914-1918

Acts of Parliament (South Africa)

South Africa Defence Act (13 of 1912)

Parliamentary Papers

British

Imperial blue book printed by command of The King Cd. 7874, 1914-16, SA Report on Outbreak of Rebellion British Colonial Office., *Union of South Africa: Correspondence Relating to the Native Land Act, 1913* (London: Colonial Office, 1914)
British Government., *Louis Botha Translation* (London: Harrison and Sons, 1901)
British Government., *Zululand: Further Correspondence Respecting the Affairs of Zululand and Adjacent Territories* (London: Her Majesty's Stationery Officer, 1890)
British Parliament., *Parliamentary Debates: Fourth Series, Fourth Session of the Twenty Seventh Parliament of the United Kingdom of Great Britain and Ireland Volume CXXVII* (London, Wyman and Sons, 1903)
Great Britain Census Office., *Census of the British Empire 1901* (London: Darling and Son, 1901)
Post Office, *Supplement to the London Gazette*, 28542, January 1911

South African

Select Committees

S.C. 7-1912. Select Committee Report. On South Africa Defence Bill

Papers printed by order of the Union Government

UG 10–1915. Report on the Outbreak of the Rebellion and the Policy of the Government with regard to its suppression
UG 46–1916. Report of the Judicial Commission of Inquiry into the Causes and Circumstances relating to the Recent Rebellion in South Africa

UG 12–1917. Correspondence and Other Documents relating to the Report of the War Stores Commission

Belgian
Belgian Ministry of Colonies, *The Fate of the Prisoners during the East African Campaign* (London: Gabriel Devreese, 1919)

Secondary Sources

Books

Akyeampong, A.K. and Gates, H.L., *Dictionary of African Biography, Volume 1: Abach to Brand* (Oxford: Oxford University Press, 2012)
Ambrosius, Lloyd E., *Writing Biography: Historians and Their Craft* (Lincoln: University of Nebraska Press, 2004)
Anderson, R., *The Forgotten Front: The East African Campaign, 1914–1918* (Stroud: Tempus, 2004)
Anglesey, Marquess of, *The History of the British Cavalry, 1816-1919* (Barnsley: Leo Cooper, 1986)
Amery, L.S. (ed.), *The Times History of the War in South Africa, Volume 1 – 7* (London: S. Low, Marston & Co, 1907)
Armstrong, H.C., *Grey Steel, J.C. Smuts: A Study in Arrogance* (London: Arthur Barker, 1937)
Anon., *Generaal Louis Botha* (Cape Town: Shell South Africa, 1979)
Anon., *Standard Encyclopedia for Southern Africa* (Cape Town: Nassau, 1970)
Badar, M.E., *The Concept of Mens Rea in International Criminal Law* (Oxford: Hart Publishing, 2013)
Barnard, C.J., *Generaal Louis Botha op die Natalse Front, 1899-1900* (Cape Town: Balkema, 1970)
Beck, R.B., *The History of South Africa* (Santa Barbara, California: Greenwood, 2014)
Beinart, W., Delius, P., Trapido, S., *The Politics of Race : Putting a Plough to the Ground: Accumulation and Dispossession in Rural South Africa, 1850-1930 New history of southern Africa series* (Johannesburg: Raven Press, 1986)
Berkhofer, R.F., *Fashioning History: Current Practices and Principles* (New York: Palgrave Macmillan, 2008)
Beukes, P., *The Holistic Smuts: A Study in Personality* (Cape Town: Human and Rousseau, 1989)
Beyers, C.J. (ed.), *Suid-Afrikaanse Biografiese Woordeboek* (Pretoria: Butterworth & Kie, 1981)
Biko, S., *Black Consciousness in South Africa* (New York: Vintage Books, 1979)
Black, J., *Warfare in the 19th Century 1800-1904* (Cambridge: Polity, 2009)
Blake, J.Y.F., *A West Pointer with the Boers* (Boston, Angel Guardian Press, 1903)

Bonner, P., *Kings, Commoners and Concessionaires: The Evolution and Dissolution of the Nineteenth-Century Swazi State* (Cambridge: Cambridge University Press, 1982)
Bossenbroek, M., tr. Rosenberg, Y., *The Boer War* (Johannesburg: Jacana, 2012)
Bouch, R.J. in*fantry in South Africa* (Pretoria: Documentation Service SADF, 1977)
Boucher, D., *Texts in Context: Revisionist Methods for Studying the History of Ideas* (The Hague: Martinus Nijhoff, 1985)
Breytenbach, J.H., *Die Geskiedenis van die Tweede Vryheidsoorlog in Suid-Afrika, 1899-1902* (Pretoria: Staatsdrukker, 1969)
Brookes, H., *General Louis Botha* (Pietermaritzburg: The Natal Witness, 1959)
Brown, J.M. and Louis W.R. (eds.), *The Oxford History of the British Empire Volume 4: The Twentieth Century* (Oxford: Oxford University Press, 1999)
Burbidge, W.F., *Field-Marshal Smuts, Soldier and World Statesman* (London: W.S. Coswell, 1943)
Cameron, T., *Jan Smuts: An Illustrated Biography* (Cape Town: Human & Rousseau, 1994)
Cannadine, D., *Ornamentalism: How the British saw their Empire* (Oxford: Oxford University Press, 2002)
Carlyle, T., *On Heroes, Hero-Worship and the Heroic in History* (London: James Fraser, 1841)
Cavanagh, E., *Settler Colonialism and Land Rights in South Africa: Possession and Dispossession on Orange River* (New York: Palgrave Macmillan, 2013)
Couzens, T., *The Great Silence* (Johannesburg: Sunday Times, 2014)
Crafford, F.S., *Jan Smuts: A Biography* (New York: Doubleday, Doran & Co., 1944)
Crosby, T.L., *Joseph Chamberlain: A Most Radical Imperialist* (London: I.B. Tauris, 2011)
Cruise, A., *Louis Botha's War: The Campaign in South West Africa* (Cape Town: Zebra Press, 2015)
Cuthbertson, G., Grundlingh, A., Suttie, M. (eds.), *Writing a Wider War: Rethinking Gender, Race and Identity in the South African War, 1899-1902* (Cape Town: David Phillip Publishers, 2002)
Danzinger, C., *Jan Smuts* (Cape Town: MacDonald, 1978)
Davenport, T.R.H., *South Africa: A Modern History* (London: Macmillan Press, 1978)
Davenport, T.R.H. and Saunders, C.C., *South Africa, A Modern History* (New York: St. Martin's Press, 2000)
Digby, P.K.A., *Pyramids and Poppies: The 1st SA Brigade in Libya, France and Flanders 1915–1919* (Johannesburg: Ashanti, 1993)
Downing, Taylor, *Secret Warriors: Key Scientists, Code-breakers and Propagandists of the Great War* (London: Little Brown, 2014)
Drew, Allison, *Between Empire and Revolution : A life of Sidney Bunting, 1873-1936* (Pretoria: Unisa Press, 2009)
Du Pisani, K., Kriek, D. and De Jager, C. (eds.), *Jan Smuts: Van Boerseun tot Wêreldverhoog, 'n Herwaardering* (Pretoria: Protea, 2017)

Elbourne, E., *Blood Ground: Colonialism, Missions and the Contest for Christian in the Cape Colony and Britain, 1799-1853* (Kingston: McGill-Queen's University Press, 2002)

Elkins, C. and Pedersen, S. (eds.), *Settler Colonialism in the Twentieth Century: Projects, Practices and Legacies* (New York: Routledge, 2005)

Egremont, M., *Balfour: A Life of Arthur James Balfour* (London: Collins, 1980)

Etherington, N., *The Great Treks: The Transformation of Southern Africa 1815-1854* (London: Routledge, 2013)

Evans, M.M., *Encyclopaedia of the Boer War* (Oxford: ABC-Clio, 2000)

Fatton, R., *Black Consciousness in South Africa: The Dialectics of Ideological Resistance to White Supremacy* (Albany: New York State University Press, 1986)

Farwell, B., *The Great Boer War* (London: Allen Lane, 1976)

Farwell, B., *The Great War in Africa 1914–1918* (New York: Norton, 1986)

Fedorowich, Kent, *Unfit for Heroes: Reconstruction and Soldier Settlement in the Empire between the Wars* (Manchester and New York: Manchester University Press, 1995)

Feinstein, C.H., *An Economic History of South Africa: Conquest, Discrimination and Development* (Cambridge: Cambridge University Press, 2005)

Fluehr-Lobban, C., *Race and Racism: An Introduction* (New York: Altamira Press, 2006)

Frazer, A., *A Roadmap for Quality Transformation in Education: A Guide for Local Education Reform Leaders* (Boca Raton: CRC Press, 1997)

Fremont-Barnes, G., *Osprey's Guide to The Boer War 1899–1902* (Oxford: Osprey, 2003)

Friedman, B., *Jan Smuts: A Reappraisal* (New York: St. Martin's Press, 1976)

Friedlander, Z., *Jan Smuts Remembered: A Centennial Tribute* (London: Wingate, 1970)

Fry, H., *The London Cage : The Secret History of Britain's World War II Interrogation Centre* (London: Yale University Press)

Fry, H., *Spymaster: The Man Who Saved MI6* (London: Yale University Press, 2021)

Garcia, A., *First Campaign Victory of the Great War: South Africa, Manoeuvre Warfare, the Afrikaner Rebellion and the German South West African campaign* (Warwick: Helion, 2019)

Garson, N.G., *Louis Botha or John X. Merrimen: The Choice of South Africa's First Prime Minister* (London: Institute for Commonwealth Studies, 1969)

Gerhart, G.M., *Black Power in South Africa: The Evolution of an Ideology* (Los Angeles: University of California Press, 1978)

Geyser, O., *Jan Smuts and His International Contemporaries* (Johannesburg: Covos Day, 2001)

Giliomee, H.B., *The Afrikaners: A Biography of a People* (London: Hurst & Co, 2003)

Gillis, D.H., *The Kingdom of Swaziland: Studies in Political History* (Westport, Connecticut: Greenwood Press, 1999)

Gleeson, I., *The Unknown Force: Black indian and Coloured Soldiers through Two World Wars* (Rivonia: Ashanti, 1994)

Gordon, C.T., *The Growth of Boer Opposition to Kruger, 1890-1895* (Oxford: Oxford University Press, 1970)

Greaves, A. and Mkhize, X., *The Tribe that Washed its Spears: The Zulu's at War* (Barnsley: Pen and Sword, 2013)
Grigg, J., *Lloyd George: War Leader* (London: Allen Lane, 2002)
Grundlingh, A.M., Die *Hensoppers en Joiners: die rasionaal en verskynsel* van *verraad* (Pretoria: HAUM, 1979)
Grundlingh, A.M., *The Dynamics of Treason: Boer Collaboration in the South African War of 1899-1902* (Pretoria: Protea Book House, 2006)
Grundlingh, A.M., *Fighting Their Own War: South African Blacks and the First World War* (Johannesburg: Raven Press, 1988)
Grundlingh, A.M., *Participation and Remembrance: South African Black and Coloured Troops in the First World War, 1914–1918* (Stellenbosch: Sun Press, 2014)
Grundlingh, A. and Swart, S., *Radelose Rebellie: Dinamika van die 1914–1915 Afrikanerrebellie* (Pretoria: Protea Boekhuis, 2009)
Gumede, W.M., *Thabo Mbeki and the Battle for the Soul of the ANC* (Cape Town: Zebra Press, 2007)
Gurr, T.R., *Why Men Rebel 40th Anniversary Edition* (New York: Routledge, 2016)
Guy, J., *The Destruction of the Zulu Kingdom: The Civil War in Zululand 1879–1884* (Pietermaritzburg: University of Natal, 1994)
Haarhoff, T.J., *Smuts the Humanist: A Personal Reminiscence* (Oxford: Blackwell, 1970)
Halisi, C.R.D., *Black Political Thought in the Making of South African Democracy* (Bloomington: Indiana University Press, 1999)
Hamilton, C. (ed.), *The Mfecane Aftermath: Reconstructive Debates in Southern African History* (Johannesburg: Witwatersrand, 1995)
Hancock, W.H., *Smuts: Study for a Portrait* (Cambridge: Cambridge University Press, 1965)
Henderson, G.F.R., *The Science of War: A Collection of Essays and Lectures 1891-1903* (London: Longmans, Green & Co, 1912)
Hill, R.A. (ed.), *The Marcus Garvey and Universal Negro Improvement Association Papers, Vol. X: Africa for the Africans, 1923*–1945 (Los Angeles: University of California Press, 2006)
Hodges, Geoffrey, *Kariakor : The Story of the Military Labour Forces in the Conquest of German East Africa, 1914 to 1918* (Nairobi: Nairobi University Press, 1999)
Hogarth, O.J. and White, R.L., *The Life of William Marlborough Carter Third Archbishop of Cape Town: Eton's gift to South Africa* (Paignton: Horsham Printers 1952)
Houghton, D.H., *The South African Economy* (Oxford: Oxford University Press, 1964)
Howard, L. and Leonard, T. (eds.), *The Frontier in History: North America and Southern Africa Compared* (New Haven: Yale University Press, 1981)
Hughes, H., *First President: A Life of John Dube, Founding President of the ANC* (Johannesburg: Jacana, 2011)
Hyam, H. and Henshaw, P., *The Lion and the Springbok: Britain and South Africa since the Boer War* (Cambridge: Cambridge University Press, 2003)
Hyslop, J., *Notorious Syndicalist : J.T. Bain: Scottish Rebel in Colonial South Africa* (Johannesburg: Jacana, 2004)

Ingham, K., *Jan Smuts: The Conscience of a South African* (New York: St Martin's Press, 1986)

Jayapalan, N., *Historiography* (New Delhi: Atlantic, 1999)

Jeffrey, Keith, *Field Marshal Sir Henry Wilson : A Political Soldier* (Oxford: Oxford University Press, 2006)

Jenkins, K., *On What is History: From Carr and Elton to Rory and White* (London: Routledge, 1995)

Jones, H.M., *A Biographical Register of Swaziland until 1902* (Durban: University of Natal Press, 1993)

Jones, S., *From the Boer War to the First World War: Tactical Reform of the British Army, 1902-1914* (Oklahoma: University of Oklahoma Press, 2012)

Jones, S. and Müller, A.L., *South African Economy, 1910 – 1990* (New York: St. Martin's Press, 1992)

Joseph, J., *South African Statesman: Jan Christiaan Smuts* (New York: J. Messner, 1969)

Kiernan, R.H., *General Smuts* (London: Harrap, 1943)

Judd, D. and Surridge, K.T., *The Boer War* (New York: Palgrave Macmillan, 2003)

Kraus, R., *Old Master, The Life of Jan Christiaan Smuts* (New York: E.P. Dutton & Co, 1944)

Krause, G.J., *Die Rol van Generaal Louis Botha in die Unifikasie van Suid-Afrika, 1902-1910* (Bloemfontein, University of the Free State, 1953)

Krüger, D.W., *The Age of the Generals* (Johannesburg: Dagbreek Book Store, 1958)

Krüger, D.W., *The Making of a Nation: A History of the Union of South Africa, 1910-1961* (Johannesburg: Macmillan, 1969)

Krüger, D.W. and Beyers, C.J. (eds.), *Dictionary of South African Biography* (Cape Town: Tafelberg, 1977)

Kuitenbrouwer, V., *War of Words: Dutch Pro-Boer Propaganda and the South African War (1899-1902)* (Amsterdam: Amsterdam University Press, 2012)

Laband, J., *The Transvaal Rebellion: The First Boer War 1880–1881* (London: Routledge, 2014)

L'ange, G., *Urgent Imperial Service* (Rivonia: Ashanti, 1991)

Lange, M., *Comparative-Historical Methods* (Los Angeles: Sage, 2013)

Lentin, A., *Jan Smuts : Man of Courage and Vision* (Johannesburg: Jonathan Ball, 2010)

P. Lewsen (ed.), *Selections from the Correspondence of J.X. Merriman 1905-1924* (Cape Town:Van Riebeeck Society, 1969), pp.285–86.

Loveland, I., *By Due Process of Law? Racial Discrimination and the Right to Vote in South Africa 1855-1969* (Oxford: Hart Publishing, 1999)

Lunderstedt, S., *'Native' Eyes: Sol Plaatje versus the Native Land Act of 1913* (Kimberley: Sol Plaatje Educational Trust, 2014)

Magaziner, D.R., *The Law and the Prophets: Black Consciousness in South Africa 1968–1977* (Columbus: Ohio University Press, 2010)

Malan, J. and Hennings, T.H., *General Louis Botha, 1862 – 1919* (Pretoria: National Cultural History and Open Air Museum, 1979)

Malherbe, E.G., *Educational Report: Education and the Poor White, Part III of The Poor White Problem in South Africa: Report of the Carnegie Commission* (Stellenbosch: Ecclesia, 1932)
Marger, M.N., *Race and Ethnic Relations: American and Global Perspectives* (Stamford: Cengage, 2015)
Marks, S. and Trapido, S. (eds.), *The Politics of Race, Class and Nationalism in Twentieth Century South Africa* (London: Routledge, 1987)
Martin, A.C., *The Durban Light Infantry, Volume 1, 1854 to 1934* (Durban: Hayne & Gibson Ltd, 1969)
Marwick, A., *The Deluge : British Society and the First World War* (Boston and Toronto: Little, Brown & Company, 1965)
Maylam, P., *South Africa's Racial Past: The History and Historiography of Racism, Segregation and Apartheid* (Farnham: Ashgate, 2001)
McKenzie, A., Du Plessis, C.N.J., Acton, R., *The Real Kruger and the Transvaal* (New York: Street and Smith, 1900)
Miller, S.M., *Lord Methuen and the British Army: Failure and Redemption in South Africa* (London: Frank Cass, 1999)
Meintjes, J., *General Louis Botha* (London: Cassell & Co., 1970)
Meintjes, J., *President Paul Kruger: A Biography* (London: Cassell & Co., 1974)
Meiring, P., *Smuts The Patriot* (Cape Town: Tafelberg, 1975)
Meredith, M., *Diamonds, Gold and War: The British, the Boers and the Making of South Africa* (New York: Public Affairs, 2008)
Millin, S.G., *General Smuts* (Boston: Little, Brown & Co., 1936)
Moore, D.M., *General Louis Botha's Second Expedition to Natal During the Anglo-Boer War, September-October 1901* (Cape Town: Historical Publication Society, 1979)
Morton, Desmond, *A Peculiar Kind of Politics : Canada's Overseas Ministry in the First World War* (Toronto: University of Toronto Press, 1982)
Mouton, F.A., *Prophet without Honour: F. S. Malan, Afrikaner, South African and Cape Liberal* (Pretoria: Protrea Boekhuis, 2012)
Murray, W.A., *Health Report: Health Factors in the Poor White Problem, Part IV of The Poor White Problem in South Africa: Report of the Carnegie Commission* (Stellenbosch: Ecclesia, 1932)
Nanus, B., *Visionary Leadership* (Hoboken: Wiley, 1995)
Nasson, B., *Abraham Esau's War in the Cape, 1899-1902* (Cambridge: Cambridge University Press, 1991)
Nasson, B., *Springboks on the Somme : South Africa in the Great War, 1914-1918* (Johannesburg: Penguin, 2007)
Nasson, B., *The War for South Africa, The Anglo Boer War 1899 – 1902* (Cape Town: Tafelberg, 2010)
Nasson, B., *World War 1 and the People of South Africa* (Cape Town: Tafelberg, 2014)
Nasson, B. and Grundlingh, A. (eds.), *The War at Home: Women and Families in the Anglo-Boer War* (Cape Town: Tafelberg, 2013)

Naugle, D.K., *Worldview: The History of a Concept* (Grand Rapids: W.B. Eerdmans, 2002)

Neumark, A.D., *The South African Frontier: Economic Influences, 1652–1836* (Stanford: Stanford University Press, 1957)

Ngqulunga, B., *The Man Who Founded the ANC: A Biography of Pixley ka Isaka Seme* (Cape own: Zebra, 2017)

Ninivaggi, F.J., *Making Sense of Emotion: Innovating Emotional Intelligence* (New York: Rowman and Littlefield, 2017)

Odendaal, A., *Founders: The Origins of the ANC and the Struggle for Democracy in South Africa* (Aukland Park: Jacana, 2012)

Okoth, A., *A History of Africa Volume 1: African Societies and the Establishment of Colonial Rule 1800 – 1915* (Nairobi: East African Educational Publishers, 2006)

Olden, J.S. and Shadle, R., *Historical Dictionary of the British Empire* (Westport, Connecticut: Greenwood Press, 1996)

Opperman, A.J.P., *The Battle of Majuba Hill* (Johannesburg: Perskor, 1981)

Orpen, N., *The History of the Transvaal Horse Artillery 1904–1974* (Johannesburg: Alex White & Co., 1975)

Overy, Richard, *The Birth of the RAF, 1918: The World's First Air Force* (London: Allen Lane, 2018)

Page, M.E., *Colonialism: An International Social, Cultural and Political Encyclopaedia* (Oxford: ABC Clio, 2003)

Paice, E., *Tip and Run: The Untold Tragedy of the Great War in* Africa (London: Weidenfeld & Nicholson, 2007)

Paice, E., *World War 1: The African Front* (New York: Pegasus Books, 2008)

Pakenham, T., *The Boer War* (London: Abacus, 1979)

Phillips, Howard, *Plague, Pox and Pandemics : A Jacana Pocket History of Epidemics in South Africa* (Auckland Park: Jacana, 2012)

Potgieter, T. and Pommerin, R. (eds.), *Maritime Security in Southern Africa* (Stellenbosch: Sun Press, 2009)

Pretorius, F., *Life on Commando during the Anglo-Boer War 1899-1902* (Cape Town: Human and Rousseau, 1999)

Pirow, O., *James Barry Munnik Hertzog* (Cape Town, Howard Timmins, 1958)

Potholm, C.P., *Swaziland: The Dynamics of Political Mobilisation* (Los Angeles: University of California Press, 1972)

Pretorius, F., *A History of South Africa: From the Distant Past to the Present Day* (Pretoria: Protea Book House, 2014)

Ransford, O., *The Battle of Spion Kop* (London: John Murray, 1969)

Raugh, H.E., *The Victorians at War 1815-1914: An Encyclopaedia of British Military History* (Oxford: ABC Clio, 2004)

Rivera, M.M. and Rivera, R.V., *Practical Guide to Thesis and Dissertation Writing* (Quezon City: Katha Publishing, 1996)

Ross, R., Mager, A.K. and Nasson, B. (eds.), *The Cambridge History of South Africa, Volume 2 1885 – 1994* (Cambridge: Cambridge University Press, 2012)

Sanderson, C.A., *Social Psychology* (New Jersey: John Wiley and Sons, 2010)
Rotberg, R.I., Shore, M.F., *The Founder: Cecil John Rhodes and the Pursuit of Power* (Oxford: Oxford University Press, 1988)
Sandys, C., *Churchill: Wanted Dead or Alive* (College Station, Texas: Texas A&M University Press, 2013)
Samson, A., *Britain, South Africa and the East African Campaign* (London: I.B. Tauris, 2006)
Samson, A., *World War I in Africa: The Forgotten Conflict among European Powers* (London: I.B. Taurus, 2013)
Sandberg, C.G.S., *Twintig Jaren onder Krugers Boeren in Voor- en tegenspoed* (Amsterdam: Amsterdamsche Keurkamer, 1943)
Saunders, C.C., *The Making of the South African Past: Major Historians on Race and Class* (Cape Town: David Phillip, 1988)
Scholtz, G.D., *Hertzog en Smuts en die Britse Ryk* (Cape Town: Tafelberg, 1975)
Scholtz, G.D., *Die Rebellie 1914-1915* (Pretoria, Protea, 2013)
Simpkins, B.G., *Rand Light Infantry* (Cape Town: Howard Timmins, 1965)
Smith, K., *The Changing Past: Trends in South African Historical Writing* (Johannesburg: Southern Book Publishers, 1988)
Smuts, J.C., *Jan Christian Smuts* (London: Cassell, 1952)
Southgate, B.C., *What is History For?* (London: Routledge, 2005)
Spender, E.H., *General Botha: The Career and the Man* (London: Constable & Co., 1916)
Stapleton, T, J. (ed.), *Encyclopaedia of African Colonial Conflicts: Volume I, A-K* (Santa Barbara: ABC Clio,2017)
Stapleton, T.J. (ed.), *Encyclopaedia of African Conflicts* (Denver: ABC Clio, 2017)
Stapleton, T.J., *No Insignificant Part: The Rhodesia Native Regiment and the East Africa Campaign of the First World War* (Ontario: Wilfred Laurier University Press, 2006)
Steyn, R., *Jan Smuts: Unafraid of Greatness* (Johannesburg: Jonathan Ball, 2015)
Steyn, R., *Louis Botha: A Man Apart* (Johannesburg: Jonathan Ball, 2018)
Stejskal, J., *The Horns of the Beast: The Swakop River Campaign and World War I in South West Africa, 1914-1915* (Solihull: Helion, 2014)
Strachan, H., *The First World War, Vol 1: To Arms* (Oxford: Oxford University Press, 2001)
Strachan, H., *The First World War in Africa* (Oxford: Oxford University Press, 2004)
Strachan, H. (ed.), *The Oxford Illustrated History of the First World War* (Oxford: Oxford University Press, 1998)
Terraine, John, *Douglas Haig : The Educated Soldier* (London: Hutchinson, 1963)
Thomson, A., *US Foreign Policy Towards Apartheid South Africa, 1948 – 1994* (New York: Palgrave Macmillan, 2008)
Thompson, J.M., *A Forgotten Patriot: The Life of Alfred Viscount Milner of St James's and Cape Town 1854–1925* (Madison: Fairleigh Dickenson University Press, 2007)
Thompson, L.M., *A History of South Africa* (Johannesburg: Jonathan Ball, 2000)
Thompson, L.M., *A History of South Africa* (New Haven: Yale University Press, 1990)

Tosh, J. (ed.), *Historians on History* (London: Routledge, 2014)

Tosh, J. and Lang, S., *The Pursuit of History* (London: Pearson Longman, 2006)

Tucker, S.C. (ed.), *500 Great Military Leaders: Volume I, A-K* (Santa Barbara: ABC Clio, 2015)

Uys, I., *Rollcall: The Delville Wood Story* (Johannesburg: Uys, 1991)

Van Damme, F., *Jan Smuts* (Antwerp: Standaard Boekhandel, 1956)

Van der Waag, I.J., *A Military History of Modern South Africa* (Johannesburg: Jonathan Ball, 2015)

Van Heyningen, E., *The Concentration Camps of the Anglo-Boer War* (Johannesburg: Jacana, 2013)

Van Jaarsveld, F.A., *Die Afrikaners se Groot Trek na die Stede: En ander Opselle* (Johannesburg: Perskor, 1982)

Van Jaarsveld, F.A., *Omstrede Suid-Afrikaanse verlede: Geskiedenis Ideologie en die Historiese Skuldvraagstuk* (Johannesburg: Lex Patria, 1984)

Walker, I.L. and B. Weinbren, *2000 Casualties: A History of the Trade Unions and the Labour Movement in the Union of South Africa* (Johannesburg, 1961)

Weltig, M.S., *The Aftermath of the Anglo-Zulu War* (Minneapolis: Twenty-First Century Books, 2008)

Weaver, J.C., *Great Land Rush and the Making of the Modern World, 1650-1900* (Kingston: McGill's-Queen's University Press, 2003)

Wilcocks, R.W., *Psychological Report: The Poor White, Part II of The Poor White Problem in South Africa: Report of the Carnegie Commission* (Stellenbosch: Ecclesia, 1932)

Willan, B., *Sol Plaatje: A Life of Solomon Tshekisho Plaatje* (Johannesburg: Jacana, 2018)

Williams, B., *Botha, Smuts and South Africa* (London: Hodder & Stoughton, 1946)

Williams, D., *Springboks, Troepies and Cadres: Stories of the South African Army 1912 –2012* (Cape Town: Tafelberg, 2012)

Wilson, M. and Thompson, L.M., *The Oxford History of South Africa* (Oxford: Oxford University Press, 1969)

Book Chapters and Journal Articles

Benjamin, L.M., 'Historical Evidence: Facts, Proof and Probability' in Godfrey D.G. (ed.), *Methods of Historical Analysis in Electronic Media* (Mahwah: Taylor & Francis, 2006)

Boje, J. and Pretorius, F., 'Black resistance in the Orange Free State During the Anglo-Boer War', *Historia*, vol. 58, no.1 (2013)

Bottomley, E.J., 'The South African Rebellion of 1914: The Influence of Industrialisation, Poverty and 'Poor-Whitism'', *African Studies Seminar Paper*, University of Witwatersrand, (June 1980)

Brookes, E.H., 'General Louis Botha', *Theoria: A Journal of Social and Political Theory*, vol.13. (1959)

Campbell-Miller, J., 'ex Unitate Vires': Elite Consolidation and the Union of South Africa, 1902-10, *Canadian Journal of History*, vol.XLV, Spring-Summer (2010)

Chanaiwa, D., 'African Initiatives and Resistance in Southern Africa' in Adu Boahen, A. (ed.), *General History of Africa VII: Africa Under Colonial Domination 1880–1935* (Berkley: University of California Press, 1985)

Davenport, T. R. H., 'The Afrikaner Bond: the history of a South African political party, 1880–1911', *Journal of Asian and African Studies*, vol.2, no.3 (1966)

Davenport, T.R.H., 'The South African Rebellion of 1914', *English Historical Review*, vol.78 (1963)

Dedering, T., '"Avenge the Lusitania"': The Anti-German Riots in South Africa in 1915', *Imigrants & Minorities Historical Studies in Ethnicity, Migration and* Diaspora, vol.31, no.3 (2013)

Dorning, W.A., 'A Concise History of the South African Defence Force 1912–1987', *Militaria, South African Journal for Military Studies*, vol.17, no.2 (1987)

Du Bois, D., 'Appraising Louis Botha's Award of a Knighthood for Frank Reynolds in 1916', *South African Journal of Cultural History*, vol.30, no.2 (2016)

Etherington, N., 'Old Wine in New Bottles: The Persistence of Narrative Structures in the Historiography of the Mfecane and the Great Trek' in Hamilton, C. (ed.), *The Mfecane Aftermath: Reconstructive Debates in Southern African History* (Johannesburg: Witwatersrand, 1995)

Fedorowich, Kent, '"The Weak Link in the Imperial Chain": South Africa, the Round Table and World War one' in A. Bosco and A. May (eds.), *The Round Table, the Empire/ Commonwealth and British Foreign Policy* (London: Foundation Press, 1997)

Fedorowich, K., 'Sleeping with the Lion? The Loyal Afrikaner and the South African Rebellion of 1914-1915', *South African Historical Journal*, vol.49, no.1 (2009)

Freund, B., 'South Africa: The Union Years' in R. Ross, A.K. Mager and B Nasson (eds.), *The Cambridge History of South Africa, Volume 2 1885–1994* (Cambridge: Cambridge University Press, 2012)

Garcia, A., 'A Manoeuvre Warfare Analysis of South Africa's 1914-1915 German South West African Campaign', *Scientia Militaria*. vol.45, no.1 (2017)

Garcia, A., 'Airpower in the Union of South Africa's First World War campaign in German South West Africa', *Historia*, vol.62, no.2 (2017)

Garson, N.G., "Het Volk': The Botha-Smuts Party in the Transvaal, 1904–11', *The Historical Journal*, vol.9, no.1 (1966)

Garson, N.G., 'South Africa and World War 1', *Journal of Imperial and Commonwealth History,* vol.8, no.1 (1979)

Gie, S.F.N., 'The Cape Colony under Company Rule' in, Walker, E.A. (ed.), *The Cambridge*

History of the British Empire: South Africa, Rhodesia and the High Commission Territories (Cambridge: Cambridge University Press, 1963)

Greef, J.M., 'Appels, Botha, Cornelitz: The ABC of a Hundred Year Old Divorce Case', *Forensic Science International: Genetics*, vol.7, no.5 (2013)

Grundlingh, L., "'In the crisis, who would tamper with the existing order?' The political and public reaction of English-speaking South Africans to the 1914 Rebellion', *Historia*, vol.59, no.2 (2014)

Guest, W.R., 'Fitzpatrick, Natal and the Unificationf of South Africa', *Natalia*, vol.11 (1981)

Hawkin, R.C., 'General Botha', *Journal of the Royal African Society*, vol.19, no.73 (1919)

Horshemke, K. and Yorre, L.D., 'Challenges of Multiculturalism in Science Education: Indigenisation internationalisation and *Transkulturalitat*' in Mathews, M.R. (ed.), *International Handbook of Research in History, Philosophy and Science Teaching* (Dordrecht: Springer, 2014)

Jewell, J.R., 'Using Barbaric Methods in South Africa: The British Concentration Camp Policy during the Anglo-Boer War', *Scientia Militaria*, vol.31, no.1 (2003)

Jonckeere, W., 'Myth and Afrikaner Idealization in Dutch Historical Novels' in, Howell, R. and Taylor, J.V. (eds.), *Publications of the American Association for Netherlandic Studies* (New York: University Press of America, 2003)

Kleynhans, E., 'A Critical Analysis of the Impact of Water on the South African Campaign in German South West Africa, 1914–1915', *Historia*, vol.61, no.2 (2016)

Lamplough, R.W., 'In Search of Mr Botha', *Natalia*, vol.12 (1982)

Le Roux, C.S., 'Schooling in the early Orange Free State: Inception to Union, 1836 to 1910', *New Contree*, vol.76, Supplement Edition (November 2016)

Le Roy, F. and Perkins, D., 'Visionary Leadership' in, Laver, H.S. and Mathews, J.J. (eds.), *The Art of Command: Military Leadership from George Washington to Colin Powell* (Lexington: University Press of Kentucky, 2017)

Meiklejohn, A., 'The Development of Compensation for Occupational Diseases of the Lungs in Great Britain', *British Journal of Industrial Medicine*, vol.11 (1954)

Miescher, G., 'Arteries of Empire: On the Geographical Imagination of South Africa's Railway War, 1914/1915', *Kronos*, vol.38, no.1 (2012)

Morrell, R., 'Competition and Cooperation in Middelburg, 1900–1930' in Beinart, W., Delius, P. and Trapido, S. (eds.), *Putting* a *Plough* to the *Ground: Accumulation and Dispossession in Rural South Africa: 1850-1930* (Johannesburg: Ravan Press, 1986)

Mouton, F.A., 'Professor Leo Fouché, the History Department and the Afrikanerisation of the University of Pretoria,' in Mouton, F.A., Southey, N. and Van Jaarsveld, A. (eds.), *History, Historians and Afrikaner Nationalism: Essays on the History Department of the University of Pretoria 1909-1985* (Vanderbijlpark: Kleio, 2007)

Mouton, F.A., '"The sacred tie": Sir Thomas Smartt, the Unionist Party and the British Empire, 1912–1920', *Historia*, vol.59, no.2 (2012)

Nasaw, D., 'Historians and Biography', *The American Historical Review*, vol.114, no.3 (2009)

Nasson, B., 'Delville Wood and South African Great War Commemoration', *English Historical Review*, 119, 480 (2004)

Nevins, A., 'The Essence of Biography: A Character Study', *The Writing of Jewish American History*, vol.46, no.3 (1957)

Nicholls, B.M., 'Rebellions in retrospect: "Die rebellie" of 1914 and the Easter rising of 1916 revisited', *South African-Irish Studies*, vol.3 (1996)

Oosthuizen, G.J.J., 'The Military Role of the Rehoboth Basters during the South African Invasion of German South West Africa, 1914-1915', *Scientia Militaria*, vol.28, no.1 (1998)4

Paterson, H, 'First Allied Victory: The South African Campaign in German South-West Africa, 1914–1915', *Military History Journal*, vol.13, no.2 (2004)

Phillips, L, 'General Botha', *Journal of the Royal African Society*, vol.24, no.93 (1924)

Penn, N., 'The Northern Cape Frontier Zone in Cape Frontier Historiography' in Russel, L. (ed.), *Colonial Frontiers: Indigenous-European Encounters in Settler Societies* (Manchester: Manchester University Press, 2001)

Pretorius, F., 'Boer Propaganda During the South African War of 1899–1902' *The Journal of Imperial and Commonwealth History*, vol.37, no.3 (2009)

Pretorius, F., 'General Louis Botha's role in the South African War, 1899-1902', *War & Society*, vol.41, no.2 (2022)

Shannon, D.A., 'The Study of History and the Critical Mind' in Lacy, E.R. (ed.), *Readings on Historical Method* (New York: MSS Educational Publishing, 1969)

Smith, I.R., 'A Century of Controversy over Origins' in Lowry, D. (ed.), *The South African War Reappraised* (Manchester: Manchester University Press, 2000)

Spies, S.B., 'The Outbreak of the First World War and the Botha Government', *South African Historical Journal,* vol.1, no.1 (1969)

Stead, W.T. (ed.), 'Review of L. Botha's article 'The Boers and the British Empire", *Review of Reviews*, vol.26 (December 1902)

Strong, E.W., 'How is the Practice of History tied to Theory' in Lacy, E.R. (ed.), *Readings on Historical Method* (New York: MSS Educational Publishing, 1969)

Stuchtey, B., 'In Search of Lost Identity' in Fuchs, E. and Stuchtey, B. (eds.), *Across Cultural Borders: Historiography in Global Perspective* (New York: Rowman & Littlefield Publishers, 2001)

Swart, S., "A Boer and his Gun and his Wife are Three Things Always Together', Republican Masculinity and the 1914 Rebellion', *Journal of Southern African Studies*, vol.24, no4 (2008)

Swart, S., 'An Irritating Pebble in Kruger's Shoe – Eugène Marais and Land en Volk in the ZAR, 1891 –1896', *Historia*, vol.48, no.2 (2003)

Swart, S., "Desperate Men' The 1914 Rebellion and the Polities of Poverty', *South African Historical Journal*, vol.42, no.1 (2000)

Swart, S., 'The 'Five Shilling Rebellion': Rural White Male Anxiety and the 1914 Boer Rebellion', *South African Historical Journal*, vol.56, no.1 (2006)

Thompson, M.D., 'Document Analysis, Oral History and Historical Methods' in Stage, F.K. and Manning, K. (eds.), *Research in the College Context: Approaches and Methods* (New York: Routledge, 2016)

Tyler, T.R. and Jost, J.T., 'Psychology by Law: Reconciling Normative and Descriptive Accounts of Social Justice and System Legitimacy' in, Kruglanski, A.W. and Higgins, E.T. (eds.), *Social Psychology: Handbook of Basic Principles* (New York: Guilford Press, 2007)

Van der Waag, I, J., 'Boer Generalship and the Politics of Command', *War in History*, vol.12, no.1 (2005)

Van der Waag, I.J., 'Rural Struggles and the Politics of a Colonial Command: The Southern Mounted Rifles of the Transvaal Volunteers, 1905–1912' in Miller, S. (ed.), *Soldiers and Settlers in Africa, 1850-1918* (Boston: Brill, 2009)

Van der Waag, I.J., 'Smuts's Generals: Towards a First Portrait of the South African High Command, 1912–1948', *War in History*, vol.18, no.1 (2011)

Van der Waag, I.J., 'All splendid, but horrible: The Politics of South Africa's Second 'Little Bit' and the War on the Western Front, 1915-1918', *Scientia Militaria: South African Journal of Military Studies*, vol.40, no.3 (2012)

Van der Waag, I.J., 'The Battle of Sandfontein, 26 September 1914: South African Military Reform and the German South-West Africa Campaign, 1914–1915', *First World War Studies*, vol.4, no.2 (2013)

Van der Waag, I., 'The First World War in Africa: Impact and Consequences' in António José Telo (ed.), *A Grande Guerra e a Construção do Mundo Moderno* (Lisbon: Academia Militar, 2016)

Van der Waag, I., 'Recording the Great War: military archives and the South African official history programme', *Scientia Militaria: South African Journal of Military Studies*, vol.44, no.1 (2016)

Van der Waag, I., 'South Africa and the making of officers, 1902-1948' in Douglas E. Delaney, Robert C. Engen and Meghan Fitzpatrick (eds.), *Military Education and the British Empire, 1815-1949* (Vancouver: University of British Columbia Press, 2017)

Van der Waag, I., 'Re-Thinking South Africa's Military past: The Curious Case of Brig. Gen. the Hon. C.F. Beyers' (Stellenbosch University: Professorial inaugural lecture, 2018)

Van der Waag, I. 'South African Manpower and the Second World War' in Douglas E. Delaney, Mark Frost and Andrew L. Brown (eds.), *Military Manpower and the Armies of the British Empire in the Two World Wars* (Ithaca and London: Cornell University Press, 2021)

Van Wyk, A.J., 'Botha en Smuts: Tweeling' in Du Pisani, K., Kriek, D. and De Jager, C., (eds.), *Jan Smuts: Van Boerseun tot Wêreldverhoog, 'n Herwaardering* (Pretoria: Protea, 2017)

Waetjen, T., 'The Rise and Fall of the Opium Trade in the Transvaal, 1904–1910', *Journal of Southern African Studies*, vol.43, no.4 (2017)

Walsh, L.S. and Lamana, M., 'A Critical Study of the Biographies of Allan Nevins', *Social Science*, vol.28, no.1 (1953)

Warwick, R.C., 'The Battle of Sandfontein: The Role and Legacy of Major General Sir Henry Timson Lukin', *Scientia Militaria, South African Journal of Military Studies*, vol.34, no.2 (2006)

Wessels, A., 'Boer Guerilla and British Counter-Guerilla Operations in South Africa, 1899-1902', *Scientia Militaria*, vol.39, no.2 (2011)

Theses and Dissertations

Anderson, R., 'World War 1 in East Africa, 1916-1918', PhD thesis, Glasgow University, 2001

Brink, L.E., 'Die lewe, werk en invloed van F.V. Engelenburg in Suid-Afrika, 1889 – 1938', PhD thesis, North-West University, 2015

Delport, A., 'Boks and Bullets, Coffins and Crutches': An Exploration of the Body, Mind and Places of 'Springbok' South African Soldiers in the First World War', MA thesis, Stellenbosch University, 2015

Garcia, A., 'General Louis Botha: Farmer, Soldier, Statesman, 1862-1919', PhD dissertation, Stellenbosch University, 2019

Gutsche, T., 'The History and Social significance of Cinema in South Africa', PhD thesis, University of Cape Town, 1946

Halstead, R.S., 'Visionary Leadership', MMAS thesis, US Command and General Staff College, 1993

Harris, K.L., 'A History of the Chinese in South Africa until 1912', PhD thesis, University of South Africa, 1998

Jones, S., 'The Influence of the Boer War (1899–1902) on the Tactical Development of the Regular British Army 1902-1914', PhD thesis, Wolverhampton University, 2009

Kamffer, H.J.G., 'Om een scherpe oof in't zeil te houden: Die Geheime Diens in die Zuid-Afrikaansche Republiek', PhD thesis, North West University, 1999

Nortier, E.W., 'Major General Sir Henry Timson Lukin (1860–1925): The Making of a South African Hero', M Mil thesis, Stellenbosch University, 2005

Schultz, B.G., 'Die Slag Van Begendal', MA Thesis, University of Pretoria, 1974

Ungleich, T.R., 'The Defence of German South West Africa during World War I', MA thesis, University of Miami, 1974

Van Aart, J.M.H., 'Die Botha-bewind in die Transvaal, 1907·1910', PhD Thesis, Potchefstroom University, 1958

Van der Waag, I.J., 'Hugh Archibald Wyndham His Life and Times in South Africa 1901-1923', PhD dissertation, University of Cape Town, 2005

Wasserman, J.M., 'The Natal Afrikaner and the Anglo-Boer War', PhD thesis, University of Pretoria, 2004

Electronic Sources

Ahmed, B., 'The Racist Behind The Rhodes Scholarship Sparks Controversy At Oxford', *Think Progress*, 14/01/2016 <http://thinkprogress.org/world/2016/01/14/3739687/rhodes-oxford/>

Anon., 'Appels, Botha, Cornelitz' : BOTHABLAD <http://home.mweb.co.za/el/elijo/afr/indexa.html>

Anon., 'Govt in favour of amicable solution to statue furore', *SABC*, 13/04/2015 <http://www.sabc.co.za/news/a/7a27118047efc3668429f74405f77b26/Govt-in-favour-of-amicable-solution-to-statue-furore->

Anon., 'Mahatma Gandhi statue vandalised in Johannesburg', *BBC News*, 13/04/2015 <http://www.bbc.com/news/world-africa-32287972>

Anon., 'No Freedom in Dishonour. How Botha Stayed a Rising. General Smuts's Story'. *The Observer*, 7/09/1919 <https://search.proquest.com/hnpguardianobserver>

Anon., 'Position of Troops in October 1899' <https://www.angloboerwar.com/other-information/16-other-information/2006-maps>

Anon., ''Statue park' not a South African solution', *PoliticsWeb*, 23/04/2015 <http://www.politicsweb.co.za/opinion/statue-park-not-a-south-african-solution--marius-r>

Anon., 'Timeline on the defacing of statues', *SA History Online*, 24/04/2015 <http://www.sahistory.org.za/article/timeline-defacing-statues>

British Battles, 'Battle of Ladysmith' <https://www.britishbattles.com/great-boer-war/battle-of-ladysmith/>

De Villiers, O., 'Steve Hofmeyr blames statue defacement on illiteracy', *Mail and Guardian*, 08/04/2015 <http://mg.co.za/article/2015-04-08-steve-hofmeyr-blames-statue-defacement-on-illiteracy>

De Villiers, O., 'Sunette Bridges protests over Paul Kruger statue', *News 24*, 08/04/2015 <http://www.news24.com/SouthAfrica/News/Sunette-Bridges-protests-over-Paul-Kruger-statue-20150408>

Ferreira, E., 'Two held for defacing Louis Botha statue', *IOL*, 09/04/2015 <http://www.iol.co.za/news/crime-courts/two-held-for-defacing-louis-botha-statue-1.1842834>

Hess, L., 'Louis Botha statue outside parliament defaced', *News 24*, 09/04/2015 <http://www.news24.com/SouthAfrica/News/Louis-Botha-statue-outside-Parliament-defaced-20150409>

Hess, L., 'Rhodes statue to be removed after UCT council decision', *News 24*, 08/04/2015 <http://www.news24.com/SouthAfrica/News/Rhodes-statue-to-be-removed-after-UCT-council-decision 20150408>

Khoza, A., 'Remove all colonial statues – Zuma's son', *News 24*, 02/04/2015 <http://www.news24.com/SouthAfrica/News/Remove-all-colonial-statues-Zumas-son-20150402>

Khoza, A., 'Statue vandalism part of a larger narrative, says Nzimande', *News 24*, 08/04/2015 <http://www.news24.com/SouthAfrica/News/Statue-vandalism-part-of-a-larger-narrative-says-Nzimande-20150408>

Kleynhans, E., 'South African Invasion of German South West Africa (Union of South Africa)' in (eds.), Daniel, U., Gatrell, P., Janz, O., Jones, H., Keene, J., Kramer, A. and Nasson, B., *International Encyclopaedia of the First World War* <https://encyclopedia.1914-1918-online.net/article/south_african_invasion_of_german_south_west_africa_union_of_south_africa>

Military History Network, 'An Acre of Massacre', *Warfare History Network* <http://warfarehistorynetwork.com/daily/military-history/an-acre-of-massacre-the-second-boer-wars-battle-of-spion-kop/>

Redelinghuys, M., '"Statue Park" not a South African solution', *DA*, 13/04/2015 <https://www.da.org.za/2015/04/statue-park-not-a-south-african-solution/>

Samson, A., 'Louis Botha' in (eds.), Daniel, U., Gatrell, P., Janz, O., Jones, H., Keene, J., Kramer, A. and Nasson, B., *1914-1918-online International Encyclopaedia of the First World War* <https://encyclopedia.1914-1918-online.net/article/botha_louis>

Santry, A., 'Rhodes Scholars Demand Removal Of Rhodes' Statue At Oxford', *The Daily Caller*, 13/01/2016 <http://dailycaller.com/2016/01/13/rhodes-scholars-demand-removal-of-rhodes-statue-at-oxford/>

Smith, D., 'Vandalism of apartheid-era statues sparks fevered debate in South Africa', *The Guardian*, 10/04/2015 <http://www.theguardian.com/world/2015/apr/10/vandalism-of-apartheid-era-statues-sparks-fevered-debate-in-south-africa>

South African History Online, 'Treaty of Vereeniging'
<http://www.sahistory.org.za/archive/peace-treaty-vereeniging-original-document?

South African Heritage Resource Agency <http://www.sahra.org.za/sahris/about/about-sahra>

Spies, D., 'Horse memorial statue moved to secure location', *News24*, 07/04/2015 <http://www.news24.com/SouthAfrica/News/Horse-memorial-statue-moved-to-secure-location-20150407>

Theletsane, W., 'Two men arrested for defacing Louis Botha statue in Cape Town', *Eye Witness News*, 09/04/2015 <http://ewn.co.za/2015/04/09/Two-nabbed-for-defacing-Louis-Bothas-statue>

Zwane, T., 'EFF and ANC at odds over 'offensive' statues', *Mail and Guardian*, 08/04/2015 <http://mg.co.za/article/2015-04-08-eff-and-anc-at-odds-over-offensive-statues-1>

Index

Wolverhampton Military Studies

www.helion.co.uk/wolverhamptonmilitarystudies

Submissions

The publishers would be pleased to receive submissions for this series. Please contact us via email (info@helion.co.uk), or in writing to Helion & Company Limited, Unit 8 Amherst Business Centre, Budbrooke Road, Warwick, CV34 5WE, England.

Titles

1 *Stemming the Tide. Officers and Leadership in the British Expeditionary Force 1914* Edited by Spencer Jones (ISBN 978-1-909384-45-3)

2 *'Theirs Not To Reason Why': Horsing the British Army 1875–1925* Graham Winton (ISBN 978-1-909384-48-4)

3 *A Military Transformed? Adaptation and Innovation in the British Military, 1792– 1945* Edited by Michael LoCicero, Ross Mahoney and Stuart Mitchell (ISBN 978-1-909384-46-0)

4 *Get Tough Stay Tough. Shaping the Canadian Corps, 1914–1918* Kenneth Radley (ISBN 978-1-909982-86-4)

5 *A Moonlight Massacre: The Night Operation on the Passchendaele Ridge, 2 December 1917. The Forgotten Last Act of the Third Battle of Ypres* Michael LoCicero (ISBN 978-1-909982-92-5)

6 *Shellshocked Prophets. Former Anglican Army Chaplains in Interwar Britain* Linda Parker (ISBN 978-1-909982-25-3)

7 *Flight Plan Africa: Portuguese Airpower in Counterinsurgency, 1961–1974* John P. Cann (ISBN 978-1-909982-06-2)

8 *Mud, Blood and Determination. The History of the 46th (North Midland) Division in the Great War* Simon Peaple (ISBN 978 1 910294 66 6)

9 *Commanding Far Eastern Skies. A Critical Analysis of the Royal Air Force Superiority Campaign in India, Burma and Malaya 1941–1945* Peter Preston-Hough (ISBN 978 1 910294 44 4)

10 *Courage Without Glory. The British Army on the Western Front 1915* Edited by Spencer Jones (ISBN 978 1 910777 18 3)

11 *The Airborne Forces Experimental Establishment: The Development of British Airborne Technology 1940–1950* Tim Jenkins (ISBN 978-1-910777-06-0)

12 *'Allies are a Tiresome Lot' – The British Army in Italy in the First World War* John Dillon (ISBN 978 1 910777 32 9)

13 *Monty's Functional Doctrine: Combined Arms Doctrine in British 21st Army Group in Northwest Europe, 1944–45* Charles Forrester (ISBN 978-1-910777-26-8)

14 *Early Modern Systems of Command: Queen Anne's Generals, Staff Officers and the Direction of Allied Warfare in the Low Countries and Germany, 1702–11* Stewart Stansfield (ISBN 978 1 910294 47 5)

15 *They Didn't Want To Die Virgins: Sex and Morale in the British Army on the Western Front 1914–1918* Bruce Cherry (ISBN 978-1-910777-70-1)

16 *From Tobruk to Tunis: The Impact of Terrain on British Operations and Doctrine in North Africa, 1940–1943* Neal Dando (ISBN 978-1-910294-00-0)

17 *Crossing No Man's Land: Experience and Learning with the Northumberland Fusiliers in the Great War* Tony Ball (ISBN 978-1-910777-73-2)

18 *"Everything worked like clockwork": The Mechanization of the British Cavalry between the Two World Wars* Roger E Salmon (ISBN 978-1-910777-96-1)

19 *Attack on the Somme: 1st Anzac Corps and the Battle of Poziéres Ridge, 1916* Meleah Hampton (ISBN 978-1-910777-65-7)

20 *Operation Market Garden: The Campaign for the Low Countries, Autumn 1944: Seventy Years On* Edited by John Buckley & Peter Preston Hough (ISBN 978 1 910777 15 2)

21 *Enduring the Whirlwind: The German Army and the Russo-German War 1941-1943* Gregory Liedtke (ISBN 978-1-910777-75-6)

22 *'Glum Heroes': Hardship, fear and death – Resilience and Coping in the British Army on the Western Front 1914–1918* Peter E. Hodgkinson (ISBN 978-1-910777-78-7)

23 *Much Embarrassed: Civil War Intelligence and the Gettysburg Campaign* George Donne (ISBN 978-1-910777-86-2)

24 *They Called It Shell Shock: Combat Stress in the First World War* Stefanie Linden (ISBN 978-1-911096-35-1)

25 *New Approaches to the Military History of the English Civil War. Proceedings of the First Helion & Company 'Century of the Soldier' Conference* Ismini Pells (editor) (ISBN 978-1-911096-44-3)

26 *Reconographers: Intelligence and Reconnaissance in British Tank Operations on the Western Front 1916-18* Colin Hardy (ISBN: 978-1-911096-28-3)

27 *Britain's Quest for Oil: The First World War and the Peace Conferences* Martin Gibson (ISBN: 978-1-911512-07-3)

28 *Unfailing Gallantry: 8th (Regular) Division in the Great War 1914–1919* Alun Thomas (ISBN: 978-1-910777-61-9)

29 *An Army of Brigadiers: British Brigade Commanders at the Battle of Arras 1917* Trevor Harvey (ISBN: 978-1-911512-00-4)

30 *At All Costs: The British Army on the Western Front 1916* Edited by Spencer Jones (ISBN 978-1-912174-88-1)

31 *The German Corpse Factory: A Study in First World War Propaganda* Stephen Badsey (ISBN 978-1-911628-27-9)

32 *Bull Run to Boer War: How the American Civil War Changed the Victorian British Army* Michael Somerville (ISBN 978-1-912866-25-0)

33 *Turret versus Broadside: An Anatomy of British Naval Prestige, Revolution and Disaster, 1860-1870* Howard J. Fuller (ISBN 978-1-913336-22-6)

34 *A Moonlight Massacre: The Night Operation on the Passchendaele Ridge, 2 December 1917. The Forgotten Last Act of the Third Battle of Ypres,* Second Edition, paperback Michael LoCicero (ISBN 978-1-911628-72-9)

35 *The Darkest Year: The British Army on the Western Front 1917* Spencer Jones (ISBN 978-1-914059-98-8)

36 *Ham & Jam. 6th Airborne Division in Normandy: Generating Combat Effectiveness, November 1942-September 1944* Andrew Wheale (ISBN 978-1-915070-85-2)

37 *Stemming the Tide. Officers and Leadership in the British Expeditionary Force 1914,* Revised Edition paperback edited by Spencer Jones (ISBN 978-1-91507-097-5)

38 *Kitchener and the Dardanelles Campaign: A Vindication* George Cassar (ISBN 978-1-915113-75-7)

39 *To Do the Work of Men: An Operational History of the 21st Division in the Great War* Derek Clayton (ISBN 978-1-804512-33-3)

40 *Botha, Smuts and the Great War* Antonio Garcia & Ian van der Waag (ISBN 978-1-915113-77-1)